Against State, against History

Against State, against History

Freedom, Resistance, and Statelessness in Upland Northeast India

Jangkhomang Guite

OXFORD
UNIVERSITY PRESS

OXFORD
UNIVERSITY PRESS

Oxford University Press is a department of the University of Oxford.
It furthers the University's objective of excellence in research, scholarship,
and education by publishing worldwide. Oxford is a registered trademark of
Oxford University Press in the UK and in certain other countries.

Published in India by
Oxford University Press
2/11 Ground Floor, Ansari Road, Daryaganj, New Delhi 110 002, India

© Oxford University Press 2019

The moral rights of the authors have been asserted.

First Edition published in 2019

ISBN-13 (print edition): 978-0-19-948941-1
ISBN-10 (print edition): 0-19-948941-6

ISBN-13 (eBook): 978-0-19-909415-8
ISBN-10 (eBook): 0-19-909415-2

Typeset in Adobe Garamond Pro 10.5/12.5
by The Graphics Solution, New Delhi 110 092
Printed in India by Rakmo Press, New Delhi 110 020

The maps in this book do not claim to represent the authentic domestic or
international boundaries of India. They are not to scale and are provided for
illustrative purposes only.

To
Jennifer Guite
For her love, patience, and endurance

Contents

Figures and Table

Figures

Table

Abbreviations

ASA	Assam State Archives
EB&AS	East Bengal & Assam Secretariat
FE	Foreign Department, External Proceedings
FP	Foreign Department, Political Proceedings
JP	Judicial Proceedings
NAI	National Archives of India
PP	Political Proceedings
sq km	square kilometre
WBSA	West Bengal State Archives

Preface

This book has been long in the making. It took toils to see some light at the end. It has always been my wish to write on the hill tribes of Northeast India not because I am obsessed with them but, more importantly, due to the way we have generally understood them. Two trends on the writings of the history of Northeast India have been disturbing me for a long time. On the one hand, the history of Northeast Indian tribes roughly begins with colonial period *as if* no history of them prior to that can be written. Thus, we have two sets of the tribal pasts—the written and the spoken/oral, the history and the myth, the state and the stateless. On the other hand, the written history of the hill tribes has been largely influenced by the dominant civilizational discourse on the 'tribe'. Our heretical view on orality, obsession with written sources, lack of 'interrogating the interrogators', and failure to read the written 'against the grain' are central. The hold of dominant civilizational narratives is so strong and its epistemic violence so powerful that it is not easy to unwind them. They are so internalized that the hillmen felt so low of themselves *as if* the chilli plant is too big to climb.

A few path-breaking studies in recent time have provoked this book. It is always easy to criticize the dominant colonial discourse but it is very difficult to provide any alternative explanation. Besides others, James C. Scott has recently shown us the way to circumvent the dominant civilizational discourse on the 'tribe'. He laid the path through which we may be able to see the history of the hill people differently and in the right perspective. To be sure, putting his boot across the rugged mountain massif is not only easier to traverse but also most fascinating one to experience. This book is the first of a series I have in mind on the history of upland Northeast India. It concerns the period when the hills were in a state of statelessness. I hope to defocus, decentre, and recast their history from the counter-perspectives of the margin and in the light of recent historiography, noted earlier, that presented the highlanders as state-evading population in the hills.

Although this had been always a long wish, I seriously began my research on it nine years back. It was a long struggle but a rewarding one. The pains are far compensated by the fascination one discovers at the forgotten fringe. My entry into this academically dark-side was making a good start with my colleagues at the Assam University, Silchar. Their hard-gained knowledge about this margin through a long research was a concrete foundation on which I began. After all, a well beginning is half done. I cannot mention all their names here but my sincere gratitude is to all of them. But of these glittering, Sajal Nag deserves a particular distinction to me. He was the one who stood beside me all the time, listening patiently of my boring (but exciting for me) arguments. He had corrected me on many counts and fattened my knowledge about the region on various counts. He was and is always a big brother as a close friend. Suryasikha Pathak was always with us, whose criticisms are always valuable to me.

I would like to acknowledge here the contribution of a great number of friends whose comments, suggestions, and criticisms helped me during the writing of this book. Some actually read my earlier papers, some wrote to me by mail, and many of them gave me their precious time over the phone. Although I cannot mention all the names here, I extend my sincere thanks to all. Of these, I cannot escape mentioning a few names: David Zou, H. Khamkhansuan, Pum Khan Pau, D.L. Haokip, Amarjit Sharma, Roel Hangshing, Robert Haokip, Bijoy Kumar, Pauthang Haokip, Bijen, Moses, Teiborlang, Joy Pachuau, Gunnel Cederlöf, Tiplut Nongbri, and Sarah Hilaly. I have also benefited from various insightful comments and suggestions I received from the participants of different seminars and conferences where I presented parts of this book. Yet, I am solely responsible for this book, for any of its shortcomings and failures.

My colleagues at the Centre for Historical Studies have been a constant source of inspiration, although my association with them was quite recent. Since this manuscript had been submitted for publication before I have had the opportunity to engage with this huge intellectual storehouse of knowledge, I can only repent for being deprived of their valuable inputs which would have made this book much better than it now is. However, their parental support over my teaching schemes and research at the centre was an important source of strength during the last leg of this work.

I am also thankful to the officers and staff of the National Archives of India (NAI, New Delhi), West Bengal State Archives (Kolkata), Assam State Archives (Dispur), and the various tribal research institutes of different states in Northeast India. I am also grateful to the staff of different libraries in Assam University, North-Eastern Hills University, and Nehru Memorial Museum and Library. There were also several people with whom I was closely engaged during my fieldwork for collecting oral sources and some primary data. I am thankful to all of them.

I thank the University Grants Commission, New Delhi, for the financial support under its Major Research Project. Part of the work is the result of this project. I am also thankful to Indian Council of Historical Research, New Delhi, for supporting part of my field trip to the NAI.

Finally, this work would not have been possible without the support of my family. My parents were a constant source of emotional and spiritual support. My three ecstatic little kids (Joye, Joshua, and Janelle), who shoved over my shoulder day in and day out, were my source of strength, happiness, and endurance. With them, my research was always lively. My wife, Jennifer Guite, a constant companion throughout these years, patiently tolerated my boring (timeless) schedules and took complete care of the family and children, all of which I was virtually exempted from. Had not her patience and endurance been so strong, I would not have been able to do anything like this. For her love, patience, and endurance, I dedicate this book to her.

Jangkhomang Guite
Jawaharlal Nehru University
New Delhi, 2018

Introduction

On Being Hillmen

History without sense is perhaps no history. This is especially so in the case of society which did not write. A sense of time, of geography, of fear and excitement, of sadness and joy, of dreams, perception, illusions, and so on, are important ingredients of history. The deceptive typology of state and civilization to its 'others', to its subalterns, and of its own cultural trope are gradually unravelled. Its epistemic violence is even clearer now. Counter-perspectives from the margin are gradually unfolding. Of this series of unfolding knowledge of the forgotten, the history of 'unlettered race' of the Zomia mountain massif has had its late but not unworthy call. The Northeast of India, part of this Zomia highland, is having its prime time.[1] The past decade has witnessed a new enthusiasm and rapid growth in the studies regarding this empire's frontier. With a geographical area of about 262,239 square kilometre (sq km), this region has emerged as an epistemological hotspot for various scholars cutting across disciplines. Historical works are behind other disciplines but, with

[1] For the concept of 'Zomia', see Scott (2009) and van Schendel (2002).

intense precision, they are nonetheless not so far from them.[2] Yet, the history of 'unlettered race', of the tribal belt in the region, is still far behind all the others. This highland massif has evolved, over a period of time, an infinite number of frameworks and constraints, of intricately fashioned 'rift and variations', making access difficult to conventional historians. It has inherited societies composed of a disparate mass of population criss-crossing the rugged landscape, of small-scale communities of recurring chores, constant worries of godly and ungodly dims and raptures, beyond and within networks of social, economic, and human exchange, diversity within and without the village communities, all suggesting a miniscule world 'out of time'. It has become a 'shatter zone' of wilderness to historians who are not able to read their sensibilities.

Yet, a world of meaning and pattern unfolds once we take the field, feel their sensibilities and perceptions, take a passage through the oral chord and codes, brood over the hill practices, and weave these facts together, all in the long view and from the counter-perspectives of the margin. The unfolding pattern of the tribal universe, which I intend to investigate here, is in no way a match to the representations made in the dominant narrative that embody the 'tribe' in primitive garb.[3] The long view referred to here suggests a methodology that grounds events and structures along the great spans of time. 'Geography has its own odyssey, which is largely imperceptible to humans, and society has its own life: human life is short and political thought, economics, and ideas are even shorter. They are layers of closely related structures, although they may also function independently at times. If geography stands as the limit around which everything gravitates, the economics and the material culture of various times fashioned the social and political formation process in which the everyday lifeways, the 'scars of events', were reflected. The dimensions of the tribal

---

[2] See, for instance, Baruah (1999), Behal (2014), Bezbaruah (2010), Bhaumik (2010), Cederlöf (2014), May (2012), S. Misra (2011), U. Misra (2014), Nag (2016), Pachuau (2014), Pachuau and van Schendel (2015), Saikia (2011, 2014), and Sharma (2011).

[3] Subsequent use of the word 'tribe' or 'tribal' may or may not show it within inverted commas. It should be read based on the view expressed here.

world of vivid passions, therefore, need to be rooted in the workings over great spans of time.[4]

I seek to describe this interesting, yet neglected, region of the world in the long view and from the counter-perspectives of the region. This is about writing *their* history, not *the* History, of the hillmen. The aim is to defocus and decentre the history of this upland region from the dominant civilizational discourse on the hill tribe, the History written from state centres, and project it from the counter-perspectives of the hillmen that re-enact the *histories* that is *said* at the margins. The historical long spans begin from their 'time immemorial' and end with the coming of colonial state in the nineteenth century, the century which this discussion would mostly draw its letters and spirit, the facts.

The study of tribal world, of the 'unlettered race', is rather difficult yet most exciting in many ways. It is difficult because there is penury of written source materials to reconstruct their past, their history. The tribals did not write, they are not even written about, until recent times. What was written about them was dominated by a civilizational bias. It is exciting because they got their *histories* in oral narratives, the corpus of which is indeed very great; it just needs to be excavated. Also, anything that the tribes have—the land, the people, the culture and agriculture, the belief, their feelings, fears, pains, angers, and so on—can form parts of the unfathomable source of information, which makes it even more exciting. We just need to be sensible to them in order to transform them into useful information. The mountains, the ecology, and the rugged landscape, which acted as the limit, can be an exciting site of surveillance into their worldview, attitude, mentality, and even their physical attributes. It not only protects, preserves, and promotes but also hinders and, in

[4] Fernand Braudel (1980 [1969]: 4) has, in fact, warned that one 'must beware of that history which still simmers with the passions of the contemporaries who felt it, described it, lived it, to the rhythm of their brief lives, lives as brief as are our own. It has the dimensions of their anger, their dreams, and their illusions ... oblivious of the deeper currents of history ... and whose true significance emerges only if one can observe their workings over great spans of time.'

hindering, it has shaped their lived world order. Space/place has been perceived, conceived, lived, and experienced through time; human actions take and make place. Therefore, the deeper we go from the brighter surface to the murkier 'depths' of the hill universe, from the eventful noises to the less perceptible silence of historical long spans, the clearer will be the picture of less and less stolid world of the hillmen.

The unfolding events and patterns from the encapsulated timelessness of the tribal universe are even more thrilling. The oral narratives of all the tribes in the region, for instance, pointed out that they came from 'somewhere else' before they inhabited their present habitat. Their fascinating memory of origin and migration would invariably take them back to the valleys surrounding their hills. They were people, the society, who had, in a series of waves—sometimes in outburst flight but in most cases a regular silent movement of people— migrated to their present habitats from the surrounding plains. The level plains of Brahmaputra, Chindwin–Irrawaddy, and Barak rivers that surrounded the Northeast highland massif, as the sea encircles the peninsula, were identified by them as their earlier home. Sometime they lived *under* 'their' own 'kings', at other times under the 'kings' of other ethnicity who decimated their power. It was often under the latter, sometime also under the former, that they found life miserable and hence their eventual flight to the margins of the state. Factors ranging from the destruction of their 'kingdom' to the pressure from powerful rivals, oppressive rulers, great flood, great darkness, great fire, and diseases were given as the different causes of their flight into the hills. In other words, they escaped into the safety of the mountain massif against state-making projects in the valleys or when worsted by their 'powerful enemies' in a competition for supremacy in the valleys. This makes the mountain massif of Northeast India the 'region of refuge' in its history and the hill people of the region the 'state-evading population in the hills' in Scott's apt term.[5]

The highland Northeast India as a 'refuge zone' provided the successive waves of state evaders the flattering air of freedom from the fury of war-machine manpower (literally, 'flesh eating' or labour

---

[5] I am drawing this argument mainly from the recent work of J.C. Scott (2009) on the Zomia, and also from the migration history of the hill people of Northeast India discussed in Chapter 2 of this book.

power) valley states, if not the abundance of honey and milk. It also evolved new patterns of social and cultural networks, lifeways and relationship, of new settlement and population distribution patterns, new social and political systems, new mode of production, and so on. Thus, we will see how an amorphous and dispersive settlement and population distribution pattern across the rugged mountain, connected only by networks of social and cultural relationship and repulsive pathways, was carefully crafted to maintain their independence in the hills. We will also observe how they fortified their villages at the top of the high ranges so as to withstand any surprise attack. The dominant social formation process was broadly plural, fluid, and porous in character. Their social and political/administrative architecture was dominated by two systems, popularly known as 'democratic' and 'chieftainship' systems, which safeguarded their rights and freedom.

Similarly, we will see that their mode of production was dominated by the multipurpose poly-cropping *jhum* cultivation system which had given them 'food sovereignty' or allowed self-sufficient economy, enhanced their freedom, and prevented control and appropriations. The primacy given to orality over writing was also another important hill factor that acted as an instrument of social control, celebrated egalitarianism, and promoted a warrior ideology. Despite social emphasis on masculinity, hill women continued to enjoy ample amount of rights and freedom. All these practices and lifeways chosen and evolved by the hillmen in the stateless highland massif of Northeast India were set on a particular line of conduct in which freedom, mobility, and resistance against all forms of control and domination was central to its essence. They are political in character and their uniqueness may be situated in terms of their potential power to prevent control and appropriations from above and from the centre of power. They are what James Scott has called the 'culture and agriculture of escape'.[6]

The primacy given to the idea of individual freedom and the safety of their hills from conquest determined their practices and lifeways. This precisely took the case of state evasion as the guiding value. Thus, while the rugged mountain ranges provided a safe haven to

[6] Scott (2009).

successive generations of state evaders, the practices they adopted in the hills prevented the control and appropriations of valley states and politically ambitious hill chieftains. Hence, the prevention of all forms of tyrannical control and oppression continues to constitute what I call the 'line of conduct'. This has been the major theme in their oral histories, which reinforced the norms and acted as a medium of social control. Thus, we have a society whose lifeways revolved around evasion and prevention of control and oppression. The general argument of this book, therefore, is that the hill society that we see in the stateless highland massif, instead of being the 'relics' and 'remnants' of 'prehistoric' primitive society, is the state-evading population in the hills and their culture and agriculture is the culture and agriculture of escape. A geographical odyssey in the region may throw ample background on how the 'culture and agriculture of escape' fashioned in times.

A Geographical Odyssey

Geomorphologically the upland region of Northeast India has a unique position in its geographical land formation. Sandwiched by the two great valleys of Brahmaputra–Barak rivers in the west and Chindwin–Irrawaddy in the east, this upland region constitutes the southward extension of the great Himalayan mountain ranges that finally sink, as it moves south, into the Bay of Bengal. This is the high point where two tectonic plates—India and Burma plates—meet, making it the turbulent highway of an earthly fissure, the 'ring of fire'. To its west lies Assam plain in the north and Bengal plain in the south, with Khasi and Garo Hills protruding in between, evolving a specific valley pattern through its two west-flowing rivers— Brahmaputra and Barak—the letter 'F' shape. To the east lies the Chindwin–Irrawaddy River valley of Burma (Myanmar) forming roughly letter 'Y' shape. Kingdoms and empires have flourished in the two river valleys from ancient times but until the later part of nineteenth century, the upland mountain massif between the two continued to be a stateless space inhabited by several numbers of hill communities. A petty highland kingdom, Manipur, at the centre of this protruding southward-moving mountain, always connected the disconnected kingdoms of the two valleys by a seasonal mule/porter's route across the massive massif as the shortest trade and political highway. Movement of military, people, and commodities between these valley states flowed through the mountain kingdom, the narrow chicken-neck Patkai Pass, and also relayed through the multiple hands of the hill tribes. Goods and people also flowed to the mountain kingdom of Tibet as far as mainland China through some passes piercing through the falling margins of the great Himalayas. Thus, despite its heights, it was always a link, a contact zone, and a zone of assemblage between the two valley civilizations. This liminality has always been the unique character of the refuge frontier. Figure I.1 shows the Northeast Indian highland bearing the names of different hills given in colonial period. It was sandwiched on both the east and west sides by two river valley system of Chindwin-Irrawaddy and Brahmaputra-Barak rivers respectively.

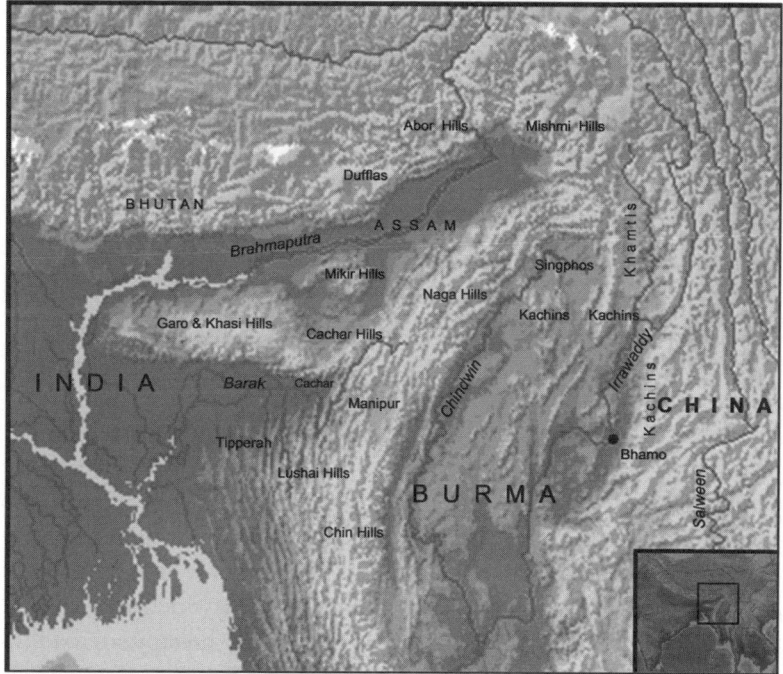

Figure I.1   Northeast India Highland
Source: Redrawn by the author from Microsoft Encarta Reference Library (2005).

Stratums of ideas begin to flow out once you engage with this hill–valley gradient. Imagine that you are at the centre of the valley state and moving towards the imposing mountain surrounding your sights. Influenced by the spherical shape of the earth, surface mirage, and tropical haze, your view and vision of the highland massif confronting you is always murky and mystifying. Your knowledge about this highland mountain is provided by a murkier view of myth and mythology, of the valley-based court chronicles (History), of the rumours that emanated from dreamers which represent the hills as the abode of wild and savage barbarians who know no 'civilization'. The cultivated part of the valley being small, your passage along the plain till the foothills was generally described as a 'dreary gloomy desolate wilderness' of a 'dark, damp, chilly, gloomy forest'.[7] You can only cross this wilderness with a very strong company of road-cutters equipped with axes and *dao*s (broadsword). The fatiguing excursion across this densely forested wilderness of the valley fringes teaches you how wilder the mountain could have been. In the foothills, you learn that you have to give away your beasts of burden and start walking on foot, carrying on your back your own baggage and food items for the whole journey (as you will not get any supply from the hill people even with liberal payment). You would require the assistance of a strong company of road-cutters, a stronger company of armed military men, and a much larger number of human porters to reach the interior parts of the hills or the other side of the mountain which normally took weeks or months.

Being fatigued and facing the imposing mountain at the foothills, nothing humbles your imagination than mulling over the wildness of the hills. Things thus appear as you learned previously at the core of the valley civilization. As you climb up the first range, your vision is firm with your lowland narrative. As you scale up the roadless height, things seem to get worse. Your daily routine now consists of dropping into the deep valley and climbing up again several thousand feet on the other side. This involves a tedious expedition over high precipices, steep acclivities, or perpendicular ledges of rock which may oblige you to take the stony bed of hill streams with precipitous banks,

---

7 Butler (1978 [1855]: 14–24, 75).

chilling rapids, slippery rolling stone, and sharp boulders. Progress is, as most colonial expedition reports would claim, 'exceedingly slow', foot becoming 'terribly lacerated and bruised' so that one will not 'easily forget the pain and suffering' in a long time.[8] However, on reaching the tip of the mountain, things change slowly from reel to reality. You would be 'utterly exhausted' due to the fatiguing journey but the view that is spread before you would soon relieve the anxiety.

Literally, you are mesmerized by the captivating views of the magnificent mountain ranges stretching before your eyes and the valleys on both sides of the mountain. The two river valleys appear imposing before your sight as if they are under your feet; on a clearer day, they appear as if on the map. The clear view of the rolling mountain ranges now completely changes your vision from a violent epistemologist to a real naturalist. Your daily fatigue seems to have gone away by magic. You think you are a different species from your fellows down there, certainly not their 'barbarians' but a person whom they would have greatly envied. Your view in the highland would be what the great sages would have called the sacred geography, of a sanctified space with immense energy of human consciousness which is the fountainhead of arcane wisdom. Your tour over the real world of the charming highland massif gives all sense of perfection and even contentment. You simply realize that your earlier views of the 'savage' mountain was mere romantic eyewash.

Let us take a brief historical excursion to this highland massif. T.T. Cooper, for instance, shared his sight of Brahmaputra valley from Mishmee Hills. After a 'long and toilsome climb', he noted:

> The grandeur of the scene from our elevated position made me draw aside from the rest of the party to contemplate it. Several thousand feet below, the plain of Northern Assam stretched far away in the distance, intersected by the Brahmapootra and its numerous tributaries, the course of each of which could be traced like the black lines denoting rivers on a map. The atmosphere was so clear that numerous forests could be distinctly seen with the shade of their trees, while the distant horizon seemed to melt into a blue haze, forming a strong contrast to the prospect to the north.[9]

[8] See, for instance, Butler (1978 [1855]: 29).
[9] Cooper (1995 [1873]: 214).

To the north was Tibet where he would find his future expansion of tea markets. From Samagudting, the initial British headquarter in Naga Hills, James Johnstone also had the same sight of the plains which were 'magnificent' and on clear days, one could see 'the dark line of the Bhootan Hills, with the snowy peaks of the Himalayas towering above them'.[10]

Just as the valley views are magnificent, one also sights the magnificent mountain ranges, and its prided population, once in the hills. Thus, Cooper was astonished to view the magnificent mountain ranges before his eyes which, one after the other, towered upwards 'in bared nakedness', many of the higher peaks crowned with snow, sparkling in the sunlight like gorgeous gems. 'All was sombre and wild.' As they descended the counter slope, which led to 'the grand but hostile regions', he took one last glance at the 'peaceful plain of Assam, recalling many a happy evening spent with kind-hearted friends'.[11] From Mount Helipong (7,280 feet) in Naga Hills, the watershed between the Brahmaputra and the Chindwin rivers, Christoph von Fürer-Haimendorf also had a similar observation. He said that the view from this mount, 'over an immense mountain country', was 'magnificent' overlooking the land of Lhotas, Aos, Konyaks (in the west) and Changs and Sangtams (in the east). The Patkai range with Mount Saramati (12,622 feet) was also clearly visible.[12]

From Mullah village (Shentlang) in the Lushai Hills, Colonel Lister also noted that the chain of mountain ranges 'runs down unbroken' from Cachar to the south till they sink in the Bay of Bengal. He could clearly see that this chain of mountain ranges, one after another, towered up towards the east from the Chittagong side, and from that direction and from Sylhet, 'numerous ranges of hills, as well as difficult swamps and unfordable rivers, would have to be crossed'. From his field glass, he could also see that the tips or spur of these hill ranges were capped and towered with villages. Villages such as Boarmolien (chief Vannoiliena village) appeared before his eyes as 'cantonment', built on regular pattern, having 'not less than'

[10] Johnstone (1987 [1896]: 14).
[11] Cooper (1995 [1873]: 214–15).
[12] von Fürer-Haimendorf (1938a: 205).

3,000 houses, and surrounded by a long stockade.[13] A view from the Thangjing ranges in western Manipur, from the Dingpi ranges in eastern Manipur, from Khasi Hills facing Bangladesh and Assam plains, from Dufflas Hills facing Assam plain, and so on, would produce similar sights.

The circumstances leading to the flight of valley population into this highland massif will be discussed in detail in Chapter 2. One anecdote will suffice here to show how such highland massif eventually becomes the safe haven to plainsmen who would like to evade punishment or oppression. The origin legend of the Kukis, for instance, has it that one day Chongthu went hunting porcupine with his dog when they were living in Noikhomang (place in lower plain). His dog entered a passage and did not return. After some time, Chongthu got into the passage himself to see what had become of his dog. The passage led him to the Chunggam (literally, 'upper world', mountain highland) which 'pleased' him so much that he eventually brought his family and kinsmen to occupy the new world he had discovered.[14] The context was such that Noikhomang was one of the famous settlements in Noimang (literally, down or lower world, meaning level plain) region and Chunggam was a highland region, meaning the hills and mountain landscape. The legend has it that Chongthu came to the Chunggam not due to a happy departure from Noikhomang but only to escape certain threats on his life. His life was in danger as the 'king' of Noimang had ordered him to be put to death. While attempting escape, he had to overcome certain dangers in the passage: *gulheupi* (a mythological snake), tiger, and *muzin* or *thimzin* (great darkness, solar eclipse) when people died if they fell asleep. His party had to traverse across the rugged mountain country from place to place in search of a better place to settle down permanently.

What is imperative to me in this origin legend is the choice made by Chongthu to escape to the mountain landscape. The choice was, as the legend shows, a compelling one and indicated a situation of adversity in which Chongthu was to choose between the hills and

---

[13] West Bengal State Archives (WBSA), Kolkata, Judicial Proceedings (JP), 27 February 1850, No. 36, Lister to Grant, 2 February 1850.

[14] Shaw (1997 [1929]: 28–30); see also Goswami (1985).

valleys, between life and death. In normal course of migration, people usually choose certain plain areas which provide them peace and prosperity. But the choice before Chongthu was the reverse. He had to leave the prosperous and populous valley settlement of Noikhomang for a harsh and rugged mountain landscape. Legend has it that the rugged mountain 'pleased' him so much because of not only the captivating imagination but more due to the free air of life. He knew that there were many odds and abysses through the rugged mountain, which manifested during the passage. However, he also knew that if he did not take such a bold step his life was in danger. He chose life in place of death. Deprived of the valley's milk and honey, Chongthu was quite content with his freedom from death. What is significant in this anecdote is the crucial role played by geography, the inaccessible mountain massif, which came to the rescue of people in danger under the intimidating gaze of power. Just as the splendour of prosperity is provided by the valleys, the mountain provided the splendour of lives and freedom to the hapless people in times of existential threat from political enemies, social prejudice, religious bigotry, economic predicament, natural calamities, and so on. In this context, the highland massif forms truly the 'region of refuge'.

The centrality of a harsh geography, such as the rugged mountains, marshland, island, desert, and so on, as a refuge zone to evade punishment and control of state or enemies is a well-established reality in history. The same is true for the mountain massif. This was mainly due to the region's inaccessibility from the core valley state and the friction of distance, which impeded the wheels of state machine. The inaccessibility was conditioned by the luxuriant vegetations and the imposing altitude of several heights, making it an 'illegible' landscape to state and civilization and hence *beyond* the pale. In this sense, the deceptive typology against the hills and its nonstate practices, studded in the narrative of dominant civilizational discourse, is largely conditioned by geography. Many instances in history show why this mountain highland was an illegible space for state builders. The Ahoms who ruled over the Brahmaputra valley for over six centuries, for instance, came from the other side of the Northeast mountain massif. They invaded Assam through the Naga Hills but apart from using this highland as their political highway to sustain their connection with their original home, these mountains were never conquered or ruled over. The illegibility of the harsh mountain country was just against its strategy of state building that depended on wet rice cultivation and population ingathering at the core of the kingdom.

The majestic sojourn of the famous Shan prince, Shamlung, across this highland in 1215 CE could not bring any change apart from introducing rice in the highland kingdom of Manipur.[15] Manipur had a long history of being the only mountain kingdom in the region, drawing its resources from the small valley formation at the height of the mountain. And like other state formations in the region, it could not succeed in scaling the mountain around the small valley, although it formed the only link with the valley states of Burma and India. David Bello has also shown how the malaria-infested Burma frontier prevented further expansion of Chinese Empire towards Burma.[16] The Burmese occupation of most of the kingdoms in Northeast region (Assam, Manipur, Kachar, Jaintia) in the early nineteenth century could not lead them to subdue the highland expanses between Burma and Bengal–Assam plains. The defeat of imperial Japanese Army during the Second World War was largely due to the daunting geography across this highland massif. The inability to overcome the harshness of geography had eventually broken the myth of unstoppable Japanese expansion towards the west.[17] Despite centuries of attempts, none of the valley states in the region were able to gain/maintain their foothold over this highland massif. Only the mighty British Empire was successful in bringing it under its imperial orbit after great efforts.

Coming back to your geographical odyssey after a brief historical excursion, you have now experienced a series of ideas available to a person who had the opportunity to travel over both the hills and valley landscape. Your only complain is about the 'strange' people you meet in the highland. Your instant encounter shows that they are 'shy' and undoubtedly different from you, practising different culture and agriculture, and so on. But as you become more and more acquainted with them, you will also realize that they could have been closely related to you 'once upon a time'. Although they did not write, you will be surprised to see them having a very strong retentive memory of their past, especially their migration histories. They would undoubtedly tell you that they came from the plain 'down there', from where you also came, before they immigrated to their present hill habitats. You may even feel that their culture is in a way mimicking your own but only in a creative, refashioned way. It is evident in their house architecture, the different signs and symbols used, the different terms employed to signify certain objects, the technology of industry such as cloth-making, handicraft, pottery, and so on.

You will be even surprised to see in each house items produced in the valleys; gongs or beads, for instance, are their core cultural items. As you go through all these, you will realize that the hills are culturally not very far away from you although they are refashioned differently. You would realize that, instead of being an isolated and unconnected wilderness, it is closely connected to your civilization that is manifesting the character of what Richard White has called 'the Middle ground' where different identities and culture actively interact to produce a 'hybrid area' or what Hannerz has called a 'Creole' or 'hybrid' culture.[18] It is certainly what Thompson and Lamar have called 'a zone of interpenetration' or what Elton has called a 'zone of overlapping' boundaries.[19] You will also learn about the strong and multiple demographic processes of radical ethnogenesis (merger), continuity (solidification), and break-up (fragmentation) of communities across the rugged landscape. The mimicry seems so strong that you tend to regard the hills as part of the valley systems, while at the same time being very clear about the distinction. Distinctive characters of the hills are especially discernible in terms of their ideological, social, political, cultural and to the extent of their economics and material culture, making the highland massif almost opposite to your own, the state. A brief discussion on such dichotomy may be helpful here.

[18] White (1991) and Hannerz (1996) respectively.
[19] Thompson and Lamar (1981: 3–13) and Elton (1996) respectively. See also Parker (2006).

On Being Hillmen, on Being Unstate

Living in the shadow of states, in a zone of interpenetrating and overlapping cultural spaces, such as the highland massif of Northeast India, was not a lifeway that was a mute, inert, and static ethnoscopic enterprise. It involved seamless activities of enactment and re-enactment of culture, customs, and traditions, of multiple demographic processes, making them all into a unique space of cultural collective. British officers, when touring the hills or during various military expeditions in the hills in the precolonial period, were stunned to discover that the various ethnic names given to the hill tribes by the valley populations were completely unknown to them. Ethnic names such as Garo, Aka, Duffla, Abor, Mishmi, Naga, Mikir, Kachari, Kuki, Chin, and Kachin, which the officers borrowed and used from the vocabulary of valley population and which arguably carried some sense of mortification, were not recognized by the hill people as their legitimate names. The officers were surprised to discover that the hill people called themselves simply, yet meaningfully, as 'man', or 'human', or 'hillmen' (for example, *Boro/Bodo*, *Achikmande, Arleng, Kyon, Chingpho, Keniak, Aor, Tengima, Zo, Yo, Sho*, or *Mizo*). On further enquiry into these self-identified names or of being 'human', they were astonished to uncover the hill sense of pride. If the idea of 'civilization' was evolved by identifying or encountering its 'others', then such pride in being 'human' or 'hillmen' can also be seen as the hill sense of civilization. Thus, just as the valley 'civilization' called them 'savage' and 'barbarians', the hill people had also developed their own barbarian 'others'. They called the valley population variously as *vai* or *kol/kawl* (in Kuki-Chin world), *dkhar* or *mynder* (in Khasis), *wansa* (in Kok-Borok), *harang* (in Nishis and Adis), and so on, meaning 'who do no belong to me', or the 'others', or 'not like me'.

Behind the idioms and expressions of the 'self' and the 'others' was a very strong sense of self-perception, a position taken by the hillmen against the dwellers of the plains or the non-tribal population. In their self-exaltation, such expressions regarded the valley population not as a culturally superior collective to the hillmen but rather as a demeaning one. In short, such idiomatic expressions represent the 'civilized' valley population as, as the expression goes, the 'pacifist', 'degenerated', or 'oppressed' collective. John M'Cosh, for instance, noted that the Khasis are: '[P]roud of their mountains, and look down with contempt upon the degenerate race of the plains; jealous of their honour, warlike and brave in action, and have a regard for their pledged word, and aversion of falsehood, little to be expected from them.'[20] Aversion to falsehood, a pledge to truthfulness, brave and warlike masculinity, and of course, their self-honour in purity of descent, in a nutshell, constituted the pride of place in the highland narrative.

Here, masculinity entered at the heart of the hillmen's self-perception and it was this that generated voluminous language of 'barbarianization' in the lowland narrative. If the dominant civilizational narrative deceptively typologized them as wild, barbaric, and uncouth, who were a 'pest' and 'nuisance' to the valley states, it was these very categorizations that the hillmen liked to make themselves known to the 'others' in sort of what Ranajit Guha has called 'reversing their values'.[21] Thus, to the hillmen, such categorizations were taken as the character of highly qualified masculinity, and in this line of thinking, the valley population were 'looked down with contempt' for lacking such 'martial' (masculine) quality. Hence, the plains population were, in the hill perception, different and 'unlike' from them by lacking hardiness, bravery, and purity of descent (ethnically mixed). In this context, what were considered to be the 'pristine savagery and hardihood' in the dominant civilizational discourse were, instead of demeaning labels, the admirable feats in highland narrative. Several interesting cases of cultural encounter between the hillmen and plainsmen were noticed during the colonial period. Two examples may suffice our purpose here.

When T.T. Cooper was strolling 'through the native bazaar' in Sadiya with some Abor men, with two of them lending their arms to him on both sides, he was stunned to discover the reaction of the people in the town: '[T]he women bolted into their houses, followed by screaming children, and even the men quietly slunk away, and every street as we passed along was quickly deserted signs of fear which

---

20 M'Cosh (2000 [1837]: 161).
21 Guha (1999 [1983]: 16).

greatly amused the Abors, who rolled along half-drunk, singing and shouting at the top of their voices.'[22] Cooper soon realized that the 'signs of fear' were not only due to the arrogant posture of the Abors but also something else. He noted that his 'public' show with the Abors earned him 'the Sahib who was going to live amongst the savages, and I am not sure that during the remainder of my stay in Sudiya I was not looked upon as a kind of half-civilised Englishman.'[23] If the hillmen were seen as 'savages' and 'barbarians' (or untouchables in the context of caste Hindu population of Brahmaputra valley), the hillmen showed themselves to be bold, brave, and warlike, which was represented by their behaviour on the streets of Sadiya. They fearlessly strolled in the streets of the valley townsmen, half-drunk, singing, and shouting at the top of their voices. In their self-exalted masculinity, they were 'greatly amused' at the 'civilized' townsmen shying away from them, not knowing perhaps how the townsmen perceived them.

On another occasion, C.T. Metcalfe also noted a Garo woman who refused to wear a cloth offered to her in the fashion of the Rajbongshis of the plains:

> The interpreters then taking it out of his hands, fastened it over her breast, similar to the way that the Rajbunsis wear it. This created disgust in the mind of the lady, for she pulled it off, saying that is how the Rajbunsis wear it. I then essayed my hand at classical drapping [sic] with better success, for she deigned to wear it till she left the hat [sic].[24]

A strong aversion to imitate the valley culture and deigning to wear one's own traditional fashion may be taken as an act of pride in one's culture, or to distance oneself from the 'others', or even a form of resistance. The Mikirs (Karbis), for instance, noted Butler, 'reproach their countrymen [Mikirs] of the plains for having adopted the

---

[22] Cooper (1995 [1873]: 129–30).

[23] Cooper (1995 [1873]: 130).

[24] National Archives of India (NIA), New Delhi, Foreign Department, Political Proceedings (FP) (A): October 1873, Nos 122–25, C.T. Metcalfe to Secretary to Government of Bengal, June 1873.

Assamese custom'.[25] It does not matter to what extent these claims are valid, the point is to show the existence of a counter-cultural narrative from the hills, a binary notion that is again made in self-perpetuation. When the 'civilized' matters of ignoble become noble to the hillmen and its noble become ignoble, we cannot pretend that there did not exist two counter-cultural narratives, two cultural world orders, between the hills and valleys. Thus, when S.E. Peal argued with a Naga warrior that killing people, especially women and children, in cold-blooded pursuit, cutting off their heads, hands, and legs, is 'unmanly', he noted that it was 'utterly incomprehensible to him [Naga]'.[26] For the Nagas, it was Peal who was unable to comprehend the way their war of revenge was taken, a strategy freely willed to prevent killing in the first place.

Therefore, to be 'human' or 'hillmen' was not only to be different from their valley counterparts, the 'others' of the hillmen, but also to be strong, hardy, and, in colonial parlance, turbulent. Here, to be masculine and warlike was necessary to be able to protect and prevent oneself from any form of control and oppression, which, in the highland narrative, was lacking in the plains under war-machine states. In this context, freeing oneself from the shackle of state control and appropriations or from any tyrant chieftains in the hills was, therefore, a much-valued idea of being the 'hillmen' or 'human'. Thus, the notion of freedom emerged most prominently in the consciousness of the hill people as 'human' or 'hillmen', implying that one should not be under subjection and oppressive control. In other words, to be 'human' according to the highland narrative is to be necessarily a free man, free from oppressive control and domination of arbitrary power. Conceptually, it is a society lacking domination relation, if categories and divisions were part of the social structure as in state society.

It is in this line of thinking that the dichotomy of the hill and valley societies may be best situated. Thus, to the hillmen, the valley populations, who were subjected to a war-machine state, were seen to be unfree or subjected population, always under state's control and oppression, whereas the hillmen were free from it. I will come back to the question of freedom in the stateless hills shortly. Here, suffice to say that to the extent they look crude, such dichotomous views on both sides only tells about a conceptual equality between the two. Therefore, one can think of two types of civilizations, rather than civilization and its unruly 'other'. In this context, they may be understood as two contesting visions of culture in the way they think about each other. State's modernity is slowly but surely removing the last remains of stateless civilization but the fact remains that until recent times, stateless world was as prolific as the world of state across the globe.

To be free from control and arbitrary power would also mean that there should be equality among all individuals within the hill society. Equality in the context of the hill society is not the absence of categories and divisions but should be understood in terms of 'cooperation and reciprocity'. This concept means that each individual must help (cooperate with) other individual and each must return (reciprocate) such help while each one of them is independent from the other. If help is to be reciprocated with help, then the conceptual equality of individuals who help and who seek help was inbuilt and the idea of domination due to 'help' was eliminated. Thus, equality in the context of stateless society is to be understood in terms of cooperation and reciprocity, say, between the chief and 'commoners', between men and women, husband and wife, master and slave, and so on. The freedom of individual was also protected within this concept. The concept of cooperation and reciprocity became the guiding principle in all walks of life in the hills and was, therefore, the survival strategy of stateless population at the margin of the states. Thus, to be 'hillmen' was also to be a great cooperator who valued human equality and freedom and renounced oppressive control and domination.

The differing worldviews between hills and valley should not, however, lead us to assume that the two worlds were completely different from each other culturally. The hill culture, archaic as it would have been from today's standard, was in a way, as noted earlier, an extension of the valley culture, just as the hill population was its offshoot. They were not only aware of the existence of coercive states 'down there' but also kept vigilance over their faux pas; they constantly acted, reacted, and interacted with them symbiotically yet indifferently. In this context, being 'human' or 'hillmen' in the highland narrative was not only about the ability to prevent state control and remain stateless but also the ability to adopt and re-enact such practices which can secure their safety. In this sense, one can talk of re-enactment of tradition rather than tradition as a radical process and *adoption* rather than innovation. Thus, what we know of the culture and agriculture of the state-evading population in the hills resembles the valley practices in many ways. However, at the same time, it indicates differences and cleavages with the valley practices.

The resemblance shows only the character of synthesis that combined adoption with a creative refashioning of things. Thus, the vigilant tribal universe was intrinsically creative and ideologically liberal. Hence, instead of an isolated world, it was intricately refashioned interregnum between two 'civilized' worlds of the past and the future (between pre-escape and after it was conquered by colonial state), and between states on all sides. It was a world in itself that dovetailed shades of two worlds but shaped it inversely and differently from them. Hence, if cultures meet in the hills and the highland massif assumed a 'contact zone', such meeting was on its own rhythm quite opposed to its origin. Its differential rhythmic cultural disposition was partly due to the contact of two 'great traditions', of the Indian and Chinese variances, and partly and more importantly due to its assertion for distinction from the state societies and to keep away from the control and appropriations of oppressive states surrounding the highland massif. This is the first pre-emptive strike to clear the possible confusion on my understanding of statelessness.

In this sense, the highland massif where the state evaders eventually settled down can be assumed to be the region or zone of reassembling and hence the *zone of assemblage*. The zone of assemblage presupposes two sets of refashioning hill practices. In the first place, it involved simply the reconfiguration of the hill society and its practices, which they brought/adopted from the valleys and by innovating some new practices. This process actually involved reordering of such practices in keeping with what I have called the hills' *line of conduct*. It breaks up into smaller pieces, yet is regularly reordered at the village level following a fission pattern. This makes the highland region a 'shatter zone' in history. It was an exercise of re-enacting their society and practices so that they acted as a breakwater against control and appropriations. It involved good sense of assimilation of valley practices only to dissimilate the valley state.

The second process was a more complex one. Re-enactment was done with reference to what may be called the state's *line of conduct* or what Scott has called state 'legibility'.[27] The hill society and its practices were refashioned in relation to the valley states that surrounded the hill habitats. It was an exercise that interrogated, negotiated, and re-enacted the very ideals of state sovereignty. In this sense, the hill society and its practices were refashioned so as to act as revolting practices that framed the state as what may be call a 'diabolical being' (from the expression in oral tradition) and its ideals as oppressive and ruinous to freedom of individuals and society. The familiar hill routines were therefore carefully crafted, or they were the 'art' in Scott's apt term so that they could constantly question and contest the ideals of oppressive state and evade its control and appropriations. As a sequel, it was also an effective instrument to prevent the formation of state and the concentrations of power in the hills. They were what Scott has called 'the culture and agriculture of escape'.

In the sense noted here, one can talk of *disowning* state instead of *anti-state* and the *unstate* instead of *stateless*. By disowning, I mean to say the process of re-enactment of the hill cultural collective so that it acted not only as a breakwater to state control but also to the emergence of state-like domination relations in the hills. Conceptually, disowning connotes the idea of unbecoming state in the hills. The circumstances in which such process of re-enactment took shape in the hills are understood as unstate. Therefore, being 'hillmen' and being 'human' in the consciousness of the hill people was not only to be strong and hardy but also to follow a specific 'culture and agriculture' so that they could prevent and protect themselves from oppressive control and appropriations from outside and inside the hill society. They adopted many practices or 'traditions' from outside (in most cases, from state space, their older

---

27 Scott (1998).

home), but refashioned and re-enacted them so that they could effectively protect and repel all forms of oppressive control and appropriations.[28] In this sense, such practices may be understood as *unstate* or *nonstate* practices and the circumstances that celebrated such practices as statelessness.[29] Unstate, as a concept, therefore connotes the state of statelessness. Under the circumstances noted above, the unstate or statelessness as a process presupposes a movement towards a particular direction. If being 'human' or 'hillmen' connotes not only the ability to prevent oppressive control and the ability to remain free, and if being free supposes a society without domination relation, then it can be said that statelessness as a process is a movement towards an egalitarian society. State is possible only if there is something called egalitarian state. Otherwise, it is a movement necessarily different from those of premodern states in the region. Also, it was a movement that could only be stopped by a political force of arms or conquest, the situation which came about with the occupation of the hills by the British colonial state in the nineteenth century.

Sequel to this notion of statelessness and in a pre-emptive strike against the dominant idea of state in the hills, we do not assume that the hill people are necessarily anti-state. Therefore, when we say that being 'hillmen' or 'human' is necessarily an interrogation and contestation to the being of state, we do not assume it to be anti-state. It was rather a tactical positioning of the hills state of statelessness as different from state. Thus, the hill people, while they were striving to prevent the control and appropriations of valley states, were also at the same time keen on control over the valley for their material requirements. The kingdoms of Kacharis, Jaintias, Tipperahs, Bhutanese, and the various hill polities controlling the state populations at the fringes of the valley, collecting *posa* (payment to hill polities by plainsmen) from them, are cases in point.[30] State formed

[28] Throughout the book, 'practice' and 'tradition' are interchangeably used in both plural and singular sense to mean the collective hill 'customs and traditions', the cultural collective of the hillmen.

[29] Throughout the book, I will use nonstate, unstate, or sometimes stateless synonymously.

[30] Detail discussion on these aspects is given in Chapter 9.

the core of their consciousness, as seen from their oral traditions, not only to be prevented (through their various 'warrior ideologies') but also to be cherished (their millenarian 'kingdom'). However, such keenness to be master of valley space as ruler, or of their 'future state', should not confuse us from the dominant notion of evading control and oppression. Thus, to be state evader is not necessarily to be anti-state; it connotes a broad projection of a society without domination, subjection, and oppression.

Stateless as a process is also therefore not necessarily an anti-state movement, but a movement that celebrates an egalitarian society that can only be controlled by political force of arms. For instance, whenever a certain hill polity became the 'king' or 'raja' of the valley population, say, the dynasty that ruled over Jaintia or Cachar, they invariably wore the booth of state sovereign in relation to the sub-dued population in the valley, and in most cases lived among them. However, his kinsmen would continue to live in the hills as *usual*, fol-lowing their celebrated set of cultural collective unhindered. Hence, the 'king' was a king to the subjected population of the valley, and to his kinsmen, he remained an equal member of the egalitarian society. In his effort to become the ruler of valley people he was, however, supported by his kinsmen from the hills; in certain cases, they even paid certain 'presents' (say, a certain number of he-goats per village in Jaintia Hills) to him annually. Thus, statelessness as a process can be evaporated only by force.

The second strike is even more interesting. As noted earlier, many of the hill practices (preferably called nonstate/unstate practices) resemble the valley practices in many ways. Take the case of, for instance, jhum cultivation that constituted one of the core nonstate practices. It also continued to remain the staple source of livelihood to a large number of the valley population in Brahmaputra and Chindwin river valleys until recent times. The question then is: if the same practices are present in both state and stateless spaces, then what makes them different from each other and also to what has been alluded to as state practices? In other words, if the same practices prevailed in both the hills and valleys, how could the former be a position that questions the ideals of state. Under such circumstances, it becomes necessary to define what constituted nonstate/unstate practices and what not, the point we now come to.

Of Unstate Practices

What constituted unstate practices is something very difficult to explain. Tracing the origin of such practices in this work would be a superfluous exercise. I neither attempt nor see any possibility in the endeavour, which would invariably end up with the timeless myths of origin which every tribe has one of. Truly, no one can say for sure they have evolved from the state evaders, and it is even difficult to say that they are the remnants of primitive society. It is simply accepted here that there are unstate/nonstate practices which had been *adopted* by hill people so as to prevent the oppressive control and appropriations from outside and inside. But the fact that they become nonstate or unstate practices is conditioned by certain historical processes in which two factors emerge prominent. First, the hill practices may be called unstate practices as they flourished in the stateless mountain massif over the centuries and had contested the control of war-machine state. If hillmen are state evaders and if being hillmen is antithesis to oppressive state, then it makes sense that their practices would also invariably become nonstate or unstate practices. In this context, they were/are deceptively categorized as primitive, uncivilized, and backward. In this line of thought, they are prehistoric, archaic, and belonging to the 'old world'. Take the case of orality, for instance. James Scott has shown how the choice of orality gave many political advantages to the state evaders in the hills, such as freedom of manoeuvre in history, genealogy, and legibility, that frustrates state routines.[31] This is similarly the case with other choices made in the hills.

The second point is even more serious. As noted earlier, the so-called unstate/nonstate practices are also equally prevalent in the valley state space. Truly, there is no such thing as state and unstate practices in a strict sense of the term. But there has always been the notion of state and nonstate/stateless practices in history on different grounds. In fact, nonstate practices have existed in history only in the eyes of the state. To state, certain practices are 'illegible' to state-making project and hence nonstate.[32] Perhaps, it may not be

[31] Scott (2009: 220–37).

[32] I use the term 'illegible' in relation to Scott's state 'legibility', which means 'simplification' and 'homogenization' of complex things in the interest of rule. See Scott (1998).

out of place to say that the longest war the state has fought in history is to eliminate the set of practices that it described as 'anti-state elements'. To the extent it has been able to eliminate such 'illegibility' and produce its 'alternatives', we say that the society is 'progressing'. If complete elimination is impossible, one can talk of dormantization of such 'elements' in state space. Freezing the striking capability of nonstate/unstate elements has been most effectively achieved through demonizing and criminalizing such practices. The various civilizational categories of the hill practices are just one set of such demonization process. Hence, within the state, nonstate practices survived but in stunted, suppressed, and parochial forms. However, in the stateless space, these nonstate practices could flourish and become *unstate* as they could effectively prevent state control and appropriations. Hence, nonstate practices are understood here less in terms of 'anti-state elements' and more in terms of anti-domination and anti-oppression practices.

What makes unstate practices different from 'anti-state' practices of the valley then? As anti-oppression and pro-freedom, unstate practices connote not only an adoption/promotion of 'anti-state elements' but, more importantly, the re-enactment of them as an effective instrument against oppressive control and domination. Thus, we can see that each of these 'anti-state' practices was re-enacted so that they cannot be transformed into a structure of domination. This re-enactment is most visible in the form of what I would call the *counter-culture conduit*, a safeguard attached with each unstate structure through which individual/family could switch over or take shelter when the system became oppressive. Hence, clan, kinship, marriage institution, political organization, and so on, were all equipped with a safe conduit system through which individuals could evade oppression with ease. These conduits came in the form of, say, free migration rights against chieftainship/village polity; liberal divorce and remarriage against patriarchal marriage institution; fluid, porous, and plural social and ethnic boundaries against clan, kinship, and ethnicity; and so on. They are the counter-culture collective of the stateless hill society in the sense that they could effectively neutralize a system when it has become oppressive; and it also forcefully prevented them from becoming tyrannical. Thus, for instance, when the chief became tyrannical, individuals could easily leave him and migrate to other village, just as he could adopt other clan/ethnicity when his clan and social system became oppressive. Similarly, a wife could easily slip out of her marriage when her husband became oppressive and get another husband with ease.

In this context, the counter-cultural collective, the conduits in each system, acts as an inbuilt mechanism to liberate the individual when the system becomes oppressive. The counter-cultural collective is even more significant as it can effectively prevent/deter the system from becoming tyrannical and oppressive in the first place. The re-enactment of nonstate practices with the counter-culture collective, the safe conduit system, therefore, makes unstate practices different from its counterparts, 'anti-state elements', in the state space. Individual freedom, therefore, emerges central to understand the being of 'hillmen' or 'human' in stateless society. Thus, it would be helpful at this stage to explain the form of freedom we will see in the stateless hills.

Of Freedom in Stateless Society

Unstate as a process centres on the question of individual freedom from oppression. Yet, there is no simple tool to define the exact meaning and forms of freedom in stateless society for certain valid reasons. When we talk of freedom in stateless society, it is different from the idea of 'unlimited freedom' in the 'state of nature', just as it is dissimilar from what we have in our liberal society. At the least, one can say that freedom in stateless society is one that is limited, interested and governed not by competition and market force but by the principle of what we called cooperation and reciprocity. If the Hobbesian notion of 'natural liberty' implies 'non-interference', or 'absence of external impediments', or 'absence of legal prohibitions', or 'unlimited freedom', then we can see that such a concept had no place in the stateless hill society.[33] Thus, while 'every man' was apparently 'his own master', 'avenges his own quarrel', 'does that which is right in his own eyes', 'follows the dictates of his own will', and can even go against 'the wishes and acts of the majority', he was always bound by the normative standard of the society enshrined in the

---

[33] For a brief and precise discussion on the different concepts of freedom, see Berlin (1969).

unwritten 'customary laws' or 'traditions'.[34] He could only avenge his quarrel or act against majority opinion based on, and within the ambit of, customary injunction. What was right in his eyes, and in the eyes of people, was dictated and determined by the same customs. Here, customary laws acted as the limit or the 'legal prohibitions' or 'external impediments' against his freedom to a great extent. They constantly 'interfered' in all decision-making process. The sacredness of 'trial by ordeal', that was his ultimate limitation, was also dictated by customs. It was within such limitations that the individual was empowered to be free in the first place.

Certain physical limitations or 'external impediments' also limited individual freedom. Take the case of the village polities, for instance. We will see that each village in stateless tribal society in Northeast had a well-established village 'government' or administrative structure. It was authorized by common people to enforce the customary laws or to limit anyone who might have infringed upon such laws. Besides, there were also some internal or psychological limitations against the free will of individuals. Take the case of threat from other individuals. Most colonial observers projected the idea that life had no value in the hills for, at the slightest opportunity, other people could kill an individual (for head or otherwise). This notion of lawlessness is not true as all tribal customs had specific rules to deal with the case of murder and other crimes. They were sufficiently effective within the precinct of the village. However, complications arose when murder took place between two or more villages, as there was no authority above the village. Individuals were often freely willed to avenge such murders, or it often caused war between two or more villages. Sometimes, revenge war dragged on for generations. However, this very celebrated idea of revenge, instead of being the source of murder, could also act as a deterrent factor against murder in the first place.

Further, we will see that the hillmen, as state-evading population, were constantly on their guard against conquerors and marauders from the valleys, as well as from politically ambitious persons in the hills. This hugely limited their freedom and even the choice of their livelihood strategies. Thus, their peculiar economic behaviours, such

[34] See Butler (1875), Woodthorpe (1882), Lyall (1997 [1908]: 22).

as valuing jhum cultivation, avoiding surplus or markets, discriminating certain crops and implements, and so on, were an act of limitation. Likewise, their liberty to choose freely was also constrained by many other factors, say, their religion, superstitions, and even the customs and traditions itself. Similarly, if the notion of 'natural liberty' implies 'non-domination' and 'self-mastery', or absence of actual interference, potential interference, and any other psychological constraints (for example, fears), then this did not hold true for individuals in stateless society.[35] Though they were free individuals, they were always under certain forms of constraint. For instance, there was always a division of people into chief–commoner, men–women, husband–wife, older–younger, master–slave, and so on. But to say that such divisions were based on hierarchy and domination relation, or non-domination relationship, will not go down well with the hillmen. These were either biological, or gender related, or occupational, and not based on grade and status.

For instance, if patriarchal society put women in disadvantaged position in the society, it could not dominate them in practice because women would not allow men to transform the relationship into domination relation. In a worst-case scenario, the hill slavery could not transform the life of a slave into a bare life. If he was subject to an occupational category of 'slave', he could buy back his liberation; in his 'subjection', he was 'kindly' treated as a normal and equal member of the master's family and in the village society. He ate, drank, dressed, slept, and worked as one of them. He worked for his master, but he was hardly deprived of the fruits of his labour. He was a different kind of slave. He struggled between domination and non-domination: a slave by category but not a slave by repression. He was, as the Lushei called him, *boi* (literally, 'who is in trouble'), someone who was 'taken care of' by the kind master.

Similarly, while there was a village 'government' in each village, it was not a regulatory regime to limit individual freedom but to protect them within the ambit of customary laws. It resembled state, but it was not a state in the strict sense of the term. Thus, each village had a headman or chief, but his authority was 'nominal'. He possessed 'no exclusive power to take cognizance of offences against the person

---

[35] For republican notion of liberty, see Berlin (1969).

or property of individuals' except those permitted by 'customs'.[36] He did not decide but presided over the village 'council' or 'assembly', which was the ultimate authority. Both the 'democratic' and 'chieftainship' systems, the two dominant forms of village 'government' in the region, were not an arbitrary power over the individual. Thus, despite the presence of 'village government' headed by a chief, each individual was 'his own king' and 'his own lord' who acted or 'self-disciplined' within the ambit of customs and traditions. Therefore, the orders of the chiefs, or headmen, or men were 'obeyed so far only as they accord with the wishes and convenience of the community' (read as custom).[37] The non-recognition of any 'superior' authority who can assume control as a matter of right implies 'absence of subjection' to any arbitrary power. In this context, what Berlin has called 'positive liberty', such as 'self-control', becomes helpful.[38]

Conceptually, we can therefore say that there was a visible presence of actual, potential, and psychological 'interference', of external and internal 'impediments', on the life and liberty of the hillmen. Thus, the idea that an individual is 'his own master' and 'follows the dictates of his own will' does not imply the notion of 'natural liberty' in Hobbesian sense. They were individuals who were always within bounds, but such boundaries were not a regime of arbitrary control but a system which protected and promoted the freedom of self-disciplined individuals.

What makes freedom in stateless society different from others is the absence of state. Several studies on the present state of freedom in liberal society have pointed out how it was gradually encroached upon by the political, the state. Individual freedoms were, for instance, constantly encroached through a series of legislative and administrative injunctions under a regime of what Agamben has called the 'state of exception' that gives primacy to the 'apparatuses of security' over the imperative of freedom.[39] Liberalism in liberal society, therefore, works not through the imperative of freedom, but through the social production of freedom and the 'management and organization of

---

36 Butler (1978 [1855]: 146).
37 (1978 [1855]: 146).
38 Berlin (1969).
39 See Agamben (2005).

the conditions in which one can be free'.[40] Thus, much ambiguity has been created between the concept of freedom as a human right and freedom as independence of the governed. In the absence of the state in a stateless society, such an encroachment was hardly possible, if not completely absent. Here, market played no or little role in the life and politics of the hillmen and its self-government. Safety and security being major concerns did indeed curb their freedom in some ways, but such limitations were easily overcome when they become oppressive.

Thus, one can talk of liberalism working not through the social production of freedom but through the imperative of freedom as independence of the governed. In this sense, we can say that if freedom in liberal society is moving towards the 'civil' and the political, the same is moving towards the 'uncivil' and the individuals in the stateless society. Unstate as a process, therefore, means the enactment of freedom as independence of the governed, a process that moves towards the individual, the uncivil, not the 'civil' of the state. It is, after all, a society which was moving towards egalitarianism or equalitarianism. The production and management of this freedom requires a vibrant counter-cultural collective. A brief discussion of these counter-cultures as a form of resistance thus becomes helpful.

On Resistance in Stateless Society

Much has been written on the forms of resistance in the state society, ranging from an open confrontation to that of low intensity, often silent, and imperceptible 'everyday forms of resistance'. While the nationalist writings have been quite successful in correcting the colonial epistemic violence on the 'others', a gradual proliferation of scholarship on 'history from below' can be witnessed.[41] It is under the latter genre of history that much of the resistance carried out by the 'subalterns' has come to the fore. Yet, until recent times, emphasis was on 'peasant movement', again in an open confrontational category. Unhappy with the idea that only an open protest against established authority qualified the concept of 'resistance', scholars like

40 See Foucault (2008: 63–4).
41 See, for instance, Guha (1999 [1983]).

James C. Scott have introduced us to a new and fertile ground of what he has called 'everyday forms of resistance'. He has noted that the 'ordinary weapons' of the weak are as powerful as open confrontation of power. They have always formed the 'dissonant political culture' of subordinated groups in state society.[42] Hollander and Einwohner have brought together different studies on resistance and suggested a 'seven-part typology of resistance' which shows the multiplicities and complexities of forms of resistance in state society.[43]

The existing theory of resistance, however, shows that resistance is either overt or covert against domination. It has meaning only when there is domination relation in a society. In other words, domination is seen to be self-articulating in nature and when it crosses a certain point, resistance is generated. This understanding, however, fails to explain the inbuilt resistance system within a cultural collective that prevented or suppressed the emergence of domination relation. The forms of resistance among the stateless hillmen are instructive in this respect. There are some studies on tribal society which have pointed out how resistance can be culturally embedded within the livelihood strategies. Jerome Levi's fine study on the Raramuris of northern Mexico, for instance, shows how they deliberately preferred their articles of everyday use, like traditional bow and blanket, as a form of resistance against the dominant political economy around them. Such material culture allowed them to be self-sufficient and independent.[44] In his recent work on the Zomia highland, Scott also shows how the state-evading hill population had chosen or evolved their culture and agriculture to resist the control and appropriations of the valley states and prevent state from springing up in the hills. He considers such ingenious practices as their 'art' and the 'culture and agriculture of escape'.[45]

Two interesting characters of resistance become apparent in the context of Northeast India highland. On the one hand, we can see that resistance was embedded in their various nonstate practices and effectively prevented oppressive control and domination. On

---

[42] See Scott (1985, 1990).
[43] Hollander and Einwohner (2004: 544–7).
[44] Levi (1998).
[45] Scott (2009).

the other, resistance was open and free from the intimidating gaze of power. The embeddedness of resistance, what I have called the counter-culture conduit, in the stateless hill society can be seen from the way they crafted their space, settlements, polities, social relations, resources utilization, and so on. Thus, the dispersive settlement and population distribution pattern, connected by difficult and repulsive pathways across the forested jungles, systematically prevented raiders, marauders, and conquerors. Similarly, the villages at the top of the hills, surrounded by stockade and guarded by hill warriors, were equally anathema to easy control and appropriations. The choice of flattened wealth (rather than capital) equally served as an embedded counter-culture collective against control, just as their 'democratic' polities and the plural, porous, and fluid social formation served the same purpose. This is one side of the counter-culture; the other side is even more fascinating.

The fascinating aspect of each choice the hillmen made for their organizational structure and relationship was the provision of an inbuilt safeguard, the counter-culture conduit, to each of them. As each of these structures could become oppressive in time, each was provided with the embedded mechanism, a conduit, not only to evade the system in case it became oppressive but also to prevent the system from becoming oppressive. Thus, if the village chief or council became oppressive, they could not do so without risking their power since the system gave individuals the right to migrate to another village at ease or people could simply disallow the chief/council to continue. Similarly, if a man became oppressive to a woman within the dominant patriarchal system or its marriage institution, he could not do so without risking his life and his marriage. This was because the same system also provided a liberal divorce and remarriage as a conduit through which the women could easily get rid of unwanted marriage. Therefore, there was a peculiar system of checks and balances by which an individual could, of his own will and without resorting to village court or somebody's assistance, make use of the inbuilt conduit to evade such oppression/domination. This counter-culture conduit system required vibrant individuals to accelerate the system.

It was, in fact, the vibrant form of resistance which made the stateless hills different from the state society. It was conditioned by the absence of intimidating gaze of power. If individuals in state society have to resist domination under the intimidating gaze of power and their action is subject to police/military repression, then the power of resistance will slide down the slippery slope, making it necessarily opaque and amorphous. This was not the case in stateless society. In the absence of arbitrary power, an individual in stateless society found no intimidating power when his/her rights were infringed. In this context, resistance was usually open and direct. His 'everyday forms of resistance' were as visible as his open 'protest' or 'rebellion'. Thus, a person who found difficulty in one social system would openly switch over to another, just as a person who found the chief oppressive would immediately and openly migrate to another village. Similarly, a wife who found her husband oppressive would immediately desert him. This not only evaded oppression but also deterred it in a major way.

Therefore, what was significant in the forms of resistance in stateless hill society was not only the structurally and culturally embedded form of resistance, a resistance through the inbuilt mechanism, the counter-culture, but it was also necessarily a resistance that was open, visible, and direct. To the extent an individual could resist all forms of domination and oppression in the open and fearlessly, freedom would continue to remain lively and vibrant and the striking capability of the political would become weak. To the extent freedom and resistance remained vibrant and collective, the stateless hill society was moving towards a certain destiny, a destiny that was an egalitarian society.

History and Orality

As noted earlier, the hillmen had a very strong retentive memory of their pasts and orality constituted the core of their cultural collective. But such oral histories remain untapped and their voices remain unheard over the centuries, partly because of the unkindly History and partly due to lack of proper methodology to deal with them. For so long, oral narratives have been put on the back burner within academic discourse in history and other social sciences. The popular oral narratives have been regarded as being fantastic, interwoven myths produced by baroque mass of illiterate, irrational, backward, and stolid population. Truth requires, as it has been argued, for its revelation a 'scientific' and 'rational' approach, which is available only in 'official' texts and documents. It never crossed the mind that a large section of the world's population has not written their histories but narrated them orally, symbolically, and metaphorically. What History has of them is what is written about them, not what they wrote for themselves. State and History have written about the peasants, the tribes, and other subaltern sections of the population. This writing is often deceptive, often stigmatizing. They have appeared in history and historical record, Scott noted, not so much as historical actors but as more or less anonymous contributors to statistics on conscription, taxes, labour migration, landholdings, and crop production.[46] The histories of the subalterns, of the consciousness of 'unlettered race', are embedded in the 'elitist' History which one can excavate only when one reads, as Guha has suggested, 'against the grain' to the elitist 'body of evidence'.[47]

But the small voices of History and the statistics can never bring much to the larger histories of the subalterns, unless their unlettered, oral narratives are taken into consideration. As Sahid Amin has declared in his famous work on Chauri Chaura, peasants 'do not write, they are written about'; it is crucial to bring to light that what is not written as well. This is particularly because what is written about them is not recorded for posterity but 'wrenched from them in courtrooms and inquisitorial trails'. By combing carefully through those 'confessions' and 'testimonies', or what Amin has powerfully termed as 'to interrogate the interrogators', historians would find some of their 'evidences'. But what is more important than courtroom testimonies in which the peasants 'cry out' under the intimidating gaze of power is what he has called the enormous 'oral accounts' expressed freely, away from power, before the 'intellectual' (who was also addressed as 'sarkar' by his peasants just like colonial policemen) not at the courtroom but in the 'field'. To access this corpus of 'oral history', he has suggested, historians must perform

---

[46] Scott (1985).
[47] Guha (1994, 1999 [1983]: chapter 1).

'historical fieldwork', sitting with bearers of history day in, day out and from place to place.[48]

What is true for peasants is even more true for the tribes. Tribals hardly write, and they are also hardly written about. Their geography has always been too far away from the core of the state: inaccessible, isolated, and often unknown. What is embedded in the History, in most cases, has been adopted from hearsay and imagination. The small voices are too stunted and too small to be recognizable; they have come in traces and, in most cases, embedded between the lines. Reading against the grain has often ended in embarrassment; it is unrewarding. Thus, the tribal universe has remained elusive, opaque, and anonymous. The obvious way of combating such bias, as Guha has suggested, is 'to summon folklore, oral as well as written, to the historian's aid'.[49] Thanks to the brave colonial officers and professional anthropologists who eventually entered the world of their 'savages' after taking so many deep breathes, trembling hundred times before asking the first question, and risking their heads in the midst of the famed headhunters, the timeless capsule of the veritable treasure of the tribal universe has been broken into. Piece by piece, we have come to know of the archaeology of tribal knowledge which got into print, visual, and audio form. Piece by piece, our knowledge of them has also been supplemented by generations of now-literate tribals themselves. Piece by piece, the corpus of oral history has piled up in our bookshelves. The time has come now where they have also found their place in History.

The rich corpus of 'oral histories' ingrained in the memory of the subalterns, waiting to be excavated, along with those already recorded in print, is indeed the *histories* of the unlettered race. They are the archaeology of knowledge which, as Marc Bloch has suggested, has become vocal only to those who can see and walk over the 'field' and are 'sensible' to their feelings.[50] Sensibility to their feelings, emotions, and even to their stereotypes is a necessary precondition to enter into the world of the subaltern universe and to be able to access the rich

---

[48] The information, including the quotes, in this para is taken from Amin (1995: 'Prologue').

[49] Guha (1999 [1983]: 14).

[50] Bloch (1973).

corpus of their archaeology. Being sensible to such voices is often to sink into the world of a discursive discourse, a counter-cultural narrative from the margins. It is an exploration; a historical odyssey into the world of what Foucault has called 'counter-memory'.[51] Juxtaposing the 'counter-memory' with that of the official and dominant discourse amounts to following a methodology involving what Shail Mayaram has called 'a clash of histories'.[52] Thus, unless the 'counterperspectives from the margins', in Mayaram's apt term, are taken into consideration, no history of the 'unlettered race' can be accessed in the way it deserves.

What remains to be asked then is how or how many of the oral narratives should find their place in history. I would say *all*. But this needs an explanation. Historians group oral traditions into memorized speech, accounts, epics, tales, proverbs, and sayings. This huge corpus of oral traditions is something which has been internalized and transmitted to children in the process of learning the language and behaviours.[53] But it is also contended that most cultures make a distinction between 'true' and 'not-true' stories, and within true stories, those with the greatest degree of chronological, historical, and geographical specificity are identified as legends.[54] But legends are few and far between compared to other categories of oral history due to its character of being non-performative and non-repetitive, limitation of human memory and information overload, and the notion of signification and interest. The last one, 'significance' and 'interest', is especially instructive because in every society, information is not a disinterested knowledge but imbued with well-defined categories involving selection, addition, omission, and even forgetting. But this process shows that oral history become closely congruent to social concerns of the *present* than the *past*. This very character of homoeostasis in orality leads many to question the 'truthness' or 'authenticity' of oral history. It has broadly divided scholars into two on the question of whether or not oral traditions should be included in history.

[51] Foucault (1977) and Misztal (2003: 64–6).
[52] Mayaram (2003: xiv).
[53] Vansina (1985).
[54] Blackburn (2003: 16).

Some historians have argued that the congruence between society and oral traditions is the product of a dynamic homoeostasis, and therefore cannot correspond to the past reality.[55] There is another group of scholars who feels that oral traditions are an indispensable source of history. Some feel that orality or memory is more 'authentic' than History and want separation of the two.[56] Others feel that orality should be taken as 'raw material' for history by removing all its 'reflections'.[57] There are still some historians who feet that oral traditions are but history by itself, although they accept the fact that some categories of orality are not at all history.[58] The two points that historians have found difficult to accept in oral traditions are its character of dynamic homoeostasis and absence of chronology. But Vansina argues that the presence of 'archaism' in various oral traditions makes homoeostasis thesis unacceptable. He shows that the first encoded message limits the decoder's interpretation. The one a researcher is confronted with is to a degree a collective interpretation.[59] Thus, one can talk about tendency towards homoeostasis, not of homoeostasis as a radical process. Vansina also argues that all cultures have their own notion of time and oral traditions and, like history, also narrate historical phenomena in 'chains of change' by taking events and situations in relative sequence. The 'chain of change' is sufficient to show how orality also has full sense of chronology.[60]

If oral traditions are not disinterested knowledge and contain truths of the past in 'chains of change', and if truth is a relative term in culture, then it does not appear that we can reject any of the oral histories. I would suggest that all those narratives, which the oral societies have represented about their past, need to be taken as true to that cultural collective. This applies both to legends and other genres of oral histories. Congruency also applies the other way

---

[55] Goody and Watt (1963).

[56] Halbwachs (1992 [1925]), Nora (1984), and Yerushalmi (1982).

[57] Le Goff (1992) and Recoeur (2004).

[58] Vansina (1985).

[59] Vansina (1985: 196).

[60] For instance, what used to be considered as 'magical chants' of the Kuki-Chin priests, for instance, narrate the legends of their migration from place to place, in sequence, till their present habitats. See Goswami (1985).

round. It connotes relevance, occurrence, and the present, or what we called significance to the present. Thus, certain legends or other oral histories become relevant or popular at certain point of time because the society needed them. By learning the message of such histories, one can find the clue or even unlock the truth of the time. They are the writing on the wall. They are what Scott has called the 'social arsenals' of the subordinated groups (the tribes in our case). They function not only as their history but also as instrument of social control, ensuring, through its social sanction, conformity with the social norms and values. These histories 'oversee' people's lives to the smallest detail and have a 'hold' over their perceptions. They are the social therapy that may encourage, evade, or evaporate joy and grievances, or respond, resist, or retaliate opponents, or it could be anything.

To the genres of orality other than legends—for example, myths, folklores, tales, ballads, sayings, chanting, proverbs, or riddles—it is to be added that they are nonetheless relevant if a researcher is *sensible* to their *feelings* and *emotions*. Subalterns often express their feelings and emotions in several ways. For example, composing songs/ballads or singing those existing one that satisfy their feeling and evaporate grievances; and composing jokes, proverbs, riddles, and so on against the powerful, the One, or narrate the existing one which generates similar message of dissent. They are not produced out of the box; they all have their contexts in a specific way. They are not disinterested knowledge. Myths, symbols, images, metaphors, and so on are very useful instruments in the hands of subalterns against their time. If history is about the narrative of facts, orality is concerned more with expression; and it is through such expressions that truth can be recapitulate. By contextualizing the contents/message/expressions of the oral narratives, such as the feelings and emotions, against the time when such narratives became popular and lively, one can actually make a useful history of the time, of that society, of that landscape. By asking why a certain set of feelings and emotions, which run through different oral tropes, become popular at a certain point of time, one would be able to judge the circumstances in which the bearers of such histories found themselves. In this context, *all* oral histories, in whatever genre one finds them, could be a valuable source of information/history. What remains to be done by historians is to excavate or extract what Ajay Skaria has called 'historical grain from mythical chaff' and join them along with what can be had from the reading of 'elitist' accounts 'against the grain'.[61]

Reading the oral narratives of the hill tribes of Northeast India will show at least two sets of oral tropes, apparently contrasting at first glance but which are actually complementary to each other (see Chapter 7). They are, to be sure, the counter-cultural narratives of the society at the margins of the state. While the first trope relates to the dissonant political discourse, the second relates to the social norms of an egalitarian society. Of the dissonant political discourse, we will see a strong presence of warrior ideology in which there was significant presence of the state, *the One*, who was always 'around'. It was sometimes seen as the One that is much envied and at other times, the One that is much dreaded. Thus, on the one hand, we will see that the stateless society was enviously looking towards the coming or restoration of their lost 'kingdom', their millenarian hope. On the other hand, they were constantly on their guard against the control of state (referring to the valley states) for which they warned people to remain alert. Both these required a strong class of warriors, and hence the predominance of warrior ideology in their various oral tropes.

We will also see that their oral tropes urged the hillmen to stick to the normative principles of an egalitarian society as a means to prevent and evade any form of control and oppression. They celebrated equality and social harmony based on egalitarian principles and renounced the mighty, the rich, and the arrogant. The two dominant sets of cultural tropes amplify not only the cultural capital that is aspiring to cope up with questions of survival and marginality but also to the question of being 'human' or 'hillmen'. While coping with the present marginalization presents the view of being state evaders, the question of being 'human' addresses the issue of survival at the margins, of being professors of egalitarianism. Both these strands are flowing in close parallel across the various layers of oral traditions. The combination of security and equality demands cooperation amongst all. Hence, the principle that governed the egalitarian society was

---

[61] Skaria (1999: 1).

what we called 'cooperation and reciprocity'. All must help and all help must be reciprocated, within which the demand of security and equality was conceived. This principle governed their lifeways and relationship in all walks of life—economic, social, cultural, political, and so on.

The Tricky Issue of Periodization

I have mentioned earlier that this work starts in the 'time immemorial' of the tribal universe but ends with the occupation of the highland massif by the British colonial state. But where are we going to put such history in the grand historical calendar of ancient, medieval, and modern is a matter that would raise eyebrows. I refrain from using any one in my title, keeping out of the tricky situation created by such periodization. However, I will be frequently using the terms premodern, precolonial, colonial, and modern in the chapters. Therefore, a small clarification becomes pertinent here to help the readers, and also to emphasize the tricky issue of subdividing history into ancient, medieval, and modern (or even postmodern). In fact, the subdivision of history into different, ideal periods is always a disturbing question everywhere. What makes European history comfortable does not bring the same sense in non-European context. Likewise, what makes the history of dominant communities or region comfortable in a national framework does not bring the same conformity to other regions or minority communities in the same country. Indeed, such periodization becomes even more uncomfortable among the multiplicity of national cultures. Perhaps, what is most comfortable for the tribal world in such periodization in general is the perceptions it comes along with, the civilizational notion of time. If modern means, for instant, industrialization and capital, the tribal world is going to wait, maybe, for another millennium. Until then, they are what we called 'ancient' and 'primitive'.

In the context of Indian history, British ascendancy in Bengal was decisively taken as the end of the old, the 'medieval', and the beginning of the new, the 'modern'. But this has been often contested on all fronts: cultural, economic, social, and even political. Thus, while larger part of India came under the British colonial regime, great swathes of Indian subcontinent remained outside it through the colonial period. If British ascendancy in Gangetic valley roughly in the middle of eighteenth century marks the beginning of the new age, this had come in Assam since 1826 and in the hills of the Northeast region in the later parts of the nineteenth century. Thus, when we say 'modern' in the context of part of India, other parts will be still reeling in medievalism. Similarly, when we use the familiar categories such as 'precolonial' and 'colonial' in the context of a certain region of India, say, Northeast region, we take it for granted that the former is pre-1750 and the latter is post-1750. This confusion will keep coming up as we go from region to region and from culture to culture. My point is not to suggest any change; far from it. But if some solution (which is not easy) can be had, it would positively serve well. My aim is, however, to underline for my readers certain terms related to periodization being liberally used in this work.

As I said, I frequently use the terms premodern, precolonial, colonial, and modern in this book, but the context in which I use them must be always taken into consideration. In the context of Northeast India, I use 'premodern' in terms of 'precolonial', that is, before the arrival of British colonial state in the region. Similarly, 'colonial' and 'modern' are synonymously used to mark the advent of British colonial state in the region. The occupation of a particular geographical space (say, Naga Hills, Lushai Hills, Khasi Hills, and so on) by the British should be taken as a benchmark to divide what I mean is 'precolonial' and 'colonial' period. Thus, larger part of Brahmaputra valley came under British control after the Treaty of Yandabo (1826), part of Upper Assam (under Purandhar Singha) was re-annexed in 1838, and Matak country was annexed in 1842. Kachari kingdom was annexed in 1832 and a small part in North Cachar Hills under Tularam Senapaty was annexed in 1854. Khasi states came under British protectorate after Anglo-Khasi War, 1829–33, and Jaintia kingdom was annexed in 1835. Part of Naga Hills was annexed in 1866; Lhota country was added in 1875; Ao country in 1889; Sema country in 1904; and Konyak country in 1910. Garo Hills came under British rule in 1873 and Lushai Hills and Chin Hills were annexed in 1889–90. The hill areas of Manipur state came under direct state control only after the Kuki Rising, 1917–19. Whereas North East Frontier Agency (now Arunachal Pradesh) and Tuensang area of Naga Hills were never under British direct control, the states of Manipur and Tripura continued to remain as princely states. Thus, when I say 'precolonial' in this book, it means before such colonization, although the same term may be very well into 'colonial' period in other parts of India.

What is described here as precolonial 'statelessness' refers up to the period when annexation actually took place. Nevertheless, it is also a moot point to argue here that much before colonialism took root in the hills, its impact was already being felt in a big way in the hills, particularly in the new political formation process, which also affected social relations. The military expeditions in the hills, the frontier policy (especially its annual durbars and melas), the intrusion of firearms, and so on had a reorienting effect on the political and social relations in the hills.[62] Thus, when the idea of statelessness is worked out until about the actual occupation, the change that might have taken place during this time since the advent of colonialism in the valley should also be considered. Hence, state control system had already entered the hills much before state actually entered there, while many forms of statelessness continue to thrive well into colonial and postcolonial period. Thus, my stricture on the calendar notion of change, such as precolonial and colonial, is not given too much weight in the making and unmaking of things here. This is particularly because the colonial state ruled over the hills not by overturning their systems but by entering into it.

[62] I have discussed this change in the case of the southern hills in Guite (2011). This was also the case in other hills. Detailed discussion on this aspect is kept for another occasion.

1

An Enormous Dead Level
Daunting Geography, Rippling States

The hills and valleys have lived in symbiosis through history. It is therefore proper to begin the history of the hills from the valleys from where, as we will learn, the hill people originally came from. The precolonial river valleys of Brahmaputra and Barak (India), and Chindwin and Irrawaddy (Burma), were the hotbed of state formation under manpower war-machine states. These states had neither the economic resources nor the requisite military power and technological support to effectively control their periphery, especially the rugged mountain margins. This was largely due to the natural friction of terrain which the modern states progressively eliminated through their distance-demolishing technology, like road, rail, air, wire, and now wireless. With the focus on Brahmaputra valley of Assam, India, this chapter shows that the peculiar feature of precolonial Assam, as in Burma, was the enormous presence of friction of terrain, mainly due to low population–land ratio, abundance of open land replenished with dense forest and marshlands, and inadequate means of transport and communication networks. The friction increased as one moved away from the core to the periphery of the state and from the navigable river corridors towards the agrarian frontier where river transport was absent. All practicable mobility for the army, bureaucracy, and marauders eventually ended at the foot of the hills or much before that. Thus, viewing from the Naga Hills, S.E. Peal, one of the earliest English settlers of Assam, described the valley of Brahmaputra River 'as flat as it was possible to be, literally a sea of jungle forest, an enormous dead level'. He estimated that the 'area under cultivation' was not more than 'one percent' of the flat plain.[1] It was this 'sea of jungle forest' which had produced the natural friction of terrain, the 'enormous dead level' in Peal's apt term. It was a significant factor in the formation of state and its spatial politics. This chapter covers the formation of valley states within such daunting geography and locates the conditions of subjected population within such manpower states.

Locating the Frontier Kingdoms

Since ancient times, a number of kingdoms emerged across the level plain of this frontier region, with different degrees of life and vitality. Edward Gait showed the presence of successive kingdoms from antiquity in Brahmaputra valley (commonly known as Assam), such as the principalities of various 'tribes' like Khasis and Kacharis (Bodos) and Kamarupa kingdom from the fourth century, followed by Kachari, Chutiya, Kamata, Ahom, Koch, and so on in the medieval period.[2] The Ahom's dominance over the valley came to an end only in the nineteenth century. In the Surma–Barak valley, hectic state-formation process similarly ensued.[3] The presence of Bodo-speaking people in its northern (Garos) and southern frontiers (Tipperahs/Kokboroks) led Gait to believe that this valley might have been initially ruled over by the same stock. One Khasi tradition of migration from Sylhet region also lends support to such an assumption.[4] In the meantime, various kingdoms such as Srihattamandalla (Sylhet) under Samatata (7 CE), Srihatta (11 CE), the Gaur, the Afghans

---

[1] Peal (1873: 317).

[2] See Gait (2008 [1905]); see also Bhattacharjee (1991) and Sinha (1989).

[3] Bhattacharjee (1991).

[4] Gurdon (2010 [1906]: 10).

(since 1303), Mughals, Tripura (since 13 CE), Jaintia (16 CE), and Kachari (18 CE) emerged.[5]

In the Chindwin and Irrawaddy valleys of Burma, waves of immigration formed different states since the early CE.[6] Ancient kingdoms under Peguin (Talaings, Mons, or Muns) groups and those of Karan, Pyu (Pru), Sak (Thek), and Mramma were recorded. Under Burmese dominance, ancient Tagaung dynasty came up in central Irrawaddy valley which emerged as Burmese (or Pagan) kingdom in the medieval period.[7] In upper Chindwin–Irrawaddy valley, there were many Shan statelets since the early CE, over which emerged the powerful Pong kingdom in the eighth century which was very soon destroyed by Burmese kingdom.[8] On the lofty height of the Great Himalayas, Tibetan kingdom existed since about the seventh century CE. In the middle of its southward-running ranges also emerged the small kingdom of Manipur under Ninthouja dynasty, which effectively took shape as a state with imperial design in the fifteenth century during the reign of Ningthoukhomba (c. 1431).[9]

The rise and fall of these kingdoms in the region has generally been studied purely from a military point of view. What has often been neglected is what I would call the sad side of such state-making projects. To be sure, none of these states were formed without first overcoming the several hurdles that opposed their emergence. While warfare and conquest were truly the core constituents of these war-machine states, their struggle to overcome opposition posited by the daunting geography, low population–land ratio, low level of technology, and so on, has been generally put on the back burner. If the nature of state has to be studied seriously, these factors are indispensable. Therefore, a brief discussion on some of these aspects in the formation of states in the region is necessary to show why state making was actually menacing to sections of the valley population,

[5] Bhattacharjee (1991: 106–22) and Gait (2008 [1905]).

[6] See Fr. Sangermano (1966 [1833]), Phayre (1967 [1883]), and Scott (2002 [1886]).

[7] Phayre (1967 [1883]: 17).

[8] Phayre (1967 [1883]: 17).

[9] For details of state formation in the valley of Manipur, see Kabui (1991) and Singh (1995).

who eventually chose to run away and take shelter in the stateless margins. Much of these aspects in Burma have been discussed by James Scott.[10] Therefore, my focus is on the Brahmaputra valley, although I will also touch upon other areas.

Assam's Agony: Rains, Rivers, Forests

Brahmaputra valley (Assam) has an area of about 24,000 square miles, with a length of nearly 450 miles (from Goalpara in the west to Sadiya in the east) and a varying breadth of about 50 miles. The valley is surrounded on all sides, save the west where it joins the Bengal plain, by high mountain ranges inhabited by different hill tribes. Thus, its climate is influenced by this geological formation to a great extent. The climate of Assam is tropical moist climate, with an annual average rainfall of 75–150 inches. The rainy season lasts for over eight months, from March to October, with heavy torrential rains from June to September. This climatic situation forms an interesting river regime in the valley. Running along the middle of the valley, in east–west direction, is one of the world's largest river, the Brahmaputra, fed by numerous tributaries on both sides. The northern streams are snow-fed and perennial, whereas the southern streams, save Dihing, are rain-fed and either shrink or dry up during the dry winter season. While Brahmaputra River is navigable throughout its course in the valley, the same is possible in its tributaries only to a short distance, mainly due to the rapids, shallowness (because of heavy siltation), and more importantly, their courses being short in the plain before they sink into the great river.

One estimate puts the total length of Assam's navigable rivers as 3,711 miles for an area of some 24,000 square miles.[11] While the volume (shallowness) and rapids set limits to most of the tributaries in the dry season, they, including Brahmaputra River, are extremely hazardous for boats other than dugout canoes in the rainy season.[12]

[10] See Scott (2009: chapters 2 and 3).

[11] Guha (1991: 9).

[12] These canoes do not use sails but have to be paddled or rowed with bamboo poles by five to six men and can cover 8–10 miles a day. The preponderance of canoes which normally carry 100–200 maunds of goods has been, thus, universal over the centuries.

This is not only because of the crashing banks with jungle covers and the floating trees they carry but also due to the torrential tropical rain in the region that raises the volume of the rivers several time higher than its normal level, making them deadly in most cases. Robinson, for instance, noted that the volume of water that Brahmaputra disembogues at its lowest ebb was about 146,188 cubic feet per second and four times more during rainy season when the river attained a height of 30–40 feet above its common level.[13] M'Cosh too noted that during the rainy season, navigation was strongly impeded because the river overflowed its banks and little or no tracking ground was left. The prevailing wind being from the east added no little impediment to the journey besides the 'rafts of pine trees, with the reeds and long grass adhering'. So, pushing along by the slowest of all processes, the bamboo, was the only means of advancing.[14] John Butler also described his disastrous adventure over the great river by a common *khelnao*[15] or pleasure-boat of the country from Saikwah to Tezpur in 1844. In the night, his boat drifted down to the middle of the river from where it was fastened at the bank. In a dilemma, he and the only servant left on the boat paddled the boat, drifted past prostrate trees and stumps, and 'whirled round and round in the numerous eddies or whirlpools' that rendered Brahmaputra most dangerous for a small boat. After the night was nearly gone and they were close to being crushed to death under the high bank of Dikhoo Mookh, they made a narrow escape by 'instantly jumping on shore' at one projecting point of the bank.[16]

On another occasion, Butler narrated the turbulent character of Brahmaputra River during rainy season when the current was so strong that it swept away 'ten paces of the bank three or four times in the course of the day'. The fall of the stupendous mass of earth into the bosom of the stream sounded like 'the report of cannon'. They had to shift their resident (which was originally about 150 yards away) at least three times against the advancing river until they finally settled down on the only high ground; and every time they shifted, they found their

[13] Robinson (1975 [1841]: 9).

[14] M'Cosh (2000 [1837]: 6).

[15] Khelnao is about 50 feet long and three-and-a-half feet wide, with a grass roof over a portion forming a sleeping berth.

[16] Butler (1978 [1855]: 7–8).

old dwelling place in the middle of the river after a week.[17] A voyage up the Brahmaputra River in dry season had its own obstacles. M'Cosh, for instance, noted that in the dry season, there were no beaten paths to facilitate tracking and the boatmen had to either force their way through the high reeds on the crumbling perpendicular bank or scramble along the bottom, or what they preferred, keep upon the shoal side of the river where the sandbank afforded good footing, though with a great drawback of the boats often running aground.[18]

In another instance, Butler also narrated his experience over one of the tributaries of Brahmaputra, the 'famed' Kalang River, that swarmed with mosquitoes. It was in August, in the midst of rainy season, when he was ordered to take the charge of Nogaong district from Tezpur. The only way to reach his new station was by boat, which usually took four days. He said that they were 'literally scarred from head to foot with sores' when they reached Nogaong because of the heat (96 degrees Fahrenheit) and mosquito bites.[19] Thus, it was due to this peculiar nature of the river regime in the valley that there were no or little riverside habitations in Assam for a very long time.[20] Early colonial accounts show no riverside town settlements 200 miles towards the lower course of Brahmaputra River from Sadiya, except in few naturally protected sites like Guwahati, Tezpur, and Goalpara. What Brahmaputra and its tributaries were to Assam, Irrawaddy and Chindwin rivers were to Burma.[21]

The time taken for a journey over these rivers was also appalling. Butler noted that one usually took 34 days from Goalpara in the west to Sadiya in the east (450 miles apart) through Brahmaputra River by a *budgerow* (kind of boat) of Bengal.[22] M'Cosh also noted that one took 35 days from Goalpara to Calcutta and eight days more (that is, 43 days in total) from Calcutta to Goalpara.[23] Thus, one took 77

[17] Butler (1978 [1855]: 2–4).

[18] M'Cosh (2000 [1837]: 6).

[19] Butler (1978 [1855]: 10–11).

[20] See M'Cosh (2000 [1837]: 2).

[21] See, for instance, Bayfield (1873), Hannay (1873), Scott (1893), and Shakespear (2004 [1914]).

[22] Butler (1847: 15).

[23] M'Cosh (2000 [1837]: 7).

days from Calcutta to Sadiya over the Brahmaputra River in normal times. Major Vetch remarked that the time taken between Calcutta and Dibrugarh (in Upper Assam) by a country boat of 1,000 maunds was as great as that of a voyage round the Cape to London by a sailing vessel.[24] This was also the case in Burma. Captain Hannay, for instance, took 46 days of 'actual travelling' from Ava, the capital of Burma, to Meinkhwon, the 'capital' of Hukawng valley in Burma's northern frontier. He travelled mainly in the opposite direction of Irrawaddy River by a large boat till the mouth of Mogaung River and by a smaller boat along the latter river till Mogaung, the capital of a frontier district by the same name, and from thence he took an overland route to Hukawng valley. But he took only 18 days to reach Ava on his return journey through the same route along the onward direction of the said rivers.[25] This means that river transport in opposite direction would normally take more than two times of the time taken in onward direction. The virulent river regime made this travel almost impossible, or greatly impeded it, during the rainy season.

Despite all these disadvantages, river transport continued to be what Scott has called 'the great premodern exception' in the region.[26] Rivers not only served as transport and communication system but also helped immensely in what Herbst has called 'broadcasting of power'.[27] Since the main military force of the state had to be stationed in and around state or provincial capitals, the effectiveness of state control depended on the efficient utilization of river transport, the type of rivers, and the direction of such rivers from the centre of power. Due to this, the state capital and provincial centres of control were normally built at the centre of the river valley, generally near the river system, from where the periphery of the kingdom/empire could be reached in a relatively equitable time scale. Considering the difficulties of travelling over this 'premodern exception', one can now well imagine the effectiveness of state control over the periphery of the kingdom.

Life during the rainy season was, in general, miserable for all. Again, Butler, sharing his experience, stated that although they

---

[24] Mills (1980 [1853]: Appendix C—Vetch to Mills, 22 June 1853).

[25] Hannay (1873: 108).

[26] Scott (2009: 4).

[27] Herbst (2000: chapter 2).

escaped the reach of the 'merciless river' by shifting to higher ground, the torrents of rain which fell daily and inundated the whole country resulted in a life of 'uttermost apparent discomfort'. He said that the only comfort they enjoyed was to feel happy with what 'providence had placed within our reach' and 'never to repine at what cannot be helped'.[28] Truly, the only 'comfort' provided to state officers during the rainy season was not to go for war and conquest, but, as Butler put it, to 'diligently' employ their whole time 'in improving their position' against the rains.[29] All official duties, including official tours and other administrative work, were usually suspended and left to 'providence'. This was particularly because torrential rain also made travelling overland equally difficult for the army and officials. The flourishing forest, impassable reeds, and unconquerable swamps normally impeded overland movement.

Evidence has shown that the vast span of Brahmaputra and Chindwin–Irrawaddy valleys, until very recently, were covered with swamps and densely forested jungles of desolate wilderness. Well in the 1820s, Wilcox, for instance, noted that large parts of Brahmaputra valley constituted 'inhospitable tract of rank jungle, without a vestige of inhabitants', and in many parts, 'rivers could afford the only means of seeing the interior of the country, the dense jungles being impassable'.[30] This situation was what Peal later called the 'sea of jungle forest'. While passing from Nogaong to Naga Hills in 1845, Butler clearly witnessed such 'enormous dead level' through the level plain of Assam. In the first two days, he passed through 24 miles of level plain, 'studded with flourishing and populous villages and gardens', surrounded by 'immense sheets of fine rice cultivation'. Beyond this cultivated zone, he was compelled to travel across the extensive plain of about 57 miles (till Mohng Dehooa) through a small track covered with 'thick tree forest and high grass or reeds unvaried by the signs of cultivation or villages'. From this point to the foothills at Dimapur was about 30 miles, 'through a dark, damp, chilly, gloomy forest', where 'neither the sky nor sun was seen throughout the day', and the forest was so thick that he could not

---

28 Butler (1978 [1855]: 4).
29 Butler (1978 [1855]: 4).
30 Wilcox (1873: 6, 24).

see beyond ten paces in the front. He described this part of the route as having no 'vestige of any habitation or a human being', 'dreary gloomy desolate wilderness' with 'a death-like stillness everywhere', and the 'earth excessively damp'.[31]

This was also the case in the eastern Bengal frontier, Barak valley. The situation of Bengal frontier in the medieval period has been described by Eaton.[32] This Bengal fringe still bore a frontier character at the dawn of nineteenth century. In 1828, the ancient land of Hairumbo (Cachar) was, for instance, described by Hamilton as an 'unprofitable country' generating only about Rs 30,000 in 1817, thinly populated, 'much overrun with jungle', lying 'under the mountains abounds with bogs and marshes', covered with 'large sheets of water' during rainy season, and 'almost impracticable' for the movement of army from March to November.[33] Likewise, in 1836, W. Griffith also described Hukawng valley in Upper Burma as 'one mass of jungle, with here and there clear patches occurring'.[34] Bayfield was compelled to travel overland between Mogaung and Hukawng valley through the pathless jungles with the help of 'road-cutters'.[35] This route was described by Captain Hannay as 'passing between defiles' with no traces of inhabitants.[36] Thus, the enormous friction of distance across the three valleys was a common phenomenon in the precolonial period. In this context, the overland route was not looked at as an important part of the state-making project. The little possibility of overland travel during dry season become almost nil once the rains started. As an example, despite the different overland roads or *garh* constructed by the Ahom state for broadcasting of power, the numerous river systems continued to serve them as the 'premodern exception'.

---

[31] NAI, FP: 23 March 1846, No. 31: Butler to Jenkins, 16 July 1846. See also Butler (1978 [1855]: 14–24, 75).

[32] Eaton (1993).

[33] Hamilton (1993 [1828]: 308–10). See also J.W. Edgar to Secretary Government of Bengal, 5 June 1872, as reproduced in Mackenzie (2007 [1884]: 472).

[34] Griffith (1873: 128).

[35] Bayfield (1873).

[36] Hannay (1873: 100).

This climatic situation also led to the formation of peculiar landforms and had an impact on the agronomy. Both Assam and Burma valleys were, no doubt, deep alluvial formations. Yet, within this locale, one can sketch soil varieties which, in turn, suggest crop patterns and agrarian practices. Brahmaputra valley, for instance, was broadly divided into three belts: *chapari*, *rupit*, and *dooar*.[37] Chapari belt was a riverine corridor of sandy alluvial tract along both the banks of Brahmaputra River, including the shoals and islands therein. It was the belt open to constant alluvial and delluvial process of the river and was generally covered with reed and grass jungles. This belt was unfit for permanent cultivation and human habitation because of annual flooding and irrepressible weeds. Except a few *pam basti*s (temporary settlements) of seasonal migrants who cultivated some winter crops like mustard, pulses, and *ahu* (dry rice), no other settlements and cultivation could be seen.[38] Dooar belt referred to the narrow submontane or *terai* belt at the outer fringes or foothills of the valley having scrubby forests and high-grass savannah. The predominant agriculture system was shifting cultivation and ahu rice. This belt also had an 'unenviable reputation' on account of its extreme unhealthiness, infested with deadly malaria, and hence uninhabitable by any 'race'.[39]

Rupit belt was the vast expanse of alluvial flatland between chapari and dooar belts. It was the most fertile part of the valley and the predominant agriculture system was the permanent wet rice (*sali*) cultivation. Although sali cultivation required intensive labour and high financial sink at the beginning (such as levelling the field, throwing up the bund for logging water, and cutting irrigation channels

[37] Guha (1991).

[38] Ahu refers to upland, dry or early rice, sown broadcast, and specific to shifting cultivation on undulating or sloping lands in submontane and riverine tracts. M'Cosh described this belt 'as dreary a trip' for one who travelled by river Brahmaputra for 'days and weeks together', with nothing else visible 'but sand-banks and water bounding the horizon, with no trace of vegetation but an endless jungle of impregnable reeds'. It was also 'without the shadow of an inhabitant, or signs of animal life but water-fowls and alligators'. See M'Cosh (2000 [1837]: 4).

[39] Damant (1880: 232) and Endle (2010 [1911]: 8).

and embankments), it was the favourite agriculture for state making for several reasons. It was permanent, required less land, needed no weeding, had higher productivity, and hence could support higher concentration of population in a small area with greater amount of surplus. Hence, it allowed high revenue flow at low cost of collection and efficient broadcasting of power over a large population.[40]

The 'Halting Place of Death'

If the dominant geographical position of Brahmaputra and Irrawaddy–Chindwin valleys was characterized by torrential rainfall, virulent rivers, and irrepressible forest infested with deadly insects and diseases, it was perhaps one of the worst places to establish a state or kingdom. Ranging from the description of the Chinese pilgrim Hsuan Tsang (7 CE) to the medieval and early colonial writings, Assam (for that matter Upper Burma) was not just the 'frontier' of empires but, as some described, 'the halting place of death'. This was true not only for empire builders and conquerors from outside but also for state builders within the region; and was mainly due to the daunting geography described earlier. Shihabuddin Talish, who accompanied Mir Jumla invasion of Assam in 1662, for instance, remarked:

> In short every army that entered this country made its exist from the realm of life, every caravan that set foot on this land deposited its baggage of residence in the *halting place of death*. In former times whenever an army turned towards this country for raid and conquests ... the wretches made night attacks on it ... drive[n] away to the hills the peasantry along the route of invasion ... The invaders, neglecting caution and watchfulness, reached the centre of the country after passing unobstructed roads full of danger, raging torrents and frightful valleys covered with *full of dangerous forests*. And by reason of [friction of] distance, the winter expired on the way and the rainy season began ... [and] from the hill tops a flood invested the army on all sides. As the saying is 'to mud tear drops are abundance of water', *if two drops of rain fall in this moist*

---

[40] For detailed discussion on these aspects of wet rice or 'padi' cultivation in valley state, see Scott (2009: chapters 2 and 3).

land, movement becomes impossible. So the imprudent army on being besieged has no power left to confront and repel the enemy and grows weaker through the failure to procure supplies of food, and is soon exterminated or taken prisoner.[41]

The detailed account of Mir Jumla's invasion of Assam was more a story of defeat than victory due to the harsh climate and topographical features. The daily marches, for instance, were 4–5 miles.[42] Once rains started, military movement became 'impossible'.

Zhou Yu's (1769) account of the disastrous Qing (China) campaigns against Burma during 1766–9 was also revealing in this respect: 'I have seen Myanmar, and it is nothing more than a southwestern tribe. Its people are neither brave nor vigorous, their weapons dull. They fall far short of Chinese troops and preserved themselves only because of *rugged terrain and virulent malaria.*'[43] No wonder, the Qianlong emperor, who presided over the Myanmar (Burma) campaigns, had to declare later (1780): 'Myanmar has awful conditions. *Human beings cannot compete with Nature.* It is very pitiful to see that our crack soldiers and elite generals died of deadly diseases for nothing. So [I am] determined never to have a war again [with Myanmar].'[44] Thus, for imperial Chinese, a weak government protected by rugged terrain, virulent malaria, deadly forest infested with diseases, and the daunting 'nature' were the uppermost images of Upper Burma, just as Assam was perceived by Gangetic valley empire builders.

The state builders in the frontier also had a difficult time insofar as control over the far-flung periphery—the impregnable forests, marshlands, and its surrounding hills—was concerned. The first Koch invasion of the Ahom territory, for instance, was compelled to retreat from Singri Hill on account of exhaustion of the provisions for soldiers, and the difficulty of obtaining them, as they had launched their campaign by the only viable means, the river.[45] The

---

[41] Gait (2008 [1905]: 147–8); emphasis added.

[42] Gait (2008 [1905]: 131–43).

[43] As quoted in Bello (2005: 283); emphasis added.

[44] As quoted in Bello (2005: 283–5); emphasis added.

[45] *Koch Beharer Itihas*, p. 89, as cited in Devi (1992 [1968]: 272).

Koch campaign of 1546–9 against the Ahoms was also disastrous due mainly to friction of distance.[46] Even the whirlwind victory of the Koch commander, Chilarai, in 1562 against the Ahoms could not hold permanent ground; the northern frontier of Brahmaputra valley that had been annexed was soon given up despite improved communication through the Gohain Kamal Ali road. The Ahom's late occupation of northern Brahmaputra valley was also due to the same factors. Geography, or more specifically the friction of distance, as a decisive factor for state making was therefore illustrative, and what was a natural barrier also became political in character. Indeed, the success of state making depended on the state's capability to control and overcome these natural frictions.

These beautiful valleys became the 'halting place of death' or, infamously, the land of 'sorcerers and magicians' mainly because of the daunting geography. If the 'raging torrents' and virulent rivers were beyond human control, the 'frightful valleys covered with full of dangerous forests' were due to lack of sufficient population to colonize the plain. There is no way to ascertain the population of Assam or Burma in precolonial period but the general picture of low population–land ratio can be gauged from the figures of early colonial records. For instance, the population of Assam (excluding Goalpara district) in 1853 was 1,059,513 persons and the total area of cultivation was 1,575 square miles out of a total area of 30,241 square miles.[47] However, one estimate put the population of Assam in 1750 at around 2.4–2.5 million, which seems to be an exaggeration, although it is true that a large number of Assam's population had migrated to other places or been taken into slavery during Moamaria uprisings and Burmese occupation.[48] Even if such later figure is taken into account, it is still so small for such a vast plain of Assam. Overall, we can say that low population–land ratio was a common feature across the region in precolonial period. No wonder,

---

[46] During this long campaign, the Koch army was badly routed, especially in the massacre of 1547, where it was said that the Ahoms stored up 5,000 heads of Koch soldiers killed in the battle at a place called Mathadang in Sibsagar district. See Devi (1992 [1968]: 275–7).

[47] Mills (1980 [1853]: Appendix-A—*Statistics of Assam, 1853*).

[48] Guha (1991: 56).

Jenkins still lamented in the nineteenth century: 'The great want of Assam is population to cultivate the soil.'[49]

The natural consequence of low population–land ratio is a familiar subject in the context of ancient and medieval states whose mainstay economy was agriculture. It was disastrous to state making because it not only encouraged but also allowed population dispersal across the vast expanse of the valley, a critical factor at the heart of state-formation process. It is known that state control and appropriations become most effective if its subjects are concentrated within an easy reach of power. Thus, to be a successful state builder in the midst of such daunting geography and low population–land ratio, one had to be able to bring together the subjected population in and around the centre of power. However, this involved large amount of force and coercions, and hence state-making projects in the region were quite oppressive and dreadful in many ways. In the following sections, I will discuss how the valley states strived to overcome the daunting geography and low population–land ratio.

The 'Dreads' of State Making

To the extent the valley states were successful in overcoming the daunting geography and low population–land ratio, one can talk about a successful state formation. However, it is also true that all successful state formation came at high human cost. Thus, one can also talk about the 'dreads' of state-making project. Take the case of one of the most successful state formations in the region, the Ahom state. The success of Ahom sovereigns was neither due to their superior military technology nor their manpower strength, both of which were indeed much inferior to the Mughals and even the Koches. Rather, the six centuries-old Ahom state was the result of its ability to control the friction of terrain to a relatively greater extent. This was achieved through its successful social and economic engineering processes. Its choice of sali rice cultivation, massive irrigation-cum-road embankment projects, ability to concentrate the subject population at close

---

[49] Jenkins (1873: 253–4). For Burma's population, see, for instance, the accounts of Bayfield (1873), Fr. Sangermano (1966 [1833]), Hannay (1873), and Scott (1893).

hand, and ability to pacify the virulent hill polities that encircled its territory were all decisive.

The Ahom's effort to introduce the superior sali rice cultivation was magnificent in many ways. Before taking up a rapid expansionist policy, the Ahoms concentrated their energy in introducing, and expanding, sali rice cultivation in its heartland for over three centuries. With heavy sink cost, much of their territory was eventually turned into a flat, levelled sali rice field. No wonder, the medieval chronicler Shihabuddin Talish was astonished to see this magnificent earthwork: 'In this country they make the surface of field and gardens so level that the eye cannot find the least elevation in it up to the extreme horizon.'[50] This gigantic earthwork went hand-in-hand with the construction of massive road-cum-embankments. On these networks, Jenkins (1833) succinctly stated: '[T]he embankments are not confined to the main lines but branch off in all directions whenever roads or bunds seemed to have been convenient or necessary, and certainly in respect to good solid embankments and commodious roadways no part of India I have visited appears to have been so well provided as Assam.'[51] In 1853, Mills also reported of the Ahom's magnificent earthworks where all the 'banks of smaller rivers were guarded by bunds, and the country was intersected with well-raised allies, or roads of great height and breadth, and which served all the purposes of bunds protecting the crops from inundation.' He also noted that these bunds were crossed by pathways joined by smaller bunds graduating down and connecting the *mouzah*s, villages, and fields. This Ahom heartland (from Dhunsiri to Boree Dehing) was, he further noted, 'exceedingly rich, and abounds in valuable products, rice, sugar-cane, muga silk, mustard seed and cotton'.[52]

But how did the Ahoms successfully convert this wilderness into the rice bowl of Assam? How did they manage to bring together large numbers of population to settle down and cultivate its vast sali fields when there was abundance of open land across the valley, both in the rupit and dooar belts? Ancient Kamarupa kingdom, or that of later states like Kamata, Koch, Kachar, Chutiya, and so on, knew

---

[50] As quoted in Guha (1991: 70).
[51] As quoted in Guha (1991: 74).
[52] Mills (1980 [1853]: *Seebsagar*, F1).

sali rice cultivation but progress was inhibited by lack of population to cultivate it. Hence, sali rice economy expanded on a very small scale in Lower Assam and the predominant agriculture practiced was, as noted earlier, the dry *ahu* rice shifting cultivation across the valley. The greatest success of Ahom statecraft was in bringing together the then scattered population of the valley and concentrating them in its sali rice fields. This population 'ingathering' process generally involved massive amount of force (war, conquest, captivity, and slavery), threat (invasion), and blandishment (offer of land, security, and employment).

Thus, the premodern states shared some common features of manpower war-machine states. They parasitically survived for all practical purposes on human labour power. The success of state building, therefore, depended on their ability to coerce, concentrate, and control the population at close hands. 'It was', as rightly noted Scott, 'the first principle of statecraft and the mantra of virtually every history of precolonial kingdoms in the region.'[53] Thus, massive warfare, mass transportation of population as captives to fill the vacant land, binding them to the soil for grain production, or destroying the enemy's subjects to reduce its supporting population, and so on, were part of the state-building project in the valleys. These are taken up separately in the following sections.

Of Warfare, Deaths, and Displacement

The hardships that the people suffered during wars is a familiar subject, especially when states are seen as war-machine manpower states. People, both the soldiers and common folks, were usually captured, butchered, or subjugated by the conquerors. They were subjected to bonded grain producers, corvée labours, conscripts, and so on. The Burmese invasion of Assam and Manipur in the nineteenth century is instructive in this respect. Burmese initially invaded Assam in 1816, only to return after pillaging villages along the line of the march. They returned in 1819, but were expelled by the British in 1826. During this period, Assam was literally robbed and devastated. The 'slaughtering' of a vast number of men, women, and children at

[53] Scott (2009: 64).

Gauhati (Guwahati) for offering opposition to them is a case in point. Butler noted that 50 men were decapitated in one day; hundreds of people were hurled together inside a building of bamboo and grass and then burned alive, in which 200 people were consumed by fire and those who escaped were tortured and killed; the earlobes of all the suspects were cut off and they were then wounded with swords so that they die slowly; and the tragedy was closed by disembowelling the wretched victims.[54]

Butler remarked that he refrained from describing all the 'diabolical acts of cruelty' told to him by people because 'they are so shocking' that he 'cannot describe them'.[55] The enormity of the situation was also visible from the *Ahom-Buranji*:

> The Burmese began to plunder our cities and villages. Many people left their home and took shelter in deep forests. The Burmese even used to haunt the forests. For days and nights they burnt down the villages. The Burmese, in a body of three to four, began to commit outrages on a single woman all at a time. Even a woman was outraged by ten men at a time. The old women, grown up women, and girls were not spared. Their outrages were so severe that a woman or a girl was not left till her female organ profusely bled. They plundered our people and made many captives. The spoils and the captives were taken to their fort.[56]

It was stated that when the Burmese were expelled from Assam, they carried off into slavery, according to the nominal returns presented to Mr Scott, 30,000 Assamese.[57] The same amount of barbarity was registered in Manipur, Arakan, and other places.[58] 'Despotism in its worst form constitute[s]', noted Fr. Sangermano, 'the very essence of the Burmese monarchy, so that to be called its king is equivalent to being called a tyrant.'[59]

[54] As quoted in Gait (2008 [1905]: 237).
[55] As quoted in Gait (2008 [1905]: 237).
[56] Barua (1985 [1930]: 384).
[57] Mills (1980 [1853]: 3).
[58] See, for instance, Brown (2001 [1873]: 61–3), Fr. Sangermano (1966 [1833]: 62), and Pemberton (2000 [1835]: 145).
[59] Fr. Sangermano (1966 [1833]: 74).

The barbarity of the Burmese state was no exception; it only represents the worst form of state-formation process in the region. The destruction or capture of rival power's manpower was as much a strategy to reduce the vanquished so that they did not rise up again as it was to strengthen the vanquisher. Thus, in the 'massacre at Jaintiapur' in 1708, 'a thousand inhabitants of Jaintia were put to the sword and Jaintiapur and all the surrounding villages were destroyed' by the Ahom Army who also took 700 Jaintia prisoners away to their kingdom.[60] In 1563, while suppressing the Chutiyas, the Ahom Army killed thousands of Chutiyas and took 3,000 captives.[61] These instances show that warfare was a source of hardships and displacement. It was under this constant situation of conflict and contestations among different principalities and kingdoms in the river valleys of the region that the movement of population in different directions took place. For instance, the repeated warfare between the Ahoms and Kacharis rendered the Dhansiri valley virtually depopulated in time.[62] Burmese occupation of Assam, Manipur, and other areas left the country desolate: 'many fled to the hills, and to Jaintia, Manipur and other countries'.[63] Regarding Burma, Fr. Sangermano recorded: 'When I first arrived in Pegu, each bank of the great river Ava presented a long-continued line of habitations; but, on my return, a very few villages were to be seen along the whole course of the stream.'[64]

Conscription and Corvée Labour

It is believed that warfare came sporadically so that people could enjoy peace during the intervening period. However, in reality, they lived in a deplorable state. As manpower state, the valley kingdoms of precolonial period wholly depended on human labour power for most of their requirements. Labour was indeed their wealth, which was accumulated in warfare in the form of captives. Thus, a thousand

---

[60] Gait (2008 [1905]: 183–4).

[61] Gait (2008 [1905]: 103).

[62] Gait (2008 [1905]: 121).

[63] Gait (2008 [1905]: 238); see also Fr. Sangermano (1966 [1833]: 101) and Mills (1980 [1853]: 3).

[64] Fr. Sangermano (1966 [1833]: 101).

'Kachari' soldiers, captured by Manipur state in the seventeenth century, were made to work as 'bugler, drummer, dhobi, mahout of elephant, syces for horses and other works according to their respective qualities'.[65] In Tipperrah, the Mugh captives from coastal Arakan were resettled in the hills in order to clear forests for cultivation.[66] The capture of thousands of people from Manipur, Assam, and Arakan by the Burmese; from Burma by Manipuris; from Jaintia, Chutiya, Kachar, and Koch kingdoms by Ahoms; and by these valley states from the hill tribes; were other astounding cases.[67]

Labour power accumulated through warfare, however, formed only a paltry amount of their labour requirement; most of the state labour power was drawn from the subjected population through a wisely engineered human labour-machine system. The institutionalization of state labour services in Assam was perhaps one of the most significant achievements of the Ahom state. It allowed the Ahoms to sustain their power for over six centuries. What was significant in Ahom statecraft was that they not only successfully converted the valley of wilderness into sali rice fields but, more importantly, were also successful in concentrating the subjected populations to extend such rice fields. This 'ingathering' process was achieved by successfully putting restrictions on the movement of people through its wisely crafted system, popularly known as *khelwari* or *khel* system. Its unique character was in clubbing together the individual, land, and labour in one triangular apparatus under state control. Guha argued that the Ahoms considered wet rice land (sali) as a 'common national pool'. From out of this common pool, the Ahom sovereigns distributed alienable tax-free land to all able-bodied adult male subjects at the rate of 2 *poorah*s (1 poorah is 2.66 acres) of land each for their lifetime. In return, they exacted compulsory labour services to the

---

[65] Singh (1995: 6). See also Parratt (2005: 1–17).

[66] Sarma and Bairagi (1938 [1724]: 30).

[67] For the Burmese conscription of labour from Arakan in the 1790s, see Hall (1955: xxviii) and Harvey (1925: 280–3). For reports of Burmese captives taken by Manipuri armies from Upper Burma, see Harvey (1925: 208). For the Burmese occupation of Manipur and Assam, and conscription of labourers by all the armies, see Barpujari (1970: 26–7) and Baruah (1993: 219–28).

state for purpose of economic production, public works, and military establishments.[68] It was, in a way, a population control machine system which bound them to the soil for production, while ensuring they were also always available for state services.

Under khel system, all the able-bodied men of the kingdom, called *paik*s, were organized into a *got* consisting of four (later three) *paik*s. The *got*s were organized under different khels, which were in turn organized under some broad division called *mel* or *dagi* consisting of 1,000–6,000 paiks each. One-third or sometimes one-fourth of the members of the khel were always on state service. Thus, one member (paik) of each *got* was obliged to be present, in rotation, for a particular state service throughout the year and the other two members would look after his paddy field and keep him supplied with food. Hence, each member would give three to four months mandatory state service in a year in lieu of 2 poorahs rent-free land, which he held on a mere usufruct right.[69] The primacy of population control to state was also reflected in different official titles. For instance, *Borah* meant lord over 20 *got*s, *Saikia* meant lord of 100 *got*s, *Hazarika* meant lord of thousand *got*s, and *Phukan* was the lord over all these.[70] There was no official designation which referred to territory. These official categories based on the number of population signified the centrality of population control in the valley of low population–land ratio. The fact that the subjected population was controlled to the minutest detail is shown by the fact that over 20 *got*s (which, by computation, was 80/60 paiks and, by implication, such a number of households) was one state officer, the Borah.

The templates of Ahom's khel system were also noticeable in other kingdoms of the region but in a simpler form. In Manipur, it was called *lallup* system. According to this, 'every male between the ages of 17 and 60' was 'to place his services at the disposal of the state,

---

[68] See Guha (1991: 44–7).

[69] Besides, each paik inherited their inalienable homestead and garden; they could also cultivate land in addition to 2 poorahs (rent-free land) for which they paid certain revenue to the state. See, for instance, Acharya (2003 [1966]: 123), Guha (1991: 44–7), Mackenzie (2007 [1884]: 6), and Mills (1980 [1853]: 2).

[70] See Mills (1980 [1853]: 2).

without remuneration' for 'ten days in every forty' days. No one was spared, except with the prior permission of the state authority.[71] The same existed in a more simple fashion in the kingdoms of Kachar, Jaintia, and the many Shan statelets of Burma, or even in the great Burmese Empire where every individual in the empire was said to be the 'born slave' of the emperor.[72] The primary objective of these systems was not only to provide a pool of corvée labour for state services but, more importantly, to put restriction on movement of population. The term serfdom may sound controversial, but the fact remains that the valley states were very particular about curbing the mobility of their subjected population as it threatened their very existence due to low population–land ratio. Therefore, to eliminate mobility or to bind the subjects to the soil constituted one of the core concerns of the state-making project in the region in precolonial period.

This peculiar labour-machine state system had virtually reduced its supporting population into what Eaton has called 'corvée militia' to the state.[73] Shihabuddin Talish's description of the Ahom's khel system was lucid:

> It is not the customs here to take any land tax from the cultivators; but in every house one man out of three has to render service to the Raja, and if there is any delay in doing what he orders, no other punishment than death is inflicted. Hence the most complete obedience is rendered by the people to the bidding of their Raja.[74]

As head count was kept and there was compulsory state service for some months annually, there was definitely a loss of freedom of movement. Thus, it was said that '[n]ot only the soil but the subject was the property of the State' in Ahom state.[75] Dalton also noted

---

[71] See Brown (2001 [1873]: 33), Dun (1992 [1886]: 36), Hodson (2009 [1908]: 63), and McCulloch (1980 [1859]: 11–12).

[72] Guha (1991: 46–7); see also Fr. Sangermano (1966 [1833]: 72).

[73] Eaton (1993: 190).

[74] As quoted in Gait (2008 [1905]: 147). Land revenue was not completely absent because one had to pay tax to state for those lands the person held beyond 2 poorahs.

[75] As quoted in Mills (1980 [1853]: 2).

that 'all subjects were considered as servants of the State'.[76] It was through this wisely crafted sali rice cultivation and institutionalized labour system that the Ahoms were eventually able to concentrate their subjected population and sufficient grain supply at relatively close hand, successfully restrict their mobility, and ensure their physical presence for state services. This equally assured the efficient broadcasting of power over their subjects and its endurance for centuries.

Slavery, Taxation, and Rebellion

Slavery as a form of production was also a rampant practice in all these kingdoms. 'The chief nobles cultivated their private estate', Gait noted of the Ahom state, 'with aid of slaves' and 'all persons of a respectable position had one or more of them, by whom all the work of the household and the labour in the fields were performed'. They were bought and sold in the open market and some 'mortgaged' themselves; 'every Native on the receipt of more than ten or twelve Rupees a month, has one or more of them'.[77] But surprisingly, slavery was seen as a better-off position than the paiks in Assam, as shown by the fact that large number of paiks 'often took refuge on private estates [of state officers] and passed themselves as slaves'.[78] It was because the slaves of noblemen and temple establishments were exempted from compulsory state services and poll tax. Absence of regular taxation was also one important source of hardship for the common man. Fr. Sangermano noted that as the king of Burma considered the property of his subjects as belonging to himself in reality, he exacted anything he pleased from them. He said that from emperor, ministers, provincial governors, *eaters* of inferior cities, till the 'Mandarins', could impose taxes to any limit on a whim. This oppression was more rapacious at the margins of the state, especially

[76] NAI, FP (B): July 1877, No. 85: Dalton to Jenkins, 19 May 1852; also see Gait (2008 [1905]: 249).

[77] See Gait (2008 [1905]: 265); see also Brown (2001 [1873]: 91–2), M'Cosh (2000 [1837]: 26), and Singh (1995: 27). Burmese had a special slave code (Burmese Code). See Fr. Sangermano (1966 [1833]: 261–5).

[78] Gait (2008 [1905]: 265).

under the 'Mandarins', where a 'dreadful oppression is put in practice'.[79]

As would be expected from the oppressive nature of the state system, some sections of the society occasionally took to rebellion as a medium of resistance against the established authority. Of the rebellions witnessed in Ahom state, the Moamarias uprising of 1789 was especially instructive as far as its impact on the people was concerned. The *Buranji* recorded how the uprising started after the incident in which one Nahar Moamaria was 'mortified' by an Ahom state officer, Barbarua.[80] But once the rebellion broke out, it unleashed a wave of brutality upon the common people. Gait noted that the people of Assam, who had hitherto enjoyed a fair measure of happiness and prosperity, were plunged into depths of misery and despair. The rebels destroyed whole villages, looted supplies, and destroyed crops. This led to a terrible famine and many people had to abandon their children. They, in fact, had to depend on wild fruits, roots, and meat of cows, buffaloes, dogs, and jackals for sustenance. Some roamed about in the jungle, while others fled to the hills and to Bengal.[81] Although such rebellions were relatively less, they really brought hardship to people whenever they happened. Regular natural calamities like flood, drought, and pestilences added to the woes of the valley population. While flood was the perennial sorrow of the plains, dreaded famine invaded Assam in 1569, 1641, and 1665, and was powerful enough to dislodge people from their home and hearths.

The Rippling States

What has been noted in the state space constituted the irony of valley civilization which generated a powerful centrifugal demographic regime. War, rebellions, deaths, displacement, and subjugation found permanent imprints in the valley, just as it was frequently visited by natural calamities. The effective instrument of concentrating

[79] Fr. Sangermano (1966 [1833]: 91–6). Thus, Bayfield (1873: 185) noted that people were so 'heavily taxed' that they became 'too poor to be either well or comfortably clad'.

[80] Barua (1985 [1930]: 293–5).

[81] Gait (2008 [1905]: 204–5, 266–7).

manpower and grain at the core of the empire, while pulling its population together in and around the capital at relatively close hand and permitting effective broadcasting of power over the nucleus of the kingdom, nevertheless, generated an equally powerful centripetal force that conspired against its centralizing and homogenizing project. While it is significant to note that large numbers of conquered populations were transplanted and resettled around the core of the state, it is also equally significant that large numbers of the state population also escaped to the frontier margins. It can even be said that the same force prevented people from outside the kingdom to voluntarily enter the nucleus area.

This centrifugal process is what we may call a population concentration effect of the state. Such concentration effect particularly becomes noticeable in a situation where there is low population–land ratio, such as in medieval Assam and Burma. In a vicious circle of desperation, the new project often turned out to be what Scott has called 'self-liquidation'. While concentration compelled flight to the margins, such flight compelled the state to press further on its grain producers so that they could not escape, which in turn forced more of them to take flight. Deprivation of sufficient population could even lead to the collapse of state/kingdom. Thus, we see the rapid rise and fall of several kingdoms in the region with varying lifespans. The long reign of the Ahoms in Assam is one exception to such general rule, although one could see similar pattern of state formation. The six centuries-old Ahom rule is, therefore, instructive in showing the actual pattern of broadcasting of power, which may be best described as 'ripple' in Wilks apt term.[82]

As noted earlier, sali rice cultivation helped in the state-making project in the valley. Thus, with the introduction of sali rice cultivation under the Ahom sovereign, the process of concentration effect especially became evident. The expansion of Ahom state during its long rule witnessed some competing frontiers, each creating its own centripetal and centrifugal forces. The Ahoms' initial political expansion and consolidation generally took the form of an agrarian expansion of sali rice cultivation, which gradually radiated from the power centre in the form of a concentric circle along the flatland.

[82] Wilks (1992).

As its political expansion continued, especially since the sixteenth century, the agrarian and demographic frontiers could not keep up with it. The political frontier now included various low hills and marshlands between pockets of cultivated flatlands connected or disconnected to the core mainland. The expansion broadly followed a rippling pattern, stopping wherever it met the hills, marshland, or impassable forest belts but re-emerged again on another agrarian frontier. In many cases, expansion followed the flat riverine corridors just like the sea meets the coast and the backwater. Consequently, the expanded territory now included multiple competing frontiers: political, agrarian, forests, and demographic.

The political frontier was the whole length of the kingdom, which was rapidly oscillating in time. The dynamics of this political frontier depended on the efficacy of other frontiers, and also the dynamics of other neighbouring kingdoms. The agrarian frontier extended slowly in and around the original seat of power (forming its main granary) and in some pockets of concentrated population connected to the core area by agriculture corridor around the connecting rivers or by mere seasonal tracks across the forest belt. Forested frontier, acting as the friction of terrain, extended from the margins of agrarian frontier along the great belt of inaccessible forestland till the foothills or between two pockets of settled territories. Demographic frontier extended along the agrarian frontier at the nucleus of the state or its pockets of settlements. There were also the scattered and mobile population roving at the margins of the kingdom, often disconnected to the nucleus core by forested frontier.

The dynamics of these competing frontiers was such that the change in one frontier simultaneously affected the other frontiers. In other words, they were inversely related to each other. This dynamic was mainly determined by low population–land ratio. The state wanted to expand the agrarian frontier as rapidly as its political frontier, but the low population–land ratio conspired against it. Hence, political expansion very soon overtook the slow pace of agrarian expansion. This compelled the state builders to bring in the scattered and conquered populations of the peripheries in and around the core area of the state. The concentration of population in the nucleus of the kingdom resulted in further expansion of the core agrarian frontier on the one hand, and the depopulation of the peripheries on the other. The major presence of such uninhabited and uncultivated forested frontier at the margins of the kingdom was, therefore, one significant aspect of precolonial state-formation process in the region. The emergence of this forested frontier at the margin was also encouraged by the political expansion itself, which caused the flight of frontier population to the more remote areas where state could not reach them, such as in the surrounding mountain ranges and glens. Few illustrations of this situation may be helpful.

Take the case of the outer fringes of Brahmaputra valley, for instance. Here, the concentration effect of population ingathering can be illustrated from its south-western and north-eastern peripheries. The Dhansiri valley, in the south-western fringe of Brahmaputra valley, for instance, was once the core region of Kachari (Dimasa) kingdom whose capital was Dimapur. This valley had been well populated until the Ahoms appeared on the scene. Against the Ahom's expansion, the main branch of Kachari population, along with its court and capital, withdrew towards the inhospitable terai landscape known as the North Cachar Hills. Thus, the struggle for supremacy between the Ahoms and Kacharis pushed the latter from Dimapur to Maibong (1536) and then to Khaspur (1750). So, in the eyes of early colonial expedition parties, the once well-populated Dhansiri valley was transformed into 'a dark, damp, chilly, gloomy forest', which was so thick that one could not see beyond ten paces in the front. It was 'totally devoid' of man, settlements, and cultivations, 'the earth excessively damp', and travelling through it was 'very depressing'.[83] The country surrounding Sadiya in the upper fringe of Brahmaputra valley was also the centre of Chutiya kingdom, well populated and cultivated, until it was destroyed and depopulated by the Ahom state in the sixteenth century (annexation in 1523 CE). Thus, Wilcox reported in his survey of Assam (1825–7) that 'beyond Sadiya, on the north side of the river, the tract is an uninterrupted jungle to the foot of the hills, and on its south side the little village[s] ... form mere specks in the widely spread wilderness.'[84] While large number of Chutiya population submitted before the conqueror, many of them

[83] See, for instance, Butler (1978 [1855]: 14–24, 75).
[84] Wilcox (1873: 27).

escaped either to the surrounding mountain ranges or to inhospitable dooar belt of the valley, which still bears the name 'Kachari Duars'.[85]

Similar was the case with Burma's Mogaung district (Hukawng and Khamti valleys) where the concentration effect of Burmese state-making project was profound. This region had been once a well-populated centre of the Pong kingdom (empire?), but the Burmese occupation gradually depopulated the area due to its population ingathering process and also due to the general flight of people to remoter places. Bayfield, for instance, noted that Mogaung district was 'a very populous district' before Burmese occupation but the people were later driven 'to the banks of the Thyen-dweng [Chindwin], and other places remote from Burmese authority'.[86] Similarly, Hannay also noted that Meinkhwon—the capital of Hukawng valley—before the Burmese invasion, 'contained 1,500 houses' but 'the exactions of the Burmese officers have led to extensive emigration, and to avoid the oppression to which they were hourly exposed the Shans have sought an asylum in the remote glens and valleys on the banks of the Khyendwen [Chindwin], and the Singfos among the recesses of the mountains at the eastern extremity of the valley'.[87] Meinkhwon had only 40 houses in 1837 when Bayfield visited.[88] No wonder, as stated earlier, Griffith found Hukawng valley in 1836 as 'one mass of jungle, with here and there clear patches occurring'.[89] These competing frontiers and population movements can be graphically represented as shown in Figure 1.1.

If sali rice cultivation helped in concentration of population at close hands, and hence the effective broadcasting of power, it also produced its own nemesis for the state. As mentioned earlier, the political expansion and concentration of population resulted in the emergence of a huge belt of uninhabited and uncultivated forest

[85] For their migration to these areas, see Endle's (2010 [1911]: 8) apt argument.

[86] Bayfield (1873: 184). The seat of provincial governor of Mogaung, bearing the same name, for instance, had only 284 'poor mat and bamboo houses' in 1836. It was also the capital of Pong Empire earlier.

[87] Hannay (1873: 102).

[88] Bayfield (1873: 192).

[89] Griffith (1873: 128).

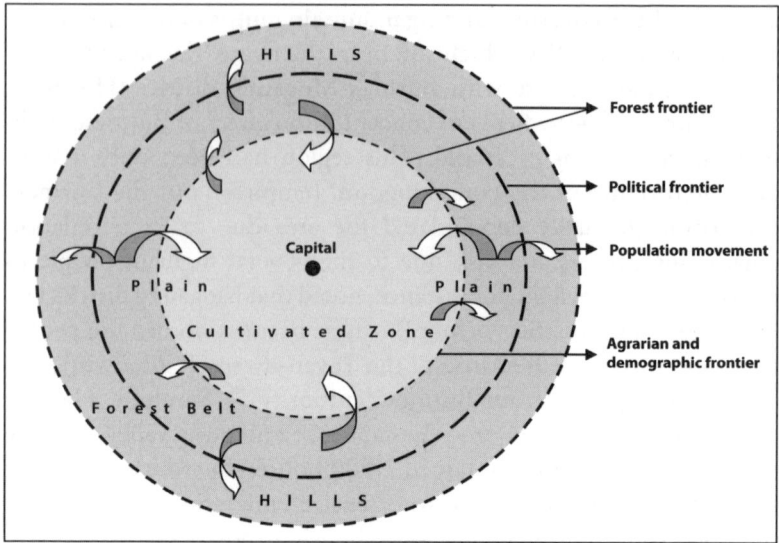

Figure 1.1   Schematic Representation of Competing Frontiers in the Valley
Source: Prepared by the author.

frontier at the margins. We have seen that forest provided a strong friction to the broadcasting of power and authority. In privileging the friction of terrain, the basic character of broadcasting of power also took the form of a ripple. While such power and authority was felt strongly at the core of the state, especially along the continuous agrarian field and riverine corridors, it became nominal, negligible, and sporadic as it crossed the limit of agrarian frontier. Along the great belt of inaccessible forested frontier, state authority was virtually absent. If such forests merged with the great forest belt of the surrounding mountain ranges, then state authority ended where the forest began at the margin of agrarian frontier. Though some nomadic communities lived within certain forest frontiers, their amorphous livelihood strategies were virtually 'illegible' to state control.

Beyond the forest frontier, there could be pockets of well-colonized areas where the presence of state again became phenomenal if they were connected to the centre by road or river corridors. Here, the rippling power of the state was visible, which dipped under the carpet of the great forest belt to re-emerge again. However, in the absence of a good communication line, the rippling power of the state was felt intermittently and was often symbolic. In any case, the rippling power of the state came to a complete end once it touched the foot of the great mountain ranges. Thus, the great mountain massif continued to remain stateless or outside the orbit of valley state regimes until the colonial state annexed it. Few examples of state power at the fringe of the valley will be sufficient to show how state actually appeared at the frontier of the state.

The case of Hukawng valley (inhabited mainly by the Singphos) and Khamti country in the northern frontier of Burma is instructive. This region had been, in theory, part of the territory of Burma but, in practice, was virtually outside its control. Burmese state authority was felt only intermittently and was symbolic. In the heyday of Ava (Burmese) Empire, Captain Hannay (1835–6), for instance, noted of this fringe:

> [T]he Burmah authorities can only enforce the payment of tribute from the Shans of Khanti [Khamti] and the Sinfos [Singphos] of Payenwen [Hukawng valley] by the presence of an armed force. In their last attempt on the latter, a Burmah force of 1,000 men was detached from Mogaung, of whom 900 were destroyed, and for ten years they had been held in salutary dread by the Burmah governors of the frontier.[90]

Bayfield also noted that 'although within the Burmese dominions', the Singphos 'pay no revenue, and are subject to no sort of control, the Burmans in fact fear them, and never go among them except on special occasions and in well armed, large parties.'[91] Hannay went on saying that Burmese authority were seen by these frontier communities, not as the 'paramount' power, but as a mere 'brigand'.[92]

The situation among the (Bor) Khamtis was even more demeaning. Hannay noted that the Khamtis were 'held in great apprehension by the Burmahs, who, about three years ago, attempted to raise revenue amongst them. The force detached on this duty, however, met with such determined resistance, that it was compelled to return, and no

[90] Hannay (1873: 99).
[91] Bayfield (1873: 222–3).
[92] Hannay (1873: 107).

subsequent attempt has been made on their independence.'[93] The situation remained the same even in 1885 when Upper Burma was finally occupied by the British. Woodthorpe, for instance, noted that when he visited the Khamti country in 1885, he was told that 'several years had elapsed since the last tribute had been paid or any Burmese official had visited them' and although they recognized Thebaw, 'they were practically independent' from Burma.[94] Yet, whenever the Burmese forces won over them, a sort of 'oath of forbearance' was usually taken by their *Tsabwas* (chiefs).[95] But such oath of submission was merely what Woodthorpe termed a 'means by which they get rid cheaply of an unpleasant visitor'.[96]

This was also the case in other frontiers. In the Chinbok areas of Burma's western frontier with the Chin Hills, for instance, the 'Burman headmen' who were sent to collect tribute from them were always 'refused' by the Chins, just as in Singpho and Khamti country.[97] The fact was that Burma was not able to maintain any permanent Burmese forces in such frontier areas due mainly to the friction of distance. Woodthorpe's description of Burmese state authority in its frontier areas was particularly precise in this context: 'In the remote districts the "paramount power" is a term utterly meaningless to the inhabitants who regard the officer visiting them to enforce their submission as some strange independent chief out on a raiding expedition on his own account.'[98]

The diminishing power of the Ahom state authority in its frontier area was also evident from the start. Until the sixteenth century, the northern Brahmaputra valley remained virtually outside the imperial ambit of the Ahom state, just as it was outside the control of the Koch and Kamata kingdoms. After the destruction of the Chutiya kingdom (in the east) in 1523 and the powerful Bhuyan chieftains

[93] Hannay (1873: 105).

[94] NAI, Foreign Department, External Proceedings (FE) (A): September 1892, K.W. No. 3: 'Note on our dealing with savage tribes, and the necessity of having them under one rule', by R.G. Woodthorpe, 1 October 1891.

[95] Captain Hannay was witness to 'oath of forbearance' taken by six Tsabwas of the Singphos.

[96] NAI, FE (A): September 1892, K.W. No. 3.

[97] NAI, FE (A): September 1892, K.W. No. 3.

[98] NAI, FE (A): September 1892, K.W. No. 3.

(in the west), this frontier area almost returned to nature.[99] Even after the construction of the famous 'Dafla-garh'/'Rajgarh' in the north, 'Mishmi-garh' in the east, and 'Naga-garh' in the south by Pratap Singha in the seventeenth century, the Ahoms control over its periphery was still precarious and incomplete. The fact that the posa system flourished at the margins of Brahmaputra valley, a point I will discuss in detail in Chapter 9, is a good case in point. The case of Khamti, and later the Singpho, occupation of its eastern frontier is another. The Khamtis initially occupied the Tengapani area in the easternmost corner of Assam valley but, in 1794, crossed over Brahmaputra River, ousted the Khawa Gohain (Assamese governor) of Sadiya, usurped and adopted the title and dignity of the ousted governor, and then reduced the ryots (peasants) to virtual subjection. The Ahom state sovereign was, remarked Mackenzie, 'compelled to acquiesce in the arrangement'.[100] The Singphos came to assist the Moamaria rebels against the Ahom state in the eighteenth century and continued to hold sway over its eastern frontier.[101]

If the authority of the valley state virtually faded away at the margins of the valley, one can now well imagine its authority in the mountain ranges where the friction of terrain was excessively prolific. These impregnable hills continued to remain outside the ambit of state's control until the British took over them in the nineteenth century. Instead, it was the hill tribes who controlled the fringe of the valley kingdoms for centuries. I will come back to this point in Chapter 9. Suffice to say here that the hills continued to remain the stateless space over the ages and provided a safe shelter to successive waves of state evaders.

A Reverse Movement

This chapter shows that the state-making project in the valleys caused seamless layers of hardship and oppression to the subjected population. Such a coercive regime made the valley space a hell to live in at times. It was under such circumstances that sections of the valley

[99] Devi (1992 [1968]: 213–14).
[100] Mackenzie (2007 [1884]: 57).
[101] Mackenzie (2007 [1884]: 61–2).

population chose to escape to the frontier margins, remote from state power, where their conquerors did not care at once to follow them up. Just as it was a perennial problem for the state to prevent its population from running away to the margins, it was also the perennial desire of many in the oppressed population to break the shackles of control system and escape to places where such control was absent. It was within these circumstances, in which the valley population found themselves oppressed under state control, that one must locate the migration of valley population to the stateless upland massif of the region. This flight to the stateless space can be called the *reverse movement*.

I use the term reverse movement to mean movement of population towards the periphery of the state, in opposition to the direction in which concentration of population at the core of the state took shape in state-making process. It was an equally remarkable phenomenon as the ingathering process was. As already noted, Ahom and Burmese state-building projects in medieval period had ejected large numbers of the valley population to the inhospitable margins of the valleys and to the hills. Ahom state-building projects led a large number of Kachari population and others to the inhospitable terai landscape at the margins of Brahmaputra valley. Similarly, Burmese state-making project also led to migration of large numbers of Kachins, Chins, Singphos, and Khamtis to the margins of Chindwin–Irrawaddy valleys. The Burmese invasion of Assam and Manipur similarly testified to the same story of reverse movement in which mass migration of population to places such as the inaccessible mountains or to nearby Cachar, Jaintia, and Bengal took place. Thus, if the ingathering process of state making involved forcible concentration of population at the core of the state, then the same centrifugal process was itself responsible for the reverse movement. This is what can be understood as the concentration effect of population ingathering in the valley states.

The people who had chosen to escape in the stateless space were people whom Endle has called 'the stronger and more patriotic spirits'.[102] They were people who held that the stateless hills provided

---

[102] Endle (2010 [1911]: 8).

them relative freedom. They were people who craved individual freedom and independence and were against control and oppression by the state. They were people whom State, History, and Civilization had deceptively categorized as 'primitive', 'savage', and 'barbarian', or simply 'tribe'. The deception was mainly because they went against the tide—against State, against History, and against Civilization. To these people, the state space was certainly no paradise; it was rather the 'halting place of death' and the hell in the heaven of civilization. To them, the flat plain was what Peal has aptly called the 'enormous dead level'. To them, the highland massif was, if not the land of milk and honey, the land of freedom from control and oppression. How they eventually escaped to the highland massif, therefore, concerns the next chapter.

2

The Great Escape

Peopling the Blue Hills

Every individual in a society is a bearer of history who not only makes but also inherits history. If you take a walk in the sleepy rural villages in the hills of Northeast India, or in the various urban centres in the region, and ask certain questions related to the origin and migration history, a prompt answer will be given to the queries. However, there will be a difference in the answers given by both young and old people. The young common folks may say, 'We came from such-and-such place' (pointing to certain hills in the area), or simply, 'I don't know'. A few educated persons may relate an elaborate story of origin and migration history that ends up in a particular 'cave', within their present hills. But you will receive a more detailed narrative from the aged and knowledgeable persons, whom the modernist categorize as 'illiterate'. They will generally start from the mythical origins of the tribe and may be able to narrate different events as well as names of places they passed through on the long march, although it is difficult to identify those names in the present. The first and second categories of oral intellectual narrate their history within the politically charged environment of the present, which compels them to omit, silence, or forget anything that points beyond their present hills. In simple, they are driven by the awful idea that 'indigeneity' is about being 'original' to the land. The second group is further informed and influenced by (through their education) the dominant colonial civilizational discourse on the 'tribe'. The researcher should stick with the third group, if he gets any. If he does not, he should still feel confident that such valuable information has been already recorded by someone in the past—think about the accounts of brave colonial officer-ethnographers.

As stated earlier, in the history of state-making project in the valley, 'reverse movement' was as important a phenomenon as concentration of population at the core of the state. Thus, when large numbers of conquered populations submitted to manpower war-machine states, the 'stronger and more patriotic spirits' escaped to the rugged mountain massif or disease-infested terai ecology of the foothills. This leads us to an important question regarding migration: why and from where (not when) did the hill tribes come immediately before they settled down in their present hills? Though much has been written or collected on the legends of origin and migration of different hill tribes of Northeast India, my aim is to find the answer through the oral narratives. But a few points should be kept in mind here. Migration in history was a continuous process and took place in series of waves: sometime in group but, in most cases, on individual or household basis. Movement of people between hills and valleys was also a continuous process and was a two-way traffic. I will thus look into the traffic that took people from the valley space to the highland massif based on the oral traditions of the local tribal communities. Although I hardly agree with the broad swathe of colonial classification, I will use it here for convenience as the basis of grouping the tribes to find out their migration history.

Peopling the Blue Hills

Most tribes in the Northeast claim that they have come from 'somewhere else', often from a very far-off place. The only difference is that certain groups came earlier than the others. These others may have been absorbed in the earlier one, or the earlier one may have been absorbed into the more dominant later groups, or the later groups may have removed the earlier one from that land, all depending upon the number and strength of the group in question. Thus, migration and movement of people from one place to another is as old as human history and is still going on. It has become one of the most controversial issues in the region today. But to see the past in the illumination of the present is to miss the point in history. It is significant that the past should be treated as 'foreign land' and history must have its deserved place in society. The migration of the hill people to their present hills marks a crucial historical juncture. As some recent studies show, it can tell us or help us re-enact their past and reorient our existing understanding of their present. In other words, it can help us refocus the history and culture of the hillmen, away from the dominant civilizational narrative.

Most of the tribes in Northeast India are broadly classified as Tibeto-Burman people. A consensus opinion on the original home of the Tibeto-Burman-speaking people has been already arrived at among the linguists. This has also been accepted by most anthropologists and historians. This original haunt was located at the confluence of northeastern Tibet, south-western China, and northern Burma, drained by four major rivers, namely, Yangtze, Mekong, Salween, and Irrawaddy.[1] It was from this region that they migrated in different directions and eventually to their present hills. It is true that all Tibeto-Burman speakers of Northeast India have a clear sense of arriving from 'somewhere else'. But from what direction did they initially come to the Northeast region remains an ongoing debate among scholars. Linguistic studies are not able to tell us much about the various routes taken by different tribal groups during their migration. But various historical and anthropological studies are able to show these routes, although it remains a debateable topic even among them. My intention is to bring these studies together mainly to locate the earlier homes of the hill tribes immediately before they came up to their present habitats.

The Kachari or Bodo Group

As per the general ethnolinguistic thesis, the Bodos, who belong to the Tibeto-Burman group of people, must have come from the east through the Patkai ranges. But insofar as the oral tradition of

---

[1] See, for instance, Blackburn (2003), Konow (1902: 136), and van Driem (2001: 410, 447).

its near-kin group, the Garos in particular, is concerned, they might have well come from the north, from Tibetan highland, through the Himalayas. J.H. Hutton, for instance, felt that the 'Bodo race' came into Assam from the north, that is, Tibet.[2] Kacharis were traditionally the rulers of ancient Kamarupa (Kamruli) and as they were worsted by their enemies in the later years, they crossed over the Bid River (Brahmaputra) in which a large section of them were washed away.[3]

The documented history of the Kachari tribes (more importantly, the Dimasas) is most instructive. Edward Gait and some fine studies in later period give a vivid account of how the 'Kachari race' was defeated by the more powerful kingdoms from the west and the east.[4] From their original seat at Kamarupa, they were pushed to the east by what came to be known as Kamarupa-Kamata kingdom. The two branches of Kachari set up separate kingdoms at Sadiya and Dimapur. Later, the Koches also destroyed the western parts of its kingdom. However, by far the most devastating for the Kachari kingdoms were the Ahoms, who established their rule over part of Upper Assam since the thirteenth century (since 1228). The Ahoms initially concentrated their energy in building their economic base and it was only in the sixteenth century that they began their expansionist policy. But this did not mean that there was no warfare at all. They, in fact, had to struggle hard against different tribes who had occupied the territories which now came under their control. Indeed, Gait noted that the Ahoms and Kachari (Chutiyas) struggled for supremacy in the Upper Brahmaputra valley for about 150–200 years. The Chutiya kingdom (of Sadiya) was finally destroyed in 1523 and the Kacharis (Dimasas) were pushed westward towards the Kalang River. Then the Kacharis were pushed out from their very base at Dimapur to Maibong in 1536. As the Ahoms continued to press, its capital was again shifted to Khaspur in 1750. The pressure from the Ahom state-making project eventually forced the Kachari mass to the inhospitable terai belt of the North Cachar Hills.[5]

[2] Mills (2003 [1922]: xvi–xvii, fn. 4).

[3] Bhattacharjee (1991: 178).

[4] See Gait (2008 [1905]), Devi (1992 [1968]), Bhattacharjee (1991), and Barpujari (1997).

[5] For detailed discussion of Kachari state-formation, see Gait (2008 [1905]); see also Barpujari (1997) and Bhattacharjee (1991).

Different observers also noted, from the remains of Kachari kingdom in their earlier settlements at Dimapur, Maibong, and Khaspur, that they had attained a certain high degree of 'civilization'.[6] Commenting on the remains at Dimapur, Gait remarked: 'the Kacharis had attained a state of civilisation considerably advance of that of the Ahoms. The use of brick for building purposes was then practically unknown to the Ahoms'.[7] From such a 'state of civilisation', the Kacharis later chose to migrate in North Cachar Hills where they could more effectively prevent the Ahom's control. The gradual process of what may be called Kachari re-ethnicization process in the long view is aptly captured by Endle:

> It may be that, whilst the great body of Chutiya (Kachari) race submitted to their Ahom conquerors, the stronger and more patriotic spirits among them, influenced perhaps by that intense clannishness which is so marked a feature in the Kachari character, withdrew to *less favoured parts of the province, where their conquerors did not care at once to follow them up*, i.e., the southern section of the race may have made its way into the districts known as the Garo Hills and North Cachar [Hills]; while the northern section perhaps took up its abode in a broad belt of country at the foot of the Bhutan Hills, still known as the 'Kachari Duars', a region which, being virtually 'terai' land, had in earlier days a very unenviable reputation on the score of its recognised unhealthiness.[8]

As mentioned earlier, the dooar belt, at the margins of the Brahmaputra valley, was the porous zone of refuge to a number of valley people from the core rupit belt where the valley state control was direct and strong. The 'Kachari Duars', of the terai ecology in general, and the hilly mountainous ranges had been indeed reputed to be an 'unenviable' and 'sterile' landscape to revenue-collecting valley states; and on that matrix, such landscapes were deliberately chosen by the Kacharis (Bodos) to evade their enemies. The undesirability of

---

[6] See NAI, FP: 24 August 1844, No. 36: Mr. Browne Wood to Captain A. Sturt, 14 April 1844; see also Butler (1978 [1855]: 24–6).

[7] Gait (2008 [1905]: 301–3).

[8] Endle (2010 [1911]: 8); emphasis added.

this tract for any useful purpose of state making was also aptly noted by Damant:

> It is a peculiarity of nearly the whole of this [Kachari] family, that they are essentially dwellers in the Terai, living, as a rule, neither in the hills nor the plains, but occupying the debatable ground between the two; a tract of country, in which no race but themselves could exist and flourish, so deadly is the malaria which arises from it.[9]

Thus, just as terai was a sterile landscape to revenue-appropriating state system, it was also a 'debatable ground' to conquerors, armies, invaders, and peaceful peasant migrants. The role of deadly malaria, for example, has been already covered in the previous chapter in the case of Chinese armies in Upper Burma. To the Kacharis, the 'illegible' terai ecology, in which 'no race but themselves could exist and flourish', became the landscape of refuge against the Ahom's imperial armies. The case of another Bodo group, the Garos, will provide this history of escape in greater detail.

The Garos

If the recorded history of the 'Kachari race' shows that they finally found the 'illegible' terai ecology as their 'manifest destiny' to evade state control, other tribes of the region found the higher mountain massif suitable for the same purpose. The Garos, the near kin of the Kacharis, also have the tradition of coming from 'elsewhere'.[10] Their legend of origin and migration has been recorded by Major A. Playfair in much detail.[11] According to this legend, the ancestors of the Garos inhabited a province of Tibet named Torua, from where they started, without any apparent reason, 'on a voyage of discovery' under the leadership of Jappa-Jalinpa and Sukpa-Bongipa. They finally reached the plain of Brahmaputra valley and started settling down at a place called 'Rangamati near Rangpur', from where they again moved to Dhubri in the kingdom of one Dhobani. King Dhobani received

[9] Damant (1880: 232).
[10] See Endle (2010 [1911]: 3–4, 81), Playfair (1998 [1909]: 7–24), and Sangma (1981: chapter 1).
[11] Playfair (1998 [1909]: 7–14).

them in a friendly manner but did not allow them to settle there permanently as he was afraid of them. Therefore, the Garos continued to move up the right bank of Brahmaputra until they reached its tributary, the Manas River, where they met their first misfortune. The 'powerful and cruel' chief of that country was attracted by the beauty of a Garo maiden, Juge-Silche, the daughter of one Kangre-Jingre, and wanted to carry her off by force. To prevent this, her fellow countrymen hid her in a cave at a place called Jugi Ghopa. A battle broke out between the Garos and this cruel chief in which the ancestors of the Garos were defeated, leading to their subjection under the said chief. Many of the Garo headmen were 'poisoned' to death by the taskmaster as a sacrifice to the latter's gods.

To escape further oppression from the chief, the Garos eventually succeeded in crossing the Brahmaputra River on rafts of plantain stems. They then defeated their enemy in the battle at Toplakhawa or Garo-mari in the Goalpara district. From Garo-mari, following the left bank of Brahmaputra River, they came into the kingdom of 'Assamese raja' Lilasing, from whom they suffered much persecution. The neighbouring chief, named Arambit, helped them out and for some time used the Garo warriors in his wars against his enemies. But very soon Arambit and Lilasing came together to reduce the Garos to slavery. The Garos then escaped to the Baghmela Pahar, a hill about 5 miles south-east of Boko in the Kamrup district. Here, they were constantly molested by tiger-men (*muchamaru*), and hence they were always obliged to carry their arms, 'with sword and shield in one hand and the implement of husbandry in the other', as their legend puts it.[12] The continuous depredations from tiger-men again compelled the Garos to migrate. This time they migrated to the west, practically retracing their steps. It was during this sojourn that the tribe broke up into several branches and settled down in present-day Goalpara district.

Here, Garos became rich and prosperous, and eventually a Garo 'kingdom' was also established, of which the first reigning prince was Abrasen. He had his palace and capital built at Sambol Ading, a detached hill not far from the village of Dakaitdol, in the present pargana of Habraghat, to which he is said to have given his name.

---

[12] Playfair (1998 [1909]: 10).

Five or six Garo kings are mentioned as having reigned after Abrasen and the last of them is said to have lived about the end of the eighteenth century. After the establishment of their kingdom, dissension soon sprung up among the Garos due to certain persons who were referred to in the story as being 'very wicked'. This compelled some of the Garos to migrate to the adjoining hills. One party, under the leadership of a chief named Abing-Noga, moved from place to place until they settled down on Nokrek, the highest peak of the Tura range, where Abing-Noga resided until his death.[13] Other Garos followed their steps in the succeeding period, whereas a large part of the Garos remained in the plains till the colonial period. Playfair also noted their legend touched upon the subject of the invasion of Assam by the Muslim army, with which the Garos become friendly as one of them is said to have married a Garo princess. He also noted that some version of the story also mentioned Aurangzeb.[14] The significance of Garo migration history is not only about their sufferings at the hands of different valley kingdoms and rulers but also their constant evasion of such oppressions which eventually took them to the rugged Garo Hills.

The Khasis

The Khasi tradition also holds that they came to their present hills from various points in the plains. Two traditions existed among them regarding the direction they came from: one pointing towards the north via Sylhet; and another towards the east via Patkoi and Brahmaputra valley.[15] The eastern tradition was, however, a more dominant one. Hamlet Bareh, a Khasi historian, showed how Khasis 'came from the east than from any other direction'.[16] He further claimed that their ancestors were 'originally connected with the Mekong river'.[17] Language connection with the Mon-Khmer

---

[13] Playfair (1998 [1909]: 10) noted: 'Signs of habitation are still to be seen there, so perhaps this part of the tale may have some truth in it.'
[14] Playfair (1998 [1909]: 14).
[15] Gurdon (2010 [1906]: 10–11).
[16] Bareh (1985 [1967]: 12).
[17] Bareh (1985 [1967]: 12).

people was also noted by Grierson's *Linguistic Survey of India*.[18] Before coming up to their present hills, as Khasi legends stated, they lived in the plains of Brahmaputra valley for a very long period. Bareh noted one Khasi tradition which mentioned that the ancestors of the Khasis 'once settled in a sea coast who came in migration via the foot of the Himalaya Mountain which they called *Mangkashang* and founded the earliest kingdoms in Assam which have been almost forgotten.'[19] He said that Nowgong, North Cachar, and Mikir Hills were once part of the powerful kingdom of the Khasis called Hadem or Mahadem (known in Tripura chronicle as Hidimba, a title which was later adopted by the Kacharis), whose capital was at Raitong Hills. Based on some literary and archaeological sources, he showed that the Hadem kingdom had trade relationship with China.[20]

Bareh also cited another Khasi tradition, that is, the ancient kingdom of Stri Rajya (a kingdom of women ruled by a queen).The ruler of Kashmir, Laladitya, tried to conquer it but was defeated, and hence he entered into a peace pact with the kingdom. He presented a turban to the queen, which is still used by Khasi kings, nobles, and dancers at state festivals.[21] Bareh also noted that Bhoi areas were always the centre of many Khasi kingdoms with adjuncts into distant plains, each having a fairly long existence, both in ancient and medieval periods. The Khasi kingdoms of Brahmaputra valley, besides the two just mentioned, were Ka Meikha (Kamakya), Muksiar, Mangkathiang or Mangkashang or Maryngkshiang, and Malngiang. They rose up about the fifth century and included a great portion of Lower and Upper Assam. He showed that the 'antiquarian remains and other historical relics still noticed in these hills and in the neighbourhood

[18] Grierson (2005 [1928]: 1–57).

[19] Bareh (1985 [1967]: 269–70).

[20] The Chinese chronicle, *Shung-shu*, mentions that the king of Kapili (identified with Hidimba), named Yuchai, sent a mission in 428 CE. A copper plate inscription also mentions a mission headed by U Ai (essentially a Khasi name) to Peking. The colloquial 'U Ai' and 'Yuchai' are the name of same person, representing the king of Hadem or head of the mission to Peking. See Bareh (1985 [1967]: 34–8).

[21] Bareh (1985 [1967]: 38–9).

such as Jaintiapur in Bangladesh, Neli, Kamakhya and elsewhere in Assam give a corroborative evidence.'[22]

Many reasons were ascribed by legends for the eventual migration of the Khasis to the hills. These ranged from 'great deluge' in Sylhet plain, 'feud' between the Mahadem and the Mangkathiang kingdoms, the revolt of Jaintias, the cessation of North Cachar to Kacharis by Jaintias, the development of horticulture and limestone excavation in Khasi Hills, the 'wickedness' of rulers in certain cases, to the shifting of power centre to the hill chieftains.[23] Bareh put the flourishing period of Khasi's plain kingdoms between 750–1000 CE.[24] This period was significant for certain reasons. It was the high noon of Kamarupa-Kamata kingdom when no other powerful kingdom in Upper Assam was known. The rise of Kamarupa since the fifth century, and on its ruin the Kamata kingdom since the twelfth century, definitely had an impact on the Khasi valley kingdoms.[25] On the other side, the rise of Kachari kingdom of Dimapur in about the eleventh century coincided with the decline of Khasi kingdoms in those areas. The supremacy of Kachari kingdom of Dimapur during this time was said to extend from Dikhow to Kallang rivers, embracing the whole tract surrounding river Dhansiri. To its east was the Chutiya kingdom and to its west was the Kamata kingdom, and this continued till the Ahom expansion in the sixteenth century.[26] Certainly, the rise of Kacharis, and later the Ahoms, had a devastating impact on the various Khasi statelets in the same areas or close by. Therefore, it would not be out of place here to suggest that the decline of Khasi kingdoms and the eventual migration of its population to the highland plateau were also closely related to state-making projects under the Kamarupa-Kamata, Kachari, and the Ahoms.

The Tanis: 'Sub-Himalayan Tribes'

Very few tribes in Northeast India have generated a heated debate among scholars over their origin and migration. Indeed, the colonial

22 Bareh (1989: 262); see also Bareh (1985 [1967]: 29–34).
23 See Bareh (1985 [1967]: 38–9, 1989: 269–72).
24 Bareh (1985 [1967]: 39, 1989: 269–72).
25 See Lahiri (1991).
26 See, for instance, Barpujari (1997) and Misra (1978: 28–9).

ethnolinguistic studies have been generally accepted as a given in most cases, and have been also supported by the oral history of the tribes themselves. But in the case of the origin and migration of the tribes inhabiting the sub-Himalayan ranges adjoining the Brahmaputra valley, there are two contrasting views which have generated heated debate. On the one hand, Roy's study on the social and cultural aspects of the Adis, for instance, reveals that the Adis migrated from the south of the Himalayas and formed part of what he called the 'trans-Brahmaputra' cultural area. In this context, the route of migration was through Patkai range, Brahmaputra valley, and their present hills.[27] On the other hand, studies based on the oral history of the Tani tribes show their migration to the present habitats from the north, through the Himalayas, passing Tibet, and then along the river corridors of Subansiri and Siang or Tsangpo (Brahmaputra) rivers.[28]

What is interesting in the debate is the basis on which they articulate their point. The first group takes on the cultural trope, especially the absence of Buddhist and Tibetan culture in sub-Himalayan tribes. The second group makes the point that such absence could be because they migrated before Buddhism came to Tibet in the seventh century. The possibility of their escape from Buddhisization process under Tibetan state is also emphasized. Nath, for instance, pointed out the similarities between 'Bon religion' of Tibet, a kind of Shamanism, and that of the tribes of sub-Himalayan ranges. He further pointed out that the Bon religion and its followers, the Bonpos, were persecuted and expelled by the rulers of Tibet after their conversion to Buddhism. This took place in about the second half of the seventh century and the migration of Bonpos to other places was put at between 800–1000 CE. He, therefore, felt that 'some batches of such banished Bonpo are the present Tani groups of tribes living in Arunachal Pradesh'.[29]

---

[27] Roy (1997 [1960]). This view is shared by other scholars too. See Chowdhury (1990: 13–18) and Nath (2000).

[28] See Dunbar (1916: 14) and Nyori (1993). Blackburn (2003) draws on Apatani legends and their material culture to prove that they came from the north.

[29] Nath (2000: 15).

Although it is difficult to reconstruct the connection between the 'banished Bonpos' and the ancestors of the Tanis, it makes sense to think that Buddhisization and religious persecution under Tibetan state was one of the primary factors for the migration of people to the rugged sub-Himalayan ranges.

Similarly, the cultural thesis also makes it clear that these tribes migrated after living in the plains of Upper Assam for some centuries. The hill Miris (Mishings), close kin of the Adis, for instance, claimed that they, along with the Chutiyas, once conquered Lakhimpur area and, after some centuries of ruling over this valley, they 'retired again with the Chutiyas into their mountain fastnesses, when they were finally defeated in the sixteenth century by the Ahoms'.[30] The Akas also claimed the prince (Bhaluka) who once ruled the valley from Ita Fort (at the foothill of the Daffla and Aka hills) was their ancestor. Ita Fort was the capital of Bhaluka who was the grandson of Ban Raja, the ruler of Tezpur (Sonitpur: 'city of blood'), said to have been defeated by Krishna. Regarding this claim, Gait remarked: '[I]t is, perhaps, not impossible that they are the remains of a people who once ruled in the plains and were driven into the hills by some more powerful tribe.'[31] Thus, it can be seen that the rugged sub-Himalayan ranges were the zone of refuge to many people who had escaped from the surrounding states in highland Tibet in the north and from states in Assam in the south.

The Karbis

The Karbis (Mikirs) also have the tradition of coming from 'elsewhere' to their present hills (Mikir Hills). Butler, for instance, noted one tradition common among them:

> [T]hey were originally [sic] settled in Tooleeram Senaputtee's territory [North Cachar Hills], under petty chiefs of their own selection. Some years ago, they were conquered by a Rajah of Cachar, from whose oppression they were driven to take refuge in Jynteea [Jaintia

---

[30] Hamilton (1997: 85).
[31] Gait (2008 [1905]: 17).

kingdom]. Meeting there with the same treatment, some emigrated to Deemoroo, Beeltollah, and Ranee in the district of Kamroop [erstwhile Khasi states]; the remainder took up their present abode in the locality described above [Mikir Hills].[32]

Charles Lyall, from the findings of Reverend Edward Stack in the 1880s, also noted their tradition which pointed to their 'original abode' in the eastern portion of the Khasi and Jaintia Hills, bordering on the Kopili River. From there they migrated to Duar Baguri or Nowgong region because they were harassed by warfare between Khasi (or Synteng) chiefs.[33] He also noted that the Mikirs 'have dim traditions of a king of their own in the good old days, whom they call *Sot Recho*, and are said by Mr. Stack to expect his return to earth'. They fought with the Dimasa or hill Kacharis, established a fort at Diyaung-mukh (the junction of the Diyaung and Kopili rivers), 'the ruins of which are still to be seen'.[34]

Lyall also discussed the further tradition of the Karbis who 'claim kinship with no other tribe in Assam'. He traced their further tradition, through their language, to the south and felt that the Karbis were 'intimately connected' to the Kuki-Chin group, especially to those living in the south of the Arakan Yoma range, and 'no such extensive affinity can be proved between Mikir and the Boro family' as it used to be held.[35] He also cited the case of close affinity between the Karbis and the Chins in their customs, both domestic and individual, such as house-building style, marriage, funeral ceremonies, disposal of death, rule of inheritance, treatment of diseases, propitiation of spirits, and festivals. He therefore concluded that the customs of Khyengs (Chins) 'presents the closest analogy to those of the Mikirs'.[36] Certain old songs of Karbis also mentioned the Borail range and Barak River, which further substantiate their further home to the south.[37] What is significant in Karbis migration history is their

[32] Butler (1978 [1855]: 126–7).
[33] See also Lyall (1997 [1908]: 4–5).
[34] Lyall (1997 [1908]: 4–5).
[35] Lyall (1997 [1908]: 153–4, 171).
[36] Lyall (1997 [1908]: 154).
[37] This emerged during an interview with Dharamsing Teron, a Karbi scholar and specialist, on 30 September 2016.

suffering under different kingdoms, such as Kacharis, Jaintias, and Khasis. They escaped the oppression under these states and eventually moved up to their present habitats (the Mikir Hills) and settled down 'peacefully'.

The Kuki-Chin Group

The Kuki-Chin[38] family is a large conglomeration of tribal groups, sharing close affinity to each other. Thus, it is difficult, and of course superfluous, to treat them separately. This is especially so if we look at their familiar legends of origin and migration. Their legends have it that they originally came from a place variously known as 'Sinlung', or 'Chhinlung', or 'Khul', or 'Khurpui', from where they 'sprung up' to the 'Chunggam' (upper world, meaning the mountain region).[39] This place has been mistakenly translated in all colonial accounts as 'cave' or 'bowel of the earth' from where they sprung up to the 'surface of the earth' or 'upper world'.[40] Most local historians have identified this old fount somewhere in China; some even felt that Sinlung (literally, stone enclosure or rampart) refers to the Great Wall of China. As already noted in the introductory chapter, Chongthu, the ancestor of some of the Kuki tribes, and his party escaped from Noimang region to Chunggam.[41] After their escape to the hills, they migrated from place to place until they settled down in 'a big valley' abundant with water, forests, and open land. They built a fortified settlement in this valley at a place called 'Mandalai' and named it 'Chungkhopi'. They called the fortified castle 'Manmasi Kulpi'. After staying for about two generations, Chungkhopi was attacked and destroyed by a 'powerful invader' (possibly the Shans). It was during

---

[38] The term 'Kuki-Chin' is a linguistic term referring to present-day Mizos of Mizoram, Chins of Burma, Kukis of Northeast India, and even the Meiteis (Manipuris). But Meitei, which formed a small state in the valley of Manipur, is excluded in this study. See Grierson 1994 [1904].

[39] For these traditions, see Lewin (1978 [1870]: 238), McCulloch (1980 [1859]: 55–7), Parry (1988 [1931]: 4), Pudaite (1963: 21), Shakespear (1998 [1912]: 91–5, 150), and Shaw (1997 [1929]: 24–32).

[40] McCulloch (1980 [1859]: 54).

[41] See Shaw (1997 [1929]: 24–5).

this invasion that they lost their long-preserved parchment (*savunjol*) on which their script was written; it is believed that the dogs ate it up when the invaders left it littered on the ground.

From Chungkhopi they followed the riverine corridor of Chinvalui (Chindwin), and finally settled down at a place called Tilmun-Tiljang where they lived for about 200 years. Here, they spread out their settlements till the foothills of Buhbangmol (literally, snow-capped mountain) and around the bank of a river (or a lake) called Leiginmaodeng. From here, they again divided into two branches. One branch moved towards the west and to Phaichungnung Gam (Manipur) and the main branch moved down to Alva (Burmese) country (Kolphaicham or Irrawaddy valley) and set up their settlements at the confluence of Chinvalui and Tuihat (Irrawaddy). After a prosperous life for some generations in this area, they were again driven out by the Burmese (Alva/Ava) towards the Jangmol Hills (that divide Chindwin and Kale–Kabaw valley). Here, they settled down in a place called Kholkip-Kholjang. From there, they moved towards the confluence of Chinvalui and Gun (Imphal River) rivers. They spread out their settlements along the corridors of the Gun River and then across the Kangmangphaicham (Kale–Kabaw valley). After living here for some generations, the Burmese expansionist policy again eventually drove them up to the Yoma ranges (Chin Hills and Manipur Hills), from where they gradually spread out to Lushai Hills and other parts of Northeast India.[42]

This was the long and tedious journey of a group of people whose memory of migration was preserved by a class of wise men called *thempu* or *puithiem*; also called *themthu* (literally, words of wisdom) in their oral histories.[43] An abstract of one such themthu of the Kukis is quoted here:

> He He He Ije Ije Ije Yah! I worship thee Heavenly God; God of seven heaven, God of seven earth, I worship thee; Look at me! Heavenly God, God of the earth; Look at me oh sun and moon; Arise from Leisanpa; Landed at Tuitobin; Landed at Kholkip-kholjang; Landed at Tuisogiet; Landed at Leiduppi-leithaopi; Make us perfect people;

[42] For details of this Kuki legend of migration, see Goswami (1985).

[43] Dalton (1960 [1872]: 112) rightly called them 'conservators of traditions'.

Abundant us with food and water; Abundant us with health; We pray, the children of Manmasi.[44]

Their songs and legends give an explicit account of their lives in the Chindwin and Irrawaddy valleys. For instance, a Mizo tradition claims that they once lived in their own 'kingdom' and built a fort palace at Khampat in Kale–Kabaw valley. They migrated to the hills after the destruction of this kingdom by the enemies. They planted a banyan tree there before they left. A prophecy associated with this was that once the branches of that banyan tree touch the ground, their ruined kingdom will be restored.[45]

Similarly, the Khyengs or Chins (Asho) have the tradition that they came down many years ago from the source of the Chindwin River, lived in a 'brick walled city' in that valley, and later escaped to their present hills.[46] One of their popular ballads is lucid in this respect:

To the upper (country of the) Kyendweng [Chindwin] (river);
To the level (plains of the) baleng and dry htoan (grasses),
To the brick (walled) city of our forefathers,
To the level (plains of the) baleng and dry htoan (grasses),
Which are so charming (lit. not a little charming),
Let us hie, come along!
Let us haste with every speed,
Oh my fairy-like young brother![47]

Dalton also noted one such tradition among the Chins which said that 'they at one time lived under a monarchical government in the plains of Pegu and Ava and their king was disposed by invaders, and retreating into the hills they formed a confederacy of colonies each under its own chief.'[48] The Hmar tradition also referred to the Himalayas, the Shan country (invariably in Burma plain), and so on, as the route of their migration. One of their priest (themthu) chant

---

[44] As quoted in Lenthang (2005: 116); translation by author.
[45] See Lalthangliana (1977: 1–26, 87–91) and Vumson (1986: 26–105).
[46] Fryer (1875: 46).
[47] As quoted in Fryer (1875: 46–7).
[48] Dalton (1960 [1872]: 112).

testified to this: 'Come from Himaloi (Himalaya) mountain; Come from Shan country; Come from Hrilia; Come from Champhai valley; Come from Chongtui; Come from Rengnu and Rengpa ground.'[49] Another ballad described the Shan country 'abundant' with harvest but described the 'Shan state' and Shan people as 'cruel'. They 'sounded out only war' so that their ancestors had to constantly fight with them and took their heads.[50]

Drawing from various Chinese, Burmese, and Shan sources, a few archaeological evidences, and with the help of other studies on Tibeto-Burman people, research on Kuki-Chin history could trace the origin of this people to the great Ch'iang tribes, the ancestors of the Tibeto-Burman people.[51] These tribes initially settled down in north-west China, but in about second millennium BCE took refuge in north-east Tibet due to Chinese hostility, and by the first millennium BCE started migrating towards the south and later entered into Burma plain and other places. The Kuki-Chin group entered Burma about the early centuries of CE, or certainly before the eighth century CE. As they entered the valley, they divided into two groups. The first group entered the confluence of Chindwin and Irrawaddy rivers, settled down there for some centuries and set up their 'kingdom', which was later destroyed by the Nanchaos (Shans) in the ninth century (835 CE). This compelled them to cross the Chindwin and settle in Kale–Kabaw–Myttha–Yaw valleys, while some of them moved towards the hills. From there, most of them migrated to their present hills about the fourteenth century in the face of mounting pressure from, and to evade, the Shans and Burmese state-building projects. The last bastion of this group was still to be seen in the 'Yaw country' (at the foothills of the Chin Hills) during the colonial period. The second group migrated southwards along the right bank of Chindwin River and reached their present hills before 1000 CE, when the first group was still struggling in the plains of Burma.

---

[49] Keivom (n.d.: 90).

[50] As quoted in Pudaite (1963: 24–6).

[51] For a detailed discussion of this historical migration, see Lalthangliana (1977: 1–26), Pudaite (1963: 21–34), Sing Khaw Khai (1995: 1–78), Verghese and Thanzawna (1997), and Vumson (1986: 33–9).

The Naga Group

The migration of Naga tribes to their present hills has been a matter of much confusion since the colonial period. This is particularly because there is no single tradition that can explain migration of all the Nagas. These varied traditions can be broadly divided into two. The first and the most dominant one is the tradition among all the Naga tribes, as in other hill tribes, which claims that they originally 'sprang up' from the 'bowel of the earth', often translated as 'cave'. This tradition can be further divided into three, based on the site of so-called 'cave' within the Naga Hills: Lungterok (literally, six stones) near Chongliemdi (by Aos, Phoms, Changs, and Sangtams); Kezakenoma (by Angamis, Lhotas, Rengmas, Maos, and Marams); and Japvo mountain (by Semas and 'Kacha Nagas').[52] The latter two groups were often known as 'Meikhelian' or 'Makhelians' as they felt that they initially dispersed from Meikhel (sometime spelt as Makhel), understood as Mekhromia in Angami (meaning 'the point/place of departure/dispersal'). The second parallel tradition prevailing among the Nagas places their earlier home beyond the Naga Hills, mostly in the plains surrounding them. The common linguistic thesis of Tibeto-Burman people which placed their origin somewhere in China is one such case.

J.H. Hutton, an authority on Naga studies, for instance, also noted many parallel traditions within Naga Hills. He cited one Angami tradition that derives the Memi Angamis from the daughter of a local god at Mekrima (Meikhel), 'impregnated by a cloud that came out of *the south*'.[53] Another Angami tradition pointed to a village, in the Tangkhul country, known to them as Piwhema, as the remotest place known to have been a fount of the Angami tribe. These two traditions point beyond the commoner's original fount at Mekrima, that is, to the south-east in the Tangkhul Naga country, bordering with the Chindwin valley of Burma.[54] Hutton also pointed out that

[52] See 'Introduction' in Mills (2003 [1922]: xi–xxxix). For different Naga tribes, see Hutton (1921a: 6–20, 1921b: 5–6), Mills (1982 [1937]: 4–6, 2003 [1922]: 3–5, 2003 [1926]: 7), and von Fürer-Haimendorf (1969: 5–6).

[53] 'Introduction' in Mills (2003 [1922]: xx; emphasis mine).

[54] 'Introduction' in Mills (2003 [1922]: xx).

Puchatsuma clan of Kohima came from the west, like the Khoiraos, while another clan came from south-west in the country of 'Kacha Nagas'.[55] Similarly, the Sezemi, Sopvoma, or Memi Angami Nagas of Mao had legends connecting them with the plain area of Manipur.[56] Butler too noted another tradition which mentions the story of the foundation of 'Angami race' by an exile from the court of Jaintiapur, who went first to Dimapur and thence into the Naga Hills. This history, he says, originated in 'an old and intelligent hill Kachari', but he could himself find no confirmation of it.[57]

Mills also noted one tradition among the Lhotas which states that the Lhotas and plainsmen were once the same people who migrated from a place called Lengka, somewhere in the north or north-west of the Naga Hills, the exact site being unknown. They soon split up into two bodies, one of which became the plainsmen of the Brahmaputra valley and the other the Nagas of the hills. One curious evidence of this tradition is represented by a long-hafted daos called *yanthang*, a few of which are still kept as highly prized heirlooms and are said to have been given to the Nagas by their 'brothers' of the plains.[58] This tradition points, noted Hutton, 'very definitely to the snows of the Himalayas seen far to the north-west as the home of their ancestors'.[59] Hutton also noted that the Khoiraos, or some of them, 'claim a western origin from the plains of Assam, and this in particular is the case with Ngari and perhaps one or two neighbouring villages, who have been less affected by the Memi Angami culture than the others, and of whose connection with the Semas there can be no doubt.'[60]

Since the Semas are closely connected to Kezama Angamis, both whose immediate origins are to be found in the Khoiraos, who traced their origin from the west (Assam), Hutton felt that Semas and Khoiraos might have, in part, some connection with the Bodos.[61]

---

[55] 'Introduction' in Mills (2003 [1922]: xx).
[56] Hutton (1921a: 7).
[57] Hutton (1921a: 20).
[58] 'Introduction' in Mills (2003 [1922]: 3–5).
[59] 'Introduction' in Mills (2003 [1922]: xxi).
[60] 'Introduction' in Mills (2003 [1922]: xviii).
[61] Hutton (1921b: 5–6).

He also said that since the Semas are connected with the two villages called 'Swemi' (one of which is still Sema, although surrounded by Angamis) and the Khoiraos of Ngari (who, as just mentioned, traced their origin in the west in Assam plain), their western origin can be established, for example, with the Kacharis, Garos, Lynngams, and Bhois. This may also, he said, apply to the Kezami-Angamis.[62] This contention, he said, is supported by one Kachari tradition which claims that Kacharis and the Nagas had originally descended from two brothers and hence they allowed the Nagas to eat and sleep in the porches of their houses, which they refused to the Kukis.[63] Hutton also cited one Sema tradition, especially those of certain clans in Vekohomi, 'who admittedly came from the country to the south-east across the Tizu'.[64]

The Tangkhuls trace their origin and migration, noted Hutton, from the point 'to the south or to the east', that invariably points to Chindwin–Irrawaddy valleys of Burma.[65] The Sangtams also, according to Hutton, 'claim to a south-eastern origin'. The northern Sangtams merely point to the south, but the southern Sangtams, he said, 'derive their origin from the Chindwin valley to the south-east of them, and have a vague tradition that their tribe has become separated into two parts of which one went apparently west, while remnants are believed to exist in the Chindwin valley still.'[66] Hutton felt that the part of the tribe which went westwards may be represented today in the Lhota tribe, who have a similar if more definite tradition about the splitting of their tribe into two parts, of which one stayed behind at the time of migration. On the other side, the Tamans of Tamanthi area in the Chindwin valley claim that they at one time lived in the hills to the east of them, but they returned to the valley, leaving some of their fellow tribesmen behind in the hills. These tribes who were left behind in the hills, Hutton conjectured, might possibly be connected with the Southern Sangtams, and hence to some of the Lhotas. Since the Tamans traced their origin to China

---

[62] 'Introduction' in Mills (2003 [1922]: xviii).
[63] 'Introduction' in Mills (2003 [1922]: xviii–xix).
[64] 'Introduction' in Mills (2003 [1922]: xviii, fn. 2, and xix).
[65] 'Introduction' in Mills (2003 [1922]: xxi).
[66] 'Introduction' in Mills (2003 [1922]: xix).

across the Irrawaddy valley, the original home of some of the Nagas can then be traced back to China.[67]

Similarly, among the trans-Dikhu tribes, there are many traditions which point to their origin outside Naga Hills, again a deviation from the commoner's tradition of the Chongliemdis. Hutton noted that there is section of the Ao tribe which claims its origin from the plains in the north-west, that is, Assam.[68] There are in Yacham, and also in some Konyak villages to the east, noted Hutton, 'apparently definite traditions of an immigration from a place called Maibang of a clan which still preserves as heirlooms certain peculiar types of spiked armlets of bronze'.[69] Likewise, part of the Chang tribe, noted Hutton, 'again claims an origin from the south, though part admits to a common origin with the Aos from Chongliemdi'.[70]

Beside Khoiraos, Konyak Nagas too have very clear traditions that point to the Assam plain. As noted by von Fürer-Haimendorf, the Konyaks have many traditions of origin and migrations. According to one tradition, the ancestors of the majority of Konyaks came from the mountain called Yengyudang, situated to the south of the present Konyak territory. Another and equally widespread tradition was of a migration from the Brahmaputra valley along the Dikhu River and into the hills flanking that river. The tradition of the people of Wakching was more specific, he noted. They believed that their ancestors came from a mountain beyond the Brahmaputra, known as 'mountain beyond the great water'. On their way from there, they crossed the Brahmaputra valley and followed the Dikhu as far as the present village of Chongwe. Finding the land there not sufficiently fertile, they and the ancestors of the people of Wanching migrated to the ridge on which the villages of Wakching and Wanching are presently situated. However, these early migrants are believed to have been only part of a tribe, the other half of which remained in the hills beyond the Brahmaputra.[71]

[67] 'Introduction' in Mills (2003 [1922]: xix–xx).

[68] 'Introduction' in Mills (2003 [1922]: xviii).

[69] 'Maibang' is a Kachari term and place name, meaning 'much paddy'. Mills (2003 [1922]: xviii, fn. 1).

[70] 'Introduction' in Mills (2003 [1922]: xxi).

[71] He, however, noted that this tradition was not shared by all and felt that some might have certainly come from the south where their spirit of the deaths goes. See von Fürer-Haimendorf (1969: 5–6).

These parallel traditions, apparently contesting, may however be seen as connected to each other in certain ways. Researches on Nagas broadly agree that the Nagas also followed the general migration route of the Tibeto-Burman-speaking people. Shimray, for instance, holds that the Nagas, as other Tibeto-Burman groups, originally came from China following a southward direction, then turned eastwards through the Chindwin–Irrawaddy valleys, and finally moved up to the Naga Hills. He feels that Makhel was the point where they originally settled down in the Naga Hills, and later dispersed in different directions.[72] If the original home of the Nagas is located, as Shimray has argued, somewhere in China, then one is tempted to draw attention to the curious resemblance of the term 'Makhel', or 'Meikhel', or sometimes 'Maikel' of the Nagas to that of 'Nmaikha' and 'Malikha' of the Kachins. The 'Nmaikha' and 'Malikha' are the two great tributaries of Irrawaddy River and many tribes in Burma, including the Kachins, claim the region around the sources of them to be their original homeland.[73] Hutton, for instance, was quite convinced on the possibility of giving local value to their old legend:

> The history of how the Naga tribes came precisely to occupy their present position has, of course, passed into the dim obscurity of vague traditions ... The legends of the Aos and of the Semas [and of course, the Angamis, Lhotas, Rengmas, and so on] give those tribes a more or less autochthonous origin, though these legends are probably the old legends of the race which have been given a local value.[74]

Citing different cases of 'marked cleavages' and strong 'penetration' of different groups into the Naga fold, Hutton concluded that Naga Hills 'has been the scene of a series of immigrations from north-east, north-west and south, and that the different stocks introduced in this way have entered into their composition'.[75] Of the possible reasons for their migration to Naga Hills, he cited the case of political struggle in the valleys: 'Indeed, in view of the struggles that have

---

[72] Shimray (1985: 12–37).

[73] For Kachin's origin story, see NAI, Foreign, Secret (E), February 1893, Nos 69–156.

[74] Hutton (1921a: 6).

[75] 'Introduction' in Mills (2003 [1922]: xxxv–xxxvi).

taken place from the fertile plains of Burma to the east and India to the west, it is inevitable that some elements of the races worsted in these struggles should have been pushed up into the [Naga] hills.'[76]

State-Evading Population in the Hills

What conclusions can be drawn from the discussion in this chapter? The history of the migration of various tribes shows that they were in the valley surrounding their present hills immediately before coming up to these hills. Most of them claim that they once lived in their own 'kingdoms', which were however destroyed by a more powerful enemy. It is under these latter kings, and sometime under their own rulers, that they suffered different hardships and oppressions. Their legends are studded with politically coercive language of control: defeat, subjection, cruelty, wickedness, oppression, enslavement, warfare, hostility, forced conversion, religious persecution, and so on, besides difficulties caused by nature, such as flood, fire, famine, diseases, and so on. A deeper research might find cases of oppressive taxation, conscription, corvée labour, and so on. Legends make it clear that it was due to all these hardships they suffered at the hands of the valley state rulers that they eventually migrated to, or escaped into, their present hills. Some of them chose the lower terai ecology infested with deadly diseases, others chose the inaccessible glens and marshlands, and a majority of them chose to flee to the rugged highland massif to escape their oppressors. Thus, the Kacharis (Bodos), Garos, Khasis, Karbis, Nagas, Tanis, Kuki-Chins, and so on migrated to their present rugged habitats to escape and evade state-making projects in the valleys of India and Burma. In this context, they became what James Scott has called the state-evading population in the hills, rather than being the 'remnants' of prehistoric society. They were the *post-* of states and civilization. They were what the dominant civilizational narrative would call 'civilizational backsliders'.

Indeed, such escape was not a wilful migration in normal circumstances but was necessarily a 'political choice' to evade the 'cruelties' of the more powerful enemy who had 'worsted' them. They are lots of what Endle has called the 'patriotic spirits' who, instead of

---

[76] 'Introduction' in Mills (2003 [1922]: xxxv–xxxvi).

submitting to their conquerors, escaped to the 'less favoured parts of the province, where their conquerors did not care at once to follow them up'.[77] In this sense, what was the 'less favoured part' of the province, such as the unforgiving *terai* ecology and the rugged mountain massif, became their safe haven, the region of refuge. If the reason for taking a flight to the rugged landscape was to evade control and oppressions, then it can be said that being hillmen and state evaders is to be necessarily a freedom-loving people. Thus, freedom and autonomy provided the ideology, individual provided the determination, the hill landscape provided the engine for social and spatial engineering process, and mobility provided the gels that drove individual freedom. To be hillmen and state evaders in the highland also necessarily meant to re-enact and refashion a new way of life that was essentially state resistant and against the concentration of power in the hills.

In the following chapters, an attempt has been made to study some of the important hill practices, that is, nonstate practices, with the aim to not only understand the very characters of such practices but also to understand the forms of freedom enjoyed by individual and groups in stateless society there. The hill settlement and population distribution patterns, their mode of production, their social and political relations, and their cultural worldviews are taken up for discussion.

---

[77] Endle (2010 [1911]: 8).

3

Divided We Stand

Space, Settlement, and Population Distribution Pattern

A traveller in the hills of Northeast India will be stunned not only by the mosaic of culture that is mesmerizing but also by the kind of a deep sense of cultural integrity in the way people express themselves to 'others'. If you ask a person, for instance, how far is the distance between two places, you would get a prompt answer, 'this much hour(s)' or 'this much day(s)', but hardly 'this much kilometre(s)'. By insisting further 'how many kilometres?', the response would be simply, 'I don't know'. A further question may make him quietly shy away. Similarly, you would hear people asking you, 'how many day(s) or hour(s) (but hardly kilometres) it took to reach such-and-such place?' and so on. This type of expression you would invariably receive from both educated and so-called 'illiterate' population. It is significant to note that such expression is not an act of innocence; it represents their deep sense of friction of terrain. It is in keeping with the hill's 'line of conduct', a conduct which determines and is determined by the sense of friction, and a conduct which opposes the dominant logocentric notion of time and distance.

Take the case of similar expressions in the past profound in their vernacular mode of measuring distance between two given points.

There is the vernacular time scale, like 'before'—morning meal, afternoon, or evening meal—'journey', or one, two, three days march; this much pipe smoking or that much time for doing certain things; and so on.[1] Kukis are, for instance, inveterate smokers and their 'few means of calculating time and distance is', noted Stewart, 'by the number of pipes he smokes'.[2] Khasis are inveterate chewers of *supari* (betel nut) and pan leaf and therefore, they often measure distance, noted Gurdon, 'by the number of betel-nuts that are usually chewed on a journey'.[3] Similarly, Lyall noted that the Karbis compute time and distance by the interval required to chew a nut. They use the phrase '*ingtat e-om-ta er*' (the time it takes to chew the nut and pan leaf red).[4] Even to explain how far some field below the village is, noted Mills among the Nagas, 'he would say how many times a man would ordinarily rest on the way up with a load'. For distances up to a day's march, he noted, the man points to where the sun was when he started and when he arrived; and for long journey, he gives the number of days required to get there. This type of distance measurement is, he rightly remarked, 'a very sensible way, too, for what really matters is not how far away the field is by actual measurement' but how difficult is the journey and the velocity it takes to cover the distance; and on that matrix, time and distance is calculated.[5] Thus, the centrality of friction of distance is again significant.

Friction of distance in the hills depends on the density of forest covers, the ruggedness of the hill landscape, the altitude, and more importantly, its position from the source of potential raiders and conquerors. Understanding this vernacular notion of time and distance and its profound sense of friction of terrain is, I think, crucial in situating the essence of settlement patterns and population distribution in the hill universe. This chapter deals with the hill notion of space and territoriality and locates the centrality of friction of terrain in their spatial distribution patterns, in the settlement and population

---

[1] These terms are still in common use among the hill tribes of the Northeast.

[2] Stewart (1855: 636).

[3] Gurdon (2010 [1906]: 5).

[4] See Lyall (1997 [1908]: 14).

[5] Mills (1982 [1937]: 317).

distribution, and in the frequency they choose to move about in the hills. Other aspects of friction of distance will be taken up in next chapter, such as the way they chose and built their villages, the type of connectivity, and the way they trained and grouped their warriors.

Irony behind the Fallen Land

Reporting after what he called a 'brief but decisive campaign' in eastern Naga Hills, Captain John Butler concluded that it was 'a campaign which I am sure will not only be *remembered for ages* to come by the tribes who suffered by it, but one of the fame of which will be handed along the whole line of Naga frontier to be *a warning* to all' [emphasis mine]. Butler was referring to the British expedition in eastern Naga Hills which took place in 1875. The expedition was in response to the 'terrible massacre' of Lieutenant Holcombe and 80 of his men in a 'most treacherous' manner at Ninu and other places in February 1874, in which at least nine villages were found to be involved. This incident took place in opposition to British interventions in general, and the topographical survey taken in that part of Naga Hills in particular. The Nagas stiffly opposed the expedition party sent to punish them in whatever way they could. The military column razed their villages to the ground, destroyed all their granaries, scorched their country, and took some prisoners. At Ninu, they found the heads of seventy-one British *sepoys* who were massacred earlier, carefully arranged in a long basket under the trees at the centre of the village where such trophies were usually exhibited.[6] It cannot be denied that such a 'contemptuous devastation' on their villages and properties continued, and still continues, to haunt the memory of many Nagas. The valley state army and marauders may have disappeared as fast as they appeared in the hills, but the memory of their cruelty remains in the hills, circulating through the folk narratives and through the medium of village site where such brutality took place. Thus, to all the Nagas, the villages of

[6] NAI, FP (A), December 1875, No. 92: Captain John Butler, Political Agent, Naga Hills to H. Luttman-Johnson, Secretary to the Chief Commissioner of Assam, 30 April 1875.

Razephemah, Ninu, Khonomah, and so on are not just villages, they are also sites of memory of colonial state violence.

Surely, the memory of such occasional military expeditions into the hills from the valley states in the past has been handed down along the whole frontier as 'a warning to all', that valley kingdoms are impending danger to the terra incognita of the hills. It is this memory of state notoriety that has always haunted the mind of the hillmen, ensuring that they do not become complacent about the danger. Take the case of Patkai (Pangsau) Pass, for instance. Travelling from Assam to Hukawng Valley (Burma) through this famous pass in 1869–70 (his previous trip was in 1868–69), Jenkins was stunned by two bewildering sights. First, the pass was without any track, let alone a road, and was covered with immense sheet of timber trees (averaging 12 feet in girth and 60–70 feet in height until the first branch) with a thick rank growth of jungle underneath. His party followed the winding natural beds of mountain streams which were 'impossible to leave' and at times, the only visible track was of wild elephants. Quite often, they got lost and his guides had to fan out in search of a possible track. They took nine days to reach Hukawng valley. Second, during this nine-day journey along the pass, there was complete absence of settlements and cultivations. After reaching Nam-yaong, the first Burmese village in Hukawng valley, he said: 'This was the ninth day since we left the last Assam village, and during this time we had seen no cultivation, not even a bit of clearance.'[7]

This famous 'pass' that linked Assam and Burma was the easiest and shortest historical route through which most migrations and invasions from the east took place. The great Ahoms, and later the Burmese, the Khamtis, and the Singphos, all used this pass to invade Assam. The Ahoms continued to use the pass as a political and commercial highway to connect with their original homeland. The Burmese, during their occupation of Assam, established a chain of military stations at every 12–15 miles along the route to maintain the pass and stock food. After their withdrawal, the route was entirely overrun by forests, although some trade was carried out on small scale (Jenkins reported three parties during that year) by Singphos and Dooanniahs traders. It was the practice among these traders to

---

[7] Jenkins (1873: 245–46, quotation 246).

set up depots of provisions along the route, in which they buried their food supply in advance and then returned for their trading loads. Otherwise, each man had to carry, along with his trading items, 15 pounds of rice for his own consumption on the journey. Jenkins was keen to open the pass for two reasons: to open up China market through this pass; and to repopulate Assam from the east.

The pertinent question now is: why was the famous Patkai Pass a desolate wilderness, deprived of any settlement? It is peculiar to observe that the Naga hillmen who inhabited the Patkai ranges deliberately avoided settling along the pass for certain reasons. On the one hand, due to the flow of goods and people, they knew that they could gain materially from occupying the pass, by providing food and shelter to traders or even collecting toll, as was the case in other passes. On the other hand, they were also aware that such economic benefits could be a prelude to physical hardship and political control of the valley states. The Nagas, over the centuries, had witnessed successive movements of valley state marauders, invaders, and conquerors along the pass. No wonder then, they could never forget the tragedies they had experienced during the invasion of Assam by the Ahoms in the thirteenth century. The more recent invasions of the Khamtis, the Singphos, and the Burmese into Assam only reminded them of the impending dangers along the pass. Besides, the frequent appearance of armed freebooters and slave raiders from Hukawng valley (and possibly from Upper Assam) during the eighteenth and nineteenth centuries was the clear and present danger to the state-evading hillmen. The political danger it could have brought to the community therefore outweighed the economic dividends.

The reason for which the Nagas avoided occupying the famous pass indicates and/or explains the way in which these state evaders visualized their space. They, in fact, imagined space as a political resource which had to be controlled, managed, or avoided. In this context, leaving that part of Patkai ranges along the pass or the state's political highway uncultivated and uninhabited was one of the effective political strategies adopted by the Nagas to avoid, evade, and avert control and appropriation of the valley state conquerors, marauders, freebooters, slave raiders, and even armed traders. These state evaders in the hills were vigilant, conscious, and wary, and always kept their eyes open for any danger from the valleys. In this sense, their notion of what was 'vacant land' and what was 'habitable land' becomes clear, and this was governed by politics rather than economics. Thus, when certain land was reclaimed by nature, it was not always a natural phenomenon. In other words, to the state evaders unclaimed, uncultivated and uninhabited land was considered to be a natural political resource to evade control and appropriations. This is what I call spatial sensibility that the stateless hillmen had evolved against their enemy. It was their line of conduct that shaped and fashioned their space and territoriality in the hills.

Space and Territoriality

The celebration of wildness in the dominant civilizational discourse denies the existence of any notion of boundary, space, or territoriality among the hill tribes. The wild, forested, and rugged mountains were considered to be inhibiting any sense of geographicity, just as they isolated, disconnected, and removed each village. The 'barbarians' were roving across the massif without any sense of direction or any respect of space. The same notion of wildness also shows that the highland massif was isolated from the valley civilization. Much has been written about their land rights, landholdings, or land use in the colonial period. However, what we learn from these accounts concerns mainly the village territory and does not cover anything beyond it. Thus, the same notion of wildness continues to haunt most colonial writings. The central problem in this dominant colonial discourse on wildness, which is also often assumed to be the only form of spatial knowledge, is the dominance of political and economic notions of space. Geography, in these writings, has been defined in terms of political regime or economic use. Any territory which does not come under any political regime or economic exploitation is but wild or wasteland and deserves no sense of geography or mapping. However, these discourses have never considered that there were also other notions of space and geography in other cultures. This denial not only limits them from knowing the unique feature of the hill settlement and population distribution pattern but also their very notion of space as a resource to be owned, controlled, or avoided.

It is true that the hillmen did choose village-based political system, but to see their geographicity only from this perspective is to miss some important points in their history. The spatial sensibility of the hillmen was much beyond any comprehension. In fact, beyond the delimited village territory, there were multiple notions of space and territoriality. At least three notions of space were possible beyond the village geography, related to social, cultural, and political space. Socially, the dynamics of clan relationship and connection mapped a different kind of geography. Culturally, their notion of the next world, the 'nether land', also set another kind of geography. Politically, beyond the village territory or contiguous to it, and also across the hill landscape, a certain notion of space and territoriality could be identified. This politically conceptualized space was most visible in the way they distributed their settlements and population across the highland massif and in the way they preserved a huge zone of forested territory at the foot of the mountain adjoining the valley state space. I will be concentrating on this politically conceptualized notion of space. But it is also pertinent here to briefly discuss other notions of space for an overall idea of space and territoriality.

Regarding the spatial distribution of village territory, I have covered the case of the Kuki-Chin world elsewhere.[8] It was similarly the case in other hills. Across the mountain massif, land was something that was very close to the hearts of the people; and it was owned, controlled, divided up for different purposes, protected, and even colonized. There was a clear notion of boundary. J.W. Edgar, for instance, noted that 'among all the tribes on the frontier there is a very strong feeling about boundaries' and 'each village has its limits which are known and respected by the tribe around'.[9] Within this village boundary, land was further divided into different clan or family holdings (among many tribes) and for different land use. Of the land tenure system, there were broadly four forms: chief land, communal/clan land, private land, and mixture of private and communal land.[10] In terms of land use, the village land was divided into

[8] See Guite (2014).

[9] WBSA, JP: August 1872, No. 220. For Garos, see Playfair (1998 [1909]) and von Fürer-Haimendorf (1969: 41).

[10] See, for instance, Gurdon (2010 [1906]: 86–88), Hutton (1921a: 140, 1921b: 155), Mills (2003 [1926]: 187–8), and von Fürer-Haimendorf (1969: 30).

at least five sectors: habitation zone (village precinct); reserve forest (around the village); cultivation zone; sacred grooves; and hunting ground.[11] Each village was sometimes subdivided into 'blocks' or 'wards'.[12] Along the fringe of the hill settlements, a vast forested belt, known as hillmen's 'hunting ground' (discussed in detail later in this chapter), was visible. There was another shared zone of valley settlement along this belt called *posaland* (detailed in Chapter 9). The above-mentioned scheme of territoriality is schematically represented in Figure 3.1.

Clan Geographicity and Governmentality

The dominant narrative understood all other sets of geographicity in tribal society as 'realm'. Let us assume that 'realm' did not connote any political boundary. Yet, it still holds that realm, for the hillmen, was a broader spatial category which may be understood in two ways. First, realm implied the mental mapping of the secular terrestrial terrain which fell under the control of a particular chief or clan members. Second, realm implied another set of mental mapping related to their spiritual or cosmological notion of the world here and to the next, often coterminous with, and a mirror of, their terrestrial world. Both operated within the dynamics of clan/tribe and constituted, in a way, the imaginative geography of the clan or tribe. Clan was, to the hillmen, an operative measure not only for their social relationships but also for their geographicity. It was a closely knit social compact which generated regular networks and communication among its members. Clan dynamics were usually substantial, which strongly influenced, and were in turn influenced by, their lifeways: of the

[11] For 'forest reserves', see Hutton (1921b: 35–6), Mills (2003 [1922]: 21, 2003 [1926]: 71), and von Fürer-Haimendorf (1969: 21). It effectively protected the village from wildfire and mountain wind, prevented landslide, sustained water resources and forest items, and, as some observers have remarked, was a good screen against enemies. For description of sacred grooves, see Carey and Tuck (1987 [1896]: 198–9) and Gurdon (2010 [1906]: 33–4).

[12] This was most visible among the Nagas. See, for instance, Hodson (2007 [1911]), Hutton (1921a, 1921b), Mills (1982 [1937], 2003 [1922], 2003 [1926]), and von Fürer-Haimendorf (1969).

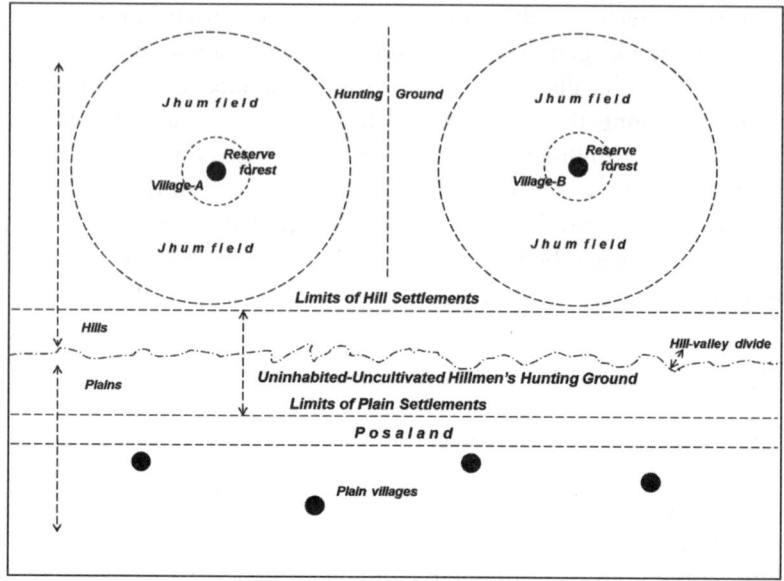

Figure 3.1 Schematic Representation of Village Territory, Its Hunting Ground, and Posaland
Source: This figure is modified from Guite (2014: 1201).

way they perceived themselves and the others, of their world, and so on. Such geographicity or the spatial worldview of the hill tribes may be called clan geographicity; and in a certain way, it involved a certain kind of governmentality amongst group of villages belonging to the same clan, which may be understood in terms of clan governmentality.[13]

The clan geographicity and governmentality should not be construed as a closely knit political geography or revenue governmentality of an administrative unit. Nor was it a subordinate–superordinate relationship of the feudal order. It merely represented the dominant

[13] I borrow the term 'geographicity' and 'governmentality' from Indrani Chatterjee's fascinating study of 'monastic geographicity' and 'monastic governmentality' in precolonial Northeast India. They connote a geography and government other than our conventional knowledge of political geography and governmentality. See Chatterjee (2013).

patterns of social and cultural networks, of relationship, linkage, affiliation, and empathy, in the stateless society that underpinned their lifeways and social conduct. In short, it conspired against the dominant notion of a world of isolation and physical disconnectedness and foregrounded the connected history of the tribal universe. Although these networks and connectedness generated contours of obligations and responsibilities to each other in specific ways, and even if such contouring connected each other on regular basis, each of these villages was politically independent from the other.

The clan governmentality was not a structure of control and appropriation, nor was it a revenue-seeking government, but a governmentality that protected and preserved the independence of the politically disconnected villages of the clan from any attempt of control from outside the clan/tribe. It was not concerned with the daily chores of the village government but was responsible for its safety from any insult. The clan governmentality was, in a way, the commonwealth of the scattered and amorphous clan villages which usually pooled, if necessary, their strength together against a common enemy or otherwise. It facilitated the circulation of warriors and, in some sense, cultural power and sovereignty between the different clan villages. This clan governmentality was governed and sustained by customary tribute and protection operated within the principle of cooperation and reciprocity which was unique to each tribe. Instead of being state–subject relation, such tribute and protection underpinned a conceptual equality between the giver and receiver of tribute. In many cases, the giver was often stronger than the receiver and it was the responsibility of the stronger to protect the weaker villages. The direction of tribute followed the lineage gradient, in which the younger gave to the elder. In a few cases, the weaker paid to the stronger village if such governmentality transformed into some kind of political governmentality, but, nonetheless, it was a very loose one in which conceptual 'friendship' or 'cooperation and reciprocity' was central.

On the other hand, the clan geographicity was a semi-cultural complex of the larger cultural universe of the hill people. It determined the mental map of pattern of networks of cultural sovereignty and customary tribute (which fell under clan governmentality), of the circulation or movement of people, culture, idea, and emotion.

In short, it mapped the 'realm' of the clan or tribe. Here, 'realm' was certainly a territorial concept, which however contested, conspired, and even opposed our modern notion of contiguous territoriality and sovereignty. It was rather a disconnected, disjointed, or often disorderly territoriality. It mapped the scattered pockets of territories belonging to different villages of a clan, often divided in between by the territories belonging to the villages of other clans.

In this geographical disconnectedness or discontinuity, the formless and amorphous villages were, however, sustained and closely intertwined to each other by the clear pattern of social and cultural networks and relationship that mirrored and mapped a particular kind of geography. This mental map or the imaginative geography of the clan, sustained by social and cultural networks, is what we call the clan geographicity. While the interaction and transactions among different villages of the clan mapped the clan geographicity, the geographies of different clans similarly dovetailed and overlapped each other at different points, as schematically shown in Figure 3.2. It is from this concept of clan geographicity and governmentality that one can actually understand the notion of space and territoriality beyond the village boundary.

Take the case of, for instance, the clan relationship and networks in the Kuki-Chin world. Here, the social and cultural networks were generated by some of their indispensable customary practices, such as the *sating* system, feasts and festivals, marriage relations, death rituals, and so on. Sating was the flesh between the upper side of the ribs and the hide of all animals killed in the ceremonies, or in the chase, which was customarily the share of, and a share to be paid by a man to his, senior-most male next-of-kin till it went up to the clan *pipa* (clan head).[14] In this, the younger son was customarily obliged to pay sating to his eldest brother, who was in turn obliged to pay his sating to his eldest brother, the chain eventually going up to the parent village of the clan (pipa) from where all of them originally split.

In this context, sating became a kind of tribute paid to the eldest brother in recognition of his superior position over the younger brothers in the clan hierarchy. In this way, the chief of the parent village emerged as the pipa (literally, 'biggest one' or 'head' of the clan/

---

[14]   See, for instance, Shaw (1997 [1929]: 65–6).

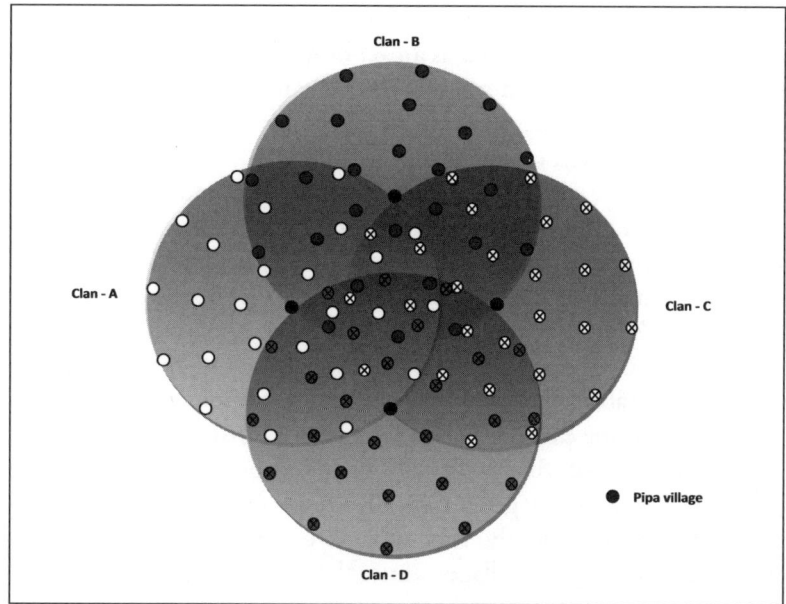

Figure 3.2   Schema of Clan Geographicity and Governmentality
Source: Prepared by author.
Note: The small circles represent the different villages connected to each other and
to the *pipa* village. But the pattern of such connections was determined by the larger
circle that represents the clan geographicity, within which such connections, networks, and relationships were patterned and operated.

tribe) over such villages. This pipa was variously known in colonial
accounts as 'principal chief', 'paramount chief', 'Rajah', or 'great
Rajah'.[15] He could be weaker or poorer, but his superior position
as the pipa over the younger villages remained intact. Stewart, for
instance, noted: 'Each of the clans have one great Rajah, supposed to
be the main branch of the original stock, to whom ... great respect
is shown by all, and acknowledgement of the superior title given,
although in power and wealth he may be much poorer than others
of the tribe.'[16] Such 'great respect' to the 'original stock' was shown
not only by way of bodily gestures but, more importantly, by a token

[15]   Brown (2001 [1873]: 48) and Macrae (1919 [1801]: 185).
[16]   Stewart (1855: 627).

payment in the form of sating. If a member did not perform this duty in the clan, it was taken as an act of rebellion and such rebellion could even lead to his dismemberment/banishment from the clan, which manifested in certain clan rituals, feasts and festivals, or in the circuit of circulation of warriors in wartime.

Since land was closely related to kinship law of inheritance, sating tribute mapped not only the clan geography but also its governmentality. Land, under Kuki-Chin jurisprudence, belonged to the chief and land transfer or inheritance invariably took the lineage gradient of the chief's family (son, eldest among some and youngest among others). Once they got sufficient followers, each of the chief's sons could also establish his own village with or without the help of his father (within the existing village territory or outside it). In this way, a good number of villages usually fissioned out from the 'original stock' and were often geographically disconnected. Although they functioned independently, they were in one way or the other connected to the original village. Thus, the geographical and political disconnectedness amongst them was overshadowed by the pattern of social and cultural networks and relationship amongst them, and with the pipa village, which reflected a particular kind of clan geography and government. I call this sating geography and sating government. It was within this kinship relationship between the 'parent village' and its successor villages, which customary sating tribute sustained, that clan governmentality could be first located. Thus, the 'great Rajah' or the pipa may be weak, poor, and his village may be the smallest of all, but his superiority over all the other villages of his clansmen was respected and never contested.

Theoretically, pipa assumed a sovereign power over the territory of his clansmen, although he did not directly control them. Such sovereignty was basically customary or cultural in character, but it could also assume political colour at times. Under a warring situation, it was in the interest of the clan that the pipa should assume political power over them to defuse the problem. Thus, a powerful pipa could insist that the successor villages pay up his share of the sating tribute or summon them for a common war whenever necessary. John Macrae (1801), for instance, noted: 'The *Rajahs* receive a tribute in kind from the tribes to support their dignity; and in cases of general danger, they can summon all the warriors to arms; but each tribe is under the immediate command of its own particular [village] chief.'[17] Once the pipa assumed his customary position as war trumpeter or protector of all the clan members, the latter could not pretend to disobey him. This was most peculiarly demonstrated, for instance, during the Kuki Rising of 1917–19, when the decision of the clan chiefs to fight against the British colonial state was obeyed by all without any sense of dissent.[18] The war between 'eastern' and 'western' Lusheis or between 'northern' and 'southern' in the 1870s, or between 'Lusheis' and 'Chins', and so on, was based on this kinship relation. For that matter, the 'Great Kuki invasion of 1860' and the great Lushei raids of 1869–71 were carried out on this line of clan governmentality.[19] Naga opposition to British forces on most occasions (say, in 1874 at Ninu, in 1879–80 in Angami Hills, and so on) shows how clan connections and its dynamics played an immense role.[20] Such clan dynamics in war and peace were also visible in the context of the sub-Himalayan tribes.

Through this kinship relationship (of tribute and warfare), clan geographicity can also be located. Thus, all the territory belonging to the villages of the same clan theoretically belonged to the clan in which the *Pipa* (clan head) assumed its ultimate head. If the clan governmentality was sustained by the customary network of sating tribute and circulation of warriors, the clan geographicity was sustained by the clan governmentality as well as the social and cultural

[17] Macrae (1919 [1801]: 185).

[18] See, for instance, Haokip (2008: chapters 12–14).

[19] For such 'raids', see, for instance, Guite (2011, 2014), Mackenzie (2007 [1884]: 287–365), and Roychowdhury (1976).

[20] Vincent discovered, by the mid-nineteenth century, that the population of the Angami Hills was broadly divided into two halves, the 'Tippremah' (clans inclined towards British government) and 'Mukpreemah' (to Manipur), and into these 'every village is divided and they are only inclined to give assistance to either Government'. There are accounts that show how some powerful Naga villages had assumed 'paramount' power over other villages who paid 'tribute' to them, who protected them from any enemy attack and whose disputes were also settled by the former. See Assam State Archives (ASA), Records of East Bengal and Assam Secretariat (EB&AS), 1850, File No. 639: Lieutenant Vincent's Diary of the Expedition to the Angami Hills in 1849.

relationship amongst them. Circulation of people between these clan villages was determined by the regularity that *sating* needed to be 'thrown' (paid), the frequency of warriors to be sent for help, and the rapidity of clan rituals and feasts performed. Thus, there was regular movement of people between these villages of the clan, such as the sating 'throwers' (payers), warriors, partakers of rituals and festivals, and so on.

Take the case of the popular 'feasts of merit', known variously in Kuki-Chin world as *chon*, or *khuangchawi*, or *thangchhuah* feasts. The 'feasts of merit' were performed by the wealthy warrior of the village (usually the chief, but could also be anyone else), in which large numbers of people were feasted for several days with a series of ceremonies. Apart from the whole village community, this was an occasion when all the near and far-off kinsmen had to participate. The need to invite as well as participate in such rituals and feasts therefore determined the clan geographicity in a specific way, and hence also governed the feasts itself. What was at play in the feasts was the ritualistic and emotional bond that each member of the clan shared in mind. It was these lineage and kinship sentiments which also compelled them to help each other in times of difficulty (natural or man-made calamities, for example).

Of the emotional mapping, perhaps the most significant case may be the funeral rites. Death ritual was, in fact, one important occasion. In olden days, the Kuki-Chin people washed the body of the dead, and then smoked it, to ensure the body did not spoil. The body was then placed, for weeks and sometimes months, in the central part of the house around the main pillar (*sutlai*). The idea was to give the deserving members of the clan, from all distances, an opportunity to pay their homage and bid a final farewell to the deceased. This showed the clan solidarity, which in turn shaped and determined the clan geographicity. Non-attendance on such occasion was a serious offence. This kinship connection also determined the physical connectivity, such as village roads/paths between different clan villages, a point which is discussed in the next chapter.

The clan dynamics could also work in other ways, say, through the marriage customs, along the hill landscape, or in terms of power relation. These could generate another kind of connection, network, and relationship between different villages, and hence different set of geography. Most tribes, for instance, followed clan exogamous marriage system which forbids any nuptial relationship between members of the same clan.[21] In a situation where most villages usually had only one or more clans, the necessity of viewing the neighbouring villages as source of or the givers and receivers of marriage partner generated a different kind of geography. Such geography, which was again based on clan relation, was conceptually a spatial order which mapped and determined another kind of clan geographicity, which may be understood as marriage geography. It continuously engaged those who had already married, the prospective suitors, and then the whole village community to see the villages which could give or take partners as part of their larger geography beyond the village and to see to it that good relationship was always maintained. Such engagement, therefore, sustained the marriage geography of the villages, and hence the clan geographicity. On the other hand, the physical feature of the hill landscape, such as hill ranges in which rivers or streams became the boundary of the clan and so on, often determined the clan geographicity. In certain other cases, a more powerful village took on the responsibility of protecting the weaker villages and collected tribute from them.[22] All the above-mentioned cases show the existence of realm, or what I call the clan geographicity and governmentality, beyond the village boundary.

Another interesting aspect of the notion of space and territoriality among the hillmen was purely spiritual or cosmological in character. On the one hand, the terrestrial order of the hill landscape was closely related to the spiritual world order. Thus, all the hills, rivers, forests, and so on were owned, controlled, and protected by certain tutelary spirits who had their own geography of control. To use certain things

[21] Tribes like Garos, Khasis, Karbis, most Naga tribes, and so on followed clan exogamous marriage system.

[22] For Lushai Hills, see 'Lister's Report, 1850', in Mackenzie (2007 [1884]: 292–3). For Angamis, see NAI, FP, 24 August 1844, No. 36: Mr. Browne Wood to Captain A. Sturt, 14 April 1844; see also Butler (1978 [1855]: 144). For Aos and other Nagas, see NAI, FE (A): July 1888, No. 122 and *Selection of Papers*: Brodie to Jenkins, 15 September 1841, pp. 286–7. For Khasis, see Pemberton (2000 [1835]: 238–9) and Robinson (1975 [1841]: 408–11).

from such forests or rivers, it was necessary to take prior approval from them or to appease them when done by mistake. In this sense, the same territory was simultaneously under the control of men and gods, in which the latter apparently were more powerful. On the other hand, an even more interesting notion of space and geographicity was visible in their concept of 'future world' or the 'nether land', the land of the dead. In the eschatology of all the tribes, their nether world was located in different places, sometime in the sky and sometime underground.[23] Thus, we have the concept of 'the seven spheres of the underworld' or 'the seven spheres of the heaven' where the soul lives. Some tribes pointed to certain local sites as the gateway to such subterranean world of the dead, where the dead person 'goes to his own village, of which there is presumably a ghostly reproduction, and lives just as he did in this life'.[24] The Wanchus, for instance, told von Fürer-Haimendorf that 'Below Niaunu there is a corresponding village, the Niaunu of the nether world, and below the chief's house there is again a chief's house.'[25] This is a different kind of imaginative geography but certainly a similar conception of space in which the shades of the present are replicated in it.

Among certain tribes, this world of the dead was located in the homeland from where the tribe originally came from. Although the place was not known, it was neither in the underworld nor in the sky; it was the real world far away from their present habitat. Thus, when a person died, the priest or priestess taught the dead about the route and what was to be done so that s/he reached her/his destiny safely. Only after such an elaborate ritual was performed, the family would give the dead a farewell. This is still the practice among the

[23] See, for instance, Hutton (1921a: 185–6, 1921b: 211–12), Mills (2003 [1926]: 226–31), Playfair (1998 [1909]: 103), Shakespear (1998 [1912]: 62–5), and Shaw (1997 [1929]: 29–30).

[24] See Hutton (1921b: 212). The Kukis put this gateway at Lhanpelkot and Thijonbung (believed to be in Jangmol ranges); the Lusheis put it at Rih Lake in Lushai Hills; the Semas, Lhotas, and Aos put it at Naruto Hills or Wokha Hills; and so on.

[25] von Fürer-Haimendorf (1969: 94). For Kuki-Chin concept of 'village of the dead' (*mithikho*), see Shakespear (1998 [1912]: 62–5) and Shaw (1997 [1929]: 29–30).

Karbis of Assam and the tribes of Arunachal Pradesh. The mental mapping of the routes to the homeland for the dead was another kind of geography, another kind of spatial concept. Thus, we can see that the notions of space in tribal universe were completely a different kind of geography, a different kind of spatial discourse, having a separate terrain of operation that mapped/formulated a different lifeworld order. They were the lens or concepts of space for seeing the world around them and served diverse purposes, secular and sacred. After appreciating these sets of what I call spatial sensitivity among the hillmen, I will next discuss the way they distributed their population and settlements and the principle they followed.

Divided We Stand: Population and Settlement Patterns

Our discussion so far shows that population and settlement in the hills are promiscuously scattered across the hills having no specific patterns. We learned that there was a certain notion of space and territoriality, of concept of boundary, landholding rights, and land use systems. But what we do not know yet is the way they actually distributed their population and settlements across the highland massif and the principle that governed such distribution. Evidences from the early nineteenth century show that, instead of grouping in few and large villages, the hill population spread out and scattered across the hill landscape. Each of them was isolated from the other, lacking any sense of communication with other villages, and sometimes shifting fairly frequently. This widely scattered population and settlement pattern was shown to be haphazardly distributed across the hill landscape having no specific rule or principle. It was felt, in general, that the split and dispersive character of population and settlement distribution pattern was determined by the physical geography and the availability of land for cultivation. But what if this character was also dictated by other factors? The geographically deterministic theory of population distribution pattern was decidedly determined by the dominant civilizational narrative, which saw the hill people through the prism of the 'state of nature'. Such narratives not only prevent us from thinking otherwise but also dangerously push us away from knowing and understanding certain facts of paramount importance regarding the hill subjects.

Available information has suggested that the essence of the dispersive hill settlement pattern was more political than geographical and economic in character. A closer examination of the hill settlement pattern shows that while the less fertile and more rugged terrain of the interior parts of the hills was more thickly populated, the more fertile lower hills along the frontiers of the plain were relatively thinly populated or sometimes completely devoid of population. The distinguishing feature was that there was an increasing propensity of concentration of population and settlements towards the interior parts of the hills away from the plains. This was evident from the accounts of early colonial officers who led expeditions into the hills. These officers first encountered the wild and desolate jungles of the plains, near the foothills (known as hillmen's 'hunting ground'), a point I shall come to shortly. This was followed by their ascent to the lower hills, with a tortuous march for few days, until they found few scattered and small hamlets as if they were the 'outposts' or 'guard villages' of the hill country. Passing through these small hamlets and after abruptly ascending and descending a number of hills in the great mountain range, they finally landed in the interior parts of the hill country. In this rugged landscape, they experienced a gradual increase in the number of settlements and concentration of population capping the high ridges of several heights. This is schematically represented in Figure 3.3.

For instance, when John Butler led an expedition in 1845 in the Naga Hills, he first travelled through the wild and desolate jungles from the last plain settlement, till his party reached the first few villages in the lower hill ranges, such as Samaguting (140 houses), Rojapomah (140), Tejamah (10), and Tokojnahmah (20), and then abruptly ascending and descending a number of hills, he landed in the interior villages, like Mozomah (300 houses) and Khonomah (500). From the heights of Mozomah, he was 'delighted' to see 'numerous villages' capping the top of high ranges, at close distance from each other. Besides others, he noticed large villages like Kohima (820 houses), Kekremah (1,000), Jotsoma (600), Kheghamah (1,600), Sopomah (2,000), and Lohjhemah (1,000). In all, there were 12 villages whose houses were 500 or more.[26] Coming back to Rojapomah

[26] Butler (1978 [1855]: 27–75, 140–2). In 1878, the number of houses changed slightly: Viswemah (530), Khonomah (600), Jotsoma (700),

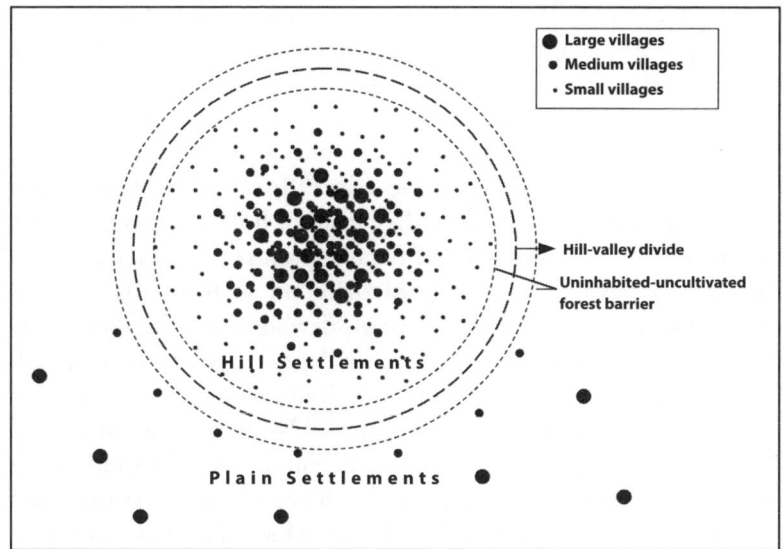

Large villages
Medium villages
Small villages

Hill-valley divide

Uninhabited-uncultivated forest barrier

Hill Settlements

Plain Settlements

Figure 3.3 Schematic Representation of Hill Settlement Pattern
Source: Prepared by author.

from the interior hills, he then moved south-west in the direction of North Cachar Hills. Along the lower ranges, he again came across villages which were scattered and thinly populated: Lehahmah (39 houses), Lakehmah (37), Beerehmah (117), and so on.[27] A similar picture could be seen among the so-called 'Eastern Nagas', with large villages like Nankam (700), Ungma (1,000), and Longsa (1,500) in the interior parts of the hills.[28] The concentration of population in the interior parts of Naga Hills especially fascinated some colonial observers. Peal, for instance, noted, 'I am aware that in some places there are hills and ranges said to be uninhabited, but I know of no

and Kohima (1,000). See NAI, FP (A), October 1878, No. 37: Captain W.J. Williamson to S.O.B. Ridsdale. See also Captain Butler's account in Mackenzie (2007 [1884]: 84).

[27] Butler (1978 [1855]: 53–75).

[28] See, for instance, NAI, FE (A), July 1888, No. 122: McCabe to Secretary to Chief Commissioner of Assam, 24 May 1888.

such places here.'[29] Thus, in 1873, the population density of Angami Nagas was 50 per square mile as compared to 23 persons in Khasi Hills and 10 in Chittagong Hill Tracts.[30]

Similarly, in the Lushai Hills, various reports of expeditions and officer tours showed that most of the hill population was concentrated in the interior parts of the hills.[31] In 1850, Colonel Lister led an expedition in Lushai Hills against Mullah (Ngura) village, Shentlang. After a tortuous and harassing journey of 11 days from Silchar and passing in southward direction through the desolate wilderness of forests and hilly terrain, devoid of any human settlement, he finally emerged at the said village. He found that the village consisted of 800–1,000 houses, 'full of grain, cotton, and other stores'. The absorbing scene across the hill landscape also astonished him. He saw that from that point of the hill towards the south, great numbers of Lushei villages capped the ridges, of which Barmooeelin (Vannoiliena) village was said to be the chief village consisting of 'not less than three thousand houses'. With his 'telescope', he could see that the said village appeared to be a 'cantonment laid out with utmost regularity'.[32]

The important Lushei villages in the interior part of the Lushai Hills on both sides of Dhaleswari River were also given in the account of one Rai Bahadur in 1858. On the west bank of Dhaleswari River, from the north to south, the villages were: Baniathangi (200 houses, most northerly point), Lalsabuta (150), Minthanga (100), Lenkhai Mantri (100), and Sailenpui (400). On the east bank of Dhaleswari, the villages were: Dausuma (50 houses, most northerly point), Lengpunga (500), Lenkhunga (200), Thangula (100), Khalkama (500), Lalpima

[29] Peal (1873: 330).

[30] Mackenzie (2007 [1884]: 84).

[31] See, for instance, Assam State Archives or ASA, Lib/RO14/51/05: *Tour Diary of North Lushai Hills District 1890–1896*. See, for instance, the various tour diaries of Shakespear and other district officers after the hills were occupied in the 1890s.

[32] WBSA, JP: 27 February 1850, No. 36: Lister to Grant, 2 February 1850. See also the abstract from Mackenzie (2007 [1884]: 292–4), Reid (1976 [1893]), WBSA, JP: August 1872, Nos 212 & 220, and Woodthorpe (1980 [1873]).

(150), Thaliena Mantri (50), Thanrima (400), Thanbang (60), Poiboi (400), Lalbura (300), Lengkam (450), Bungteya (300), Bungteya's Mother (150), Lalruma (100), Poiboi's Mother (150), Lunglema (300), Kairuma (400), and Nikama (200).[33]

These settlements in northern Lushai Hills merged with other Lushei villages of the south, known variously as 'Howlongs' and 'Sylos', and then the 'Poi' villages.[34] To the west of this Lushai Hills settlement was the Chittagong Hill Tracts, and to the east the Chin Hills, with certain vacant spaces (a point I shall discuss shortly) in between the hill settlements continuing in both directions. Towards the Chin Hills, their settlement again was mainly concentrated in the interior parts of the Chin Hills on both sides of the Gun or Manipur River. From this zone of concentration, the settlement and population gradually decreased towards the plains. A zone of 'uninhabited and uncultivated' forest belt in the lower hills continued into the plains, leading to the plain settlements of Kale–Kabaw valley proper. Several small villages conglomerated around some large villages in the interior parts of the hills.

Some of the major settlements in Chin Hills, from north to south direction, were Losow (300), Tingtam (80), and Lonpi (70), followed by Kamhow-Sukte and Siyin villages of Koset (90), Limkai (90), Molbem (80), Wunkathe (108), Laitui (100), and Tunzang (100). This northern area led to the Shunkla villages, such as Falam (500), Hmunli (150), Klangrong (180), Kwungli (250), Laiyo (300), Lyente (200), Minkin (250), Rumklao (200), and Shunkla (200). South to Shunkla areas were the Haka-Klangklang (Poi) villages, such as Haka (255), Faron (150), Hreinhrein (150), Wantu (150), Klangklang (150), Kapi (180), Kwahrang (180), Longrang (140), Lotaw (140), Lungno (200), Naring (280), Shurkwa (200), Thetta (180), and so on.[35] Thus, when the British took over the Lushai Hills and Chin Hills in the 1890s, they were surprise to see a good number

---

[33] As cited in a report by government, entitled *The Lushais* (2008: 18–21).

[34] For the account of the settlement of these groups of people, see, for instance, the tour diaries of British officers such as John Shakespear in the early 1890s.

[35] See Carey and Tuck (1987 [1896]).

of interior villages having a large number of houses. Shakespear, for instance, noted that when Lushai Hills was occupied, 'the country villages of 400 and 500 houses were not uncommon, and there were two or three of 800 houses'.[36]

Larger villages in Garo Hills, like Tura, Arbella, Rongrengiri, Dowa, Swangiri, and so on, were also in the interior parts of the hills. Some part of Garo population settled down in the valley, such as in some parts of Goalpara and Mymensingh frontiers. The Garo settlements in the hills were separated by a vast forested jungle from the plain settlements, as seen in other places. Similarly, major concentration of population and settlements was at higher altitudes of Khasi Hills. Major settlements like Nunklow, Kyrim, Churra, Nurtung, Nuspung, Muriow, Mahram, and Ramrye were indeed at higher altitudes and in the interior parts of the hills.[37] In the sub-Himalayan ranges, similar settlement pattern was visible. Early survey reports and expedition accounts of the colonial officers attested to the fact that concentration of hill population in this part was also not at the foothills close to the plains, but in the interior parts of the hills along the various corridors of the river regimes.[38] The hill people avoided the higher mountain ranges due to the rugged terrain, snow capping, and more importantly, the difficulty in accessing their cultivation in lower ranges. However, they still chose the higher and inaccessible ground to set up their villages. In any case, they were well protected, like other hills, by the vast span of 'uninhabited tract' of forest and marshland between them and the valley settlements. The hill settlement patterns in the region become clear from the case of certain hills given in Figures 3.4 and 3.5 (redrawn based on the expedition and survey maps of the 1870s).

The evidence given here gives a clear picture of the general settlements and population distribution pattern across the hills, which

[36] Shakespear (1998 [1912]: 19). For details of houses and settlement pattern, see the tour diaries of British officers after Lushai Hills was occupied, and before that the expedition field diaries.

[37] See Mills (1985 [1853]).

[38] See, for instance, Griffith (1873) and Wilcox (1873). See also Needham and Hamilton (1997) accounts of Abor Hills, Cooper's account (1995 [1873]) of Mishmee Hills, and so on.

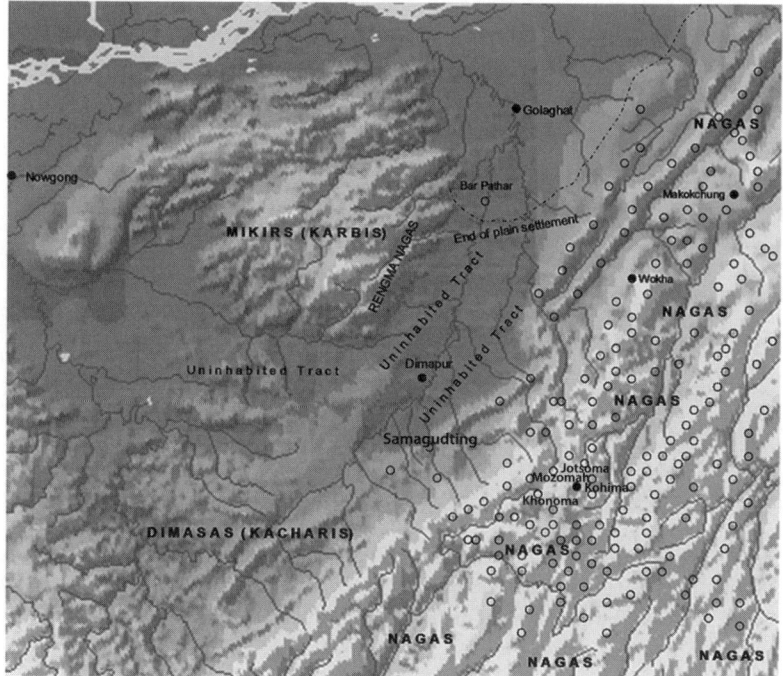

Figure 3.4 Settlement Pattern in Naga Hills (also showing 'uninhabited tract' in southern Assam)

Source: Redrawn by author from maps of Lower Assam, Naga Hills, and North Cachar Hills.[39]

can be characterized as small, scattered, and dispersive, but following certain geometric pattern as shown in Figure 3.3. Hence, a person moving from the interior parts of the hills towards the plains found that the higher concentration of population in the interior parts of the hills gradually dovetailed, diminished, and eventually fizzled out in the lower ranges bordering the plains. These frontier villages were generally small, scattered, and dispersive, appearing as if they were the 'guard villages' or 'outposts' of the hill people. Beyond these

[39] See ASA, Map Section, No. 15: Indian Atlas, Sibsagar, Naga Hills, Naga Tribes, 1878 and No. 509: Sketch Map of Naga Hills Showing the Localities of the Various Tribes, 1877.

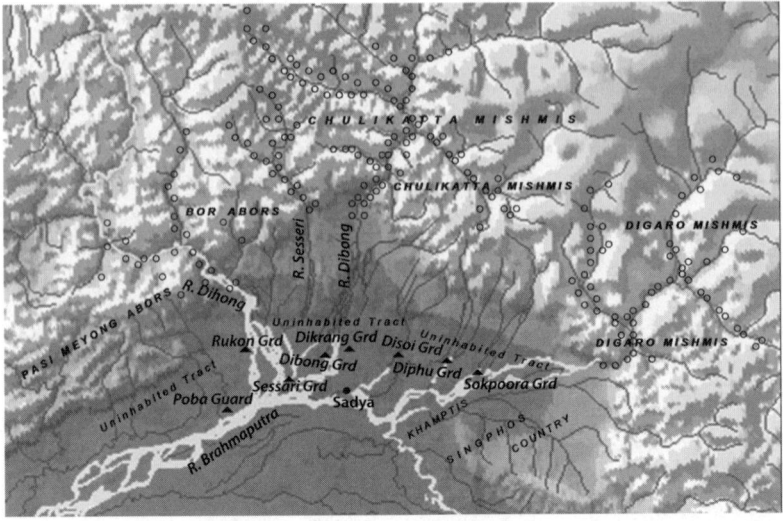

Figure 3.5 Settlement Pattern in Sub-Himalayan Ranges (also showing 'uninhabited tract' in Upper Assam)
Source: Redrawn by author from the map of North East Frontier of Assam, 1879.[40]

villages, one came across a vast belt of uninhabited, uncultivated forest zone, in the hill–valley continuum, over which the hill people claimed authority. This forested belt was their 'hunting ground'. The whole pattern revealed the fact that certain parts of the hills were habitable and certain parts were not, and what mattered also was the size of the village. How can this peculiar behaviour of the hillmen in relation to their settlement and population distribution pattern be explained then?

The one thing that immediately strikes the mind is the hillmen's relationship with the valley states. The settlement and population distribution pattern was thus shaped and fashioned in relation to the valley states surrounding their hills. In this sense, such a distribution pattern was political in character rather than a haphazard split

[40] See ASA, Map Section, No. 413: Map of North East Frontier of Assam Comprising Country Inhabited by Abors, Mishmis, Singphos, and Khamtis, 1879 (based on Duffla Expedition Map of 1874, Captain Woodthorpe's Survey, 1877–8, and Captain Beresford's Exploration Party, 1879).

dictated by geography and economic imperative. This is proved by the fact that the hillmen refused to come down to the valley where land was abundant even when there was a furious 'internecine warfare' in the hills and when the British government was offering land with incentives.[41] No wonder, Reverend Bronson lamented for the Nagas: 'I am sorry to say that they do not; neither do I think that they could be induced to come on the plain, I have repeatedly offered to feed and clothe them if they would do so, but have never succeeded.'[42] Why did they choose to struggle in the rugged, interior parts of the hills, leaving the more fertile and favourable landscape of the lower ranges, adjoining the plain, virtually uninhabited. Why did the hill people refuse to concentrate in few large villages or why did some villages shift frequently when the land was able to support such concentration for centuries, as was shown by many villages in the hills? The list of questions against the geographically and economically deterministic theory is indeed long.

Under such circumstances, the political factor emerges prominent. Here, the notion of hill people as state-evading population becomes instructive. Two alternatives were open to the hillmen in their history: live in the hills with few supplies; or go down to the plain of plentiful harvest. They chose the hills because it gave them many political advantages, even if they lacked the economics of honey and milk. As noted earlier, these hill people were those who had escaped from the valleys against state-building projects there and who were always vigilant not to fall into the trap of valley states but to prevent its control and appropriations. Therefore, it is evident that they would be certainly reluctant to go back to the valleys to become the subjects of the state. Hence, if the hill people dispersed over the hill landscape instead of settling down in one big village in the hills, or coming down to the plain to replenish their economic needs, then

---

[41] They would come down only when they were in grave danger, only to return to the hills when the situation improved there. Thus, those Kukis who took shelter in Cachar under British rule and who had been settled in different 'punjees', reported Edgar, secretly 'slipped away' to the hills later. See Guite (2011: 358–66).

[42] NAI, FP, 22 November 1841, No. 124: Bronson to F. Jenkins, 9 September 1841.

such dispersive population and settlement pattern had nothing to do with what nature could have provided.

The pattern of population and settlements distribution thus reflected their perennial political concern for safety and security against the control and appropriations of valley states and state-like political formation in the hills. In other words, the settlement pattern visible in the hills was politically framed to prevent, repel, and deter the control of valley states, as well as the formation of state in the hills. So, the concentration of population seen in the fastness of interior mountain ranges, with the settlements and population gradually decreasing and eventually fizzling out towards the outer ranges of the hills close to the plain, showed the essence of such settlement pattern (as shown in Figures 3.3, 3.4, and 3.5). This political strategy is supported by four facts.

First, the small and dispersive character of population and settlements was in stark contrast to valley state-making project where ingathering of population in and around the centre of power was the order. By dividing and spreading their population and settlements across the rugged landscape, the hill people ensured that the hills became amorphous and illegible to potential raiders and conquerors. Any expedition to the hills therefore became politically and militarily prohibitive. Its cost far exceeded the benefit it offered to any state, as shown by expeditions carried out during the early colonial period. Therefore, for the valley states, the hills were literally a 'sterile' landscape and its population the no-touch-able due to such settlement and population distribution pattern and other strategies (discussed later).

The second was the very appearance of the frontier villages (villages in the lower ranges), described as small, scattered, and poor. As mentioned earlier, they usually appeared as 'guard villages' or 'outposts', which were economically unattractive to the raiders and marauders. This pattern of not building large, rich, and permanent settlements in the lower ranges adjoining the valley, which would have invariably acted as a bait for valley state potentates and raiders, was an effective political strategy to keep the valley states away from the hills. By their appearance, these settlements kept the richness of the hills in the interior opaque, invisible, and unattractive, thereby keeping the danger at bay.

The third reason was what has been civilizationally dubbed as 'nomadism'. Certain tribes were seen shifting their settlements quite frequently, moving from one place to another after a period of time. This, instead of being an act of primitivism or migration for better land, was also a political choice for some of the hillmen in order to evade control and appropriations. Indeed, it can be seen as a strategy for becoming formless and invisible in the eyes of state officers, the case clearly shown in the early colonial period. For instance, Cooper noted that 'it is impossible to give a geographical position to any village' and 'renders it difficult to find one's way through the country'.[43] Butler also noted that Karbis nomadism needed the administration 'to make a new settlement every year with their chiefs'.[44] Hutton also felt that the Kuki way of splitting up villages and frequent migration was an 'administrative nuisance'.[45] Therefore, 'nomadism' was decidedly inconsistent with state sense of 'legibility' and 'simplification'.[46] If mobility was an 'administrative nuisance' for the state officers, then that is exactly what became 'a line of conduct' for the state-evading population in the hills.

The fourth factor is even more striking. As noted earlier, the settlements came to an abrupt end at the lower ranges, to emerge again in the plains at certain distance from the foothills. The intervening space was uninhabited and uncultivated forest belt of what was known as hillmen's 'hunting ground'. This belt provided an immense friction of terrain to potential conquerors and marauders from the valley, and hence acted as a screen against such unwelcome intruders. In this context, the essence of this belt also was political in nature. As this belt was an important part of the hillmen's strategy to keep away the valley states from the hills, a detailed discussion is given in the following section.

[43] Cooper (1995 [1873]: 228–9). See also NAI, FP, 6 March 1837, No. 67: Griffith to Jenkins, 20 January 1837 and NAI, FP, 28 March 1845, No. 141: Lt. Rowlatt to F. Jenkins, 1 January 1845.

[44] Butler (1978 [1855]: 126, 132, 135).

[45] Shaw (1997 [1929]: 23, fn. 1).

[46] For the concept of state 'legibility' and 'simplification', see Scott (1998).

Of the Hill Screen

It has been noted earlier that space was not only the economic resource of the tribal community but was also their social, cultural, and political capital. What is significant from their notion of space and territoriality is not only the way they valued, distributed, and managed their space but also the way they valued the friction of terrain. Their notion of friction of terrain in relation to the valley state invaders is perhaps best shown by the impassable forest zone that divided the hills from the plain settlements. Evidence from early colonial survey and expedition reports shows the profound presence of an extensive belt of 'uninhabited and uncultivated' densely forested jungle, often above a hundred or so miles apart. It consisted of both the lower hills and adjoining plain areas along the hill–valley continuum, between the inhabited hill settlements and populated lowlands, and over which the hill chiefs claimed authority. This belt was popularly known in colonial account as the hillmen's 'hunting ground'.

Wilcox's survey of Assam in 1825–7, for instance, noted that the fringes of upper Brahmaputra valley, adjacent to the hills of the Dufflas, Abors, Miris, Mishmis, and Nagas, were densely covered with forested jungle: 'Beyond Sadiya, on the north side of the river, the tract is an uninterrupted jungle to the foot of the hills, and on its south side the little village[s] ... form mere specks in the widely spread wilderness.'[47] This situation remained the same in the 1870s, as evident from the reports of later surveys and expeditions. The map of North East Frontier of Assam, 1879 (Figures 3.4 and 3.5), also showed a vast belt of 'uninhabited tract' along the foothills of Assam. This was also visible from various revenue and exploration surveys of Assam and the hills surrounding it, undertaken between 1860 and 1890.[48]

[47] Wilcox (1873: 27).

[48] See, for instance, ASA, Map Section, Sl. No. 953: Topographical Map of Miri Hills, 1879, Sl. No. 510: District Lakhipur and Miri & Mishmi Hills, 1889, Sl. No. 206: Lakhipur & Sibsagar District, Sadiya Frontier Tract, Tribal Territory (1867–1890), 1899, Sl. No. 15: Sibsagar, Naga Hills, Naga Tribes, 1878, Sl. No. 509: Sketch Map of the Naga Hills Showing the Localities of the Various Tribes, 1877, Sl. No. 512: Lushai Hills, Pakokku, Upper Chindwin District & Unadministered Area, 1853–1908, and Sl. No. 663: Topographical Map of Lushai and Manipur, etc, 1899.

Butler's account (1845) of the frontier of Assam with Naga Hills (about 30 miles from Mohng Dehooa to Dimapur), as given earlier, stated that it was covered with 'a dark, damp, chilly, gloomy forest' of desolate wilderness with 'a death-like stillness', unbroken except by 'occasional barking or halloo of the Bobell or ape'.[49] The existence of such forest belts was also shown in the frontiers of Cachar, Chittagong, Burma, and Manipur with the Kuki-Chin country.[50] In southern Cachar frontier, for instance, Lister (1850) described the belt as 'a mass of dense jungle, without inhabitants, or the material of supplies of any kind'. The 'country' of the 'Luchye Kookies' (later Lushai Hills) was 'some nine or ten marches south of Cachar' and the nearest village was 'some eight or nine days' away.[51] His party took 11 days (from 4 January to 15 January 1850) to reach Mullah's village (Shentlang), the northern-most hill settlement in that part, and the distance was 'upwards of a hundred miles, utterly uninhabited'.[52]

Edgar also described this 'tract of forest', the 'Kuki hunting ground', covered with 'dense jungle, of swampy cane-brakes', and was 'uncultivated and uninhabited', except for a few tea gardens (which came up recently) which were 'merely specks in the great forests that surround them'.[53] Same forested belt of 'hunting ground' existed between Tipperah state, Chittagong Hill Tracts district of Bengal, and Arracan and Akyab districts of Burma with Lushai Hills, and between Chin Hills and Kale–Kabaw valley of Burma. It was variously described as 'uninhabited and uncultivated tract', 'so difficult, so hostile, so unknown', and 'hopelessly inaccessible' from administered districts and the distance was roughly 8–10 days march.[54] Thus, there was visible existence of the 'great belt' of forested landmass

[49] NAI, FP: 23 March 1846, No. 31: Butler to Jenkins, 16 July 1846.

[50] See Guite (2014).

[51] WBSA, JP: 27 February 1850, Nos 33–4.

[52] WBSA, JP: 27 February 1850, No. 36.

[53] J.W. Edgar to Secretary, Government of Bengal, 5 June 1872, as quoted in Mackenzie (2007 [1884]: 472). A similar account of the 'Kuki hunting ground' was also given by other British expeditions, such as Blackwood, Raban, Hopkinson, Edgar, Lewin, and so on.

[54] See Guite (2014). See also J.W. Edgar to Secretary, Government of Bengal, 5 June 1872, as quoted in Mackenzie (2007 [1884]: 335, 359, 472–4); WBSA, JP: August 1872, No. 212, December 1870, No. 172, November

that encircled the hill settlements and divided them from the valley settlements (see Figures 3.1, 3.3, 3.4 and 3.5).[55] But how can we understand the profound presence of such an extensive forest belt at the margins of the valley?

It has often been assumed that such forested belts along the frontier were either due to tribal raids or a mere extension of the hill forest. Pemberton (1835), for instance, reported that the Kukis of Cachar frontier 'frequently made incursions into the border villages along the line of frontier, and in Cachar', that the 'whole tracts of fertile country were, up to a very recent period, deserted, from an apprehension of these attacks'.[56] This view was shared by most colonial authorities on all other frontiers as well. Other evidences, however, suggested that the essence of such forested belt at the margins of the valley was political in character and the political situation in the valleys had a strong bearing on it. The previous chapters showed how Dhansiri valley and the country around Sadiya, which were once the core areas of Kachari and Chutiya kingdoms respectively, were depopulated and reduced to nature not because of tribal raids but due to Ahom state-formation process.[57] Similarly, the accounts of Wilcox and Butler, cited earlier, noted that these two regions continued to remain in state of nature. But it was also visible that the Ahom state, like its predecessors Kachari and Chutiya, maintained a friendly relationship

---

1866, Nos 97–112, WBSA, PP (B): September 1891, Nos 1–55, File L/8 of 1889, Captain H. Hopkison, Commissioner of Arracan, to the Secretary Government of Bengal, 7 May 1856, as quoted in Mackenzie (2007 [1884]: 531–6).

[55] The Bengal frontiers with Khasi and Garo Hills apparently showed settlements merging up. In the former case, Jaintia kingdom had control over a part of the plains, so a closer commercial relationship was possible, but most of the prominent Khasi villages were found in much interior highland. In the latter case, the Garos inhabited both the hills and adjoining margins of the valleys, and eventually the existence of such forested belt was less visible, although the principal chiefs were also in the interior parts of the hills. For discussions on Khasi and Garo frontiers, see Cederlöf (2014), May (2012), and Misra (2011).

[56] Pemberton (2000 [1835]: 18).

[57] See Chapters 1 and 2 of this book. See also Gait (2008 [1905]).

with the hill people in its frontier areas, hence tribal raids were not a cause of concern.

The symbiotic hill–valley relationship under the Ahoms was visible from the cases of revenue rights given to the hill polities at the margins of the valley, variously known as *khat*s, or *perganah*s, or what I called posaland.[58] This presupposed the merging of hill–valley settlements in certain frontiers. However, by the eighteenth and early nineteenth centuries, the whole frontier of Upper Assam was again apparently reduced to jungles; those khats, perganahs, or posaland under the hill people were also deserted. This was largely attributed to the political turmoil in the valley due to internal conflicts, Moamaria uprisings, Burmese occupation, and finally, the advent of the British.[59] Such political turmoil indicated that the hill–valley relationship had also eventually turned sour. It was from this period onwards that tribal raids over the villages in the plains were visible. The worsening situation during this time resulted in two important developments in the frontier that led to the strengthening of the 'hunting ground'. First, the political turmoil in the valley compelled the hill people to withdraw their settlements towards the interior parts of the hills and strengthen their 'hunting ground'. Second, as the hill–valley relationship worsened and tribal raids became imminent or frequent as a strategy to strengthen their 'hunting ground' or otherwise, the valley populations also withdrew to the core of the valley. The mutual withdrawal of settlements towards their respective core areas eventually strengthened the forested belt at the margin.

Significantly, what emerges from the given context is that the political situation in the valley largely determined the extent of the hillmen's 'hunting ground'. It narrowed down or contracted when peace prevailed in the valley and hill–valley relationship was convivial, but it expanded when the situation worsened or when a formidable power, unkind towards hill people, rose up in the plains. The case of Cachar frontier in early colonial period, for example, was illustrative of this process. Evidence suggested that the limit of Lushai Hills settlements in precolonial period was much advanced than their position

---

[58] These points will be discussed in detail in Chapter 9.

[59] For detail discussion on these aspects, see, for instance, Gait (2008 [1905]).

in the colonial period. This was illustrated by the presence of many old village sites belonging to those Kukis who had later fled to Cachar plain due to internal conflicts in the hills. J.W. Edgar, then Deputy Commissioner of Cachar, was surprised to see many of these old sites close to the plain of Cachar during his tour in 1870 and during the great Lushai Expedition, 1871–2. This was further corroborated by the fact that Kachari kingdom had a close relationship with hill Kukis during their heydays, often employing them as mercenaries against their enemies in battles. Pushed from behind, the Lusheis (Kukis) appeared in Cachar frontier in the 1840s and pushed out other Kuki tribes who were living at the margins of the valley. But finding a formidable British colonial power in Cachar, they eventually shied away. Edgar noted that the Lusheis had 'given up' their intention to occupy these 'old sites' in the face of the British power. He said: 'while the Lushais showed some desire to keep on good terms with the Cachar authorities, they perhaps accidentally followed *a line of conduct* which looked as if they *suspected and feared* of us.'[60]

He noted that the principal villages of Lushei chiefs such as Sookpilal, Mora (Ngura), and others—whose villages before 1849 had advanced north of Chatterchoora Peak and 'old Kholel'—were withdrawn by degrees towards the south, in the interior parts of the hills, close to the 'Sylhoos'.[61] Towards the frontier, they established what they called the 'guard villages' on points commanding different routes and discouraged 'all intercourse' between the plains and the hills; valley traders and woodcutters were 'obliged' to go only by water to certain points.[62] 'In this way,' Edgar remarked, 'the Lushais

---

[60] WBSA, JP: August 1872, No. 220; emphasis added. See also NAI, FP (A): August 1872, No. 70.

[61] WBSA, JP: August 1872, No. 220. See also NAI, FP (A): August 1872, No. 70.

[62] The 'routes' in question were not so much the easily passable roads or cut pathways. They were the ridges or river courses passable only during dry season. There were five such 'routes' from Cachar which expeditions normally took: Silchar–Tipaimukh route (ferry over Barak till Tipaimukh); by the Sonai River route (ferry till Sonai bazaar, 12 days); by Dhaleswar River route (ferry till Changsil bazaar, 12 days); by Kolasib and Rengti range (overland route); and by Parsonsib and Langai range (ferry and overland).

succeeded in putting between our frontier and their villages *a tract of forest* which was not only unexplored by us, but to a great extent unknown to any of our Kookies, except a few old men who had not been over the grounds for years' [emphasis mine].[63] This 'tract of forest' was popularly known in colonial account as 'Kuki hunting ground'. The British appropriation of their 'hunting ground', or their attempt to transform it into tea gardens, resulted in incessant 'raids'.[64]

What this case of Cachar frontier suggests is that the limit of hill village settlements towards the valley kept on shifting with time and was largely determined by the political situation in the valley and the hill–valley relationship. It shifted towards the interior when hill–valley relationship deteriorated or when a powerful state emerged in the valley. It shifted back towards the valley, sometimes almost to the foothill, when on good terms with the valley rulers or when there was political vacuum in the valley. In certain circumstances, the hill polities extended their control over parts of the valley, as in the case of Tipperah, Jaintia, and Kachari kingdoms.[65] Raid as a means to put fear into and split the valley population was incidental to the changing political temperature in the valley and was utilized by the hillmen to push the encroaching valley settlements away from the frontier in order to strengthen their 'hunting ground'. Thus, the shifting pendulum of the limit of hill settlements at the frontier and size of their 'hunting ground' was strongly political in character. The 'fear' and 'suspicion' of the valley states was indeed always very strong in the consciousness of the hill people. Thus, as the hillmen preferred to remain isolated, this barrier had to remain strong and any attempt on the part of the plainsmen to encroach upon it was resisted.[66]

This then leads us to the question: how did strengthening their 'hunting ground' help the hill people? This basically concerns friction of terrain. As noted earlier, the hillmen strengthened their control

[63] WBSA, JP: August 1872, No. 220. See also NAI, FP (A): August 1872, No. 70.

[64] See Guite (2011, 2014).

[65] See Sinha (1989: 177–211, 243–305); see also Bhattacharjee (1991).

[66] Guite (2014).

on the hunting ground when the political situation was not favourable in the valley, relaxed it when relationship was friendly, extended their authority when there was political vacuum, and immediately withdrew when stronger power emerged again. This meant that the impregnable forest belt was seen as a political capital which generated friction of terrain for valley state invaders and marauders, providing them safety and security against such invasions. In fact, a dense forest provided a very strong friction of terrain to imperial army, raiders, and marauders. Crossing such densely forested jungles, devoid of road, was akin to walking against the knife. All military expeditions into the hills needed a strong sapper brigade to cut a path through this forest belt, along with a company of coolies (porters) to transmit their food items. The harrowing journey across the hillmen's 'hunting ground' can be seen from the following military expedition reports.

An expedition party under Butler (1845) took 10 days—and under Lister (1850), 11 days—to cover the pathless and densely forested hillmen's 'hunting ground'. This belt, the Dhansiri valley, was the common 'hunting ground' of the Nagas, Mikirs, and Kacharis against each other, as well as for the valley state of Assam. From the foothills to the first Naga village, his party had to wend its way along the bank of Deboo River. Their days were occupied with 'cutting open a footpath through a dense forest'. They struggled over some high precipices, many steep acclivities, and perpendicular ledges of rock, which obliged them to take the stony bed of river with precipitous banks on both sides, chilling and rapid water, slippery rolling stones, and sharp boulders. He described their progress through this forest belt as 'exceedingly slow'; also, their bodies became 'excessively cold' and shook to such a degree that they could hardly stand and their feet were 'terribly lacerated and bruised'.[67]

The pathless jungles in the hills also had other deadly components. The hunting grounds harboured deadly and venomous animals and insects that spared no one who passed through its flourishing forest covers. Thus, when Lieutenant R. Wilcox passed through the lower ranges of the Mishmee Hills, he had to struggle against leeches, besides

---

[67] NAI, FP: 23 March 1846, No. 31: Butler to Jenkins, 16 July 1846. See also Butler (1978 [1855]: 279).

other difficulties. He reported that some 30–40 leeches needed to be plucked off a person's ankles after every 600–800 paces, which caused profuse bleeding and severe fever. His companion, Lieutenant Balton, was among those mowed by leech bites; he suffered from severe fever.[68] Cooper too faced the same ordeal during his trip to Mishmee Hills.[69] Surely, it was the ordeals of friction of terrain, the hillmen's 'hunting ground', the forest, the geography, that denied and repelled easy intrusion. In this context, the impassable forest tract around their hill settlements definitely served as a protective screen against valley state conquerors, marauders, and raiders in a great way. It could effectively check state's control and appropriations. It was for this reason that I called this forested belt the hill screen, a screen that inhibited movement, a screen that discouraged the valley state conquerors and marauders to venture over the hills, and the screen that was the purveyor of their freedom in the hills in the long view.

[68] See Wilcox (1873: 68).
[69] Cooper (1995 [1873]).

4

Pathways, Citadels, and Sentinels of the Hills

As a tourist in the hills of Northeast India, you will not only be unnerved by the vicissitude of roads and pathways but, at the same time, also be excited by the beautiful sight across the rolling mountains. An occasional flash of light emanating from a certain summit or spur of the hills could be another wonder. If you want to see this, take special note of what you see on the top or spur of the hills. It would be visible only on a bright sunny day. If you see such a flash of light, it could be the hill villages or it could also be something else. Most of the hill villages which used to be at the top of the hills, connected with narrow and repulsive hill paths, have been moved *down* to the 'national highways' or 'district roads' and are, in most cases, hidden and invisible from horizontal view. What could this 'something else' be then? When you sight such a flash of light, feel happy and safe because you are being watched. This flash of light, in fact, is not from a watchtower or any lighthouse station; it comes from what is popularly known in the region as the 'Sepai Camp', the temporary or permanent stations of the armed security forces. The light is the mere reflection of sun on the white tin roof of the buildings in such 'camps'. These 'camps' are the bases of the force proclaimed as 'Sentinels of Northeast India' and are studded and scattered across India's 'disturbed areas'.

The striking feature of these 'camps' is their elevated position on the summit/spur of the hills or ridge, a strategic site commanding and overlooking the routes of potential attack from nonstate elements, popularly known as 'insurgents' or 'underground'. From their elevated position, these 'camps' keep constant surveillance over the main arteries (roads) of the hills. They are usually fortified, surrounded by a deep pitch, and the sides of the hills frequently scarped; inside the fortified camp are ranges of military barracks and quarters where the soldiers and officers stay day in and day out. All such matters as water supply and shelter from the wind are secondary. Daily patrolling of the area, keeping an eye on 'enemies', and protecting the state 'subjects' or 'citizens' from being troubled by 'nonstate' elements are central to such an establishment. In this way, the 'Sentinels of Northeast India' keep constant vigilance over any indiscretion by armed 'insurgents' and prevent the 'foreign hands' from entering the field. Here, to keep the peace means to keep the nonstate elements out or to prevent them from having any control and appropriation over the citizens. Citizens and protection of their freedom and peace are, therefore, at the heart of the state universe.

Now, take this image of the 'Sepai Camp' back into the dim past of the Northeast hills when there was no state. You will be surprised to find a replica of it (of course, no flash of light). The setting of hill villages in the precolonial period will show the mirror image of our 'Sepai Camp', although the present context is quite different, such as the people who man them and the purpose it has been built for. These hill villages at the summit of the hills were the 'sentinels' and 'citadels' of the hillmen (not nonstate elements because there was no state) when there was no state structure in the hills, when there were no such state forces, and when people were in a state of statelessness. They were constantly watching over the movement of state forces. The enemy of the stateless 'sentinels' then was decidedly not its 'insurgents' (because it did not have one) but the valley 'state' forces which threatened their very existence as nonstate society. Such sentinels were meant to keep a constant surveillance over the movement of state army, conquerors, raiders, marauders, and freebooters from the valley states. It was about stateless people defending themselves against 'state' elements in order to keep their stateless hill country away from state control and appropriations. This aspect of the hill villages, and its political temperament, is what is covered in this chapter. The chapter, therefore, discusses the way in which stateless hill people chose and built their village fortresses, the way in which they connected them by narrow paths, and the way in which they disciplined and trained their 'warriors' so that they remained sentinels of the peace and freedom of stateless people in the hills.

The Road Most Taken

Reading his paper before the Royal Geographical Society of London on 10 December 1860, Dr M'Cosh pointed out five overland routes across the Northeast frontier, between India and China. The five routes were: the Dihong Pass; the Mishmee route; the Phungan Pass (to Manchee in China); the Pathkoy (Patkai or Pangsau) Pass (to Bhamo in Burma); and Manipur route (to Bhamo in Burma). He urged for an expedition to be despatched to explore these passes and begged the influential Royal Geographical Society to put pressure on the Government of India in furtherance of his proposal. Accordingly, he provided some information for each pass. Regarding the Dihong Pass, he said that it was normally used by pilgrims who reached Mah-loo, the frontier town of Tibet, in 16 days, and four days after that, a populous city called Eho-shee-mah, under regular Chinese government. The pass was, he remarked, 'always difficult, and impracticable except in summer'. The Mishmee route was, he said, 'very practicable, but little commerce is likely to flow along it'. The Phungan Pass led over the Wang-leo-bum mountain range at an altitude of 8,400 feet, through a dense jungle of oak, pine, rhododendron, and juniper. No footpath was to be seen. Venomous flies and swarms of land leeches infested the forest. Guides, who followed notches in trees they had made in a previous journey, had led Wilcox and Burlton. Patkai Pass was, he remarked, 'by far the most practicable line from Assam to China'. At Bhamo, it met 'great stream of Chinese commerce between that country and Burma'. Caravans of 30–40 mules or bullocks and about 500 Chinese constantly arrived every year at Bhamo and transacted business to an amount of 700,000 l. However, in both the cases, he noted, 'the natives were the obstacles'. Of Manipur route, he said that one passed by the line of the Barrak River to Bans-kundee and thence by land route over Munipur till Monfu on the river Chindwin (Ningthee), and to Bhamo.[1]

What is interesting about M'Cosh's description of the passes is the impracticability and obstacles that precluded the possibility of having a regular traffic. These passes did not appear as a trade route in strict sense of the term. They rather indicated a mere natural pass, seasonally used by the hill people while visiting the plains, or used by troops, ambassadors, traders, pilgrims, monks, or missionaries with the assistance of the hillmen. As noted in the previous chapter, the 'most practicable' route, the Patkai Pass, did not amount to a trade route at all, although some traffic was observed. Manipur route was more regularly used due to the existence of Manipur kingdom in the middle of the mountain. But it was also equally harsh and seasonal, mainly driven by human porterage. Hence, great emphasis on the role of these passes or trade routes in the process of exchange and transaction between India and China or Burma, in the past, was misleading and may have been an exaggeration. These types of passes even excluded the possibility of valley traders passing through the highland massif without the assistance of the hillmen. One is even tempted to question whether the valley traders had ever scaled up, by themselves, the heights of the highland massif for trading purpose. Exception to this rule was the route between Bhamo (Burma) and Maintha (China) which, Bayfield noted, was used by traders after paying 'small presents' to Kachins for 'safe passage' and also to obtain a guide from them. The five ranges between the two places were inhabited by the Kachins who were, according to Bayfield, 'very numerous' that 'no party considers itself safe without an escort' of 50 or 60 men.[2]

Cooper's description of 'Mishmee route' was instructive in this respect. He said that he was 'utterly exhausted' when he reached the first Mishmi village:

> At time our path, which was often scarcely discernible, led along the almost perpendicular sides of the hills, which as we advanced, became

---

[1] Dr M'Cosh (1860: 47–55).

[2] See Bayfield (1873: 176). This route formed part of what is known as the 'Southwestern Silk Route'. See Anderson (2009).

veritable mountains. Often we scrambled, monkey-like, along their declivities, holding on by means of tangled roots, which formed a network sufficiently strong to bear our weight; occasionally we crossed deep chasms by means of bamboo scaffolding rudely constructed by the guides ... and in some places long plaited bamboo ropes, let down over horrible precipices, afforded the only means to descent to the valleys below.[3]

Despite these 'impracticable' routes across the highland massif, there is sufficient evidence to show that several trade items from China, Tibet, and Burma actually found their way into India's frontier region in large amounts, just as Indian goods also reached them. Take the case of, for instance, the bell-metal gong, which formed part of the core cultural items among many communities in the region. Other items like beads, ornaments, utensils, agriculture implements, and so on were also found in large quantities. Considering the type of passes across this highland frontier, it is doubtful, or even impossible, that these items came through these passes only. There may, in fact, have been other possible channels through which these items found their way into the region. In this regard, a study of the roads or paths between the hill villages and of the role played by the hillmen in the transit of the items from village to village, involving many hands, will be helpful. The presence of social and cultural networks across the hills that compelled regular movement of people between villages, sometime covering large distance, has been noted earlier. Such movement presupposes not only the existence of regular paths in the hills but also the networks through which circulation of goods could have taken place across the highland massif and with the valleys surrounding them.

Recent studies on connected history have pointed out that the Northeast highland massif was, instead of being a barrier to movement, a channel, a contact zone, through which culture, commodities, and communities flowed over the ages. The role of what was known as the 'Southwestern Silk Route' has been especially given great important as the link between India and China via Burma.[4]

---

[3] Cooper (1995 [1873]: 186).

[4] See, for instance, Anderson (2009) and Cederlöf (2014: chapter 4).

In this, the role of hill people who lived in those highlands has been either completely ignored or deliberately sidestepped in the interest of organized trade. While such routes were important, the assumption that connection and circulation of goods and people between India and Burma–China took place only through such routes seems overrated. It, in a way, takes for granted the dominant discourse on disconnectedness and isolation of the hill villages (among each other and with the valley settlements). But considering the difficulties of such passes and the obstacles posed by the hill tribes to the free flow of goods, any study on connected history across this highland massif that does not take into account the system of networks and communication among the hill villages is likely to be incomplete or even misleading. As these so-called passes across the hills were but natural passes across the wilderness, there is little evidence to suggest that flourishing trade had ever taken place through these passes in the Northeast frontier. What can be more beneficial to this regime of connection and circulation across the massif is to look into the connectivity that binds the scattered hill villages, which, in a way, conspires against the dominant notion of isolation and disconnectedness.

Evidences from early colonial accounts show a regular traffic of goods between the hills and valleys through several routes other than the above-mentioned famous passes. Here, the village paths connecting different hill villages have been shown to be critical for circulation. If the social and cultural networks produced regular pathways/roads between the hill villages, the need for valley goods in the hills produced some routes between the hills and the valleys, although the character of pathways in question was of a different kind. Peal, for instance, noted a Naga path which the Nagas used while visiting Assam valley. He remarked: 'the traffic had worn down the rock into a narrow passage, where only one at a time could pass, and also into holes and steps, very well for Nagas to grip with their bare feet, but slippery and unaccommodating to thick-soled boots.'[5] I will come back to the regular flow of goods between the hills and valleys in Chapter 9. However, I would like to give some attention here to the process by which the valley goods might have entered the rugged highland.

[5] Peal (1873: 317).

If the so-called passes were mere natural pathways studded with many harsh realities, the role of hillmen who were well acquainted with such rugged terrain becomes profound. Major chunk of the valley goods may have taken the village paths, rather than the passes, in the form of relay trade, that is, goods were passed through different hands in the hills. Thus, instead of the valley traders taking their goods across the mountain terrain, one can think of relay trade through the hill people as middlemen or go-betweens. Thus, a kind of peddling trade and the role of hillmen as peddler of valley goods, transferring the items from one village to another across the hills, through the social and cultural networks, cannot be simply brushed aside. In this context, Wilcox's remark of the Mishmi's 'habit of trafficking' is significant: 'every man among them is a petty merchant'.[6] This remark is equally applicable to most of the hill tribes in the region. I will show in Chapter 9 how the hill people annually visited the frontier *hats* (markets); some tribes like Falam Shunklas (of Chin Hills) even monopolized certain trade items. While the hillmen frequently visited the valley markets, I would like to point out here that all of them could not freely access these markets from all distances. Although there is evidence to suggest that certain hillmen travelled a wide distance for trading purpose, the general pattern of transaction in most cases took the form of a relay trade, in which the border villages would take goods from frontier hats and pass them up to the next set of villages, which in turn transferred the goods to the next, and so on.

Considering the importance of controlling the flow of goods into the hills, the border villages, on the basis of sheer military power, appropriated the rights of exchange in the frontier hats, and hence set a train of monopolistic transaction across the hills until such items found their way into the interior villages or on the other side of the mountain. Peal, for instance, noted, although indirectly, that only 'few Nagas reach the plains but those living on the border'.[7] About those Nagas who could not reach the plains, he noted, 'they are extremely anxious to do so' and 'Asam to them is like a goal, always in sight, but never to be reached'.[8] Thus, when the British occupied

[6] Wilcox (1873: 36).
[7] Peal (1873: 330).
[8] Peal (1873: 332).

part of Naga Hills and encouraged trade, large number of Nagas from interior villages came down for trade in the valley hats; 1,904 Nagas passed through Samaguting in 1875–6 to trade at Dimapur, Golaghat, and other places in the Assam plain.[9] Hence, it was the 'jealousy' of border villages who wanted to monopolize the flow of goods at the frontier which was responsible for such exclusion; this exclusion was not due to internecine warfare and isolation. And it was this jealousy that eventually generated a kind of relay trade across the hills. This relay transaction invariably took the different routes, which I have called the social and cultural pathways, that connected various hill villages. Since circulation of goods was determined by the network of pathways across the hills, the next section talks about how the hill people conceived their roads/pathways and how such pathways which connected different hill villages can be characterized.

The Art of Menacing Distance

The discussion on space, settlements, and population distribution pattern in the previous chapter presumed two contrasting consequences: the absence of roads in the hills on the one hand, and its existence on the other. Considering the phenomenal role of friction of terrain in spatial engineering and demographic distribution patterns, the existence of paths seemed unthinkable. If elimination of such friction was one primary objective of state-making project in the valley in the interest of rule, the hill line of conduct determined to strengthen such natural friction as a political choice to evade control. Here, nature's wrath was considered the frame, the support, in the interest of safety. Hillmen, therefore, banked on the support of the rugged terrain, altitude, forest covers, hills, swamps, and so on. Hence, this line of conduct excluded road as an important part of its spatial engineering process, thereby drawing us close to the dominant narrative of an isolated and disconnected world order. Yet, this was not the case in reality. The paths did exist in the hills in their own way, although these pathways in the hills were quite different from the way road communication was projected in the state space.

---

[9] NAI, FP (A): September 1876, No. 143: *Naga Hills Administration Report, 1875–76.*

As noted earlier, the clan or cultural dynamics necessitated regular networks and communication between its members. This, in turn, presupposed the existence of road/pathway between different villages, conspiring against the dominant notion that hill villages were isolated and disconnected for centuries. But, not surprisingly, the pathways generally found in the hills were, unlike in the state space, the most 'difficult' and 'repulsive' type. Whenever there was bridge, it was similarly repulsive; the Mishmi or Abor cane bridges were one extreme case.[10] The hill paths were mere narrow footpaths, passable by a single file, mostly seasonal and slippery, and in most cases, easy for ambuscade. Their daily routine of travelling in the hills, as the early British expedition reports tell us, consisted of dropping into the deep valley and climbing up again several thousand feet on the other side. The progress was 'exceedingly slow' and completely exhausting.[11] Hutton, for instance, described the 'Naga paths' which were the usual pathways across the hills: 'The Naga paths that link up one village to another some miles away are usually the tracks of men going in single file over hill and through jungle in the most direct route possible.'[12] Colonel Woodthorpe similarly described the Naga paths leading to the village as 'long narrow tortuous lanes, with high banks of stone and earth on either side, tangled creepers and small trees meeting overhead, preventing an escalade, and admitting only of the passage of one man at a time'.[13] These intricacies of the narrow hill pathways were the norm rather than the exception. Cooper's account of the pathways in Mishmee Hills, given earlier, also said that they were 'scarcely discernible'.[14] 'Utter exhaustion' was the usual result of travelling on those pathways.

[10] For description of such cane bridges, see, for example, Wilcox (1873: 41–2).

[11] See, for instance, Butler (1978 [1855]: 29).

[12] Hutton (1921a: 46).

[13] Woodthorpe (1882: 63). For Garo paths, see NAI, FP (A): October 1873, Nos 122–5: 'Annual Administration Report of the Garo Hills, 1872–73', C.T. Metcalfe to Secretary to Government of Bengal, June 1873.

[14] Cooper (1995 [1873]: 186). See also description of Mishmi paths in Griffith (1873: 116). He said that jungle was most troublesome on the path and Mishmi would 'risk their necks than take the trouble of cutting down the underwood'.

The hill paths thus were not roads in the strict sense of the term. They were not conceived as a political highway for warfare, control, and revenue collection, or economic network for trade and commerce, but as a social and cultural network. As noted earlier, the clan geographicity and governmentality actually operated in such a way that it necessitated a regular movement of people (married couples, their families, potential suitors, lovers, matchmakers, warriors, feast and ritual partakers, tribute throwers, and so on), goods, and culture between the hill villages, and hence the need for regular pathways. But the hillmen were, at the same time, conscious of the vulnerability it would cause to their hill abode from raiders and conquerors if they opened up the road networks. The hill paths were, therefore, the result of reconciling culture and security: while these pathways helped them fulfil their social and cultural responsibility as members of the clan or family, they were deliberately made difficult and repulsive for raiders and marauders. Griffith rightly noted that 'the natives seem to think that the more difficult paths the better, a greater security being thus obtained from foreign invasion'.[15] Circulation of goods and commodities also took these difficult paths when necessary.

To what extent these pathways were conceived to prevent control and appropriations requires some explanation. Several evidences point to the fact that the 'long narrow tortuous' hill paths were, besides giving security, patterned for difficult accessibility and easy defence. In 1840, for instance, when E.R. Grange's expedition party was passing a narrow 'Naga path' beneath 'the almost perpendicular rocky range' on which Yang or Tzukquama village stood, they were attacked by the Nagas, who rolled down stones and boulders over them, which they narrowly escaped.[16] Captain Butler was, in fact, killed in such a surprise ambuscade along the narrow path. After Butler was speared, Woodthorpe noted, the Nagas appeared in large numbers and started attacking them:

[W]ho now and then came charging down the paths towards us, appearing and disappearing, as if by magic, through the narrow outlets ... A spear had fallen a few yards before us on the path, and the head constable stepped forward and picked it up, when at once a Naga appeared as if out of the ground, flourishing a dao over his head, and he escaped.[17]

To avoid such ordeals by following the narrow hill paths, a new path (which came to be popularly known as 'political path/highway') was usually cut through the wilderness by most British expedition parties.

These pathways, however, should not be confused with other categories of routes among the hills, such as the paths leading to jhum fields, to the water-pent, or the war paths. While the paths to water-pent and jhum fields were cut properly and relatively well maintained, war paths or hunting routes followed secret paths through the jungles. If roads were made between all friendly and related villages, only war paths were possible between two or more rival villages. Thus, in between village Mekula (a Lhota village) and Changki (a Hatigoria or Ao village) in Naga Hills, noted Hinde, the road was 'merely a jungle tract, worn by the warriors of the two villages in their raids on each other, and is studded with pitfalls and panjies, as our advance-guard discovered to their cost.'[18]

If pathways were extremely bad between most hill villages, the case with the frontier 'outposts' or 'guard villages' was worse. As described by Dalton (1872: 26), these villages were built to 'resist encroachments and prevent marauding expeditions', and hence were almost devoid of any pathways. If the impassable forest covers, the excessively difficult hill terrain, and unattractive border 'outposts' still tempted the valley invaders to go up to the interior hills, then every effort was made by these 'guard villages' to stop them at the foot of the hills. The party was refused any guide, all facts about the interior country were concealed, or in certain cases, they were attacked/ambuscaded. Thus, when Wilcox's party was in the Abor Hills for a survey, 'numerous body of armed men' of Pasi and Padu Abors encamped near them to oppose their progress towards the Bor

[17] NAI, FP (A): January 1877, No. 148: R.G. Woodthorpe to W.F. Badgley, 15 June 1876.

[18] NAI, FP (A): January 1877, No. 148: Appendix C: Hinde to Woodthorpe, 7 May 1876.

Abor villages. Wilcox noted that the 'vengeance of the tribe [in the interior] would fall on them, they said, if they dared to permit our advance'.[19] Griffith also noted that his attempt to reach the frontier of Tibet did 'prove completely futile' since 'no tribes, no promises would induce any of the chiefs to give me guides even to the first Mishmee village belonging to the Meezhoo tribe', 'without whose assistance in this most difficult country, I need scarcely say that all attempt to advance would have been made in vain'.[20]

Whenever hill guides were obtained, often under duress, it was even more problematic. These guides invariably took the party along the most difficult and repulsive tracks, possibly with the idea of harassing the party in a different way. Thus, when Butler was over the high ranges in Naga Hills in 1845, he realized that the Naga guides and interpreters were 'determined to take us by the most impassable routes', which could have been easily avoided if he had known the country before.[21] Butler attributed such behaviour to sheer ignorance of the Nagas about good roads. But he did not realize that his Naga guides were actually harassing him by taking his party through the most difficult paths. Similarly, Wilcox also noticed what he called a 'marked instance of their jealousy' among the tribes of Mishmee and Abor Hills during his survey: 'they had no intention of showing us the commodious path which we afterwards discovered on our return'.[22] Griffith also noted that although better paths existed, he was taken by his guides through 'the very worst' paths.[23] Thus, all efforts were made to discourage, or even resist, the entry of 'foreigners' into the interior parts of the hills. This line of argument is further substantiated by the way the hill people conceived their hill villages, a point discussed in the next section.

[19] Wilcox (1873: 54).

[20] NAI, FP: 6 March 1837, No. 67: Griffith to Jenkins, 20 January 1837; also see Hamilton (1997: 88–9). For Lushai Hills, see WBSA, JP: 27 February 1850, No. 36: Lister to Grant, 2 February 1850.

[21] Butler (1978 [1855]: 57). See also his report in NAI, FP: 23 May 1846, No. 31: J. Butler to F. Jenkins, 16 January 1846.

[22] Wilcox (1873: 53).

[23] NAI, FP: 6 March 1837, No. 67: Griffith to Jenkins, 20 January 1837.

Masada of the Hillmen

Reporting on an attempt to capture Khonomah 'Fort' in Angami Hills on 10 December 1850, Major Butler noted that the British forces, with a total number of 354 troops, two three-pounder guns, and two four-inch mortars, found it impossible to breach it. From 2 p.m. onwards, they started firing mortars: first, at a distance of 600 yards; then, with two three-pounder guns within 150 yards; and finally, within 70 yards. But they were not able to 'injure' the stockade, 'strongly constructed of stone and timber', even after 'many rounds of shot and canister had been expended'. As there was no hope of breaching the stockade, and the day was coming to a close, the whole party advanced to escalade the position. But on reaching the defences, 'a deep and wide trench stopped all further progress'. As the fort was flanked at each end by an abrupt precipice, and exposed to showers of spears, musketry, and stones, the troops were obliged to retire to the spot where the guns first opened fire. They bivouacked there for the night. To prevent a surprise attack from the Nagas, a desultory fire was kept up during the night on the enemy's position. The British troops took possession of the fort the next morning when it was found that the Nagas had evacuated it during the night. 'Thus fell', Butler proclaimed with pride, 'one of the strongest forts ever seen in Assam, after a siege of sixteen hours' duration.'[24]

Khonomah Fort (see Figure 4.1) was not the kind of fort as seen in the valley state where rulers and soldiers lived. It was neither the power centre of a great kingdom. It was rather a mere hill village of some Angami Naga clans for centuries. The fortification in question was part of the tradition commonly shared among most Naga tribes and, to an extent, by most stateless hillmen in the highland massif of the region. There were many reports of British expeditions in the hills of Northeast India where the hill villages had been taken only after a long fight. This was usually due to a strong stockade around the villages and the very difficult position of the villages, that is, normally perched on the summit of the precipitous hills. Carey and Tuck's description of the fortification in the southern hills (Lushai and Chin Hills), and especially that of one Vaiphei fortification, is interesting:

[24] Butler (1978 [1855]: 198–9).

Figure 4.1 View of Mozemah Valley, Overlooking Khonomah (inset: sketch plan of Khonomah Fort)
Source: See Butler (1978 [1855]: 193 [valley view], 199 [inset]).

Perched on the summit of precipitous peaks they build their villages, and if the approaches were not almost perpendicular they proceeded to so cut away and block the paths that friend and foe alike could only ascend to the heavily stockaded gates in single file. On the summit of Lunglen peak is found the remains of an ancient Vaipe [Vaiphei?] village, which was defended in a most extraordinary manner by boulders and sungars. Finally, just in front of the fortified gate, the rock had been cut perpendicular for 10 feet, which necessitated the use of a ladder before it could be scaled.[25]

If the ordering of the hill space was conceptualized following certain principles and keeping the 'line of conduct' in mind, that is, to prevent and evade control and appropriations, then it also makes sense to argue now that the setting of hill villages was also done on the same basis. Truly, the hill villages could not escape the general 'line of conduct' followed in the hills because it was literally their

[25] Carey and Tuck (1987 [1896]: 174).

'base camp', the microcosm of their stateless universe, which needed to be guarded as the last stronghold. From the point of its conception and the arrangement of its specific location across the hills, the hill villages, until colonial occupation, were peculiarly political in nature. This was mainly because the general setting of the hill villages gave the impression of a defensive posture. Surprisingly enough, this was also the view shared by most colonial observers, although they differ from our general understanding. Thus, most of the hill villages were established on the summit of the hills, on a high saddle, or perhaps, more frequently, on the ridge of some spur running down from the high range. They were generally fortified, surrounded by a deep ditch studded with *panjies* (piece of sharp bamboo stuck upright in the ground), and most of them had one or more bachelor's dormitory (variously known as *morung, zawlbuk* [Figure 4.2], and *mosup*) where unmarried men of the village stayed during the night.

C. Holroyd, for instance, noted about the Naga villages:

Naga villages are without exception situated on the tops of precipitous hills with commanding views of all approaches; they are generally

Figure 4.2 A Lushei Zawlbuk (bachelor's dormitory)
Source: Taken from Shakespear and Hodson (1909: 390).

fortified by a ditch, and many by a succession of ditches having a stockade on the inner side; the sides of the hills are also frequently scarped where the path-way winds round a shoulder of the hills overhanging a steep precipice, a breast-work or flanking defence being here erected to defend the pass.[26]

Colonel Woodthorpe also added that the 'stiff stockades, deep ditches bristling with panjies, and massive stone walls often loopholed for musketry, are their usual defences'. He further described the village gates: 'closed by strong, thick, and heavy wooden doors made out of one piece of wood', 'fastened from the inside', and 'are protected very often by raised look-outs' on which 'a watch is kept up day and night'.[27] Keating even said that 'every village is a fortress, into which the intrusion of strangers is warmly resented ... The average elevation of the villages near the existing political path is 5,000 feet.'[28]

In the Chin Hills, Carey and Tuck also described the Chin village fortification which consisted of a narrow, fortified gate and rifle trenches hidden by growing grass and ferns at a distance of 100 yards to 2 miles from the village. A zigzag path and often a tunnel had to be entered to reach the gate and 'at each turn in the path and at both sides of the gate are stone and wooden sungars and stockades overgrown with briars, cactus, and thorny bushes, which render entrance in face of resistance impossible'. Besides the gates, they said, 'cactus and stiff thorn hedges, palisades, stone breastworks and rifle-pits surround and defend the village'. In the Siyin-Sokte country, they said that 'large trenches are dug and roofed with heavy timber flush with the ground inside the villages; these trenches are maintained as

[26] Mills (1980 [1853]: cxiii). This report was adapted from several expeditionary field reports, like that of Brodie in 1841 and 1842 (see NAI, FP: 17 August 1842, No. 186), Butler (1978 [1855]), and so on. See also Woodthorpe (1882: 63). For other hill tribes, see, for instance, Carey and Tuck (1987 [1896]), Needham report on Abors in NAI, FE (A): March 1885, No. 253, Reid (1976 [1893]), and Woodthorpe (1980 [1873]). See also colonial ethnographical works on all the tribes for details.

[27] Woodthorpe (1882: 63).

[28] NAI, FP (A): October 1878, No. 28: 'Memorandum of the Chief Commissioner of Assam Giving Detailed Account of His Visit to the Interior of the Naga Hills', 23 January–14 February 1878.

a refuge for the women and children in case of sudden attack'. The entrance hole is 'blocked up and there are some dozen loop-holes through which the defender shoots down any who approaches his underground block-house'.[29]

In Lushai Hills, Shakespear noted that the Lusheis also 'perch his village on the top of a ridge or spur' and were 'surrounded by one or more lines of stockade made of timber, with several rows of bamboo spikes outside it'. He also said that at each gateway was 'a block house, and others were built at suitable places on the roads along which enemies were expected to come, and were occupied whenever an attack was apprehended.'[30] Parry too noted that the Lakhers 'generally built on some high slope in an easily defended position' and 'every village had its fort or *ku*, to which the people retired on news of a raid'. Their ku was built in the middle of the village, and consisted of a strong stockade of tree trunks and saplings about 10 feet in height in two or three rows. All around the stockade, a trench was dug and sown with bamboo stakes called *seu* (panjies), and was crossed by a drawbridge, which was raised and lowered by cane ropes. Some distance from the village, the jungle was cut at all vulnerable points to render surprise more difficult, and sentry posts were established on all the paths to give timely warning. As a further defence, stone traps (*longpa*) were built at suitable places on paths approaching the village.[31]

Although some tribes did not put up fortification, the idea of defence and security from enemy's attack always dominated the founding of a village. This becomes especially clear in the case of those hills where the topographical setting of the hills could afford natural defence system, such as, in the sub-Himalayan ranges and the Khasi Hills. In the sub-Himalayan region, village sites were normally chosen along the river valleys (as the higher altitude did not allow any settlement), but they would invariably choose the higher slope where the physical setting afforded them maximum security. For instance, Membu, an Abor village, was described by Wilcox (1825), Dalton (1855), and Needham (1884), noting particularly its defensive

---

[29] Carey and Tuck (1987 [1896]: 175–6).
[30] Shakespear (1998 [1912]: 19).
[31] Parry (1988 [1931]: 60–4).

position against enemy attack.[32] Needham noted that the village site was 'marvellously well chosen':

> On its southern and western sides the hills rise perpendicularly from the bed of the Siku to a height of about 800 feet, and they are quite bare, while to the north and westward the hillsides are cut up by deep ravines, and they are likewise so perpendicular that it would be impossible to ascend them ... the only possible way of getting into the village would be by the path we were taken *viz.*, from the southward, and there are numerous deep, though narrow, artificially made ravines to be crossed as well as several steep ascents to be made ere the village is reached, each of which might, if necessary, be so defended in turn by a resolute body of men as to make it an exceedingly difficult matter for any enemy to enter the village.[33]

Stockade was not completely unknown. Needham noted that the Abor villages near the river valley were strongly stockaded. Bomjir was, Dalton also remarked, 'on a high bank overlooking a western branch of the river, strongly stockade, and was evidently placed here an *outpost* of the confederate Padam states' [emphasis mine].[34]

Citadels against State

What is significant from the given village built-up is the importance that was given to the safety and security of the village against enemy attack. It was a fact that all colonial authorities also recognized. For instance, Carey and Tuck said that village sites were chosen 'solely for the defensive advantages which they offer' and 'all such matters as soil, water-supply and shelter from the wind were secondary considerations'.[35] Shakespear also noted the Lusheis perched their villages on the top of a ridge or spur, 'chiefly, I think, in order to get

---

[32] Wilcox (1873: 49) and Dalton (1960 [1872]: 27) respectively.

[33] NAI, FE (A): March 1885, No. 253: 'Needham Report of his Visit to Abor Hills', Needham to Deputy Commissioner, Lakhimpur, 27 October 1884.

[34] Dalton (1960 [1872]: 26).

[35] Carey and Tuck (1987 [1896]: 174).

a good defensive position'.[36] Similarly, Stewart noted that the Kukis 'generally perched their villages on the tops of hills, not from any particular love for such elevation, but as offering greater advantages for defence.'[37] Of the Naga villages, von Fürer-Haimendorf also remarked that 'strategic considerations were certainly uppermost in the minds of most village founders'.[38]

But who was the enemy against whom such defensive posture was erected? Woodthorpe felt that the Nagas built their villages in commanding positions and fortified them 'owing to the almost constant state of war'.[39] Brodie similarly felt that Naga village 'defences are made chiefly, if not altogether, in consequence of feuds and warfare among themselves'.[40] Keating remarked that the 'terrible insecurity of life which prevails has made the Nagas perch their villages on the highest summits'.[41] The Kuki-Chins were also seen as 'cognate but warring tribes'.[42] This situation, it was further contended, had existed in the hills since 'many centuries' before.[43] But what if the hill tribes also perched their fortified villages owing to the threat they felt from the valley state conquerors and marauders? In that case, the concept of 'internecine feud' fails to give the total picture of the hill situation. It also badly fails to explain why the same defensive posture was erected even when there was no internecine warfare and/or even after the hill rivals had been subdued or after a weaker village had submitted to a more powerful one.

It is true that there was very strong 'internecine warfare' among the tribes when such village setting was recorded in the early

---

[36] Shakespear (1998 [1912]: 19).

[37] Stewart (1855: 635).

[38] von Fürer-Haimendorf (1969: 21).

[39] Woodthorpe (1882: 63).

[40] NAI, FP: 17 August 1842, No. 186: T. Brodie to F. Jenkins, 9 April 1842. See also Damant (1880: 229–30).

[41] NAI, FP (A): October 1878, No. 28: Memorandum of the Chief Commissioner, 23 January–14 February 1878.

[42] See McCulloch (1980 [1859]), Edgar (quoted in Mackenzie 2007 [1884]: Appendix-E), Lewin (1978 [1870]), Shakespear (1998 [1912]), and Carey (1987 [1896]) accounts for details.

[43] Brown (1851: 157).

colonial period. But to assume that such warfare had happened among them 'many centuries back' is not only simplistic but also loaded with civilizational prejudice. Elsewhere, I have shown that such warfare was but the product of colonial intervention, directly or indirectly, during the same time, and not the hangover of the past centuries. The reconfiguration of power and social relationships due to the interventions of colonial states was rather central to such 'internecine warfare'.[44] On the question of the 'fortresses', evidence has suggested that such village built-up was already in existence since a long time ago, so much so that it had become part of their 'custom'. As noted earlier, the Kuki-Chin legends always talk about their 'old forts' or ramparts. The Kukis cannot not forget their Chungkhopi Fort; the Mizos show uncompromising elation in their old 'Khampat Fort'. Sinlung, or Chhinlung, or Khul, if it is taken as a fort, is always lively in the memory of Kuki-Chin people. Fryer has also recorded one time-tested ballad of the Khyeng (Asho) which cherished the old, 'brick walled city' of their forefathers which was so 'charming'.[45] Fortress as a defensive posture against enemy has been, therefore, well known to the tribes, probably before they came to their present hills. In any case, their constant association with the valley states could have taught them the importance of fortification.

An interesting case from the Naga Hills brings out how such village fortification was a very old tradition among the hill tribes, deeply embedded in their customary practice. Hutton, for instance, noted among the Sema tribe that even after the colonial government banned village fortification, symbolic fortification system was continued quite religiously:

> The village from time to time, say once in three to five years, does a genna for fear that the wrath of some spirit might afflict them by reason of their *having given up a former custom* [of fortification]. They therefore turn up a little earth by way of digging a ditch, just scratching up the mould in two or three places, and put in a few harmless panjis for roughly-pointed bamboo and a few sticks to represent the

---

[44] For a narrower discussion on this issue, see Guite (2014).
[45] See Fryer (1875: 46–7).

fence. A pig is slaughtered and divided, and a share given to every male in the village.[46]

If village fortification had formed part of their 'custom' and giving up such custom was believed to cause 'the wrath of some spirit', then it was indeed a very old practice prevailing in the hills. Unfortunately, there are very few archaeological remains in the hills, partly because most of the fortifications were built of perishable material, and partly due to the migratory habits of the tribes as another strategy of state evasion.

Even if it is still assumed that such village fortifications were made due to 'internecine warfare' over a long period of time, there are still some pertinent questions which require appropriate answers. Why did the hill people, instead of going to the nearby plains, choose to remain in the hills and suffer the brunt of such 'internecine warfare'? Why, as mentioned earlier, did they continue to put up their fortification when there was no 'internecine warfare' or after they had submitted to the more powerful village and so on? The migration of Miris to the plain of Assam during the colonial period was specific to the relative freedom granted to them there than under the hill polities. Few Kuki populations had also taken shelter in the plains of Manipur and Cachar due to internecine warfare in their hills, but they very soon 'slipped away' to the hills once the situation was better, just as the Mikirs had slipped away from the shelter they received from the Ahoms earlier. Apart from such few cases of taking shelter under the valley states, there is no evidence to suggest that the hill populations, in general, migrated to the plains due to 'internecine warfare' in the hills. In fact, such movement from the hills to the valleys in the past could be seen only as part of their effort to control and rule over the valleys, rather than be subjects of the valley states.

The hillmen responded to the 'internecine warfare' of the nineteenth century in the hills in two ways. First, the hill people, instead of going to the plains, strengthened their village defence, as described earlier, or they came together in one village, or joined the 'grand clan/village', to defend or overpower their rivals. This involved flight from one village to another, invariably to the more powerful village.

---

[46] Hutton (1921b: 35); emphasis added.

Such migration especially became quite common in the nineteenth century.[47] The concentration of a large number of mixed populations under the popular and powerful chiefs voluntarily, or by the circumstances of 'exterminating warfare', was, therefore, one response against the so-called internecine warfare. Hence, regrouping within the hills rather than migrating to the plains was one clear response against internecine warfare. Second, the weaker villages submitted before a more powerful one without shifting their settlement so that they could enjoy the latter's protection or at least prevent its attack. Thus, in Naga Hills, some large villages like Khonomah, Mozemah, Kohima, and Lopshehma became 'the head of the Angamee tribes', and all the small villages were 'subjected' to them, paid 'annual tribute' to them, and 'they are the arbitrators in all disputes, and without their approval nothing important can be done'.[48] Interestingly, both the paramount and subjected villages continued to put up their fortifications as usual. Thus, a strong disinclination to go 'down' to the plains was exhibited.

If fortification continued with or without 'internecine warfare', then it can be said that there was some imminent danger, other than their hill rivals, in their consciousness that perpetually compelled the hill people to remain on the alert. The fact that they refused to go to the plains despite such major warfare in the hills shows that the valley

[47] I have discussed such migration in the southern hills elsewhere. See Guite (2011). Similar situation was reported in Naga Hills. See, for instance, NAI, FP: 25 May 1840, No. 118: Sg. E.R. Grange to Lt. H. Bigge, 29 July 1840.

[48] See NAI, FP: 24 August 1844, No. 36: Mr. Browne Wood to Captain A. Sturt, 14 April 1844; also see Butler (1978 [1855]: 144). Similar role was assumed by Ungma, Longsa, Nankam, Mooloong, Chunguye (Changnoe), Jaktung, Tablung, Namsang, and Wakching among 'Eastern Nagas'; by Nunklow, Kyrim, Churra, Nurtung, Nuspung, Muriow, Mahram, and Ramrye in Khasi Hills; by Falam, Haka, Klangklang, and Teddim in Chin Hills; by Sailo chieftains in Lushai Hills; and by Kuki chiefs in Manipur Hills. See Brown (2001 [1873]: 480), Carey and Tuck (1987 [1896]: 118–64), Dun (1992 [1886]: 32–4), NAI, FE (A): July 1888, No. 122 and *Selection of Papers*, pp. 286–7: Brodie to Jenkins, 15 September 1841, Robinson (1975 [1841]: 408–11), Shakespear (1998 [1912]: 1–8), and WBSA, JP: June 1871, Nos 206–7.

state was always one factor against whom their fortification and other security measures were constantly kept up over the ages. This, again, supports the idea of the hill people as state-evading population in the hills. If they constantly kept up their 'hunting ground' and distributed their population and settlements so that conquerors, raiders, and marauders from the valley found difficulty in controlling the hills, then it also makes sense to argue that the choice of village sites and its fortification were for the same reason.

Therefore, when the hillmen made their strongholds in the hills as strong and defensive as possible, it was not only to secure themselves from their hill rivals but also, more importantly, to keep themselves safe from the control and appropriations of the valley states. In this context, securing their villages from any surprise attack was another 'line of conduct' for the state-evading population. While putting themselves up at the summit of the hills gave them an advantage of having a commanding view of the approaching enemy, such fortified villages also protected them from any surprise attack. Here, the importance given to safety and security of the people against human 'enemies', over the disadvantages of improper water supply, exposure to strong winds, and so on, becomes quite clear. What was suitable location for their village was therefore determined by the requirement of their political security against human enemy, and not by geography or economics. In this sense, the hill villages were the citadels of the hillmen, the state-evading population. The popularity of morung ('bachelor's dormitory') among the hill tribes further explains why political security was so central to the hillmen.

Warriors, Morungs, and Sentinels of the Hills

When Grange was in Beremah village in the Angami Naga Hills in 1837, several Naga villagers visited him in a 'friendly spirit'. Besides other things, he was fascinated by the attire of Naga warriors. In this respect, he was particularly impressed by the powerful chief of Mozemah, one Ikkari, who was said to have led most of the 'raiding' parties in Assam. He was described to be 'a perfect savage, wild and suspicious, wearing a collar fringed with hair of his enemies scalps'.[49]

---

[49] Mackenzie (2007 [1884]: 104).

Grange did not understand the significance of Ikkari's collar. He did not know that it was no ordinary attire but one exclusively worn by a famed warrior—a status gained after a long course of dedication to the cause of the community as a 'warrior'. It was a symbol of the prowess of a great warrior, and all men aspired to achieve this in their lifetime. This collar spoke to the Nagas that Ikkari was an admired, respected, and influential person in the Naga Hills, or at least among his kinsmen. In eastern Naga Hills, the same custom of bestowing social recognition to a great warrior was followed in the form of tattooing the body parts. Thus, every British expedition party in the Naga Hills had come across such 'gaily-dressed warriors', who studded the forest or the hill villages and whose fighting spirit and war strategies were well recorded. In the Lushai Hills, warriors who defeated the enemy and brought home their heads as proof of that prowess, or who brought live captives and plunder during the war against the enemy (or even that of big game), were 'publicly decorated, each man's hair being bound with a thick white cord, at the ends of which knots of black and red thread were fastened'. This thread was called *arkezen* in the Lusheis and was highly prized, carefully preserved, and transmitted to their descendants as 'proofs of the prowess of their ancestors'.[50] The fame of a named warrior lasted for generations.

While this is not the right place to elaborate on the concept of 'warrior', and so on, a short explanation here would make things clear.[51] A society which was constantly reeling under a sort of invasion from outside definitely needed a class of warriors who could defend and protect the community from attack or take revenge when it was insulted. Thus, warriors became the community's social capital: they were celebrated; could hold high social status, but not dominate others; as well as hold certain positions in the village government. As mentioned earlier, certain dresses, ornaments, or tattoos could be worn by warriors only. If orality glorified the name of the famed

[50] As quoted in Mackenzie (2007 [1884]: 325). For a similar account, see Shakespear (1998 [1912]: 57–8), Shaw (1997 [1929]: 78–81), and Soppit (1976 [1887]: 20).

[51] In Chapter 7, we shall see the predominance of warrior ideology in their oral histories and who can be called as 'warrior' to the community.

warriors in order to promote the idea of warriorhood, there were also different ways society trained and magnified the image of such warriors. For instance, each community prescribed the ways in which one could become a named warrior. Thus, killing an enemy and bringing his head home was one common way to become a warrior. A person could also become a warrior by being a great hunter and so on. On the other hand, if a man could not fulfil such prescriptions, he could not become a warrior and there were certain penalties. For instance, people would call him 'boy', 'girl', 'woman', or otherwise, and force him to wear women's clothes and associate with women only, as in Lushai Hills. Besides, no girl would marry him if he could not become a warrior, a point discussed in Chapter 8.

The main concern here is to show how the stateless hill society trained their young boys to become good warriors and why they valued them so much. In this, the role of morung in training and disciplining their young ones becomes significant. As 'Sepai Camp' without soldiers has no meaning, the hill village fortification without its 'warriors' is useless. Thus, every hill village had some way of organizing its warriors so that they remained active and alert. Of these, the most unique was the young man's or bachelor's dormitory system. Almost every tribe in the Northeast had a certain form of 'bachelor's dormitory' system in the past, popularly known as the morung (in Assamese). It was known in different tribes by different names: zawlbuk (Lusheis), *som* (Kukis), mosup (Abors), *champo* (Lhotas), *arichu* (Aos), *ban* (Konyaks), *maro* or *terang* (Karbis), *nokpante* (Garos), *kichuki* (Angamis), and so on.[52] Morung was generally understood as the common sleeping place of every boy in the village from the time he left his house to enter morung until he got married. In the nineteenth century, morung system was clearly visible among certain tribes as a well-established social institution, whereas its existence remained symbolic among others tribes.

Among the Aos, Lhotas, Konyaks, Abors, Garos, and Lusheis, morung was a well-established institution, although its role and functions varied from tribe to tribe. Among the Aos, Mills noted that 'from the cradle to the grave a man is part of a machine' in

[52] Certain tribes like Aos, Abors (Adis), Konyaks, Noctes, Gallongs, and Khamti had 'girl's dormitory' as well. But we are not concerned with this here.

which morung played a central role. Every three years, a new batch of boys entered the morung and hence formed one age group. They continued to remain part of this age group throughout their life.[53] Each stage of this age group had specific communal responsibility assigned by customs. Fellowship under the command of the elder ones was the essence of this age group system. From the first stage in the morung, each individual was trained and disciplined for the next stage so that at the fag end of his life, he would be able to rule the village effectively as a councillor. A few of them were expected to eventually take up the duty of village priest (*patir*). 'Only on these lines', Mills rightly noted, 'could a village of perhaps two thousand souls, without king or chief, be run.'[54] Among Konyaks, von Fürer-Haimendorf noted similar age group system, 'whose members worked, danced, and played together until the time when the obligations of family life loosened the close links between members'. Morung as a powerful 'cooperative institution' was well recognized by all colonial observers.[55]

Morung served a variety of functions, such as sleeping place and educational institution for boys (where 'younger boys are under discipline' and 'that the old men tell of the great deeds of the past'), 'council room' for the village, rest house for travellers, and at times sanctuary for criminals.[56] It was always the largest building in the village and each village was very proud of it. Needham, for instance, noted that the Abors were 'excessively proud of their "Mosup"', where 'all important topics are talked over and disposed of in it'. Membu morung was 80 yards long and 10 yards wide, having 24 fireplaces, and was entirely open along the whole length with one front and

---

[53] Among the Changki Aos, these age groups were successively known as *nozabarihori* (unripe gang), *iukapbahari* (ripening gang), *chuchenbahori* (morung leaders gang), *okchangshamicharihori* (pig's leg eaters), *kidongmabang* (clan leaders), *khonri* (load carriers), *tatari* (councillors), *maozambatelakba* (assistant councillors), *maozamba temamba* (councillor-dross), and *patir* (priest).

[54] Mills (2003 [1926]: 73–4, 176–80).

[55] See von Fürer-Haimendorf (1969: 48).

[56] See Mills (1982 [1937]: 49, 2003 [1922]: 24), Parry (2009 [1928]: 8–12), Playfair (1998 [1909]: 37–8), and Shakespear (1998 [1912]: 20–1).

back exit. He said that it could hold about 500 men.[57] Among some tribes, morung system was merely symbolic, although they all claimed that it had been in full shape earlier. Among the Karbis and Semas, the chief's house formed the village morung; and among the Kukis group, young boys chose their som (morung) in the house of a young lady until her marriage.[58] Among the Angamis, morung house was merely used for occasional ceremonies and *genna*s (sabbath of village); and among the Semas, it 'practically non-existent' except in a 'miniature form'.[59] Yet, the function of morung was carried out with similar efficiency among these tribes.

There are different opinions regarding the essence of this institution among the scholars. Some scholars feel that it was a mere 'survival' of 'pre-marriage communism' from the past having no 'definite purpose', whereas others feel that its essence lay in the sexual life of the people such as to prevent or permit 'pre-marital sex' or to prevent the children from witnessing the sexual privacy of their parents.[60] However, from the evidence of nineteenth century, it is clear that morung emerged as a composite institution that combined social, economic, and educational roles. Its importance as a political or military institution was projected sometimes, only to be jettisoned soon. It is true that this institution was very old and it diversified its role in the village society with time. But from its essence, the importance of morung as a political or military institution cannot be overlooked.

Central to the morung system was its role in disciplining and 'hammering into shape' the young boys of the village. Mills, for instance, noted among the Aos that boy 'fags for other boys and is taught his duties in life and generally hammered into shape'. The

---

[57] NAI, FE (A): March 1885, No. 253: 'Mr. Needham Report of His Visit to Abor Hills', from Needham to Deputy Commissioner, Lakhimpur, 27 October 1884.

[58] Hutton (1921b: 37) and Lyall (1997 [1908]: 11).

[59] See Hutton (1921a: 49, 1921b: 37). Among Semas, a model of morung was built in times of scarcity as they felt that such scarcity took place because they had 'neglected to conform to a custom which has been abandoned'.

[60] See the colonial accounts cited earlier. See also Peal (1893), Srivastava (1990), and von Fürer-Haimendorf (1938b).

morung took the place of his father 'as a disciplinarian'.[61] The boys were 'hammered' not only to be good followers but also fearless warriors. Mills also noted that during the first few years of entering the morung, the boys were 'very severely disciplined'. They were to supply firewood and water, massage the bigger boys, make pipes, sharpen daos, besides doing everything else they were told.

> They were, for instance, held over the fire and compelled to endure the heat without a cry. Or, they were made to show their pluck by being sent alone on a dark night to fetch a bamboo from a certain clump ... Or, again, a boy would be sent to leave a torch at some particular spot far away in the jungle and come back alone in the dark without a light.[62]

In Karbi's morung disciplinary system, Lyall noted, 'they used to roast those who shirked their share; now they beat them for failure to work'.[63] No one, including their parents, was allowed to interfere in the affairs of the morung.[64] Among the Lusheis, Parry noted, discipline was 'strictly enforced in the *zawlbuk* and no interference from outside is tolerated'. If any parent interferes due to complaint of ill-treatment from their son, he noted, 'all the inmates of the *zawlbuk* combine to punish the father of the sneak'.[65]

What was central to this disciplinary system was the promotion of what is popularly known as the esprit de corps. Von Fürer-Haimendorf, for instance, rightly noted of Konyak's morung system, which had played a central role in promoting the 'corporateness of a morung community': 'Members of a morung cooperated in

---

[61] Mills (1982 [1937]: 50).

[62] Mills (2003 [1926]: 179–80).

[63] Lyall (1997 [1908]: 11).

[64] Mills (2003 [1926]: 180).

[65] 'They go off to the offender's house sit down on the floor, catch hold of the posts and away [sway] their bodies to and fro until the whole house sways with them and nearly falls down. After having thoroughly frightened the householder they go away. This punishment which is known as *Sawi* is intended to show the man they are punishing that they have no respect for him and do not care if he migrates to another village or not.' See Parry (2009 [1928]: 11).

numerous social, economic and ritual activities. The intimacy prevailing between all the inmates of a men's house facilitated the smooth operation of joint activities.'[66] Lyall also noted that Karbi youth all ate together, worked together in the fields by going on the round of the fields in the village, practised dancing and singing, and kept alive the village usages and tribal customs.[67] Similarly, Guha felt that besides disciplining the young men and developing the spirit of cooperation among them, the morung of the Abors also developed a 'spirit of responsibility, alertness and habit of taking risk in the face of danger which are essential for the existence of the tribe'.[68]

This brings us to the question: why did the hillmen need the spirit of cooperation then? Some scholars feel that the spirit of cooperation was required for their economic activities, whereas others feel that it was due to social and cultural needs. These points are sound but not the primary concern of morung system. They merely constitute the consequence, the incidental of the political particulars. Among others, two factors emerge significant for our purpose here. First, it is possible to see that the village fortification, which was a clear expression of defence, and the morung were closely related to each other, just as 'Sepai Camp' and the soldier's barracks. Immediately after the British occupied the hills, village fortification was banned but not the morung. Christian missionaries saw morung as a site of vice and immorality, but the colonial administration wanted the institution to remain as it was the pivot through which they could similarly discipline, hammer, and control the turbulent hillmen. However, morung could not transform into another colonial tool like the chieftainship institution despite the encouragement given. It could not survive the ban on fortification. It was as if it had no meaning to stand alone without the village fort or without any danger from the enemy. It died a slow death on its own. The end of statelessness and eventual evaporation of threat from outside attack led to the natural death of this time-tested institution.

Second, despite the death of morung institution, the hill villages continued to carry on their economic, social, and cultural activities

---

[66] von Fürer-Haimendorf (1969: 48).

[67] Lyall (1997 [1908]: 11).

[68] Guha (1953: 53), as quoted in Srivastava (1990: 121).

as usual. The spirit of cooperation remained vigorous in these fields, although it was definitely not the same as it used to be. In fact, morung was not everything for the village community. Even in the heyday of morung life, the family was always responsible for the child from the cradle to the grave. For the children, parents and grandparents were always the main disciplinarians. Morung only served as the site of convergence of family–base education system. But what the family did not impart was the art of warfare and warrior tradition or the esprit de corps among the young men, which the morung amply provided. In this sense, the essence of morung can be situated in the realm of politics rather than economic or social. It was conceived, conditioned, and shaped by the persistent demand of stateless society for security against the control and appropriations of valley state and other hill enemies.

Two illustrations of how the esprit de corps actually worked in emergency situation will suffice here. Dalton (1855) recorded one interesting case in Abor village where a widow lost her children in the field. The said widow, with her two children, had gone to the field. She tied the infant on the back of the three or four year-old boy and went to work. But after coming back from work, she found them missing. Not finding them, she went back home hoping her children had gone there. When she did not find them at home, she was upset and her cries could be heard throughout the village. Her cries soon reached the morung where the village youth and men sat round the blazing hearths carousing. But at the sound of this poor widow's sorrowing cry, they at once arose and went forth, 'prepared to pass the night searching for the lost children'. Dalton remarked:

> There was no discussion; no mandate was sent forth, no apathy was shown, no excuses were made. The widow's appeal was at once responded to by benevolent action. There was no delay except to prepare torches, and in a very few minutes a band of not less than 100 young men, armed and equipped, followed the woman to the scene of the disaster.[69]

John Owen (1844) also noted one instance at the morung of the Nagas. He got the chance to stay the night in one of the morungs.

---

[69] Dalton (1960 [1872]: 29).

Except for a few young men on guard all night, the rest slept soundly until the wee hours of the morning when they were awakened by a 'shrill scream from the party on the guard'. He remarked that it was the 'customary morning call' for work, which was followed by a rapid descent below, and 'in less than five minutes not a single person was to be seen'. He also noted that in case of any sign of an attack, 'a password is given, and every man is instantly on his legs, carrying his battle-axe and spear'. 'The brief period of time in which they all muster', he remarked, 'is incredible'.[70]

Yes, it was incredible indeed. The kind of discipline imparted in the morung was so 'incredible' that at any sign of attack, in any shape, 'every man is instantly on his legs'. There was no discussion, no mandate was sent forth, no apathy was shown, and no excuses were made. Every appeal was responded by 'benevolent action'. However, there was no need for such incredible alertness and promptitude in carrying out peaceful economic, social, and cultural activities, although the spirit of cooperation would have been quite helpful for these. This level of preparedness would not be essential unless such spirit was prompted by political necessity of defence. Thus, morung was valued by the hillmen for ensuring alertness, vigilance, watchfulness, or ever preparedness, with the spirit of cooperation. In other words, defence, protection against attack, and unity against rivals were the yardsticks, and hence it was political in character. If such discipline was inculcated and the morung continued to flourish even when the tribes were on good terms, then we can say that such esprit de corps was also but an antidote to the imminent dangers from the valley states. The fact that the system met its natural death after the occupation of the hills by the colonial state closely suggests that such an institution was founded against state control and ceased to become relevant once the state succeeded in controlling the stateless territory. In this sense, morung can be regarded as the hillmen's 'barrack', where the sentinels of stateless society were disciplined, hammered, and fielded.

[70] Owen (1844), as quoted in Elwin (1959: 40–1).

5

A Pleasurable Toil

Food, Freedom, and Livelihood

In 1873, an English merchant adventurer, T.T. Cooper, was deputed by East India Company government to take a journey from Assam to Tibet, through the Mishmee Hills, in order 'to open new routes for commerce', especially for Assam tea. A route through the Mishmee Hills was thought to be 'very practicable', the people were considered 'friendly'. Tibet annually imported about 6–8 million pounds of China brick tea. The prospect of his mission was very high as he had himself expressly floated the idea again and again. A sum of Rs 6,000 was unanimously voted towards defraying the cost of his mission. Before he started from Assam, his guide warned him of the 'dearth of food' in the hills. But he refused to listen because he thought he had enough money for his small party. He was accompanied by a guide, an interpreter, a cook, and a few coolies. To his surprise, he found that his guide was actually right. He had sufficient money but no one was willing to give him food even for an exorbitant payment. His party had to face starvation for many days. He narrowly escaped to the plain after a protracted struggle for life: daily fatigue against the massive friction of terrain, starvation, and the surliness of people. Inflicted with fever due to leech bites, he was literally carried by his coolies and would have died if not for his medical knowledge which saved him in time. He was, as he expressed, 'utterly exhausted'. The 'dearth of food' appeared to him an extreme one. He said that he had 'scarcely expected to find the Mishmees living such a hand-to-mouth existence' and 'they are often reduced to great straits for want of food'.[1] Before him, Wilcox had experienced a similar situation where his offer of triple payment, in kind, at Sadiya, or a large price in money, was unable to get him any supply from the hillmen.[2] Were the hills really suffering from a 'dearth of food'?

In 1876, H.M. Hinde, the Extra-Assistant Commissioner of Jaipur, who had assisted Lieutenant R.G. Woodthorpe, in-charge of Naga Hill Survey, reported that the Nagas were tired of them. He said that the Nagas were 'by no means inclined to accord us the cheerful welcome we had received from them on our first visit'. They even refused to show them water. One old man said to them: 'Why should we show you water? Why are you here again? You said last time you were here you had come to make a map. What are you looking for now? *Have you no rice in your own village, that you travel about to eat?*'[3] These apparently sarcastic questions actually addressed and reflected the deeper current of the state of hillmen's mind in relation to travellers from the valley state. They reflected the apprehension commonly shared by them against the valley state officers, marauders, and travellers. And even if a state officer had a good explanation for his presence, he was always viewed with suspicion and his presence in the hills was thought to indicate an ulterior motive for rule, revenue, or wealth gathering. Thus, in 1870, when J.W. Edgar met Lushei chief, Khalkom, at Bepari Bazar in Lushai Hills, he said that despite giving 'full proof of his amicable intentions ... still the predominant feelings in Khalkom's breast were fear and mistrust'.[4] Wherever survey was carried out in the hills, it was seen as a prelude to control and revenue collection. 'Mistrust' of any visitors from the valley was central to the consciousness of the hillmen. Hence, food

---

[1] Cooper (1995 [1873]: 206–7).

[2] Wilcox (1873: 60).

[3] NAI, FP (A): January 1877, Nos 146–51, Appendix C: H.M. Hinde to Lt. R.G. Woodthorpe, 7 May 1876; emphasis added.

[4] *Pioneer* (newspaper), 19 July 1870, as quoted in Mackenzie (2007 [1884]: 566).

or any kind of supplies would be refused to them so that there was a 'dearth of food' everywhere, although it could be seen in heaps in the hillmen's granaries and there was always something for starving hill travellers.

Studies of the hill economy during the colonial period, which continue to dominate our understanding of the situation even today, supported the notion of 'subsistence economy' revolving around jhum cultivation, described to be 'primitive mode of agriculture', a 'rude system', and a 'very wasteful method of cultivation'.[5] Three contradictory arguments were given. Hill people were described to be extremely poor, wretched, and overworked population, working very hard for a 'bare subsistence' through the year, with no leisure time.[6] Second, they were described to be extremely poor and destitute: they lived a 'hand-to-mouth existence' and in 'permanent scarcity'.[7] Third, they were said to be extremely poor because of their 'inferior' technology, 'indolent' habits, and the habit of 'improvidence'.[8] This was

[5] Such descriptions can be seen in most ethnographical works and other reports of colonial period. See, for example, Butler (1978 [1855]: 126, 132, 135), Cooper (1995 [1873]: 228–9), Hutton (1921b: 59–60), Parry (1988 [1931]), Playfair (1998 [1909]: 34), Shakespear (1998 [1912]: 31–3), and Smith (2002 [1925]: 40). See also, for instance, various official reports like NAI, FP: 6 March 1837, No. 67: Griffith to Jenkins, 20 January 1837, 28 March 1845, No. 141: Lt. Rowlatt to F. Jenkins, 1 January 1845, and 24 August 1844, No. 36: Wood to Sturt, 14 April 1844.

[6] Mills even said that 'every day is like the last' and 'one day is much like another'; and Parry remarked that 'his day is full, and he has no opportunity of experiencing the boredom of having nothing to do'. See Mills (1982 [1937]: 126–7, 2003 [1926]: 160–1) and Parry (1988 [1931]: 75). See also Rowney (1882: 167–75), as quoted in Elwin (1969: 101), Hutton (1921b: 116–18), Lewin (1978 [1870]: 142), Robinson (1975 [1841]: 389), Shakespear (1998 [1912]: 16), Stewart (1855: 636), and von Fürer-Haimendorf (1969: 38).

[7] See, for instance, Cooper (1995 [1873]: 206–7), Hutton (1921b: 59–60), Parry (1988 [1931]: 75), and Smith (2002 [1925]: 45).

[8] See Butler (1847: 157–8), Cooper (1995 [1873]: 206–7), Hutton (1921a: 104), Lewin (1978 [1870]: 142), Parry (1988 [1931]: 75), Pemberton (2000 [1835]: 17), Playfair (1998 [1909] : 4), Shakespear (1998 [1912]: 16–17, 31–2), Smith (2002 [1925]: 45), and Stewart (1855: 636).

a value-loaded civilizational discourse which saw the hill economy not in terms of what it had but in terms of what it *lacked*—lacking state, lacking surplus, lacking market, lacking technology, and lacking industry. It was a state of incompleteness.[9]

However, such arguments are decidedly inconsistent and contradictory. On the one hand, the hill people were described to be perpetually engaged in back-breaking work throughout the year for a bare subsistence, and on the other hand, they were shown to be extremely lazy, idle, and indolent. Similarly, they were also described to be poor, wretched, and destitute on the one hand, and extremely improvident, extravagant, and prodigal on the other. The truth is that it cannot be both; these are self-defeating statements. Either a person depends on subsistence economy, spending full time in search of meagre food, or else he does not depend on subsistence economy and enjoys plenty of food and leisure time. Similarly, one cannot be simultaneously poor and prodigal, wretched and improvident, or destitute and extravagant. Either one remains poor and has no means of being extravagant or one leads a prodigal life without being wretched and destitute.

Further, this notion of technology is also decidedly civilizational. The hill people were said to be poor or lack surplus because they *lacked* technology or their technology was 'inferior'. They practised at least three methods of cultivation: *jhumming* (dry shifting cultivation), *panikhet* (wet terraced cultivation), and *lailo* (dry terraced cultivation). Universal implements of husbandry were dao, hoe, some wooden and bamboo implements, and in some cases, axe and sickle. These few, simple, rude, and primitive implements, as the expression goes, were said to be 'inferior' because they were different from the technology seen in the 'civilized' valley states. But to see the differences in the context of superior–inferior complex and reduce the hill technology by calling it 'inferior' to that of the plains is to deny the logic of *efficiency* and the cultural value attached to such implements. Pierre Clastres argued that technique/technology can be best understood not in terms of men's absolute mastery over nature but their mastery over the natural environment 'suited and relative to their

---

[9] For a detailed discussion on this subject, see, for instance, Clastres (1977 [1974]), Freid (1975), Kuper (2005), and Scott (2009).

needs'.[10] *Satisfying one's needs* have become the keywords for technology. Therefore, the only measure of how well a society is equipped with technology is its ability to meet its needs in a given environment. In line with this thinking, I will discuss the jhum economy as practised in stateless hill society and explain why the hillmen chose this method of husbandry. Before that, a brief discussion on their notion of wealth is necessary.

'Who Will Give Us if He Does Not': Wealth as Communal Resource

As in many culture, wealth was understood broadly in two ways among the hill tribes of Northeast India: alienable and inalienable. In the Kuki-Chin world, for instance, there was a concept of '*nei-le-gou*' (literally, property and heirloom). Under the category of *gou* (heirloom) came some of their priceless and inalienable possessions, like offspring, land, gongs, ornaments, and trophies. They were to be passed on from generation to generation. The centrality of offspring and land was significant. Sometimes, certain valuable items, say, gun, could also be called gou, although they were substantially *nei* (property). All the other possessions of a person came under nei which was alienable. Both nei and gou constituted the wealth of a person. Although a person could be very rich, his house was called 'empty' if he had no son, or he was called *ingam* (literally, house-empty). Similarly, in a purely agrarian society, one could not live in the hill village without a land to cultivate. As long as a person lived in a village, the use of land and forest resources could not be refused. Among the tribes following chieftainship, the village land exclusively belonged to the chief as owner of the land. Yet, no one can be refused the use of land and resources for livelihood that support the family. Refusal in this case is 'uncustomary' and each individual, in a way, assumed it as a right not to be refused. Among the tribes following 'democratic' village government, land was divided into clan and common land (sometime added by chief land, among Khasis). While clan (chief) land was exclusive to clan members, common land belongs

---

[10] Clastres (1977 [1974]: 161).

to the whole village community in which all assumed the right of use. In all the cases, each village had their own modicum of use or set of rules, in which the preservation of natural resources was at the pinnacle of practices. It was the responsibility of each individual to maintain the rules while they used the resources for the benefits of the family. Under the circumstances noted, one can talk of shared or common resource, if the term communal ownership is a little tricky. The normative value of wealth as common resource thus remains. Overall, resources or the wealth of the hills were what we know them as 'the commons', accessible to, and managed by, all individuals for personal and collective benefit of the village community.[11]

A simple way to understand the wealth of the society as common resources of the people, and how their distribution took shape in the society, is by looking at the system of wealth accumulation and redistribution. The egalitarian hill society, for instance, normatively talked about equality in all respects. However, this principle did not stop a person from accumulating wealth and becoming rich. In fact, it was the natural aim of everyone to become rich in their lifetime. Thus, there were generations of rich men in the hill society whose wealth became legendary in the local society. Yet, the object of such wealth accumulation in the hills was different from what is normally understood. Here, wealth was considered to be a communal resource and if a person accumulated beyond a reasonable level, he was expected to redistribute it to the needy through 'charity' or to the people at large by throwing communal feasts. In this sense, wealth was accumulated in the hills only to be redistributed to the people. To the extent that a person would redistribute his wealth, his name and fame, or his defamation, would be celebrated, or ridiculed, in the local society. So, wealth was, instead of an economic capital, seen to be a social capital and, among certain tribes, a cultural capital as well.

The distinguishing character of the rich people in the hill society was broadly philanthropic and prodigal. They considered their wealth not as an economic capital meant to generate more wealth, but as a social capital to gain social recognition as 'big man' and as

[11] There is a lot of literature on 'the commons' since the past few decades. See, for instance, the classic exposition of 'the commons' by Ostrom (2015 [1990]).

the citizen of the 'abode of bliss' in the next. 'Charity' was seen to be one important channel to redistribute wealth and attain fame. It took the form of 'help' given by the rich to the poor in the shape of, say, food, rice, meat, and clothes. Thus, every rich man or the chief of the village would consider giving charity as a social obligation. The society, in turn, was also expected to give charity in the form of gifts or presents to the chief. T.H. Lewin, for instance, noted that the Lusheis considered 'any presents given to the Chief are common property' and 'his people walk off with them' whenever they needed them. He quoted them saying: 'He [chief] is a big man, and will get lots more given to him. Who will give us if he does not.'[12] He went on to say that the chief's house was 'a harbour of refuge' for the poor and needy.[13] Shakespear (1892) similarly remarked that the 'chief house was the house of charity'. The normative value of economic relation in the hills was that 'help' could not be refused when it was sought. Thus, if a man 'helped' in charity, he would be celebrated as 'big man' or 'wealthy man' (*haosa* in Kuki). However, if he refused to 'help', he would be frowned upon as 'greedy' (*milop*) or 'stingy' (*kilose*, literally, earning-bad), or people would spew slandering lines like '*hao ngailou hao anai*' ('wealth is pain'). People would stop going to his house, 'refuse to eat with him', even stop speaking to him, and so on. This 'public mockery' would not only cause him to 'lose face' but would also, very soon, tarnish his name in the local society, which would make him miserable. If he was a chief, his people would desert him and he would be a king without subjects. If he was an ordinary rich man, the public act of disagreement and backstage accusation would be so strong that he would eventually give up his wealth for public consumption.

Interestingly, 'charity' also operated within the principle of 'cooperation and reciprocity'. For instance, the Kukis used the term '*kithopi*' when they sought 'help' from the chief or someone else. *Kithopi* literally means 'to loop-upon' or 'double-up', which means 'to cooperate' or 'to assist'. Thus, when a person sought help, he said, 'please cooperate/assist', not 'please help'. Similarly, when a person 'helped', he uttered, 'I cooperate/assist', not 'I help'. This verb

---

12 Lewin (1978 [1870]: 140).
13 Lewin (1978 [1870]: 141).

invoked the principle of 'cooperation and reciprocity', within which the term 'help' ('to cooperate') implied an equivalent (if not identical) return of favour by the recipient at some later date. To make this 'return' journey clear, consider the case of the giver of help seeking help from the receiver and not receiving it. In that case, the giver would invariably invoke what he had given originally, hence causing serious conflict between the two. Thus, help was two-directional and 'repayment' was structured within 'help' itself. One example of this was the 'gifts' or 'presents' given to the chief by the villagers. Here, the circle of 'help' given by the chief and the 'return' with 'presents' clearly identifies the channel through which communal wealth flowed. People pooled their wealth into the chief's granary as 'presents' and 'walked off with them' whenever they needed it in the shape of 'help'. If the chief risked his chiefdom by refusing 'help', the villagers risked expulsion from village by refusing 'return' or 'presents'.

In the above-mentioned context, 'charity' was not a disinterested act but actively interested and obligatory behaviour, just as 'presents' was. It was, as Marcel Mauss noted among many 'archaic' society, a 'formal pretence and social deception'.[14] Thus, when the chief proclaimed himself as a great philanthropist and people uttered, 'who will give us if he does not', it was a mere 'pretence' and 'social deception'. This was mainly because the chief knew that he could not refuse 'help' and the poor man knew that it was his right to receive 'help' from the chief/rich man. The whole episode of 'help' and 'presents' operated within the normative order of an egalitarian society, governed by the principle of cooperation and reciprocity. As the principle of 'return' or 'repayment' was inbuilt within the system of 'help' or 'charity', the conceptual equality between the giver and receiver was sustained and the domination of the former over the latter evaporated.[15]

The second major mechanism of redistribution was communal feasting and festivities. Take the case of the famous 'feasts of merit' common to all tribes. It was a series of progressive feasts given by a

[14] For a classic discussion on the nature and forms of 'gifts' in 'archaic' society, see Mauss (1966: 1).

[15] This system of exchange reminds us of the situation in Malay peasant society. See the classic work of Scott (1985).

rich man to the whole village community for several days. It involved considerable expenditure for the giver (called performer) in the form of rice, meat, drinks, and other properties. This occasion was strictly an occasion for redistribution of wealth to the people, in exchange of which the performer received the highest distinction the society could give in this world (universal to all), in addition to a greater comfort in the next world (among some tribes). He would be decorated with certain warrior insignias, such as special clothes (common) and tattoos, in addition to a window (Lushei and Garo), forked posts (common) in front of his house (see Figure 5.1), and so on.[16] Among the Angamis and cognate tribes, noted Shakespear, 'the performers of these ceremonies seem almost a class apart'.[17]

The 'feasts of merit' was strictly a redistributive performance not only because of the lavish expenditure in providing feast for a large people but also for the fact that the wealth of the performer was actually distributed among the people. For instance, among certain tribes,

Figure 5.1 Khawtlang Forked Post in Lushai Hills
Source: Shakespear (1998 [1912]: 64–5).

[16] For a general discussion on these 'feasts', see Shakespear (1922: 274–81).
[17] Shakespear (1922: 278). See also Shakespear (1998 [1912]: 87–90).

the wife of the performer performed a symbolic act of distributing wealth to the people by throwing down things from a raised platform or palanquin. Among the Lusheis, for instance, real, good items like gongs, brass basins, money, clothes, and other things were thrown down from a platform not only by the wife but also the performer, his family members, and some village elders. Among the Lakhers and Fanai, the throwing was merely symbolic: Lakhers took back the real items thrown and the Fanais just used symbolic gifts.[18] Thus, the 'feasts of merit' literally cleansed the accumulated wealth of the rich man such that his wealth was reduced to the normal level. However, this lavish expenditure was not without a reward. The reward was in the form of distinct social recognition as 'big man' (if not to dominate others) and spiritual solace in the next world.[19]

In the sense noted in both the cases, one can say that the wealth accumulated by a person in stateless society was a social and cultural capital, rather than economic. It was not related to markets, but constituted a common wealth of the community. If every prodigal was 'a public enemy' and every frugal 'a public benefactor' in Smithsonian terms in a capitalist society, then the reverse was exactly true for the stateless society. Within this notion of wealth as a communal resource, I will now locate the various economic activities of the hillmen in stateless society.

Time, Work, and Labour

A researcher working on jhum cultivation in the hills would be mesmerized by the mosaic of knowledge inherited by the *jhumers*. Almost every question asked would be answered with authority and accuracy, including the relationship between the size of land, labour, seeds, forest and soil types, and harvest. They would be decidedly the best authority on all these counts. However, the issue of concern here

---

[18] See Parry (1988 [1931]: 376–7, 2009 [1928]: 107–8).

[19] Among the southern tribes, a person who performed 'feasts of merit' had the spiritual licence to enter *Pial-ral* or *Peogal* (beyond mithikho, village of the death), which was understood as the 'abode of bliss' where 'food and drink are to be obtained without labour'. See Shakespear (1998 [1912]: 62–4).

is work, labour, and leisure in relation to time. If you ask a person about the size of his jhum field, he would tell you in terms of number of workdays or number of seeds sown, and not by any modern measurements. A Kuki, for instance, would tell you that the size of his land is 'such-and-such *tha*' (literally, flesh/energy, meaning physical labour a person can do in one day). If he says 30 tha, it means the size of his land is what 30 persons can cut in one day or one man in 30 days.[20] In a rugged landscape, this is, I think, by far a more scientific and accurate way of expressing than an actual measurement. What is interesting is the centrality of tha (labour) in his worldview when it comes to work. Even more interesting is the fact that when he uses the term tha or labour, it is always related to work (*na-toh*, literally, work-doing) and 'work' (*na*) is always invariably related to agriculture work (*lou natoh*).

Thus, tha is used in *khotha* (village labour in jhum), *haosatha* (labour for the chief in jhum), *kithaneh* (eating-labour together or cooperative labour in jhum), and so on. If he is going for agriculture work, he would say, 'I am going for labour' (*tha-kon*, literally labour-going/doing); and if he is going for non-agriculture works, he would say, 'I am going for such-and-such thing' (say, hunting, fishing, trapping, trading, and so on), not tha-kon. Similarly, if a person is engaged in agriculture work, he would say 'I am working' or 'I am doing work' (na-toh or *tong*, literally work-doing); and if he is engaged in non-agriculture works, he would say, 'I am doing such-and-such thing' (say, hunting, fishing, trapping, trading, and so on), not na-tong. Thus, to the hill people, 'work' and 'labour' means agriculture. In other words, all other works not related to agriculture are not 'work' and the labour they endure with such works is not 'labour' in the conceptualization of 'work' and 'labour'.[21]

Therefore, the opposite of tha (labour) is *tha-kichol* (literally, labour-easy, meaning leisurely labour); not 'no-labour' or 'rest'. Similarly, the opposite of na or na-toh (work) is *choldo* (literally,

---

[20] This is the older expression. Today, people are more used to speaking in terms of the amount of seed sown, often expressed in terms of *tin* or basket. This is an ordinary way of expressing among the common folks.

[21] A person not willing to work in agriculture is called *thase* (literally, labour-bad, meaning lazy).

tire-easy, meaning leisurely work); not 'no-work' or 'free'. The term 'easy' in both 'labour-easy' and 'tire-easy' connotes a lesser labour and lesser work, which means a non-engagement in agriculture or engagement in non-agriculture works is considered to be 'easy', although the fact of the matter may be different. What is 'easy' in the context of the hills division of work and labour relates to non-agriculture works and is, in turn, related to 'leisure', not 'rest'. There is no place for 'rest' or 'laziness' in the conceptualization of time, work, and labour in tribal universe. Idleness is itself a form of labour and occupies large part of their time. Thus, even when they are engaged in leisurely mannerisms, such as the loafing around the village, smoking, drinking, gossiping, talking scandal, or basking in the sun, or in the feasts and festivals, the hillmen consider themselves to be engaging in something else. Truly, no person, except children, remains idle even when s/he is engaged in gossiping at the 'gossip platforms' of the village; their hands will be always engaged with something, say, basket-making and so on, and the gossip itself is important as part of a learning process. In this context, 'leisure' in the hills has a wider connotation. It is not only related to merrymaking during feasts and festivals but also when they are engaged with non-agriculture activities which normally do not have any pressure on tha.

The jhum exceptionalism with 'work' and 'labour' is not necessarily to indicate its 'monotony', but rather to put it on a high pedestal as the cradle of their livelihood strategy. Thus, every effort is made to 'enliven' this core livelihood practice, so much so that it also becomes leisurely instead of monotonous work. Thus, despite its tedious toil for a time, jhum cultivation has a pleasurable side for the hill people. Lewin, for instance, noted the 'pleasurable toil' of jhum cultivation in relation to the 'moiling toil' of the 'monotonous cultivation of the dwellers in the low-lands'. He rightly noted the pleasurable 'surroundings', such as the shade of jungles, the lofty eminence, rich and varied scenery of the forest, and the hill breeze and the buzzing bees, that enlivened the spirit of hill people. More importantly, he talked about the role of cooperative labour system which 'enlivened' the spirits, 'lightened' the labour, and rendered the work 'pleasurable': 'He is surrounded by his comrades; the scent of the wild thyme and the buzzing of the forest bee are about him; the young men and maidens sing to their work, and the laugh and joke goes round as they sit down to their mid-day meal under the shade of some great mossy forest tree.'[22]

This is also what most ethnographers had noted among different tribes during the colonial period. Von Fürer-Haimendorf, for instance, noted the Konyaks 'cooperative labour system': 'To enliven the monotonous task of weeding, boys and girls of different morung joined forces and worked side by side ... Many romance began in the rice fields at weeding time, and wherever such mixed labor groups were at work, there was much laughing and joking.'[23] The fullness of social life in jhum field was, therefore, the rule rather than the exception, so much so that the idea of wretchedness and monotony at work was unfounded. Von Fürer-Haimendorf even remarked that 'the social life of the village was transferred to the fields', where family worked with family and 'labor gangs' were employed on a basis of 'cooperation and reciprocity'.[24] In the southern hills, whole village communities, except the old and infirm, usually transferred themselves to the jhum houses and lived there until the agriculture season was over, except on certain 'genna' and 'festivals'. The social life in the field revolved around the 'labour gangs'. It was due to all this 'pleasurable toil' that one may talk of leisure in jhumming.

The actual time spent in 'work' and 'labour' (that is, in agriculture) would conspire to give the idea of overworked wretches and monotony. Several studies across the globe have shown that the so-called tribal societies were one of the happiest communities, with maximum amount of leisure time at their disposal. In contrast to the dominant discourse, they engaged with work for a relatively short time to get their food supply. They worked for an average of three to four hours a day to satisfy their requirements. Clastres noted that the 'Indians devoted relatively little time to what is called work. And even so, they did not die of hunger.'[25] This was also the case with the Northeast tribes, whose actual engagement with 'work' (that is, agriculture) was for a little time and they got plenty of time for leisure and other activities. Evidences from colonial ethnographic

---

[22] Lewin (1978 [1870]: 14–15).
[23] von Fürer-Haimendorf (1969: 33–6).
[24] von Fürer-Haimendorf (1969: 36).
[25] See Clastres (1977 [1974]: 163–4).

data show an average of five to six months of relaxation from strenuous agriculture works, and hence plenty of time for leisure if they so desired.[26] This average goes up if one considers the actual working hours or days a particular cultivator would invest in a year to meet his ends.

The sample collected from different parts of the Manipur Hills in recent times presents an interesting case (see Table 5.1).[27] The broad figures arrived from the study of actual working days for an individual in all stages of jhum cultivation show roughly an average of 118 days for tree forestland and 111 days for bamboo forestland. Generally, these workdays ranged from 100 to 130 days depending upon the size of the family. It was during such working days only that the hillmen had their 'pretty full day' work, not the whole-year round as it is believed. If this data is taken seriously, then it can be said that the hill people have plenty of 'leisure' time, say 235–65 days in a year, to attend to non-agriculture activities or leisure. This time can also be utilized for surplus production, if they so desire.

The contemporary data, inserted here for comparison, is rather in a degenerative form considering the increasing shortage of land for jhum and the deteriorating forests, although the method of husbandry remains unchanged and technology also remains more or less the same. But it is evident that jhum cultivators still have plenty of time for 'leisure' in a year. This can be used for merrymaking, or sitting idle, or if they wish, for hunting and fishing expeditions, repairing house, engaging in handicrafts, organizing trading expeditions, and so on. Besides, this time can be used for surplus production in the field if they so want. Therefore, to say that the hill economy was 'monotonous', 'subsistence', and lacking any 'leisure' time is to merely follow an epistemic violence of the dominant colonial discourse.

---

[26] See Hutton (1921b: 59–67), Mills (1982 [1937]: 75–89, 2003 [1926]: 110–24), Playfair (1998 [1909]: 34), Shaw (1997 [1929]: 88), and von Fürer-Haimendorf (1969: 29–37).

[27] Table is based on case study carried out in some villages in four hills districts of Manipur in 2014. Criteria of villages chosen were bad connectivity, distance from markets, and full-time engagement in *jhum* cultivation as source of livelihood. I am grateful to Nemminthang Lhouvum for assisting me in collecting data.

Table 5.1 Average Annual *Actual* Workdays for an Individual in Jhum Field

Jhumming Phase	Full-grown Tree Jungle (months)		Average Workday (called *tha*) by One Person	Full-Grown Bamboo Forest (months)		Average Workday (called *tha*) by One Person
	Zoulou	Simlou		Zoulou	Simlou	
Cutting (*louvat*)	December	January–February	15	February	March	10
Burning (*louhal*)	March/April	March/April	1	March/April	March/April	1
Clearing (*mongse*)	April	April	9	April	April	4
Sowing (*butu*)	May–June	May–June	15	May–June	May–June	15
Weeding–1 (*aham* or *hampi*)	June–July	June–July	17	June–July	June–July	17
Weeding–2 (*athol*)	August–September	August–September	13	August–September	August–September	15
Weeding–3 (*aphoi*)	September–October	September–October	12	September–October	September–October	13
Reaping–1 (early rice or *changpal*)	October	October	4	October	October	4
Reaping–2 (late rice or *changtah*)	November	November	15	November	November	15
Transportation (average of 2 trips a day @ 7 tins)	November–December	November–December	17	November–December	November–December	17
Total average workdays in a year for one person			**118**			**111**

Source: Based on data collected from some villages in the hills of Manipur in 2014.

Note: *Zoulou*: higher-altitude fields; *Simlou*: lower-altitude fields.

Being Improvident, Being Prodigal

Despite spending so little time on jhum, there was a sense of plenitude in the hills. The idea of poverty and wretchedness was a stubborn prejudice. Most colonial observers were stunned to see that scarcity was 'rare' and famine was something 'unknown' to the hill people. Famine did not occur, they explained, because of the favourable and caring character of nature, the fertile soil, rich forest reserves, and so on. Among the Garos, for instance, Playfair noted:

> There can hardly be another aboriginal tribes in India more easily circumstanced than the Garos. *Real famine never touches them*, for even if the rice crop fails, they have so many other cereals and *edible roots* on which to fall back, and the jungle supplies them with so many more of the latter, that it must be a bad year indeed when the Garo has to go hungry.[28]

Similarly, Dalton remarked of the Abors that 'seasons of scarcity are rare with them'.[29] Mills also noted that among the Aos, 'though times of scarcity occur, real famine is rare or unknown'. Famine occasionally (once every 20–30 years) visited the southern hills of Northeast India due to natural bamboo flowering cycle leading to disproportionate growth of rat population that invariably fell on the standing crops. Yet, this apart, scarcity was rare and famine was generally unknown there too.[30]

If famine was rare, scarcity relatively unknown, and people engaged in agriculture for a relatively short period, then the idea of poverty and wretchedness in the hills falls on hard ground. People rather spent more time in activities other than agriculture. Evidences show that the hill people, despite giving little time to work, had plenty of food to eat, enough to support them for at least a year with all sense of plenitude. This plenitude was expressed most profoundly in their habit of what was known as 'improvidence'. Most colonial ethnographic accounts attested the fact that the hill population, in

---

[28] Playfair (1998 [1909]: 4); emphasis added.
[29] Dalton (1960 [1872]: 31).
[30] Mills (2003 [1926]: 107); Nag (2007).

general, had their daily three full meals (morning, noon, and evening); and drinking rice beer (*zu*) was universal. There was also a long chain of rituals and ceremonies, feasts and festivals; the famous 'feasts of merit', mentioned earlier, was a celebrated custom. Besides, people gave huge amount of their wealth in charity and in appeasing the ever-seeking malevolent spirits. Some of them also took their jhum produces to the frontier markets (hats) for exchange with valley goods. If the idea of surplus meant something beyond what one needed for survival or beyond his daily meals, then the series of expenditures on drinks, rituals, charity, feasts, and festivals may be taken as surplus. Indeed, expenditure on these counts was usually very high, so much that one can actually talk about production beyond subsistence. All these expenditures were borne by their poly-cropping agriculture project, commonly called jhum. Thus, it was by no means a primitive accumulation but an accumulation which presupposed an affluent society.

Two important factors contributed to this affluent lifestyle: production and productivity of the land. On the first, the poly-cropping pattern in jhum cultivation provided almost all the items the hillmen needed for survival. A multitude of crops was grown promiscuously on the same field, such as rice (staple to most tribes), millet and Job's tears (staple to Changs), taro (staple to Konyaks), maize, arum, yam, sweet potatoes, cotton, tobacco, and a range of most cereals and vegetables.[31] In this, the predominance of root crops was significant. They not only cultivated root crops in large amounts but also developed a peculiar tradition of dribbling a seed on the same ground after harvest, only to remain there without further attention. These seeds continued to grow wild in the old fields and also the forests, leading to certain forests studded with remains of root crops.[32] These

---

[31] See, for instance, Carey and Tuck (1987 [1896]: 210), Gurdon (2010 [1906]: 43–8), Hutton (1921a: 76–7, 1921b: 60–1), Lyall (1997 [1908]: 10–11), Mills (2003 [1922]: xxix, 56–8, 2003 [1926]: 124–3), Parry (1988 [1931]: 75, 81–2), Playfair (1998 [1909]: 45–7), Shakespear (1998 [1912]: 32), and Shaw (1997 [1929]: 87–8).

[32] The only enemy of these root crops was wild animals. But it is interesting to note that the wild animals also had the habit of leaving a certain amount of what may be also called 'seed' on site, just as the hillmen did.

underground edible roots formed a huge food reserve that the hill-men normally banked on during scarcity. Therefore, a very strong sense of 'food security' was seen in the hills, though most colonial ethnographers stated otherwise.

The fertility of the soil was also central. Francis Buchanan (later Hamilton), for instance, noted that an ordinary family could easily raise 100 baskets of rice besides cotton, yams, arum, tobacco, and others in proportion.[33] He, therefore, felt that the hills were able to 'maintain many thousand inhabitants in ease and abundance'.[34] Shakespear also noted the average yield of rice in a jhum was 50 baskets for each basket of seed, and where the soil aspects were good, 100 baskets, and in exceptionally good years, 150 baskets.[35] Certain hills, like the highland plateau of Khasi Hills, were relatively less productive for rice; yet they still received a good yield from the soil. One study put it at 9.4 mounds of rice per acre.[36] This 9.4 mounds is about 773 pounds, which was not very small amount compared to the production figure for the valley of Assam, that is, 800–1,000 pounds per acre.[37] The combination of the two factors thus made life easy, affluent, and prodigal.

It is little wonder then that these hills produced successive gen-erations of rich people who performed the famous 'feasts of merit', which every village had more than one. In fact, Buchanan was sur-prised to see that the jhum cultivators 'have the good things of the world in greater abundance than the cultivators of the plains, or at least they are more willing to part with them'.[38] Lewin even went on to say that 'by his comparatively pleasurable toil, the hill man can gain two rupees for one which the wretched *ryot* of the plains can painfully earn'.[39] Generosity, or the will to part with what one

---

[33] van Schendel (1992: 88).

[34] van Schendel (1992: 133).

[35] WBSA, PP: August 1893, Nos 4–6, File No. L/49 (1–3): *Administration Report of South-Lushai Hills for 1892–93*, p. 17.

[36] See Gurdon (2010 [1906]: 44). The figure was the result of 667 experimental crop cuttings during 15 years preceding 1898.

[37] Guha (1991: 72).

[38] van Schendel (1992: 88).

[39] Lewin (1978 [1870]: 15).

has, can be both an act of plenitude as well as point to the world of surplus. Its essence, however, had more to do with a lived world order at the margins of the state, where saving and selling was not so much the concern but sharing and caring for the needy was central. If the hill village was 'full of grain, cotton, clothes, etc.,' during the post-harvest season, they were left with little or nothing before the next harvest.[40] Much of the surplus produce was used up for the series of expenditures noted earlier. Shakespear remarked that the hillmen were 'contented with their state, and have no desire to improve it'.[41] Thus, they exhibited perfect prodigal behaviour in Smithsonian terms.

The Art of Being 'Lazy': Healthy People, Happy People

Rigorous and season-bound activities, such as jhum cultivation, require ample time to *disconnect* from work to ensure health and happiness. In this respect, the hillmen had their peculiar 'disconnected time' from work. This important time of 'doing nothing' was often seen in derogatory terms by civilization. Thus, they were said to be lazy, idle, and indolent to the extreme. The problem was considered to be particularly severe among the men who passed their days in complete enjoyment, loafing about the village, lying in the sun, and assembling round the fire, smoking, drinking, telling stories, and talking scandal. After their crops were reaped, the village folks indulged in feasting and unrestrained merrymaking.[42] Thus, their 'disconnected time' related to extreme leisure moments, completely away from rigorous agriculture works.

The importance of 'disconnected time' from work has been gradually appreciated in many industrialized societies today. The Italians have a concept of good living called '*La Dolce Far Niente*' (the sweetness of doing nothing). It is the concept that ridicules our fear

[40] In 1850, Colonel Lister found that the Mullah (Ngura) village was full of grains. See WBSA, JP: 27 February 1850, No. 36.

[41] WBSA, PP: August 1893, Nos 4–6, File No. L/49 (1–3): *Administration Report of South-Lushai Hills for 1892–93*, p. 17.

[42] Hutton (1921a: 104), Lewin (1978 [1870]: 142), Pemberton (2000 [1835]: 17), Shakespear (1998 [1912]: 16–17), and Stewart (1855: 636).

of being lazy and teaches the smarter way to live and work. Some scholars feel that 'doing nothing' can indeed calm the soul, create peace of mind, and generate meaningful action.[43] Recognizing its importance for national health and wealth, countries like France have passed a law which gives citizens the 'right to disconnect' from office after office hours. Thus, for certain, the 'art of doing nothing' has found an increasing appreciation in the depressing world of 'businesses'. The search for peace from depression, creativity from redundantness, natural instinct from routine matter, and so on, has found its answer from doing nothing over a period of time between routine works. This is what the yogis and generations of ascetics were performing as a bodily practice since ancient times. Such innovation, such creativity, and such peace of mind has even outlived the storming modernization process. Therefore, if the tribal people of the great mountain massif in the eastern world were doing the same thing, it was not without substance. It gave rest to their bodies after tedious labour and helped to regenerate strength for the next season. More importantly, it avoided possible 'work fatigue' from the tedious agriculture work.

It may sound ridiculous when it is said that toiling over back-breaking jhum was 'pleasurable', but it would be equally ridiculous not to accept the fact that the hillmen were, instead of being wretched, half-starved, and overworked individuals, happy and contented human beings. The ability to produce sufficient food in a relatively little time, with sufficient amount of time for leisure, was at the heart of the happy population. In other words, the prevailing concept of 'disconnected time' or the meticulous dispensation of the art of doing nothing produced a happy and healthy population. The rich ethnographical data during the colonial period show that they were one of the healthiest populations, better than those living in the plains. The men were generally described to be strong, sturdy, powerful, and turbulent. The women were said to be squat, stout, strong, lusty, healthy, hardworking, and industrious. Despite high child mortality rate (due mainly to lack of proper childcare), the grown-up

---

[43] See Cliff Hsia, 'The Art of Doing Nothing', 9 September 2014, available at http://www.huffingtonpost.com, accessed on 5 April 2017.

children were described to be healthy and active beyond any human. There is not much data on the general lifespan of the hill population but a few passing references show an interesting health index. Lewin, for instance, noted: 'The average duration of age is from 70 to 80 years; but it is by no means uncommon to see among them white-haired and bowed old men, of whose age all count has been lost. Women die at a comparatively early age, owing to the constant labour, which their sex entails upon them.'[44]

If this is taken as the benchmark, then it can be said that the hill population were a healthy people. Healthy people are invariably happy people. In this context, the hill population were relatively an affluent community, enjoying sufficient calories of dietetic food, with reasonable level of labour and sufficient amount of leisure at their disposal. Carey and Tuck, for instance, noted:

> It is popularly supposed that the Chin is a wretched, half-starved, overworked and generally unhappy individual. The reverse is the case, and if we analyze his labour in agriculture, which is the hardest work he is called on to do, we find that in reality he has an easier time than the farmers in the west of America and in the colonies ... The Chin, instead of being pitied, is to be congratulated that he can make his living so easily ... and he has always three meals a day, a roof over his head at night, and all the clothing he needs.[45]

Surely, the hillmen deserve appreciation for being able to produce a happy life out of the rugged mountain topography. If not necessarily a prosperous life, the stateless hillmen certainly lived a relatively healthy and happy life.

Restricting Surplus, Limiting Choice

There were some interesting characteristics of hill agriculture. One interesting quality of the agriculture system was the hillmen's sense of 'a rooted disinclination' for surplus. As noted earlier, unless a person was striving to accumulate wealth for 'charity' and communal feasts,

[44] Lewin (1978 [1870]: 111).
[45] Carey and Tuck (1987 [1896]: 213).

the normative order of the society was to produce just for household consumption, not for the markets. Smith, for instance, noted that the Nagas did not prefer to become merchants and spent very little in the shops of Marwaris. Instead, each household 'produces practically all that is needed, so that it is practically independent, while beyond this limit very little is produced.'[46] In a worst-case scenario, among the hill tribes of Tripura, the 'surplus' from unexpected bumper harvest was not sold or taken to the markets but was left out in the jhum field for wild animals. Indeed, they refrained from producing anything beyond their wants—a practice they religiously followed. So great was their irritation regarding such surplus that they were described to have a 'rooted disinclination' to produce 'in excess of their immediate wants'.[47] The fact that they refrained from producing surplus for markets when market system was brought into the hills during the colonial period shows that excess production was, in principle, against their sense of living in the hills.

Another interesting characteristic regarding hill agriculture was the peculiar discriminatory economic behaviour of the hill people. They were receptive to certain new additions and opposed to others. For instance, with the entry of New World crops like maize (Indian's corn) and sweet potatoes, agriculture implements like axe and sickle were welcomed by the hillmen. The colonial state, meanwhile, was seriously attempting to transform the hill economy as part of its 'civilizing mission' by introducing new crops (wheat, tea, potato, apple, orange, garden vegetables, and so on), new methods of cultivation (wet rice, terrace, among others), and new implements (like plough). However, all the schemes failed. O.A. Chambers, while preparing an official *Handbook of Lushai Country*, for instance, lamented that 'several attempts to introduce plough cultivation have met with little successes'.[48] This was also the case with the Angami's terrace cultivation, where an attempt to introduce plough and cattle was a failure.

In the Khasi Hills, however, potato was partially successful. This was probably because of the poor out-turn of rice in those hills, as noted earlier (9.4 maunds per acre), which compelled them to import

---

[46] Smith (2002 [1925]: 39).

[47] See, for instance, Choudhuri (1996: 120 [vol. I], 37 [vol. II]).

[48] Chambers (1899: 61).

from the plains. In contrast, the out-turn of potato was five times the quantity of seed use (that is, 63 maunds per acre of 9 maunds seed used), which enabled them not only to export in great volume but also supplement the quantity of their staple rice immensely. Thus, until the appearance of potato disease in 1885–6, the export of potatoes from the Khasi Hills rapidly grew. For instance, in 1881–2, the export of potatoes was as high as 126,981 maunds; and from 1886–7, export gradually decreased until in 1895–6, when it touched as low as 8,296 maunds. This trend gradually picked again from 1900–1.[49] This success story of potatoes in Khasi Hills was rather an exception than the rule. In all other hill districts, such projects were not successful despite the fact that the soil profile there was also quite suitable for mass production. Indeed, the failure of all its schemes to 'improve' and 'enrich' the hill economy perplexed the colonial administration.

The hill people, in fact, had a strong 'passion' for their mode of agriculture. Lewin, for instance, noted that 'the hill people have a passion for their mode of life, and regard with absolute contempt any proposal to settle down to the tame and monotonous cultivation of the dwellers in the low-lands.'[50] This 'passion' was undoubtedly sweeping as they even refrained from adopting the method of their neighbouring tribes. Parry, for instance, noted the Lakher method of harvesting by 'pulling up the plants by the roots, and then beating the grain off the plants'. He called this 'clumsy and laborious' but a Lakher is, he remarked, 'very conservative, and prefers his old ways to new-fangled methods'.[51] This was also the case with Semas, Garos, Lynngams, and Bhois who refused to change their 'process of stripping the grain by hand', which is 'painful and causes much bleeding'.[52] Similarly, eastern Nagas like Changs and Konyaks refused to cultivate rice, although their land was quite suitable for it, and stuck to their staple crops, like millets, Job's tears, and taro.

---

[49] See Gurdon (2010 [1906]: 44).
[50] Lewin (1978 [1870]: 14–15).
[51] Parry (1988 [1931]: 81).
[52] See Hutton (1921b: 63–4), Playfair (1998 [1909]: 34), and Gurdon (2010 [1906]: 40).

Jhum as Agriculture of Escape

How can the peculiar economic behaviours of the hillmen be explained? As mentioned, the hillmen had plenty of time to produce surplus if they so wanted, but they restricted themselves to producing only for their household and had a 'rooted disinclination' to produce surplus for the markets. Some people did, however, produce large amount of surplus, only to give it back to the community through charity and communal feasts. The hillmen also highly valued the root crops which could grow with little attention in the harsh geography, but not those which required constant attention (say, potato). Besides, they regarded with 'absolute contempt' any attempt to change, enrich, or improve the existing method of cultivation, crops, and implements. But, at the same time, they graciously accepted certain new crops and implements. Their 'passion' for their mode of agriculture was also sweeping. The dominant colonial discourse expressed that all this was due to their 'laziness', 'indolence', and lack of 'industry'. As noted earlier, 'laziness' did not indicate disinterested behaviour. It can be further stated that laziness was not disinterested behaviour towards work in general, and to a particular kind of work in particular.

To understand these selective and discriminatory economic behaviours of the hillmen, a completely different kind of understanding is needed. James Scott, for example, showed that such behaviours were determined by the political choice they made in the hills as state-evading population. It was their 'agriculture of escape'.[53] Based on this line of thinking, the nature of the hill economy can be explained. For instance, it can be said that the hill people refused to produce surplus to keep the control of markets, state, raiders, and marauders out of the hills and to prevent social stratification based on wealth. Surplus necessarily demanded markets for circulation and it was clear that control and appropriations from state normally came through the market regime. Besides, stocking surpluses in heaps, and stocking them for future use or markets, also made a particular village vulnerable to attacks and raids from wealth-gathering marauders. Certainly, rich and prosperous hills acted as a bait for potential conquerors,

[53] See Scott (2009).

just as the poor hills structurally deterred raiders and conquerors in a big way. Wealth also restricted mobility and was, hence, against the normative values of the state-evading population who chose to move frequently. The 'dearth of food' in the hills was one of the most powerful deterring factors to invasion. This was testified by the various military expeditions into the hills during the early colonial period.

Production of surpluses and accumulation of wealth beyond a certain level were also a prelude of the formation of state and social stratification in the hills. In other words, the 'dearth of food' literally dismantled the formation of state in the hills. Though the advent of firearms in nineteenth century incited many hill chiefs to take up a new political formation process, the lack of sufficient surplus and a strong resistance from the stateless population did not let them form state in the hills.[54] Similarly, as mentioned earlier, if the chiefs or certain individuals accumulated wealth beyond the normal, the society would force them to redistribute it among the people through different mechanisms, such as 'charity' and communal feasts. Equality among all individuals in the hills was central to the hill social formation, and therefore prevention of economic disparity was considered to be central to such an egalitarian end. Thus, the hill people's choice for safety and social equality against wealth was evident; and it was because of this preference for freedom and security that they remained materially poor and not because they lacked time, technology, and industry.

There is a similar explanation for why they discriminated against certain crops, implements, and methods of agriculture. The hill people were quite aware of the implication of colonial 'civilizing' projects. It was known that the colonial idea of 'improvement' and 'enrichment' was aimed at changing their livelihood strategies, rather of improving it. The new agriculture scheme, which encouraged them to cultivate mainly cash crops, would have compelled them to depend on the markets for all means of production, for exchange of their produces, and even for their food items and other family requirements. This, in turn, would have strengthened the hold of state and

---

[54] In the context of the southern hills, I have discussed this elsewhere. See Guite (2011).

markets over their freedom. The idea of control through 'enrichment' was clear from the start. For instance, Francis Jenkins, Agent to the Governor-General, North-East Frontier, urged the Government of India to support Reverend Miles Bronson's scheme to introduce tea cultivation and other crops, like wheat, potatoes, cotton, and apples, in Naga Hills because it would 'bind the Nagas to the Company' and ensure that British 'supremacy gradually extended over the hills'.[55] Thus, if state 'enrichment' project was aimed at controlling the hill people more firmly through their food chain, the hillmen opposed the schemes to prevent market forces from controlling their food system. In other words, the hillmen avoided the cash crops so as to avoid depending on the valley markets for all their requirements and, in the process, protect their freedom.

They were receptive to certain crops like maize and sweet potatoes for different reasons. The popularity of these crops was not only due to their ability to thrive well in most ecological conditions, including different elevations, temperatures, and soil profiles, but, more importantly, because they were, as Scott noted, pro-mobility, pro-nomadism, and hence pro-state evasion. Both the crops matured quickly, had higher calorific value, were altitude friendly, needed little attention, and were less prone to disease. In addition, sweet potato was less accessible to raiders and marauders and could easily substitute rice and others in times of scarcity.[56] Besides, both of them were of less commercial value in the state space. Above all, these crops had the potential to replace their staple crop, rice or millet, and they did not require markets for their outlets as they could be consumed locally in large volumes. They were, like rice or millet, independent crops that ensured the freedom and isolation of the people in the hills. It was due to all these characteristics of adaptability and independence that they were quite popular in the hills.

The political character of sweet potatoes also emphasizes the importance of root crops for the state-evading hillmen. As noted earlier, the hill tribes had a typical tradition where, after harvesting

---

[55] See NAI, FP: 23 May 1846, No. 30: Major F. Jenkins to J.H. Maddock, Secretary to GOI, 14 April 1840, NAI, FP: 11 May 1840, No. 128: Reverend Bronson to Major F. Jenkins, n.d.

[56] See Scott (2009: 199–207).

the root crops, they dropped a seed on site, which remained there without further attention. This formed a huge reserve of food for the hillmen during scarcity. This hill 'food security' system was peculiar to the hillmen and as a result, there was hardly any famine or scarcity in the hills from natural processes. This now leads us to the political essence of this system. If the state-evading population in the hills were always on their guard against invasions from raiders and marauders from the valleys, then it makes sense to argue that such food security measure was also part of the same strategy. Scott noted that root crops, inarguably, repelled the control of the state as they, in general, survived the raiders and marauders by virtue of being hidden underground.[57] Therefore, when the British expedition parties 'punished' the hill people by destroying their villages and granaries (in the village as well as the ones hidden in the jungle), they were stunned to see that such 'punishment' did not cause famine, nor bring the hill people to submission. Instead, to the surprise of the same officers, the devastated villages soon regained their normal life. This was possible mainly because of the root crop reserves in the old fields and in the jungles. The case of Kuki Rising, 1917–19 is especially instructive in this respect. The Kukis fought the British forces for almost two years across the 7,000 square miles of rugged mountains, mainly surviving on wild roots and root crop remains in their old jhum fields that survived the colonial scorched-earth policy. The same mode of survival was visible during the Second World War in the region. Thus, the importance of root crops as their hidden food reserve, invisible and indestructible to empire's army, becomes clear.

The next question is: what was so special about jhum cultivation for the stateless hillmen? Jhum, undeniably, played an important role in 'dismantling' control and appropriations. As mentioned earlier, mobility and population dispersion were the central principles of state-evading hillmen, and jhum facilitated these concerns in a different way. When any individual found the chief becoming tyrannical or oppressive, he immediately migrated to another village to evade such control and oppression. This migration was easy and possible mainly, if not exclusively, because of jhum cultivation. The few and

[57] Scott (2009: 199–207).

simple implements of husbandry in jhum cultivation included the universal daos and hoes, and occasionally an axe, sickle, and other bamboo or wooden implements. Since these implements could be carried everywhere with ease and, with it, one could begin a new field with little amount of labour and capital sink, any household or individual who felt oppressed and threatened could easily move to a new village and start a new life. Therefore, the great political advantage of jhum over sali (wet rice) cultivation was due to the simplicity, efficiency, and effectiveness of these few implements. In this sense, jhum prevented control and oppression.

There was also another dimension of jhum cultivation. As mentioned earlier, a scattered and dispersive settlement across the hills was one strategy employed by the state-evading population to evade control and appropriations. As jhum required shifting the agriculture field annually or biannually, it mechanically dispersed the hill settlements into small, scattered villages. Until very recently, the average jhum cycle was put at around ten years or more. If this is taken as the benchmark, the land required for a single village would be always more than ten times greater than the land required by the same size of population in the plains. Suppose a medium-sized family in the hills requires, say, 5 acres of land in a year, then the same family would require 50 acres of land for agriculture rotation. This is a very large area of land for a single family. The land required by each hill village for jhum, forest reserve, sacred grooves, and hunting ground, would be, therefore, quite great. Thus, concentration of large population in a single village with jhum as their source of livelihood would be naturally difficult. As the population increased, it had to break up into smaller groups. Therefore, jhum, by its nature of shifting, mechanically dispersed the population across the hill landscape.

Another important factor for which the hillmen valued jhum cultivation was its ability to sustain forest cover, and hence ecological sustainability. If population pressure and commercialization have made jhum practice ecologically unsustainable today, we cannot say the same for the past. Thus, in a situation when rotation of jhum field took more than ten years, the practice of shifting cultivation hardly affected the forest cover permanently. Centuries of its practice neither removed forest cover nor disturbed its ecology, or fertility of the soil, to any great extent. Its ability to provide sufficient food and yet sustain the forest environment was undoubtedly one of the main reasons why the hillmen were so passionate about jhum. In fact, to condemn jhum cultivators as anti-environmentalist is not only to make a simplistic argument but also to expose our shallow understanding of the practice. Seen from their customary, religious, and livelihood practices, one can clearly see how the hillmen valued their forest and strived to preserve as much as they could. The forest, as noted earlier, played an immense role in the life of the hill people economically, culturally, and politically. Thus, in all possible ways, forest was central to their life. It was due to this that preservation of forest was central in their consciousness. For instance, there was a strong belief among all the tribes that every forest, sometimes every tree, has its own sylvan deities who need to be appeased before cutting or using it. Some tribes (for example, Lusheis) even believed that trees and plants were once human beings who transformed during the Great Darkness (*Thimzing*).[58] Thus, the idea of being 'rude' and 'reckless' to the standing forest did not arise.

The Kuki ritual of *Daiphu* is instructive in this respect. To seek permission or to appease the deities of forest, the Kuki priest (thempu), for instance, performed certain sacrifices: *tolthen* (cleaning the ground) before cutting the forest for jhum; Daiphu sacrifice after burning the field; and so on. William Shaw recorded Daiphu sacrifice as follows:

> After the field has been cut and burnt *Daiphu* is performed. For this the *thempu* has to make small earthen images of the following:- *Saipiha* (elephant's tooth), *So long nupa* (slaves), *Vengke* (Partridge), *Thoche* (Squirrel), *Shel* (Mithun), *Khichang* (Ear bead), *Langbel* (Mica). With these he takes an egg and some cotton and goes to the field and *asks Pathen to excuse the cultivator of that field for all the damage he has done by cutting and burning the land.* All the objects are then placed on the hole of a tree and the *thempu* then returns to the village. The day following nothing is done but the day after that the *thempu* goes to the field to see whether the objects which he placed there are still where he left them. If any of the images are missing or broken it means that someone of the household will either die or suffer illness *as Pathen has*

---

58 Shakespear (1998 [1912]: 93).

considered the damage done excessive. Consequently, *kilhalho* [sacrifice] will be performed in the village to ward off any ill effects which may be expected from the *thempu's* interpretation of the *Daiphu*.[59]

If cutting down the standing forest for jhumming was a necessary evil for survival, the fear of death or illness caused by *Pathen* (God) as a result of 'cutting and burning the land' and the 'excessive' damage done to the natural environment was but a powerful restraint against its reckless destruction. Among the Abors and Miris, Dalton also noted that they avoided 'breaking up fresh ground' for cultivation due to 'dread of offending the spirits of woods by unnecessarily cutting down trees'.[60]

Due to their earnestness to let the forest regain its full growth in the shortest possible time, the hillmen also followed a peculiar tradition of not cutting the bigger trees in the jhum field or merely looping or trimming its branches. This practice let the forest regain its growth sooner than if they were cut down entirely.[61] Hutton too remarked about 'the excellent Lhota practice of stripping the trees of all their branches and leaving a bunch of green leaf at the top so that the tree does not die, but branches out again when the two years' cultivation is finished'.[62] He went on to say that the 'value of the practice is obvious, as it gives the trees a chance of seeding and so of restocking the cleared ground and making it fit for jhuming again'.[63] 'Excessiveness' was something the hillmen avoided over the ages when it came to their natural environment. This was particularly because they wanted the forest to remain strong not only to sustain their livelihood strategies in the hills but also to provide maximum friction of terrain against control and appropriations from valley state conquerors and raiders.

---

[59] Shaw (1997 [1929]: 77); emphasis added.

[60] Dalton (1960 [1872]: 31, 38).

[61] Aos and Lhotas, for instance, 'merely lopped' and 'trimmed' or few branches were left 'uncut at the top'. See Mills (2003 [1922]: 46, 2003 [1926]: 110). This was also common among other Nagas and in the Kuki-Chin world.

[62] Hutton (1921b: 60).

[63] Mills (2003 [1922]: 46, fn. 1). Associated advantages were that it provided shade from the blazing noon sun, supported many high climbing vegetables, and so on.

Jhum provided them the best method of agriculture for both. Scott precisely put down the overall importance of jhum to state-evading population in relation to states as follows: 'Shifting cultivation was a sterile form of agriculture: diverse, dispersed, hard to monitor, hard to tax or confiscate. Swiddeners were themselves dispersed, hard to monitor, hard to collect for corvee labor or conscription. The features that made swiddening anathema to states were exactly what made it attractive to state-evading peoples.'[64]

The argument thus far takes us close to the current notion of 'food sovereignty'. For instance, the 'Declaration of Nyéléni' defines 'food sovereignty' as follows:

> Food sovereignty is the right of peoples to healthy and culturally appropriate food produced through ecologically sound and sustainable methods, and their right to define their own food and agriculture systems. It puts those who produce, distribute and consume food at the heart of food systems and policies rather than the demands of markets and corporations. It defends the interests and inclusion of the next generation. It offers a strategy to resist and dismantle the current corporate trade and food regime, and directions for food, farming, pastoral and fisheries systems determined by local producers and users ... Food sovereignty implies new social relations free of oppression and inequality between men and women, peoples, racial groups, social classes and generations.[65]

These important aspects of 'food sovereignty' are, I think, part of the familiar livelihood strategies of the hillmen in the past, in which jhum cultivation played a central role. The hill economy then was familiar with the concept of 'food sovereignty' in at least three important ways. First, the concept of 'food sovereignty' is about the control of food systems by the producers and resisting or dismantling the intrusion of 'corporate' food regime. Second, it implies a social relation free of oppression and inequality. Third, it projects the need for a sound and sustainable ecology for future generations. These three parameters were strongly present in the livelihood practices of the stateless hillmen, as noted earlier.

---

[64] Scott (2009: 191).

[65] For 'Declaration of Nyéléni', see https://nyeleni.org/spip.php?article290, accessed on 27 July 2016.

What, therefore, becomes evident from the above discussion is that the hill people in general were following, instead of a 'primitive' and 'subsistence' economy, an economy that was peculiar to the state-evading populations in the hills. They were, instead of wretched, half-starved, and overworked population, affluent communities who reaped sufficient amount of food (to eat, feast and drink, or to pay the chief or to feed the needy) from their *jhum* land with little amount of labour and within the existing implements of husbandry. They developed a 'rooted disinclination' to produce surplus and opposed introduction of new crops, implements, and methods of husbandry not because they were lazy but because they wanted to prevent the control and appropriations of markets and state. They chose jhum cultivation as it mechanically dispersed the population, permitted maximum mobility, prevented social inequality, ensured freedom from oppression and control, sustained the forest covers, and facilitated huge root crop reserves for any eventuality. Above all, jhum cultivation not only provided the state-evading population healthy and culturally appropriate food produced through ecologically sound and sustainable method, but also offered the right agriculture to prevent, resist, and dismantle state control and appropriations. In short, jhum cultivation epitomized the food sovereignty of the state-evading hill population in the highland massif.

6

Chiefs, Commoners, and the Babel of Tongues

When J.W. Edgar, then Deputy Commissioner of Cachar, was at Bepari Bazar in the Lushai Hills during his famous tour in 1870, Lushei chief Khalkom, son of Sookpilal, with his 200 strong warriors, visited him. His arrival was announced in advance by 'the clash of barbaric music chiefly gongs', as reported. He was brought in on a *dooly* (palanquin) and after the conference with the deputy commissioner, he was 'scuttled off in a dooly with visible symptoms of relief'.[1] Some weeks later Edgar met Sookpilal, one of the most powerful Lushei chiefs, and presented him with what the local tradition would call the 'robe of honour' (but deceptively reported as 'clad in gorgeous raiment to delight his barbaric soul'). It was reported that the chief was so excited that he 'grew, vain, smirked, grinned and finally fairly melted', and eventually 'flung himself on Hurri Thakur's neck and hugged him like an ecstatic bear'.[2] The interesting point is the parody that the hill chief mimicked the court culture of the valley

---

[1] *Pioneer*, 19 July 1870, as quoted in Mackenzie (2007 [1884]: 566).

[2] *Pioneer*, 19 July 1870, as quoted in Mackenzie (2007 [1884]: 568). The robe consisted of: 'green pyjamas with scarlet and gold flowers, a purple coat with green and gold embroidery, an indescribable hat of green and white silk, a necklace of glass buttons and gold beads, and two glass earrings.'

state/kingdom, such as the use of palanquin, a march with a clash of music and followers, and the excitement (honour) over the robe of honour. These were the symbols of power and status associated with the valley kingdoms.

Appropriation of such courtly symbols and gestures of the valley states by the hill chieftains was one of the political pretences in the hills in relation to the 'others'. There were many other such courtly insignias that were appropriated by the hill chieftains *as if* they were really powerful. Thus, a turban with a plume of king crow feathers, distinct apparels, choice of marriage, colour, and so on were kingly culture.[3] In many cases, they also assumed certain valley titles like raja, king, and so on. As noted earlier, distinctive clothes and other rights adorned famed warriors. The colonial state officers were also equally enthusiastic to define the hill chiefs as 'king', 'raja', 'rajah', or 'monarch' and their village polity as 'state', 'republic', or 'government'. Shakespear, for instance, defined the hill polity of Lushai Hills as: 'each village is a separate State, ruled over by its own *Lal* or chief.'[4] Lal was an important political title across the Kuki-Chin world, which was a common noun for 'king', 'lord', or even 'emperor'. It was adopted by the village chiefs as their title in relation to the commoners. In common people's expression, the term lal was always uttered with *leng* (king). Thus, when a person described the chief or the rich and wealthy people, in a slandering way behind their back, he would utter '*leng le lal*' (king and lord). It was also often used by the commoners on the face of the chiefs or wealthy people as the basis of appeal for 'help'. It was always the flattering self-image of the elites and even commoners.

However, the use of such state and civilization categories like 'state', 'king', or 'raja' to define the hill polities had its own political dynamics, which dangerously jeopardize our understanding of the hill political system. While the colonial specialist liked to see them as powerful or make the powerless look powerful, the hill chiefs also appropriated these terms so as to pretend to be really powerful among

---

[3] Dalton (1960 [1872]: 52), *Pioneer*, 19 July 1870 and *Observer*, 25 February 1871, cited in Mackenzie (2007 [1884]: 566–8, 572), McCulloch (1980 [1859]: 65), Reid (1976 [1893]: 226), and Shakespear (1998 [1912]: 10, 25, 49–50).

[4] Shakespear (1998 [1912]: 42–3).

their people. To the frontier officers, the success of making the hill chief as a 'despotic' authority was a travesty. It was aimed to create an enabling situation in which they may be able to rule over the hillmen through the powerful chiefs. So, they would always ask for a 'government' which could control the hills with an iron fist like the 'king'. This was justified by showing the hill chiefs ruling like the 'king' over the hill population, who were painted as 'turbulent' and 'lawless brigands'. Thus, Johnstone had little sympathy for the powerless Kuki chieftainship system that he defined as 'strictly monarchical, and their chiefs are absolutely despotic, and may murder or sell their subjects into slavery without murmur of dissent'.[5]

Many of the frontier officers in nineteenth century, such as Lewin, McCulloch, and Johnstone, were no doubt the product of English romanticism and believed in 'personnel government'. Act XXII of 1860 implemented in Chittagong Hill Tracts was an act that enabled the district officers to administer the hills 'suited to its conditions'. Thus, while many of Johnstone's friends considered his posting in Northeast frontier as 'punishment', he thought it otherwise. He was happy to be posted in a region where personal government could be effected. He said that he was 'one of those old-fashioned Anglo-Indians who still believe in personal government' and who felt that 'the machine-like system' of government was 'ill adapted to the requirements of these Oriental races, and blighted in its effects'. The type of government in the plains was, he remarked, 'distasteful to the native mind'.[6] By describing the hill polities as 'personal government' under the chief, these officers wanted to score the point that the new government under the British should also be just like that. There was, to be sure, no such government in the hills that could be called 'personal government' and the notion of 'despotism' they put in the character of the hill polity was largely unfounded.

The problem with such statist categories in describing the hill polities was that it imposed the idea that the hill chief was like the 'king' of the valley kingdom who treated the people as 'semi-slaves' or bonded 'serfs'. The logical conclusion was that there was no personal freedom, no social equality, and no freedom at all in the hills; and

---

[5] See Johnstone (1987 [1896]: 27) and Stewart (1855: 626).
[6] Johnstone (1987 [1896]: vii–viii).

the subjection, bondage, and oppression, which they had evaded in the valley, continued to be in full force in the hills. However, the reality was very different from these possible conclusions arrived at by employing such valley state categories. It was true that the hillmen had a clear notion of 'state', 'king', and 'warrior', but the way they conceived them in their worldview was quite different from the way they were represented in the dominant discourse. For the hillmen, their 'king' was dead but *he* was always remembered in many ways.[7] As mentioned in Chapter 2, most tribes once had their own 'king' or lived under another 'king' within the state. For them, king, kingship, state were thus just memories, and they struggled to prevent its formation and control in the hills. 'Kingship' as an institution was always understood to be despotic and authoritarian, and to be evaded.

In this context, one common adage in the Kuki-Chin world is instructive. A Kuki proverb says, '*lal ngailou lal anai*' (it is also sometimes said, 'hao ngailou hao anai'), which I translate as 'kingship is tyranny' (and 'wealth is pain'). The literal rendering of 'lal ngailou lal anai' means 'never in power is painful when in power', meaning power is corrupted by pain or oppression. Considering the predominance of 'king' in the consciousness of the state-evading population in the hills, I use 'lal' as 'king' here. Thus, in a narrow sense, the saying means 'he who was never a king will become tyrant if he be one'. In a broad sense, it means 'a king in the land of no king would be tyrannical/painful'. Both the senses presuppose 'kingship is tyranny'. Today, this proverb is used in myriad ways, connoting its popularity and dynamism in the Kuki-Chin world. It was used, for instance, in relation to village chieftaincy; and sometimes in relation to the leadership in new democracy, to the wealthy people, and so on. It was mainly used as a means of social control. Thus, when someone became unduly tyrannical or oppressive (or in the other sense, extravagant), this proverb was spoken to warn him in clear terms that it is unwanted/unwarranted/taboo.[8] In this sense, 'kingship' was seen to be hugely

---

[7] In Chapter 7, I will show from their oral traditions the profound presence of the idea of 'king', 'state', and a warrior ideology.

[8] Hmar also, for instance, use the term 'Remember Sinlung!' for the same purpose against anyone who becomes, or shows the intent to become, tyrannical in his dealing with other people.

corrupted by the idea of oppression, just as 'wealth' was also seen on the same lines. The popularity of the saying not only indicates how a society controlled, or was vigilant about, the intrusion or emergence of 'kingship' in the hills, but also determined its notion of, or its goal to preserve, a society free from control and oppression.

On the other hand, the term 'king' was also appropriated in different ways. Thus, an individual was spoken of as 'his own king', 'his own lord', and 'his own master'. To be one's own king was not to be only above everyone, or there was no one above, but also to assume the character of a 'king' whose was the final arbiter in all decisions related to his personal affairs. Thus, the idea of valley kingship now emanated from every individual. Similarly, the gesture that the 'subjected' showed to their 'king' in the valley was mimicked in many respects. Thus, the 'self devotion' and 'loyalty' the Kuki populace showed to their chief, who was the 'main branch of the original stock', was as if he was their 'king'.[9] But while such a gesture was appropriated and constituted the core cultural expression of the people to their pipa, it could not be construed in terms of domination relation as in valley state. Such an act of loyalty was a mere pretence, a symbolic gesture, the mimicry of the valley state practices. Thus, when the Khasis appropriated the term 'king' to mean their *syiem*, they did not construe him to be the tyrant 'king' of the valley kingdom. It was an act of giving self-importance to their institution and to themselves vis-à-vis the valley states. It was a self-actualization process. Overall, the term 'king' was appropriated not as the goal of society or individual in life, but to score the point that everyone must feel they are 'their own king'. It is from this line of thinking that would I like to proceed on a reading of the various political and social institutions and customs of the hillmen.

The 'Purest Democracy'

Egalitarianism or what is popularly known as 'democracy', with degrees of variation, was one set of polity prevailing among the tribes in Northeast India in the precolonial period. This was the case with

---

[9] Stewart (1855: 626).

some Nagas, Khasis, Abors, Dufflas, Mishmis, Garos, and so on. Each of the villages had a recognized head or chief assisted by elders or councillors among certain tribes, or just a body of councillors, to run the village administration. Among the Angamis, for instance, Butler noted that each village community has a head or chief whose 'authority is nominal' and whose 'orders' were obeyed when they accorded with the 'wishes and convenience' of the people. They 'do not collect revenue' and do not possessed any exclusive power against the person and property of individuals.[10] In this context, the position of the chief was what Butler called 'primus inter pares' (one among equals).[11] The chiefs were, according to Woodthorpe, 'chosen for their wealth, bravery, skill in diplomacy, powers of oratory, etc.'[12]

Among the Khasis, Robinson also noted that every village had its own chief who was 'king in name' and who obtained 'more than nominal respect', with 'powers being much circumscribed'.[13] Likewise, Abors and Karbis also had a recognized chief/headman (gam in Abors and sar-the in Karbis) who was 'chosen for his personal character by the householders' and who presided over the village council (me). Both of them also had a 'great council' (me-pi in Karbis) consisting of all headmen.[14] Among the Aos, there was no recognized chief but the village administration was run by a body of councillors (Tatar) which was manned by a peculiar age group system. The whole body of councillors went out of office at once, and no one could be re-elected however influential he might be.[15] Both the council system and nominal headship were followed by many other tribes in the region, thus making the 'democratic' form of polity the dominant form of political organization.

As just seen, each of these villages had a council headed by a chief. This council ran the village administration and presided over the

[10] Butler (1978 [1855]: 145–6).

[11] Butler (1875).

[12] Woodthorpe (1882: 68).

[13] Robinson (1975 [1841]: 410–11).

[14] Lyall (1997 [1908]: 22) and Robinson (1975 [1841]: 359).

[15] Mills (2003 [1926]: 183–4). The 'Old Kukis' also had a council manned by 'elected managers of the community'. See Butler (1978 [1855]: 81–2).

village assembly where all the members of the village participated. Among the Khasis, for instance, Robinson noted that the 'business of the state' was transacted 'at public meetings' in which 'subjects affecting the welfare of the parties, are canvassed, opinions advanced and maintained by the king and his counsellors, and the question decided by a majority'.[16] Among the Abors, he also noted that 'each clan or village forms a democratical republic by itself, and is governed by the laws enacted by all the inhabitants in a formal meeting.'[17] 'These singular people acknowledge', noted Wilcox, 'no other authority but that of the "Raj" or people generally, who make laws at the Councils, assembled in the Morang, where everyone has an equal vote.'[18] Lyall also noted among the Karbis that 'should the dispute not be settled in this manner, the majority prevails'.[19] Among the Garos, 'the village met in conference to decide any matter in dispute' and when 'evidence could not be adduced', the recourse was 'trial by ordeal'.[20] Therefore, it was the people at large, or their elected councillors, who met at the durbar to decide matters as the ultimate authority. In this context, the chief's position in all democratic systems, as Hutton noted among the Angamis, 'gave him no power except on the warpath' and while his leadership in war gave him much 'influence', it did not give any 'authority' in the village in times of peace.[21]

---

[16] Robinson (1975 [1841]: 410–11). Gurdon (2010 [1906]: 66–7) also noted that the Khasi Syiem's power was 'much circumscribed' because he 'can perform no act of any importance without first consulting and obtaining the approval of his durbar (executive council), upon which the state *mantris* sit'.

[17] Robinson (1975 [1841]: 359).

[18] Wilcox (1873: 51). For further account of Abor's 'Councils' at the morung (mosup in Abor language), see, for instance, the reports of Wilcox, Dalton, and Needham in *Selection of Papers*, pp. 49–51; also see Dalton (1960 [1872]: 26–33) and NAI, FE (A): March 1885, No 253: JF Needham to Deputy Commissioner, Lakhimpur, 27 October 1884.

[19] Lyall (1997 [1908]: 22). For Angamis, see Butler (1978 [1855]: 145–6).

[20] Playfair (1998 [1909]: 74). For Aos and 'old Kukis', see Butler (1978 [1855]: 81–2) and Mills (2003 [1926]: 183–4).

[21] Hutton (1921a: 142).

Thus, the position of the chief or headman did not give any power and authority and his orders were obeyed only when they were in accord with the 'wishes and convenience' of the individual and community at large. He *did not decide* but only *presided* over the village council or assembly, where 'everyone had an equal vote' and where questions were 'decided by a majority'. If evidence could not settle any dispute, they took recourse to 'trial by ordeal', which was considered to be sacred and absolute. If the chief did not possess any 'exclusive power' against the 'person or property of individuals', then it can be said that the system revolved around preservation of individual rights and freedom, not the chief or king power. Here, *individual* was so pronounced that even when questions were decided by majority vote, an individual or minority could disown such a decision if he/they thought otherwise. Among the Angamis, Butler noted that if the minority wishes were not in accord with the majority opinion or if they felt that majority opinion was against the fact of the matter, they would not 'hold themselves bound in any way by the wishes and acts of the majority'.[22] Lyall noted among the Karbis that the 'dissident households, if they do not acquiesce [with the majority view], may remove elsewhere, and set up for themselves as a new community with a *gaonbura* (headman) of their own.'[23]

Butler went on to note that 'every man follows the dictates of his own will'.[24] Woodthorpe also noted that 'virtually every man does that which is right in his own eyes, and is a law unto himself' and 'every man is his own master, and avenges his own quarrel'.[25] Even if this was a little exaggerated tuned towards Hobbesian's twist, it still held up an extreme case of individual rights and freedom granted by the system. In this context, individual was the ultimate hero and at the epicentre of the whole village 'democracy' system. Such system may be understood in terms of what Butler called 'a form of the purest democracy', a democracy which was certainly not in 'state of nature' but something different from it. It was a democracy 'which it is difficult to conceive of as existing for a single day, and yet that it

[22] Butler (1875: 314) and Woodthorpe (1882: 68).
[23] Lyall (1997 [1908]: 22).
[24] Butler (1875: 314).
[25] Woodthorpe (1882: 68).

does exist here is an undeniable fact'.[26] I will come back to this point in relation to freedom of individual in the concluding chapter.

Among the Khasis, the notion of 'public' in public durbar was rather interesting, as reflected in the village crier's proclamation for a durbar called *khangshnong*:

> *Kaw*! thou, a fellow-villagers; thou, a fellow-creatures; thou, an old men; thou, who art grown up; thou, who art young; thou, a boy; thou, a child; thou, an infant; thou, who art little; thou, who art great. *Hei*! because there is a contest. *Hei*! for to cause to sit together. *Hei*! for to cause to deliberate. *Hei*! for to give intelligence together. *Hei*! about to assemble in durbar. *Hei*! for to listen attentively. *Hei*! ye are forbidden. *Hei*! ye are stopped to draw water then not to cut firewood then; *Hei*! to go as coolies then; *Hei*! to go to work then; *Hei*! to go a journey then; *Hei*! to descend to the valley then; *Hei*! he who has a pouch. *Hei*! now appear. *Hei*! the hearing then is to be all in company. *Hei*! the listening attentively then is to be all together. *Hei*! for his own king. *Hei*! for his own lord, lest destruction has come; lest wearing away has overtaken us. *Kaw*! come forth now fellow mates.[27]

This proclamation is indeed revealing. It was a very powerful constitution and represented the very conceptual fountain of tribal 'democracy'. Apart from paying unquestioned attention to the proclamation by all, the message it conveyed was surely a democracy of different kind. It was truly the people's democracy where 'contests' were heard and settled not only by the *named* chief, his councilmen, 'old men', and 'grown up' men of the village, but a democracy that also included the 'young', the 'boy', the 'child', the 'infant', and women of all ages. They were all urged to 'sit together' in 'company' at the durbar not only to 'listen attentively' to cases but also to 'deliberate' and 'give intelligence'. The proclamation was a call not only to the 'great' but also to the 'little'. Hence, no one *was* left out; in fact, everyone *was* included. They were all considered to be fellow villagers, fellow creatures, 'fellow mates' in the affairs of the community. What is even more fascinating is its conceptualization of individual in the society. Everyone was 'his own king' and 'his own lord'. The

[26] Butler (1875: 314).
[27] Gurdon (2010 [1906]: 91–2).

expression '*lest*' indicated a kind of the 'irrevocable law' where the presence of *everyone* was a must and the absence of *anyone* seemed to cause 'destruction' and 'wearing away' of the whole community. Each individual, 'from the cradle to grave' in Mills apt term, was not only part of the system but each of them was the pivot of the society. This is the perfect example of a democracy where individual is at the centre of the universe.

To the extent the system revolved around *individual*, it goes without saying that the hill democracy was against all forms of control and oppressions within the village society. But to what extend this system was an antidote to control and appropriations from outside, from the valley states, is a matter of debate. If control from above and from the centre, being facilitated by homogenous political and bureaucratic structures across several hundred or thousand villages, was central to state system, then the hill democracy was surely an antidote to such control. Each village government was completely independent from other village or any higher authority. Hence, there was no central power through which control from above and centre could be affected. More importantly, the so-called village chief possessed no power and authority over the rights and freedom of individuals so that any state authority, to affect any control over the people, could not use him. In this context, it can be said that the hill 'democratic' system was perhaps the most effective instrument to prevent, repel, and evade any form of control and oppression from above and from the centre. Macgregor, for instance, noted that the 'great difficulty in dealing with the Naga tribes is that there is no recognized head, and that each village is often divided into three or four parties'.[28]

Wilcox also noted that there were certain influential persons among the Abors who could be bribed for 'gaining of any point at issue with them', but 'the extreme jealousy of the "Raj," and vigilant watchfulness to preserve their democratical rights, render it a matter very difficult to manage to bribe these influential men.'[29] That was

---

[28] NAI, FP (A): October 1878, No. 21: Diary of Lieutenant C.R. Macgregor during his Tour through Naga Hills in 1878, quotation from 2 February 1878.

[29] Wilcox (1873: 51).

the insurance of, and an assurance provided by, the village democracy in an egalitarian society which rendered it 'very difficult' to control. The creation of a powerful chief in each village therefore became necessary if any extension of state control was to be effected over them. R.B. McCabe, then Chief Commissioner of Assam, even suggested that the government should encourage the chiefs to become 'despotic' as 'it facilitates the extension of our [British] control'.[30] It was in this context that the colonial state, after annexation of the hills, recognized a certain person as *gaonboorah*/headman, who was endowed with power and authority hitherto exclusively possessed by the village durbar to collect 'taxes' due to government (with certain percentage as commission) and who had to occasionally attend the durbar of the political agent (later deputy commissioner).[31] Thus, we can say that the village democracy was chosen by the state-evading population to evade all forms of control and oppressions in the hills.

Chieftainship without Power

If the 'democratic' system ensured freedom of the individual, then to what extend did the so-called chieftainship system provide a similar space to them? Most colonial observers of the nineteenth century believed that the chief in chieftainship system was 'despotic' and 'authoritarian'. The hereditary chief was shown to be at the centre of the village polity and he was often the last arbiter in all matters. His council members, appointed by him, normally assisted him in village administration. This system was followed among the Kuki-Chin tribes and some Naga tribes like Semas and Konyaks.[32] In the Kuki-Chin world, the position of the chief was, in most cases, hereditary. He collected 'taxes' from villagers, enforced forced labour, coerced people into a state of 'semi-slavery', obtained obedience from

[30] NAI, FE (A): July 1888, No. 122: R.B. McCabe to Secretary to Chief Commissioner of Assam, 24 May 1888.

[31] NAI, FP (A): December 1866, No. 138: 'Naga Administration', from Col. H. Hopkinson to Secretary to Government of Bengal, 14 September 1866.

[32] See Hutton (1921b: 121–2, 147–50) and von Fürer-Haimendorf (1969: 40–64).

all, and above all, his word was the law. As noted earlier, his decrees were honoured by the people with 'no murmuring voice'. Johnstone even said that Kuki polity was 'strictly' monarchical and their chiefs were 'absolutely despotic' who may murder or sell their people into slavery.[33]

Among the Chins, Carey and Tuck noted that the 'position of the Chin Chief in regard to the people is very similar to that of a feudal Baron.' The chief was the 'lord of the soil and his freemen hold it as his tenants and pay him tithes, whilst they in common with the slaves are bound to carry arms against all his enemies.'[34] In Lushai Hills, Shakespear also noted that each village was like a 'separate State' ruled by a chief (*lal*), who was assisted by the council members, called *upa* (elderly men), whom he had appointed. He presided over the council which discussed all matters of the village and decided on all disputes, for which they received fees called *salam* from the party who lost the case.[35] Thus, it was shown that individuals under the Kuki, Chin, and Lushei chiefs lived in a state of what Shakespear has called 'semi-slavery' or what Carey has called as 'vassals' or 'tenants'.

If such colonial accounts are taken seriously, then it can be concluded that freedom of the individual was completely curbed. The 'despotic' chief not only ruled with absolute power but he could even kill or sell his 'subjects' into slavery. This was an extreme view, which completely overshadowed the reality of chieftainship system. In the rebellion against all forms of absolutism and divine kingship, the colonial observers saw the chieftainship system through the lens of the dominant discourse on 'oriental despotism'. At most, it represented the theoretical position of chieftainship system in the eyes of colonial observers. However, the functioning of this institution at the ground level was quite different; the system of 'oriental despotism' hardly existed in reality. Even from the theoretical position prevailing among the tribes, such absolutism was never to be seen unless one had become the slave and bonded servant of the chief. It is, therefore, necessary to observe this institution from the point of the hillmen who valued their freedom from control and oppression.

[33] See Johnstone (1987 [1896]: 27) and Stewart (1855: 626).
[34] Carey and Tuck (1987 [1896]: 201).
[35] Shakespear (1998 [1912]: 42–3).

It is true that serious effort was made by many chiefs to circumvent the rights and freedom of the individual, which became quite apparent in the nineteenth century. In fact, it can be said that the situation described above only represented the changing situation in the colonial period. Elsewhere, I have noted that the entry of firearms from Burma and Chittagong during this period induced massive 'internecine warfare' among different clans/tribes, leading to the emergence of few powerful chieftains.[36] Before this period, however, a 'democratic' form of government seems to have dominated the landscape, which was now overshadowed by the chieftainship system. There is evidence of 'elected' system in the Kuki-Chin world before they became 'despotic' and 'authoritarian'. In the late eighteenth century, Macrae, for instance, reported that the Cucis (Kukis) who inhabited the Lushai Hills had a number of independent villages under the immediate command of an 'elective' chief.[37] This is also supported by the legends of how Lushei chiefs came into prominence. Thus, Zahmuaka, the ancestor of the great Lushei rajahs, was initially chosen by the people (*hnamte*) as their headman. It was from him that the generations of Lushei chieftains came into prominence and ruled over the greater part of Lushai Hills in the nineteenth century.[38]

As noted in the previous chapter, the term for 'tax' or 'revenue' was surprisingly absent in the tribal vocabulary, although many chiefs were known to have 'collected'. This was known commonly by the people as 'shares' or 'presents'. In the colonial period, the Kukis, for instance, invented the term *kai*, which meant house tax paid to the government, and later on it was also used to signify what their chiefs had collected from them. But it had a very strong negative connotation: kai literally meant 'pull' or 'rob', referring to the 'pulling away' (of animals from someone) or 'robbing'. In fact, it implied not only a deviation from the custom but also its off-putting social offence. For instance, when the chief employed the mandatory labour of the whole village (three or four days in a year) to clear or clean his jhum field, which was called 'khotha' or 'haosatha' in Kuki (literally,

[36] This changing political situation has been discussed in much detail in Guite (2011).

[37] See Macrae (1919 [1801]: 185).

[38] Vumson (1986: 64–8).

flesh-of-the-village, meaning labour given by the village), it was not said 'he taxes' or 'he takes', but it was invariably said, 'he eats the flesh of the villagers' (*khothaneh*). The term 'eat' was also commonly applied to all that the chief had exacted or taxed from the people.[39] The generic use of the negative term 'eat' to all that was exacted/ imposed by anyone to other, say, father for his daughter's bride price and so on, connotes a significant political discourse of the stateless society which underpins not only its absence in the past or deviation from norms but also the social disapproval of it. I will come back to this point later.

Even judged on the basis of nineteenth century evidence, the chieftainship system, instead of becoming as notorious as it was painted in some colonial accounts, did not curtail the freedom of individuals in any substantial way. Every individual, except slave and bonded labourer (which I will come to later), was guaranteed maximum freedom of mobility within the chieftainship system. Although the so-called 'despotic' chieftainship was in theory 'absolute', none of the tribal customs endowed him any power to stop or prevent any individual or family when they decided to shift from his village to another village. In other words, no chief, however powerful he might have been, was empowered by custom to compel his villagers to be 'bound to the soil'. This irrevocable right that an individual in the hills possessed is what I call *migration right*. It was customary across the hills that everyone had the liberty to migrate from one village to another. Migration right acted as a powerful weapon of the individual—or as a customary shield or the safe conduit—through which one could easily get away from any oppressive control. Thus, whenever the villagers found that their chief had become or was becoming tyrannical and oppressive, they would immediately leave him and migrate to another village. It was a kind of insurance of the freedom of the individual, just as it was against, and an antidote to,

---

[39] Kuki chiefs 'robbed' and 'ate' many different kai (rob, meaning 'tax') in the later period, say, *changseo* (one *dan* of rice by each family household), *su-kai* (payment to chief when a bride is taken away from his village), *shelkot-kai* (paid by seller of *mithun* to chief), *lam-kai* (paid by purchaser of mithun), *thilkot-kai* (payment from export of goods), *shamal* (right hind leg of all animals killed), and migration dues. See Shaw (1997 [1929]: 62–5).

tyranny and oppression of the chief and, for that matter, any person in the village. In this context, migration right was the counter-culture of the village society. It was also the counter-culture in the sense that it prevented the chief from becoming tyrannical.

Every chief would therefore restrain himself from becoming oppressive but acted, as permitted by custom, as the 'protector' and 'helper' of his villagers in all adversities. If he neglected his community responsibilities or became tyrannical, he very soon found himself a 'king' without any subjects. Shakespear rightly noted this in the Lushai Hills where one of the most powerful and 'despotic' chieftainship systems existed: 'The chief was, in theory at least, a despot; but the nomadic instinct [read, migration right] of the people is so strong that any chief whose rule was unduly harsh soon found his subjects leaving him, and he was therefore constrained *to govern according to custom.'*[40] To him, the chief's position was 'anomalous' due to the wide gap between theory and practice. In reality, 'his power was very much circumscribed' because 'his subjects could so easily transfer their allegiance to some rival chief'. The amount of power he wielded, therefore, depended 'almost entirely on the personal influence of the chief'. Thus, he said that a strong ruler, 'who governed mainly *according to custom*, could do almost anything he liked without losing his followers, but a weak man who tried petty tyrannies soon found himself a king without any subjects'.[41]

Shakespear was right in acknowledging the 'nomadic instinct' of stateless people, which was indeed one of the most powerful weapons to prevent or evade any tyrannical regime. To the hillman, migration was not only his customary right but also a powerful weapon of resistance against oppressive control, just as it was his right to live under a chief who 'governed according to custom'. Indeed, such 'instinct' marked the continuing relevance of the older 'custom' of the stateless society. Thus, ruling 'according to custom' was the key to understand the chieftainship system, just as in 'democratic' system. In this context, 'to govern according to custom' meant to avoid 'petty tyrannies' and respect the individual's rights and freedom. As long as the so-called 'autocratic' chieftain ruled according to 'custom', it was

---

[40] Shakespear (1998 [1912]: 43); emphasis added.
[41] Shakespear (1998 [1912]: 44).

considered that he was within the *line of conduct* and had not yet converted his hereditary position into political authority. The real position of the chief among his people as one among equals was shown by some evidences even during the peak of so-called 'despotism'.

Lewin noted one interesting case among the Lusheis. In 1866, when he was standing and talking to one of the leading Lushei chiefs on the village path,[42] a drunken Lushei came stumbling along and finding them in the way, 'seized the chief by the neck and shoved him off the path, asking why he stopped the road'. Lewin was stunned to see this behaviour and asked the chief for an explanation of 'such *disrespect* being permitted' [emphasis mine]. The reply of the chief was quite interesting: 'On the warpath or in the council I am chief, and my words are obeyed; behaviour like that would be punished by death. Here, in the village, that drunkard is my fellow and equal.'[43] The reply was revealing insofar as the position of the chief in relation to his people was concerned. It was only on the warpath, and in the council, that the real power of the so-called 'despotic' chief became 'authority'. In the village, outside the council or warpath, the position of the chief was, however, not different from others: he was an equal member of the village community, having equal rights and power as his fellow villagers. Other members, including the drunkard, were his 'fellow and equal'. His 'authority' was not absolute but circumstantial, and greatly circumvented by the rights and freedom enjoyed by other individuals.

What is even more interesting in this case is the strong presence of resistance against any form of domination. Here, the chief could have been easily spared from such a humiliation before the dreaded British officer, but the Lusheis valued their rights to such an extent that even the chief was not spared. Thus, what appeared to Lewin as 'disrespect' was the legitimate power of an individual against another individual who went against the tide of egalitarian order. His right of way was asserted here. To the hillman, an open space outside the warpath and courtroom was a liberated zone, free from control and domination, where everyone was equal. It was improper to 'stop the road' and everyone, even the drunkard, must have his way. The idea

---

[42] The village path was normally a narrow footpath used in single file.
[43] Lewin (2004 [1869]: 140).

of equality and individual rights was so strong that the so-called 'despotic' Lushei chief was speechless before a drunken man. In this case, the chief was wrong, not the drunkard, because he had stopped the road. He just could not pretend to be powerful and tyrannical before his people lest he found himself a king without any subjects, for the irrevocable migration right or the 'nomadic instinct' was so very strong among the people.

Therefore, the 'chief', or 'headman', or 'king', whatever we may call him, in both the 'democratic' and chieftainship systems was the mere *leader* of the village community due to what Clastres has called his 'technical competence' alone, or sometimes by virtue of birth. But his, and always *his*, words did not carry the force of law because *he* could only 'persuade' and *his* 'prestige' did not signify 'power' and 'authority' because the stateless society, and their social norms and custom, would not allow him to change his 'technical superiority' to 'political authority'.[44] So, it was always the individual who triumphed in case of conflict of interest with the chief. Individual became the pivot of the stateless society and polity and all things revolved around him/her. Thus, they had a chief without authority and a society free from control and oppression. The idea of mobility and individual freedom becomes more pronounced if we consider the general social formation process in the hills, the point I shall come to now.

Being 'Slave', Being Member of the Family

It is difficult to say whether 'slavery' existed among the hill tribes in the past. However, at the turn of nineteenth century, 'slavery', if the term may be so used, did appear as an established institution. The early colonial accounts are witness to the existence of slavery in the hills among all tribes, which I will discuss in greater detail later. Here, I would like to draw attention to the very character of 'slavery', such as the degree of the subjection of slaves. Folklores and legends have often mentioned some kind of bondage among most tribes, but they were not 'slave' in the strict, classic sense of the term. They

[44] This 'technical competence' included his oratorical talent, his expertise as a hunter, and his ability to coordinate martial activities, both offensive and defensive. See Clastres (1977 [1974]: 175).

were largely 'servants' or 'bonded labour' (also called debt bondage or debt slavery) who had lost their freedom due to certain criminal acts, indebtedness, or in most cases, poverty (orphans, widows, poor, and destitute). It was a form of 'charity' given by the wealthy householders to the poor and needy who offered themselves up for 'help'. Their subjection, under most circumstances, was temporary in nature, unless the 'slave' chose to become part of the 'master's' clan. It was customary for the 'slaves' to live in the house of the 'master' until an independent source of livelihood was available and s/he could pay 'freedom price' to the master. In the southern hills, for instance, the customary price for liberty was one *mithun* (*Bos frontalis*).

In the Lushai Hills, Francis Buchanan (1798), for instance, was told by the Kukis (Lusheis) that 'they have slaves in the same manner as the Ma-ra-mas'.[45] As per the practice, one became a slave to someone due to his debt and, accordingly, he had to provide free labour until he could pay the debt. During this time, he was provided a monthly allowance by the master. He could not be sold by his master, but he could move to another master if the latter paid the debt. Often, the wife became slave for her husband's debt and children for their parent's.[46] More categories were added later such as criminals, destitute and war captives. 'Slaves' were broadly classified into two: 'boi' and *sal*. Boi or *bawi* (literally, who are in trouble, who need help) was a common term for those who voluntarily offered themselves to the chief's house or other rich men due to poverty (known as *inpuichhung* boi), crime (*chemshen* boi), and defeat in war (*tuklut* boi). Although they were bonded, most of them lived in separate houses; and in that context, they did not appear to be 'slave' in strict sense of the term. Sal referred to those who were captives of war and raids. While the bois could purchase their freedom, the sals were 'personal property of their captors', who might own, sell, or even kill them as they pleased. All children born of slaves became slaves (boi or sal as the case may be).[47] In the Chin Hills, Carey and Tuck also noted two classes of 'slaves': one formed by captives of war

---

[45] van Schendel (1992: 93).

[46] van Schendel (1992: 89–90).

[47] Shakespear (1998 [1912]: 50), Nag (2016).

and raids; and another formed by the poor and criminals.[48] Similarly, there was slavery among the Garos, Aos, Semas, Lhotas, Angamis, sub-Himalyan tribes, and so on.[49]

It is difficult to provide the number of slaves in the hills. At the most, it can be estimated that they were relatively a very small part of the population. Even in the nineteenth century, when it was recorded, their numbers seem to be negligible. In the worst-case scenario, the Kachin tribes of Upper Burma were found to be possessing large number of slaves. A. Symington, for instance, noted that 'as a rule, in a Kachin village the slaves are more numerous than free persons'.[50] This was an exception rather than the rule. One area where a large number of 'slaves' were kept was the Chin Hills and Lushai Hills. In both the cases, the number of slaves liberated after the occupation was very small. For instance, the boi census taken in Lushai Hills in 1923 put their number at 362 in-dwelling or inpuichhung bois (95 males and 267 females and children) and 941 houses of out-dwelling or *inhrang* bois in Aizawl subdivision and 476 in-dwelling or inpuichhung bois (119 males and 357 females and children) and 1,110 houses of out-dwelling or inhrang bois in Lungleh subdivision.[51] Whatever the numbers may be, they were largely the product of nineteenth century conflict situation in the hills, a point I have discussed elsewhere.[52]

In its classic sense, slavery connotes domination relation where slaves are subject to extreme abjection and have to spent a 'bare' life. However, this was not so much the case in the context of the stateless hill society even during the nineteenth century. The slaves lived within certain degree of domination and, for that matter, subjection.

[48] Carey and Tuck (1987 [1896]: 203–4).

[49] For Garos, see Hamilton (1993 [1828]: 563). For Nagas, see ASA, EB&AS, 1850, File No. 639, Butler (1978 [1855]: 189), Mackenzie (2007 [1884]: 104), and Mills (2003 [1926]: 211). For slavery in sub-Himalayan region, see Robinson (1975 [1841]: 354) and Thakur (2003). For Kachins, see NAI, FE (A): September 1892, Nos 140–4.

[50] NAI, FE (A): September 1892, Nos 140–4.

[51] ASA, Appointment and Political Department, Excluded Areas Records, No. 8, Pol-A: September 1923, Nos 3–19.

[52] See Guite (2011), Nag (2016).

In fact, the idea that slaves in the hills were also subject to abject conditions, as normally indicated in colonial accounts, was largely a parody, again a civilizational plot, to criminalize the nonstate practice. It is true that some kind of bondage, conveniently called slavery, prevailed in the hills, but their situation was not as bad as it was projected. Instead, various ground reports indicated that the so-called 'slaves' were 'kindly' treated as members of the family. An inventory taken in Kachin Hills in early 1890s was revealing in this respect. Rae, for instance, noted that among the Kachins, 'as a rule slaves were treated well, and it frequently happens that they become members of the creditor's family by marriage, and on this event occurring the slave is considered free.'[53] Elliot also noted: 'On the whole there is very little hardship in their life. They are well clothed, well fed, and well looked after, and their work is so light that it is questionable whether they are worth their upkeep to their owner.'[54] Symington even went on to say, 'I have never heard of a case in which a Kachin has lost slaves through their running away. They are treated well and are well cared for and have no wish to leave their owners. Slavery among the Kachins is not like the "blood and thunder" slavery of which we read in books.'[55] H.F. Fertz said that 5 per cent of the slaves would not leave their master if they were given freedom.[56]

What was seen in Kachin Hills was also the general condition of 'slaves' among all the hill tribes of Northeast India. In Lushai Hills, for instance, Lewin noted many of the captives taken from the plain refused to be released. He attributed this to the 'remarkable' kindness the 'slaves' received from their hill captors, which was described by all the rescued slaves as 'kind in the extreme'. Lewin remarked:

In no case has it been ascertained that any violence had been offered to female captives, while, as the list shows, many of them have actually married, and becoming incorporated with the tribe, decline positively to be released. The captives given up by the Southern Howlongs had to be brought forcibly into the camp, and clung to their Lushai

[53] NAI, FE (A): September 1892, Nos 140–4.
[54] NAI, FE (A), September 1892, Nos 140–4.
[55] NAI, FE (A), September 1892, Nos 140–4.
[56] NAI, FE (A), September 1892, Nos 140–4.

friends, weeping piteously and entreating that they might not be made over to us.[57]

His interpreters ascribed such 'unnatural feeling' of attachment being influenced by 'Kookie magic'. But Lewin rubbished such idea, saying: 'Magic, it is true, but I imagine that it was the white magic of kindness and human sympathy.'[58] It was this 'white magic of kindness' which made the hill slavery system quite different from what was found in the surrounding valleys or to that of the classical slaves in the West. 'The residence of a powerful Chief', Lewin went on to say, 'is generally surrounded by the houses of his slaves, who marry and cultivate, enjoying undisturbed the fruits of their labour.'[59] Mills also noted among the Ao Nagas that the slave 'became the absolute property of his master' and 'became in a vague sort of way a member of his master's clan'. They all 'lived in their master's houses' and 'on the whole slaves were kindly treated'.[60] Hence, it was not strange to observe that the 'slaves' of sub-Himalayan tribes were often sent to the markets of Assam for trade and other purposes.

Under the above-mentioned circumstances, it is difficult to say whether the 'slaves' of the hillmen were slaves at all. The refusal to be released, the circumstances in which they were kindly treated as equal member of the master's family, the eventual membership of his clan, and the amount of freedom they enjoyed, all made the hill slavery system different from the classical slaves or those of the valleys in the region. One can therefore talk of slavery, but not as a radical process that contested the prevailing egalitarian system in the hills. In this sense, there was a domination relation without oppression. Here, the Lushei's use of the term boi (those who are in need of help or those who are taken care) becomes helpful. Thus, instead of looking at hill slavery in terms of exploitation, it may be better seen as a domination

[57] WBSA, JP: August 1872, No. 212.

[58] WBSA, JP: August 1872, No. 212.

[59] Lewin (1978 [1870]: 132). Shakespear remarked that 'any man may take a person into his house and feed him in return for his work'. WBSA, PP: August 1893, Nos 4–6, File No. L/49 (1–3): *Administration Report of South-Lushai Hills for 1892–93*, p. 18.

[60] Mills (2003 [1926]: 211).

relationship governed by the principle of 'cooperation and reciprocity' in which the rich looked after the needs of the poor and needy. As noted in Chapter 5, the rich were obligated by the egalitarian norms to 'help', or could not refuse 'help' when asked, and the poor had the right to seek 'help' when needed and, in turn, reciprocate with 'help' (labour in this case). While a few cases of slavery were by force and punishment in character, the majority of the cases, instead of being a form of exploitation, were in the form of cooperation and reciprocity, the 'charity' of the rich. This is not to celebrate the system but to show, thus far, the worst case of domination relation in the stateless highland.

Babel of Tongues, Borderless Ethnicities

How did language and ethnicity come to be divided? Each tribe had its own likely explanation. Some pointed to their different origin stories and others came out with an interesting nuance of their cosmological worldview. But in each case, multiplicity was a fact recognized by all; and interestingly, this fact was well cherished, each asserting the distinction as given and each intended to go further away from the main branch. Yet, the commonality of all human being, at one point of time, was recognised by all.

> Ukepenopfu was the first human being. Her descendants are very many. Instead of dying she was raised to heaven. Later on her descendants thought to communicate with her by building a tower up to heaven from which they could go and talk to her. She however, knowing their thoughts, said to herself: 'They will all expect presents, and I have no presents for so many men. The tower must be stopped before it gets any higher'. So she made all the men working at the tower talk different languages so that they could not understand one another, and when one said 'Bring a stone', they would fetch water or a stick and so forth, so that all was confusion and the tower was abandoned. Hence arose the different tongues of the various tribes of man.[61]

This was not the story of Babel tower from the Bible; it was not a rendering of the same by people who already knew about biblical

[61] Hutton (1914: 479).

Babel. It was purely a local folktale collected from the Angami Nagas. Similar renderings of the folktale were circulating widely among different tribes in the region, say, in Sikkim, Garo Hills, Mikir Hills, Chin Hills, and in Manipur among the Zalengrongs.[62] This 'Babel' story, in fact, emphasizes the multiplicity of languages and ethnicities in the region.

As noted earlier, the village was the basic social unit in which the state-evading population organized themselves in the hills. While this village often formed the social unit, there existed a vague idea of clan/tribe organization beyond the village based on kinship ties. These kinship ties were often based on language, the fulcrum of ethnic grouping. But it would be a mistake to consider that the boundary of this ethnic or linguistic grouping was closed, bounded, and compartmentalized in the past, as is seen today. The freezing point may be located somewhere during the later colonial period or after that. Certainly, there was a different kind of ethnicity in the hills before the advent of colonialism, which may be best described as multiple, porous, and fluid. The guiding principle of the state-evading population in the hills, as mentioned earlier, was to spread out widely and in smaller groups. This was necessarily a political choice to keep the valley state conquerors and some politically ambitious persons in the hills at bay. The dispersive social formation of the runaway population was not only shaped by their principle of 'divide against imperialism' but was the mirror of it. The broad swath of social formation process showed multiple ethnic groupings which almost lacked borders in any strict sense of the term. This borderless ethnicity was best shown by the porous and fluid ethnic boundaries through which individuals and groups kept moving back and forth as the circumstances allowed them.

The colonial ethnographical accounts were very clear on the subject of multiplicity. Despite the tendency to see the hill societies through the coherent lens of social evolutionists, the actual disposition the colonial specialists encountered in the hills was more

---

[62] See Haokip (2011: 101–3, 156–8), Hutton (1914: 479–82), and Lyall (1997 [1908]: 72). 'Zalengrong' is a new ethnic nomenclature evolved to substitute a rather colonial derogatory term like 'Kacha Naga' or 'Kabui'.

prismatic than homogenous. 'Of the Naga alone', noted Damant, 'there are not less, and probably more, than thirty different tribes, all speaking different languages, and mutually unintelligible one to another.' In some instances, he said that 'a few may be reduced to the rank of dialects, but in the majority of cases they are essentially distinct languages, and often no connexion or similarity is to be found between them, as, for instance, Angami and Lhota are so entirely different, that it is difficult to believe they belong to the same family.' He went on to state that amongst the 'Eastern Naga', greatest confusion existed: 'There is such a multiplicity of tribes, each speaking a different dialect, and they are so small in numbers, sometimes consisting of only one small village, that, without visiting each village personally, it is *almost impossible to define the limits* of each tribe with any approach to accuracy, or even to say precisely how many tribes there are.'[63]

The colonial administration was utterly unsuccessful, despite great efforts, in mapping or defining such 'limits'. The 'impossibility' of defining the limits eventually ended up in 'lumping' and 'dubbing' them together under some broad classifications.[64] Although some tribes comparatively showed more inherent unity than the Nagas, the situation that existed in Naga Hills depicted the general ethnic situation in the hills of the region. For instance, among the Garos, Playfair found at least 12 clear divisions of the Garo tribes.[65] Of the Khasis, Gurdon noted at least five broad divisions. These broad divisions represented 'collections of people' speaking dialects which were 'so dissimilar to the standard language as to be almost unrecognizable'.[66] Among the Kukis, Lusheis, and Chins also, there were several divisions and subdivisions, each having their own dialect, often unintelligible to each other though syntactically very close to each other.[67] Thus, there was a multiple, scattered and often disconnected ethnicity throughout the hills.

---

[63] Damant (1880: 229–30); emphasis added.

[64] I have discussed this process of lumping elsewhere in detail. See Guite (2018).

[65] See Playfair (1998 [1909]: 59–62).

[66] Gurdon (2010 [1906]: 62).

[67] See, for instance, Grierson (1994 [1904]).

Different opinions were expressed for the emergence of these multiple identities. The dominant view was centuries of isolation and disconnectedness. Nathan Brown (1851), for instance, felt that the Nagas were 'divided into a great number of independent tribes, often hostile to each other, and speaking a variety of dialects' because they 'have remained in their present scattered and disconnected state for many centuries'.[68] Damant also noted that this 'immense number of dialects has undoubtedly arisen from the isolation, in which each community is forced to dwell.'[69] This idea of isolation denied any possibility of social mobility and interaction between different groups and implied that each one of them was a stiffly partitioned ethnic identity, as seen in today's context. But to say that plurality was the result of isolationism and disconnectedness is to negate the fact that there was continuous movement of people and goods between villages and communities in the long view. This was noted in the context of clan geographicity and governmentality, which mapped the pattern of social, cultural, and even economic and political relationship, network, and communication in the hills. It was within these networks and relationship that there was constant movement of people, commodities, culture, ideas, and so on, between different, scattered, and dispersive villages and communities in the hills. Thus, the theory of isolationism and disconnectedness could not be substantiated.

But if there was a constant network of interaction and communication among the scattered villages, why did the society appear to move away from the 'parent stock' and form a new identity rather than coming together? In other words, if there was regular interaction among different groups, why was there a tendency towards split social formation, rather than a homogenizing one? Scott contended that this was a political choice at the margin of the states, a strategic positioning to evade control and appropriations.[70] Truly, there can be no other good reason as to why the hillmen had to split up if they were not socially and culturally isolated than to say that it was a political choice. This will become profound if other ethnic factors are

---

[68] Brown (1851: 157).
[69] Damant (1880: 229–30).
[70] Scott (2009: 208–19, chapter 7).

taken into account. Besides plurality, there were two other important ethnic or social factors, namely, fluidity and porosity, which were as dominant as 'multiplicity of tribes'.

The fluid and porous social and ethnic situation in the hills as another dominant character of the tribes was evident from many colonial accounts. Woodthorpe, for instance, noted about the Nagas in Naga Hills that the cultural 'distinctions between the different tribes are so slight' and 'their villages are so mixed up together' that he was doubtful 'very much' whether any 'tribal limits could ever be successfully adopted'.[71] He was referring to the 'dovetailing' ethnic situation among all tribes which conspired against the drawing of the limits of any ethnic boundary. Captain Butler clearly remarked:

> These various tribes all dovetail into each other in a most remarkable manner, and it is impossible to assign to them any hard-and-fast limits, or to say that beyond certain limits a tribe does not extend; for not only do we often find men from two or even three tribes living in the same village but in many cases villages belonging to the same tribe are separated from each other by those of several other tribes.[72]

He went on to say that 'portions of the dialect, manners, customs, and dress of any one tribe we may like to take up will constantly keep cropping up in other tribes as we go on.'[73] Each tribe across the highland massive thus dovetailed with the next; and eventually, all the tribes could be even considered as one large family group. This was how the term 'Tibeto-Burman' family came to be invented. In this context, defining the limit of tribal boundary based on language or otherwise became certainly 'a very variable quantity' and any attempt was studded with 'doubt' and 'uncertainty'.

The dovetailing situation was largely due to the 'continued admixture' of tribes and clans in a village in which a certain clan settled down in the village of another clan for different reasons. They

---

[71] NAI, FP (A): January 1877, No. 148: Lieutenant W.F. Woodthorpe to Captain W.F. Badgley, 15 June 1876.

[72] As quoted in Woodthorpe's report in NAI, FP (A): January 1877, No. 148.

[73] As quoted in Mackenzie (2007 [1884]: 85).

eventually, through acculturation, became one of them, or the new migrants (more in numbers) absorbed the earlier one, or together they formed a new identity built on the previous ones, making the village a site of radical ethnogenesis, the 'hybrid area' or 'middle ground' in Richard White's apt term. In many cases such absorption or acculturation took place by choice but, at other times, it could also be by compulsion. Thus, as noted earlier, a certain tribe called 'Dhansee' of Khonoma became Angami tribe 'from their continued admixture with that tribe whose superiority obliged them to seek protection by a union with them'.[74] In a village of Namsang, McCabe also noted, 'one *khel* of about 20 families call themselves Ahom, and have decidedly an Assamese cast of feature.'[75] Hutton too noted that those tribes who had been strongly influenced by the powerful Angami tribe and 'Angami culture' showed the tendency of becoming Angamis. He noted that 'there has been an infiltration, often a very strong one, of the same stock (Kuki), into most of the Naga tribes', like Maring, Tangkhul, Angami, Ao, and Sema.[76] Hodson noted that Yang-Khulen or Chekwema people directly claimed 'relationship with the Kukis'.[77] Shaw also noted that the village of Toushem claimed that they were originally Lenthang Kukis who were absorbed into Naga community on reaching Maram. He further suspected that the people of Liyangmai might also be of Kuki origin as they too claimed to have come from Maram.[78]

The dovetailing situation was thus visible among all tribes in the region, say, the Marings, Anals, Lamkangs, Koms, and so on in Manipur and the Lynngams and Dkos of Khasi Hills. The former group, for instance, incorporated both the culture and tradition of Nagas and Kukis, so much so that they were described either as Kukis or Nagas by different ethnographers. They were the so-called 'bridge-tribe' between the two. Thus, the Khoibu section of Maring

[74] NAI, FP: 25 May 1840, No. 118: Grange to Bigge, 29 July 1840.

[75] NAI, FE (A): July 1888, No. 122: 'Mr. McCabe's Promenade through the Ao Country, 1888': McCabe to Secretary to Chief Commissioner of Assam, 24 May 1888.

[76] Shaw (1997 [1929]: 17, fn. 1).

[77] Hodson (2007 [1911]: 17).

[78] Shaw (1997 [1929]: 17).

tribe claimed themselves as an offshoot of the Falam Chins in the Chin Hills, whereas other sections claimed to be autochthonous to their present hills.[79] The combination of two or more different ethnic groups normally formed one such ethnic group like Maring. Many such groups existed across the region, such as the Saihrem or Faihrem of Barak valley.[80] Gurdon also remarked that the Lynngams were 'half Khasis and half Garos' and the Dkos 'are Garos who observe the Khasi custom of erecting memorial stones'. Similarly, he noted that the Jinthong, Mynri, and Ryngkhong subdivisions of the Bhoi division of Khasi Hills 'are not Khasi, but Mikir'.[81]

Recent studies on this 'ethnic borderland' between Khasis, Tiwas, and Karbis found how such social baptism/miscegenation has been still going on. Philippe Ramirez, for instance, noted three forms of 'adoption rite' still prevailing among the Karbis which admit other clans/tribes into their clan/tribe: *deng-pharlo* (cult–group-change), *kur-pharlo* (title/clan-change), and *bang-kur-kepon* (another-title/ clan-taking). While the first two relate to changing of clans within the Karbi tribe, the third relates to non-Karbis entering into one of the Karbi clans.[82] I have not come across any such elaborate 'adoption rite' among other tribes in the region. But it is interesting to note that each tribe has a ceremony of 'adoption', which suggests its importance in the past.[83] However, evidences also show that in the past, without resorting to such formalized ceremony, social mobility was as common as the freedom of physical mobility. Adoption, in fact, took a reverse format from its formal order. An individual adopting the clan of other, instead of a clan adopting people from other clan, was a more common form. In this way, fluidity became the order rather than the exception. Families and individuals moved

[79] See Gimson (1926).

[80] Saihrem is an ethnic group which was formed out of conglomeration of different clans and tribes of the Kukis who were expelled from the Lushai Hills in the middle of the nineteenth century.

[81] Gurdon (2010 [1906]: 62).

[82] These sets of 'purification' rites are discussed in Ramirez (2014: 67–71).

[83] For instance, the Lusheis called this adoption ceremony *sa-phun* and the Kukis called it *phunkai*.

freely and willingly from one clan/tribe to another clan/tribe in certain times. Such mobility was part of their social world.

The evidence from Lushai Hills is perhaps the best example of such a fluid, porous, or 'dovetailing' ethnic situation. Shakespear noted that those 'consanguineous communities', using a 'dialect of their own', before the Thangur (Lushei) chiefs had risen in Lushai Hills were 'quickly absorbed' and 'now form the majority of the subjects of the Thangur chiefs'.[84] He further stated: 'The population of a village ruled by a *Thangur* chief at the present time is composed of representatives of many tribes and clans, which have all more or less adopted the language and customs of their rulers.'[85] Here, the people were 'adopting' the language and customs of their 'rulers'. The 'rulers' had not forbidden such adoption but instead, apparently, encouraged the proceedings as it added to their political power and glory.

It was not only the 'language and customs' that were adopted; many of them also adopted the clan or family names of their 'ruler' Lushei chiefs. Shakespear, for instance, noted that the arrival of the British in the Lushai Hills 'put a stop in certain cases to this process of absorption', but it badly failed to disentangle the existing arrangement. During the census of 1901, he noted, an unsuccessful attempt was made to get a complete list of the clan families and branches. An old man sarcastically ridiculed him for hoping to get a complete list of family and branch names: 'Can you count the grains in that basket of rice?' The reason for the difficulty, he noted, was not only because there were too many clans but, more importantly, because of 'the ignorance of the people themselves as to what clan or family they belonged to and the tendency to claim to be true *Lusheis*'. He observed: 'Everyone knew the name of the branch to which he belonged and as a rule the family name would be correctly given, but in many cases the clan name was altogether omitted or *Lushei* was entered against families which had no real claim to that distinction.'[86]

If a group of people or an individual family deliberately ignored or omitted their clan's name and instead willingly entered the name of other clan or willingly entered through ritual channel to be one

[84] Shakespear (1998 [1912]: 5, 40–1).
[85] Shakespear (1998 [1912]: 40).
[86] Shakespear (1998 [1912]: 41).

of them, often that of the dominant clan/tribe, then there could be one possible reason: they were not truly ignorant of their clan/family's name but rather pretended to be so in the face of others or the census enumerators. Hence, many of the families who pretended to be ignorant of their family names and their earlier languages and customs later reclaimed them when new, favourable circumstances permitted them to do so. Many of them thus 'returned', claimed Shakespear, to their earlier position when they regained their independence under the British regime.[87] In this context, what was 'true' and 'real' to Shakespear was not really the case with the people of Lushai Hills. For them, it was a political or social choice to 'claim to be true *Lusheis*', instead of remaining with their own and being marginalized under Lushei domination. Thus, when a new situation arose, they also shifted back to their old position. The ethnic history of Lushai Hills is, therefore, a fascinating site for observing the up and down and back and forth movement of people between different tribes/clans in history.[88]

But it is also important to note that such 'claims'—'adoption', 'absorption', or even 'return'—were only possible because of the systemic porosity. Thus, if a Kuki could become a Naga and a Naga could become a Kuki, or if Angami could become Lhota and Lhota Ao, and so on, it meant that the ethnic boundary of each tribe, clan, or family was porous and unrestricted. As just mentioned, in Lushai Hills, many non-Lusheis had claimed and adopted Lushei language, customs, and clan names, and came back to their old position when the situation permitted. But this was possible only when it was acceptable to the Lusheis. The fact that many other clans/tribes could claim or adopt and become one of the Lusheis suggests that the Lusheis liberally allowed such adoption. Parry, for instance, noted that the 'striking characteristics of the Lushais is their capacity for absorbing other races'. He said that this process had started 'before they came under British rule and has continued ever since'.[89] Thus, the situation was such that an individual could freely choose to move

---

[87] Shakespear (1998 [1912]: 40).

[88] Comparative study of census reports of colonial and postcolonial period would show this interesting case.

[89] Parry (1931: 134).

from one tribe/clan to another and the system also permitted such social and ethnic mobility with ease. In this context, it can be thus said that the fluid and porous social relationship was the order than the exception.

Truly, multiplicity, fluidity, and porosity became one of the normative social standards, or what I have called the 'line of conduct', in the stateless society of Northeast India. One even wonders whether there was any social boundary at all. This social system provided the individuals maximum choice and permitted maximum mobility from one tribe or clan to another as the situation demanded. Imagine a social system that froze social hierarchy and social mobility, as was often the case in many valley states and civilization system, where such movement was unthinkable. In comparison, the social situation in the hills of Northeast India before the colonial occupation was, to be sure, an extreme case of ethnic multiplicity and fluidity. Thus, instead of a closed and compartmentalized social system, what the hills had was a system that was not only plural but also porous and fluid to the extreme. This porous social order among the tribes of the region was best described by J.H. Green in the 1931 Census of Burma: 'Some of the races or "tribes" in Burma change their languages almost as often as they change their clothes.'[90] Thus, this was a social world that was uncut by history of a dispersive and scattered population, of people isolated and disconnected by geography of road and wire.

How was this social situation related to the state then? The best way to link this situation with the irony of state is to see it from a political rather than a social lens. Mobility was a necessity in a society which opposed any oppressive control or for an individual who valued freedom. The lack of mobility was, in fact, one major source of oppression in the valley states. The lack of social mobility in many societies, such as caste-ridden society, or feudal society, or slaving society, condemned a large section of its population to 'inhuman' conditions. This was often understood to be a common feature of the state society in the valley. In this context, such discrimination became purely political or extra-economic, and hence the loosening of such social compartmentalization became political in character in the context of the stateless society. Providing free social mobility was,

---

[90] *Census of India*, Vol. II: Burma, Part II, 1931: 245.

therefore, one effective political instrument to prevent the intrusion of oppressive control from above and from the centre. Thus, a large number of minor clans/tribes, say, 'Dhansee' of Khonoma, Kukis of Naga Hills, 'consanguineous communities' of Lushai Hills, and so on, 'adopted' the culture, customs, and clans of the dominant and what Shakespear called the 'prevailing race' or their 'rulers', just as the latter would 'absorb' them to strengthen the clan/tribe. Green rightly remarked about such political manoeuvring: 'Languages are changed by conquest, by absorption, by isolation, and by the general tendency to adopt the language of a neighbour who is considered to belong to a more powerful, more numerous, or more advanced tribe or race.'[91]

If the choice of a social system that permitted mobility was political in character, then it is easy to see how this choice would give such political dividends to state-evading population. Looking from the lens of state-evading population in the hills, plurality, porosity, and fluidity were surely the gels that upheld individual freedom. Plurality provided maximum choices; porosity provided the channel for mobility or free movement of individuals; and fluidity provided the possibility of social engineering process. They were, indeed, the essence of hill social formation. Mobility was possible only when there were maximum number of choices. The hill people were indeed provided with multiple choices in the form of multiple number of clans/tribes/ethnicities, with extremely porous and fluid boundaries. This situation of multiplicity, porosity, and fluidity, therefore, provided the stateless society maximum amount of freedom, with the individual and family now and then moving from one clan/tribe to another whenever they felt threatened by remaining in the one they were presently attached. In this sense, plurality, porosity, and fluidity again become the counter-culture of the stateless hillmen.

Therefore, despite the 'clannishness' that epitomized the hill society, a strong political undercurrent in the process of miscegenation, absorption, adoption, wilful submission, alteration, and omission and commission of one's identity and lineage could be identified in the long view. The 'dovetailing' situation was, therefore, another line of conduct enunciated to prevent any oppressive control and appropriations from above and from the centre of power. Thus, when

[91] *Census of India,* vol. II: *Burma,* part II, 1931: 245.

one can change ones identity at ease it cannot be said that there was strict social isolationism and disconnectedness among the scattered and dispersive state-evading population of the hills.

The Fuzzy Social Customs

The jelly-fish character of the tribal social system was further reinforced by their fuzzy customs said to be intensely irritating to the state officers. Hutton, for instance, felt that the Kuki's 'irritating ways of making a fuss about the unpaid price of his defunct second cousin's great-grandfather's sister's bones are not calculated to endear him to a district officer'.[92] He regarded them as 'administrative nuisance'. Not only did every single tribe have their separate customs that differed from the next, but each clan/family within a tribe would have or maintain some kind of distinction from the other clans or families. Attempts to simplify and codify them during the colonial period failed badly. The volumes of written customary laws recorded by several British officers remain unused till today. Each tribal community/clan still relies on the oral interpretations of their customs by the clan elders. 'Desperation' may be the best word to describe the position of district officers in the midst of the hills and in the courtroom. Shakespear, for instance, noted that he was 'many a time ... driven to desperation, when trying a case.' He said:

> Sometimes two Lushais would come and wrangle for an hour about a gyal; after much trouble I would arrive at a decision, and the parties would go off, and return and ask—'What is to be done with the girl?' 'What girl?' 'Why the girl that the case was about?' "But you never mentioned any girl, you talked about a gyal'. 'Of course, we thought you *knew* about the girl,' they would say; 'the gyal was her mother's price,' and then the whole thing would have to be begun again.[93]

There was one classic instance at the court of the subdivisional officer of Mokokchung where a case was decided on the question of the 'Dog's Share'. Hutton remarked: 'In this case the Sub-Divisional

---

Officer of Mokokchung ... has to decide claims for "dogs' share" of a deer which has been killed by someone who is not of the hunting party chasing the deer, and has refused to give up the share due to the dogs that put it up'.[94] Here, the dog's pleader narrated the tale of 'The Dog's Share' in full length before the court in order to justify his claim of the dog's share in the chase. Insisting that the court should give order for the dog's share, the plaintiff ended his address to the court as follows: 'Now from of old we Semas, after hunting game, do not forget the dogs' share. And now, too, we represent to our father Sahib that the dog's share be not forgotten. So now, too, give order not to forget the dog's share.'[95]

Folktale as a legitimate source to decide matters at the district court was perfectly incomprehensible to a district officer. Folktale, for an officer, was a myth having no legal sanction in any manner. Providing justice to animal was even more unintelligible to the sahib. But this was not so to their 'savage' and 'simple' people. When the plaintiff was stubborn on this issue, what could then the officer do best to resolve the matter? Truly, he could not pick any legal holes or find any legal flaws in the case. He could not simply dismiss the authenticity of the folktale either. He could not also give any adverse 'order' against the socially accepted custom of 'Dog's Share'. So, for 'prompt and vigorous justice', he could only use his 'legitimate influence' as 'father Sahib' and make 'the best of the situation' to control any commotion. His decision may be fraudulent to his position as a state officer or to the legal system he represented, but he had to do what was best to control the situation. Thus, most colonial officers working among the hill tribes were equipped with the old English legal tradition of 'broad equity' where personal and legitimate 'influence' of officer for a 'prompt and vigorous justice' was central. This literally dismantled state laws and its overarching bureaucracy.

I would like to close the discussion on customs with another interesting case of litigation at the court of the deputy commissioner of Lushai Hills district. A certain Chunga had complained that he had given a pregnant mithun as dowry to his sister apparently with the idea of taking back the calf when she gave birth. With that intention,

---

[94] Hutton (1921b: 338).
[95] Hutton (1921b: 338). See also Shakespear (1922: 270–1).

he took back the mithun to his house before the calf was born. However, the mithun died along with the unborn calf. Now, the village court ordered him to compensate the calf with another mithun. Dissatisfied with the decision, he brought the matter to the district court. His complaint letter read as follows:[96]

> Kindly consider my petition:-
>
> Nuii is my sister to whom I gave a Mithan on her marriage day as dowry for her. I wanted to take it back before it was one year and during that time the calf of the Mithan paid by me nearly become grown up. This young Mithan was regarded to be the gain or profit. But the gain or profit was dead along with its mother Mithan, after I have taken the mother Mithan back with me. The young calf was dead in the year I gave its mother to my sister as her dowry.
>
> Now! Sir! Do Mithan give birth twice during a year's time? Why did the Elders give the Mithan which belonged to me to her? The Mithan which I gave to her as dowry brought up its calf which they called the 'gain of the dowry'. The gain was dead when it was in its mother's stomach before it was formed along with its mother.
>
> —Chunga, 9.2.1939

Now, how on earth could a district officer decide on such a litigation? Should he rely on tribal laws or penal laws? Was there any law that dealt with 'intention' or gain of dowry or otherwise? The matter was beyond legal comprehension. But he could not simply dismiss it either when the litigant was insistent. In such cases, the officer probably had only two options: either he could subscribe to the decision of the Elders (chief's court), which he anointed as *decentralised despot*, or he could use his 'legitimate influence' as 'father Sahib' of the tribe. Thus, in every way, the fuzzy tribal customs and disputes were not only legally 'irritating' for the district officers but, in many cases, defeated/dismantled the state bureaucracy and its legal apparatuses. Here, a brief note would be helpful regarding the conditions of the colonial period.

After occupying the hills, the colonial state introduced a new system of administration to establish control over the hills. The new administration differed from that seen in the plains and may be best

---

[96] As quoted in McCall (2003 [1949]: 163).

described as 'personal government', to use Johnstone's apt term. The colonial officers were able to dispose of thousands of disputes/cases not through the interpretation of colonial laws but the judicious admixture of tribal customs and their 'personal influence'. In fact, from the beginning, most frontier officers were opposed to bringing the hills under the legal system of the valleys due to their experiences in other hilly parts of the colonial world. Therefore, the frontier officers were instructed to follow a certain form of administration while dealing with the hill tribes. The experiences they gained from other tribal areas were incorporated in the various 'Hill Regulations' (for example, Chin Hills Regulations, 1896) which positioned the district officers as the virtual potentate of the hill districts. Thus, the district officers were not required to rely on legal penal codes of the colonial state but to use their personal influence while settling disputes.

Such instructions were already given to frontier officers even before the hills were occupied. One order, in 1871, to the frontier officers of Assam is instructive in this respect.

> It is not for them to pick legal holes and find legal flaws, and to affect a pedantic legality. They should *make the best of the situation*. Some districts have been exempted from the Regulations and Acts … to enable them to administer a *broad equity* … for tempering a too harsh administration of any law … Above and beyond, or it may rather be said before law, is the *legitimate influences* which a good district officers may and should exercise. There are very many cases in which, by a *judicious personal interference*, matters may be arranged, or in which the path of law (where a resort to law becomes absolutely necessary) may be smoothed over … The Lieutenant-Governor does not think that to be within the law it is necessary to be slow, exacting, and unintelligible to simple people, he may do much *prompt and vigorous justice within* the law, especially, as has been said above, when he combines all powers in his own person. The Lieutenant-Governor trusts that you will impress these views on the officers of your division, and try to make them act upon them in cases in which *savage and simple people* are concerned.[97]

The message was clear. A 'good' district officer who served among the 'savage and simple people' should not 'pick legal holes' but

---

[97] As quoted in Mackenzie (2007 [1884]: 30–1, fn. 1).

'make the best of the situation' at his disposal by making a 'judicious personal interference', utilizing his 'legitimate influences', and administer them with the principle of 'broad equity'. This was, as asserted, for a 'prompt and vigorous justice' among them. Hence, the effectiveness of a district officer among the hill tribes relied not on the legal paraphernalia of the state but on his personal influences. This was not due to the simplicity of tribal laws but rather largely due to the complexity of it. If the 'slow' and 'exacting' legal system of the state was 'unintelligible' to the 'savage' and 'simple' people, the dizzying masses of tribal customary laws were even more 'unintelligible' to the district officers who were there to administer them. The only solution to such 'unintelligibility' was to 'make the best of the situation' and use the personal influences of the district officer who should combine all power in his own hands. Thus, Johnstone was content to settle cases or pass orders at Samagudting in Naga Hills as a statesman, but often with a loaded revolver in his hand, so that the 'wild savage' did not dispute his authority.[98] It was through such 'colonial despotism' or 'personal government' that the stateless hills could be taken over. No wonder, when Shakespear introduced himself to the chiefs of Lushai Hills, after occupation, as their 'King' and told them that 'as long as you obey me you will not be hurt', it did not raise any eyebrows at the centre of power.[99] That was exactly the manner in which a district officer was expected to show himself to the 'savage' hill people. Hence, it was only through force, fear, and obedience that the stateless hillmen could be subdued, and in subduing, the legal apparatuses of the state had to be given up, dismantled.

[98] See Johnstone (1987 [1896]: 39).

[99] NAI, FE (A): March 1892, No. 201: Diary of the Superintendent, South Lushai Hills, for the Week Ending 2nd January 1892 (diary of 1 January 1892).

7

Between the Worlds Upside Down

Summoning Folktales

In history, orality has been a powerful political tool in the hands of many subordinate groups. Several studies around the world have shown the inherent power of orality for the peasants, slaves, and so on.[1] James Scott, for instance, shows at least four varieties of political discourses prevailing among the subordinate groups in which orality played an immense role. Of these, the vibrant political culture of disguise and anonymity is instructive for my purpose here. It constitutes a range of rumours, gossip, folktales, jokes, songs, rituals, codes, and euphemisms. They are spoken or said in public but are designed to have double meaning.[2] Orality as a source of knowledge and power in a 'face-to-face' society, such as the tribal society, was particularly strong.[3] While orality survived as a 'veiled' culture and 'voice of unreason' before the intimidating gaze of power within state or in domination relation society, it flourished as an open and direct face-to-face discourse in stateless egalitarian society, like in precolonial

---

[1] See, for instance, Amin (1995), Guha (1999 [1983]), and Scott (1985, 1990).

[2] See Scott (1990).

[3] See, for instance, Vansina (1985).

Northeast Indian highland. In the latter, orality indeed formed the bedrock of public discourse and had the legitimate social sanction as the national constitution of the time. However, the free flow of such knowledge and its appeal gradually declined with the coming of colonial state in the region. The advent of literacy and the colonial epistemic violence on orality and tribal knowledge most powerfully constrained the natural appeal, and the disseminating power, that oral traditions had had in the past. With this, the values and valuable knowledge that oral traditions had stored and projected for the society were also gradually undermined. Orality lost its natural propensity so rapidly that what can actually be accessed today is a paltry amount of the huge corpus of oral traditions that used to exist in the past. From what can be accessed, I aim to find out the dominant political discourse the stateless hillmen had 'hidden' in their oral traditions, in relation to power and authority.

What is true for the peasants in a subordinate position in the state may not directly apply to the stateless hill tribes. However, the contours of subordinate group politics are a good place to begin. Here, what is subordinate before the intimidating gaze of power becomes the dominant discourse. Gossip is, to an extent, one fertile ground where hefty discoveries of such political discourses can be made. But, unfortunately, historians are not blessed with the fortune to explore such social grapevine of the past neighbourhood. Nonetheless, several studies have found that gossip also usually entered the structured forms of knowledge in every society and often took the form of social norms.[4] Or that gossip, based on its core principle, is a reflection of or is expressive of the norms, values, and ideology of a given society.[5] Either way, one can excavate gossip of the shared grapevine in a community. For the historian, the best way to explore the gossip of the past is to dive deep into the structured knowledge of the community, such as in the legal and customary norms and values of the society in a particular time.

[4] See, for instance, an interesting study of 'gossip' in classical Athens by Hunter (1990).

[5] See, for instance, Scott (1990: chapter 6). On the importance of 'gossip' in tribal society, see, for instance, an important work of Besnier (2009).

Among the 'unlettered race', their social customs and oral traditions therefore become immensely important. Oral traditions, such as legends, myths, folklores, ballads, proverbs, riddles, sayings, and so on, become indispensable to reconstruct the political discourse of tribal society. Like gossip in a neighbourhood, behind every piece of tribal oral tradition is an implicit statement of rule or norm which has been asserted or broken. Like gossip, tribal oral tropes are never disinterested; it is a partisan effort by them to advance their claims and interests against those of the others. It involves statements that make moral judgements, which censure individual conduct, and which thereby ensure appropriate standards of community behaviour. Like gossip, they function as a means of social control, ensuring, through its social sanction, conformity with those rules. Overall, they keep alive the sense of community and the preservation of its claimed highest values.[6] This chapter looks into those highest values that the stateless hill society had claimed for itself at the margin of states and empire, particularly their dominant political discourse in relation to power and authority.

Oral Traditions as Democratic Voice

Oral traditions of the hill society relied, for their expressions, on the shared social grapevine of the community where different modes of dissemination took shape: 'face-to-face' conversation between persons within the family and outside of it in public 'hang-outs' or 'gossip platforms'; and 'open speech' in public gatherings of the village. While women were seen to be less interested due to the burden of works bestowed upon them, they had their own 'inner circle' within the family relations and among the women in the jhum field, where they 'talked' while walking/working. Children had their 'bedtime discourse' from their parents or grandparents. Gossiping, as central to the social belonging of the male folks, was especially pronounced. Among the tribes which had an established bachelor's dormitory (morung) or girl's dormitory, such dormitories constituted their 'gossip platforms'. Among certain tribes (say, Abors), a separate

---

[6] For a masterly discussion on these aspects, see Scott (1990: chapter 6).

'hang-out' for aged persons was established. Among the tribes which did not have the morung system, there was, however, a clear presence of 'gossip platforms', just as each family built a platform of their own for family and friends in their house in the village as well in their 'jhum house'. Most men (also women) spent their days in these 'gossip platforms' whenever they were free from agriculture works.

They allowed themselves prolonged hours of leisure in these platforms, smoking, drinking, and gossiping, and usually brought their small crafts (such as baskets and weaponry) to work on. 'In some village', noted Hodson among the tribes of Manipur, 'the only relic of the institution [of morung] is the gossip platform in the centre of the village where the elders gathered and discuss politics over a pipe.'[7] 'The daily life of the Angami' is, remarked Hutton, 'to loaf about the village all day doing nothing but drink zu and eat thirst-raisers' and 'assemble in the verandahs of houses, where they sit on planks round a wood fire made on the ground and tell stories or talk scandal.'[8] Among the Kukis, Stewart remarked that 'the men like the Nagas ... love to sit on high platforms raised for the purpose in the villages, and pass the day in conversation and smoking.'[9] Lewin also remarked that the Lushei men were 'generally to be seen lounging about, cleaning their arms, drinking, or smoking'.[10] Shakespear too noted that they were fond of passing the days with 'complete enjoyment, lying in the sun, and smoking'.[11]

Assembling in the village 'hang-outs' or 'gossip platforms', such as in the verandahs of the house, or the high platforms, or at the morungs of the villages, and passing off the day by talking scandals, gossiping, drinking, smoking, and in complete enjoyment provided a fertile ground for dissemination of tribal political discourse. It also proved to be the lifeblood of an unlettered oral society on which the totality of their history and culture hinged. It was here that an appeal to a shared normative standard of the society was vociferously made.

[7] Hodson (2007 [1911]: 76).

[8] Hutton (1921a: 104).

[9] Stewart (1855: 636).

[10] Lewin (1978 [1870]: 142). For the various raiding expeditions, see Mackenzie (2007 [1884]).

[11] Shakespear (1998 [1912]: 16–17).

It was here that their village gossips recalled their history, culture, social norms and values, and reinforced and reordered them into a structured oral trope. In this sense, oral traditions were the potential source of power; they became what Scott has called the 'social arsenal' of the group/community. They were the product of what Habermas has called an 'ideal speech situation'. As in all oral societies, there was apparently a deep sense of anxiety about 'what people will say'; and when what they said was contemptuous or ridiculed a person, it not only caused him to 'lose face' but also made him miserable. The sense of 'public mockery' being a powerful social therapy empowered the oral traditions of 'unlettered race' literally to 'oversee' people's lives down to the smallest detail.[12] In a situation where such traditions reached deep into individual lives, their hold over people's perception was understandably strong. In other words, in appealing to the shared normative standards and values of the society, oral traditions declared what was essential to be a good individual and what not.

Such oral traditions were a kind of 'democratic voice' in the absence of dominant power that could impede its dissemination. It was necessarily 'democratic' in the sense that people at large, from the cradle to the grave, cherished the stories, and hence the political discourse it was likely to disseminate remained lively across the social spectrum. It was also 'democratic' in the sense that it was the dominant discourse in a stateless egalitarian society. Therefore, to be 'democratic', oral traditions needed to create or generate sensation so that everyone became not only the consumer but also an effective retailer. This made legends and folklores a storehouse of incredible stories. If 'incredibility' caused problem with the club of 'authenticity', the same produced a continuous relevance and significance within a particular culture. This is not to say that oral traditions lacked 'authenticity' but to emphasize the tendency towards creating incredible stories for mass consumers and retailers. In other words, it was the tendency towards homoeostasis, not of homeostasis as a radical process. Thus, the 'archaism', to use Vansina's apt term, remained intact. Such stories were full of sensation so that the very 'archaism', the authentic discourse, may reach maximum number of story-starved consumers.

---

[12] For a wonderful discussion on this, see Hunter (1990).

It was for this objective of 'archaism' that oral traditions, in order to be effective and appealing, relied on 'incredibility'.

At the same time, such 'incredibility' should not be taken as completely irrelevant to the discourse. In fact, the incredibility itself had a double meaning and could perhaps influence more strongly the consciousness of a person than a straightforward message. Thus, there were so many incredible stories of incredible characters in which men and animals, or men and gods, or small and big animals, or small/weak/poor men and big/powerful/rich men, and so on, would be put together in a particular fashion. What was more incredible about these stories was that the small/the weak/the poor always triumphed over the big/the powerful/the rich. Trickster stories of this kind were the most popular. This was not only to appeal to 'public' sensation or democratic social domain but also to put the moral message, or political discourse, or normative standards of the society in right and clear perspective. Orality, therefore, focused more on expressions than facts, and it was with such expressions that truth was reconstituted. In this context, oral traditions represented a 'point of articulation', a democratic 'climate of opinion' for the individual, family, and community in totality. They were indeed the cultural capital of the community.

Politics Over the Pipe

Of the different genres of oral traditions, folklore is apparently the best place to locate the highest value of the community at the margin of states. As a counter-cultural narrative, folklore was an implicit statement of moral fact and the measure of heresy in the tribal society. Across the oral spectrum, at least two sets of oral tropes, apparently contrasting at first glance but actually complementary to each other, became significant. While the first trope related to the dissonant political culture at the margin of states, the second trope related to statement of rules or norms that centred on an egalitarian social order. Of the latter, there were sets of folktales ranging from trickster story, love story to animal tales, that acted as medium of social control and a measure of deviation or heresy. They orally chipped away the reputation of the mighty and the powerful in the society and celebrated the weak, the poor, and the commoners. The former similarly chipped away the reputation of valley state power and celebrated the warriors who could protect and prevent the community from their control and appropriations.

Of the dissonant political discourse, there were at least two competing political ideologies, running side by side along the social grapevine, which complemented each other by promoting the warrior ideology of the community. Here, 'State' constituted one important element of the oral trope; it was always 'around'. On the one hand, it appeared as a symbol of fear and danger, which had to be prevented; and on the other hand, it was surprisingly shown to be a much-envied idea. Thus, the stateless society was enviously looking towards the coming or restoration of their lost 'kingdom', their millenarian hope. On the other hands, they were constantly on their guard against the control of 'State' (referring to the valley states) for which they warned people to remain constantly on alert. The first was a set of political discourse that was, crudely put, the longing to become a 'king'. The second was, on the other hand, a set of oral tropes that was, again crudely put, the fear of a 'king', the One, who was to be defeated or prevented. But the 'king' of the former was different from the latter, with the latter clearly denoting those of the valley states surrounding their hills. The former 'king' could be of two kinds.

First, the hill people always wanted to become the rulers of the valley if the situation permitted, even if they flatly refused to be the 'subjects' of any other ruler. Thus, some hill potentates ruled over the valley whenever there was power vacuum and withdrew to the hills when a more powerful force appeared. The states of Jaintias, Tipperahs, Kacharis, and so on are cases in point. Second, most tribal communities believed in the coming 'state', the 'Raj', where everyone would live 'equally' and 'happily' without any discrimination. This 'Raj' was a prophecy, their millennial hope, in which their hero-king would be born again from amongst them. Thus, Karbis talked about their *Sat Recho*, the Mizos talked about the restoration of their Khampat 'fort' or 'kingdom', Kukis always dreamt about the 'Raj', the Chins were keen to see the 'rise of the Chin Hills' (the mortal remains of their Babel tower), Dimasas fought the British under Sambhudan Phunglo in 1881–2, and the 'Kacha Nagas' (today Zalengrongs) had also already fought for their own 'Raj' under Jadonang in the 1930s.

The society required heroes and warriors who could take the community to the coming 'state' and who could prevent the control and appropriations of the valley states *down* there and avenge any insult to the community. It was in this context that the warrior ideology of the stateless society became significant. In fact, the predominance of hero stories in many of the folktales is a testimony to the importance given to such warrior ideology. Thus, each tribe produced a good number of legendary heroes who had done things no ordinary warriors could do. For instance, in the Kuki-Chin world, there were legendary heroes like Galngam (Ralngam), Hangsai (Hrangsai-puia), Laangchal (Hrangchala), Dapa (Tlandrokpa), Benglam (Chhura), Mualsavata, Keichalla, Vahrika, Lalrunga, and so on. Also, as noted earlier, a prominent position was given to people who could perform the 'feasts of merit'; and the performers obtained a great social consideration in this world and in the next.[13] All this shows the importance of warrior ideology. A brief illustration of this warrior ideology in relation to the One would be helpful.

Ridiculing State, Celebrating the Hill Warriors

If there was a warrior ideology in the stateless society, then it is natural that there was an enemy; I term it 'the One', who was to be prevented or defeated. Yet, surprisingly enough, the folktales were silent about and/or did not directly mention who the enemy, the One or the Mighty, was. But this apparent absence should not lead us to the assumption that there was no enemy at all or the One did not exist. The apparent absence was rather due to the peculiar style the oral trope had taken to enact their political discourse. This was in keeping with the appeal of the democratic voice, which preferred incredible stories for an incredible time. In this, representation of human enemy with an animal character was most popular and its origin can be possibly traced to the traditions of subordinate group politics under domination relations in the valley. Thus, the

---

[13] See, for instance, Hutton (1921a: 230–3, 1921b: 227–8), Mills (2003 [1926]: 136–44), Shakespear (1998 [1912]: 87–91), and Shaw (1997 [1929]: 76).

representation of the One was visible in the form of animal or half-animal–half-human being. In this context, tiger or tiger-men became quite popular among the hill tribes of Northeast India. Almost every tribe had some kind of folktales about tiger, who most prominently appeared as the One, the dreaded one.

As the tiger killed and ate men, it was natural that this beast became the 'king' of the jungle in their worldview and was feared most by all. But it would be wrong to assume that it became such a popular character in the various folktales due only to its power to kill people. The same power and fear, however, made tiger a metaphorical image and the personification of the One, not himself being the One. This is said because the way they framed the tiger or tiger-men in their tales was devastatingly different from its reality. For instance, tiger was depicted as a person who was arrogant in disposition but very simple and stupid too. He was always defeated by men and other small but shrewd animals, which was not the case in reality. The arrogance and stupidity of the tiger was central to the representations of the fearful animal. It was to be feared but it was also easily defeated by application of trick and shrewdness. The following tales bear out this character of the tiger.

Take the case of a popular Kuki folktale called 'Moltinchaan' (Kungori in Lushei tradition). It showed how, by his magical power, the One, the fearful enemy called Khalvompu who belonged to the people of tiger-man (*lhomi*), bewitched a beautiful lady, Moltinchaan, with the hope of marrying her. After deceiving her mother, he carried her away and took her to his village, known in the story as the 'village of tiger-men'. A great gathering took place to find out the most powerful man, a hero, who could rescue Moltinchaan and avenge the insult. Only poor Laangchal and his brother Pujil (Hrangchala and Hpohtir in Lushei tradition and Rangchar and Fachirang in Kolhen tradition) cleared the tough test. They were then sent to tiger-men village where Laangchal killed Khalvompu and rescued Moltinchaan. On their way back, his own brother deceived him, leading to his imprisonment in 'mithi-kho' or 'Khuavang village', which was underground and whose passage was sealed with a large stone boulder. He, however, managed to escape from 'Khuavang village' after many years; also, while in the village, he married the daughter of Khuavang chief and had some children as well. On his return to his village, he killed his brother and married Moltinchaan.[14]

In another story, Khalvompu was courting a widow who told him to go instead to 'the most beautiful women' of the time, Lenchonghoi. She taught him a deception to get Lenchonghoi to open her ten-folded iron (*thihpi-thosom*) door behind which she lived during the absence of her seven brothers. Khalvompu, using the trick (by pretending as one of her brothers), eventually succeeded in convincing Lenchonghoi to open the iron door. He then captured and carried her away to his village. Six of her brothers, finding the iron door shut, died while attempting to open it. The youngest brother succeeded in opening the door. He went and rescued his sister, Lenchonghoi, and killed Khalvompu. In another tale, Khalvompu was courting two beautiful sisters, Jawllhing and Jawlphal. However, by deception, Jawllhing was able to push him into the fire and he died.[15] Folklore always associated the famous Khalvompu, the tiger-man, with luring and capturing beautiful women, whom he would then carry away by force. He was dreaded and hated by all, and no social or marriage relationship was permitted between them. The tiger-men, and Khalvompu, were often depicted in various tales to be the 'enemy' who lurked in the vicinity of the village and jungle, targeting lonely people. Whenever 'tiger-man' was associated with kidnapping women, he was invariably nicknamed 'Khalvompu'.

This association of Khalvompu with kidnapping beautiful women is significant on two counts. First, the Burmese and Shans of Burma valley were historically notorious among the hillmen of the Chin Hills for carrying away their beautiful women. In fact, the origin of tattooing the face of their women was said to be related to this notorious Burmese adventurism. Fr. Sangermano, for instance, explained the origin of 'tattooing with black the faces of the [Chin] women' as follows:

During the time that the residence of the Burmese kings was in the city of Pagan, they were accustomed frequently to despatch their

---

[14] See Haokip (1998: 1–91). In Lushei tradition, Laangchal's role was played by Hpohtir and vice versa. See Shakespear (1998 [1912]: 177–82).

[15] See, for instance, Singson (1997: 124–7).

soldiers into the country of the Chien [Chin] to carry off the most beautiful women and girls. It was in order to free themselves from this disgraceful oppression that the Chien adopted the practice of thus disfiguring [tattooing] the features of their women.[16]

Second, in the Kuki-Chin world, there was a strong belief that the thigh (*khal*) of Burmese and Shans was dark/black (tattoo), and hence they called them *khalvomte* or *khalvomtepu* (people/man with a dark khal or thigh). Thus, 'Khalvompu' or 'tiger-men' was a nickname or slandering name given to the Burmese and Shans who were infamously known in the Kuki-Chin world as raiders and marauders.

The Kukis, for instance, said that when they were living at Lhanpelkot and Thijonbung (identified in the Jangmol ranges in Burma, between Chindwin and Kale–Kabaw valleys), and then at Molphai (identified as the valley at the confluence of Chindwin and Imphal rivers in Burma), they were constantly harassed and oppressed by the lhomis (tiger-men, identified as Burmese) who fed on their 'mithun, pigs, fowls, etc.'. They also threatened to attack if they were not supplied with human flesh. This order was, however, not carried out; but, by deception, many of them were killed (when in a state of drunkenness). Eventually, a treaty or oath was concluded between the two communities 'by throwing down *gahoh* (bean seeds) and cutting *moulthing* (a small plant) while swearing future friendship'. This was done, and 'so peace was declared', as per the legend.[17] It is to be noted that the reference to 'tiger-men' in their legends came during their stay in this region, and later in the Chin Hills, when they were associated with the Burmese or Shans of the valleys. In this context, the infamous Khalvompu in Kuki folktales referred to the notorious Burmese/Shans of the valley states.

In fact, the various court chronicles of the valley states in the region testified to incidents of raids into the hill villages by valley state potentates; they usually returned with a number of captives or slaves. The court chronicle of Manipur, *Cheitharol Kumbaba*, for instance, was studded with such instances of Manipur kings taking their forces into the hill villages, raiding them, and returning with

---

[16] Fr. Sangermano (1966 [1833]: 42–3).

[17] Shaw (1997 [1929]: 42–3).

several captives/slaves.[18] If the Burmese were fond of capturing beautiful women, it also became fashionable for most manpower war-machine valley states to send their forces occasionally to the hills to capture slaves and captives for valley production. Thus, the valley state forces remained a clear and present danger for the hill people in the region. But, surprisingly enough, the hill people did not represent this potent force of the valley states by their known names, like *kawl* (Burmese) and so on. Instead, it was fashionable for the composers of folktales to represent them as certain powerful animals, which they dreaded the most, just as they feared the valley power. Hence, as mentioned earlier, tiger, which was feared the most and considered to be the 'king' of the jungle by the tribes, became famous as a metaphorical image of the notorious valley potentates. In this context, the association of tiger-men and Khalvompu with the Burmese of the valley states was evident.

The Garo migration legend, mentioned in Chapter 2, also stated that they had to be vigilant all the time against the tiger-men (muchamaru). The fear of depredations from tiger-men forced the Garos to always keep their arms with them, and to work, as the legend put it, 'with sword and shield in one hand and the implement of husbandry in the other'.[19] It was also because of the depredations from tiger-men that the Garos had to move towards the west, practically retracing their steps backwards. This association of tiger-men with state conquerors and marauders was a well-established fact in other tribes too. Playfair, for instance, felt that 'the movement of the Kacharis ascribed by Mr. Gait to the invasion of the Ahoms, may in some way correspond with the western movement of the Garos, which the latter attribute to fear of the demons (*muchamaru* or tiger-man) who inhabited the tract of country assigned to them by the Assamese raja.'[20] The Lamkang tradition also had that two brothers went to avenge the death of their parents. However, instead of killing the tiger, they came to a compromise and took his 'two golden *dolais*'(litters or palanquins, associated with valley rulers) on

[18] See Singh (1995).
[19] Playfair (1998 [1909]: 10).
[20] Playfair (1998 [1909]: 16).

which they rode back to their village.[21] Chakesang story noted certain Metshi who, in his exile, lived together with the dreaded tiger.[22] When he died, his tiger friend came for his funeral service.[23] Thus, in all the tales, the tiger was not related to the animal but to a certain human being, enemy, or friend. In fact, the association of tiger or tiger-men with someone (the One in my terminology) appeared fashionable across the hills.

As the association of tiger-men and Khalvompu with the marauders from the valley states was strong, it is now easy to assume that the folktales of tiger or tiger-men were not a mere depiction of the dreaded animal but had more to do with its metaphorical being, the fearsome valley state rulers, raiders, and marauders. Their association with capturing the beautiful women of the hills became a legend in order to warn their succeeding generations of the impending disaster from the valley marauders if they did not remain alert. The dread of the valley marauders was depicted in the character of the tiger or tiger-man, who was so powerful that no ordinary person could take him. A hero with exceptional qualities could only take him, as shown in many folktales. Thus, there was only Laangchal or Lenchonghoi's youngest brother who passed the test to avenge Khalvompu. Similarly, a popular story of Lengbante (vine-cutter), in which the seven brothers died while fighting tiger-man, was common among many tribes. Only the son who was born later through the god's bow finally avenged the death of his father and seven brothers.[24]

However, these folktales also made it clear that tiger or tiger-men, despite their power, were stupid and easily defeated by trick and deception. Interestingly, the tiger-man was shown to be more stupid than the stupidest person known across the hills. The Kukis called this magnetic character Benglam; and he was known by different names in different tribes and formed one of the most popular folktale characters across the hills. The Lusheis knew him as Chhura,

---

[21] Shakespear and Hodson (1909: 411–12).

[22] Laloo (2011: 152–7).

[23] See Laloo (2011: 148–51).

[24] See Shaw (1997 [1929]: 119–28). For a similar version of Lamkang, see Shakespear and Hodson (1909: 411–12) and for Chakesang version, see Laloo (2011: 152–7).

the Angamis as Matsuo, the Lhotas as Apfuho, the Semas as Iki, the Karbis as 'Simpleton', and so on. The famous Benglam, known to be the 'fooliest' person of the Kuki-Chin world, for instance, once asked the tiger to help him out of a quagmire. He promised to let the tiger eat him if he got him out. After the tiger did so, Benglam obtained a moment's grace to clean himself from the mud, and then to clean his bowel. After this, he cut a cane in order to tie himself to a tree, explaining that an awful storm was coming. The stupid yet arrogant tiger, fearing the storm, forced Benglam to tie him first to the tree. Benglam did this and then departed, leaving a mallet by the tiger with which the passers-by might beat him. After this, the wildcat (*sangah*) came by, and the tiger pleaded friendship and fraternity and was released. However, instead of thanking the wildcat, the merciless tiger tried to kill him; however, the wildcat played various tricks to get away. When the tiger caught his leg, the wildcat told him that he was holding the root of tree instead of his leg, so that he let him go. He also bluffed the tiger to eat his own paw, which caused him much pain. He then asked him to go to Benglam's house at night with a torch to steal some fowls. And finally, he fooled the tiger into rolling down to a waterfall to cool himself after he was doused with boiling water by Benglam when he went to steal the fowls. The great stupid tiger died after rolling down into the waterfall.[25] Similarly, Lhota's Apfuho and Sema's Iki had also once fooled the tiger on different occasions until he died.[26]

Fooling the tiger was also common by other small animals and birds. For instance, the Jaintia tale of 'Tiger and the Fox' similarly narrated how the fox fooled the tiger on several occasions and the tiger, tired of running after the fox, eventually died.[27] The Tangkhul story of 'Monkey and the Otter' also showed how tiger was successively fooled by the otter and the monkey and finally, by the little young bird.[28] A common tale of Angamis, Semas, and Aos noted how the tiger was deceived to live in the jungle by his brothers, man,

[25] For this story, see Shakespear (1998 [1912]: 208).
[26] See Mills (2003 [1922]: 177–8) and Hutton (1921b: 319–21), respectively.
[27] Laloo (2011: 109–13).
[28] Shakespear (1922: 271–2).

and spirit/god.[29] Thus, seen from its penetration across the spectrum, the ridiculing of tiger as a foolish, stupid, and defeated character was well established through the medium of folktales and received much political significance in the making of warrior ideology. Folktales became a medium through which the notoriety of the valley state conquerors and marauders was projected. They not only chipped the reputation of these intruders but also urged the people to remain alert against them because they were lurking around their settlements, day in and day out, as the stories put it. As a warrior ideology, they propagated the idea that those heroes who could prevent these intruders, or avenge an insult to the community, would get the highest distinction any warrior could get in life. In other words, these tales urged the young ones to remain strong and powerful as warriors so that they would be able to prevent or avenge the invaders. The idea of stupidity was not only to ridicule the fearsome intruders but also a means to generate hope and fearlessness in the minds of the hill warriors.

Celebrating the Weak, Re-enacting Egalitarianism

Complementing the warrior ideology, there was another set of discourses on moral code of conduct. Good numbers of folktales on animal tricksters, 'love stories', and so on, acted as a measure of social conduct. The animal trickster tales, for instance, also had two contesting characters: the weak, the small and the powerful, the mighty (the One). It was the weak who invariably won the game. Take the case of the Lushei's story of 'Bear's Water Hole', in which the monkey played a trick leading to the death of bear and tiger and the monkey, in turn, was outwitted by a quail. The bear made a water dam and entrusted the monkey to watch it. When the thirsty tiger came for water, instead of stopping him, the cunning monkey told him to drink it, knowing that tiger would bite the bear when the latter got angry. He told the tiger, 'The water belongs to the Granddaddy Bear. If you dare to drink, drink. If you dare to suck, suck.' Not fearing the bear, the tiger sucked up all the water, leaving the dam dry. A long fight ensued between the angry bear and the tiger in which both

---

[29] Hutton (1921a: 261–2).

died. Out of their bones, the cunning monkey made a *Rot-chhem* (a musical instrument of flute type). When he played this, the quail came and persuaded the monkey to let him play a bit. The monkey replied, 'Oh no! you will fly off with the *Rot-chhem*.' The quail bluffed him and said: 'If you fear that, hold me by the tail.' The monkey did this and gave up the instrument. The quail then flew away with the instrument and the monkey pulled his tail clean out. The monkey demanded a ransom of eight mithuns but the quail preferred to go tailless and flew away with the Rot-chhem.[30]

In a Kuki tale of 'Hare and Buffalo', the two tricked each other and, eventually, the hare, the weaker one, won the game. Initially, both joined hands to steal milk from the milk seller, water jars from a boy, and then rice from an old woman. They cooked the stolen rice, but the buffalo ate it up all alone by deceiving the hare. The angry hare ran after the buffalo who, time and again, fooled him but, finally, the hare succeeded in taking his revenge. This happened the one time when the hare was beaten so badly that his body was swollen. His friend buffalo came and asked him how his body was 'so nice and plump?' The cunning hare told him that since the rajah fed him daily two fowls for waiting on the roadside, he had become fat. The stupid buffalo believed him and requested to change place for one day. The hare then tied the buffalo to the tree trunk and beat him with stick until the buffalo was nearly dead. He put up a notice by the trunk: 'To all who pass by, this Buffalo is to be well beaten with sticks'. Everyone who passed by then beat the buffalo with stick.[31]

There are many more trickster stories but the two tales given here are enough to show the set of discourses that could be extracted in relation to power and domination. Trickster stories in stateless society ridiculed the arrogant, dominating, and oppressors. They celebrated the tricksters who were represented as commoners, the equals, who would use trick and deception only to counter anyone pretending to be, or who had become, tyrannical and oppressive. They did not promote treachery and deception as a radical social process but aimed to inculcate the idea that equality among all individuals was the moral code for the society. They warned that all attempts to control and

---

[30] Shakespear and Hodson (1909: 412–13).
[31] See Crace and Hutton (1960: 180–3).

dominate would end tragically. Thus, in all trickster stories, the weak and the small (read as commoners) always won over the powerful and the mighty, which in real life is impossible. These tales socialized the spirit of resistance.

There was another genre of folktales, which was about contestation between individuals, again between the weak, the poor versus the powerful and the rich. For instance, the folktales of tribes like the Karbis were mostly of this category. Like in animal tales, the rich and powerful people were always shown to be stupid and arrogant, whereas the weak and the poor were good and intelligent. Take the case of one popular 'love story' common in the Kuki-Chin world. The Kukis named it 'Ahsijolneng story' and the Lusheis called it 'Tlumtea and his brothers'.[32] In the Kuki version, the competition was between Changkhatpu (an orphan boy living with his widow mother) and the Punchate (the many, the family of many boys); and in the Lushei version, the competition was between Tlumtea (the youngest) and his brothers. The tale was about courting the most beautiful woman, Ahsijolneng (Vanchung maid in Lusheis), of a distant village. On their way, they came across different people who needed help, such as *lomlhangho* (group of cultivators), *gitchate* (a kind of chickadee bird), *gulngongsan* (red-necked snake), *huise* (storm), *meilhang* (cloud), *sumsuipa* (mortar-maker), and *thingponu* (widow who gathered firewood) (in Lushei's tale: bamboo rat and red-necked snake only). Changkhatpu helped each one of them, whereas Punchate refused to help any and harassed them in different ways. Ahsijolneng welcomed the sober Changkhatpu and treated the proud Punchate badly who, out of shame, returned the next morning.

Although Ahsijolneng chose Changkhatpu, her father (a chief) disapproved of it merely because he was poor, orphan, and commoner. Therefore, he had to undergo certain ordeals from her proud father who was the chief of that village. Besides being abused, he was put to test before the village council. But the mortar-maker and poor widow, whom he had helped on his way, rescued him by ridiculing the chief's intemperate behaviour and winning public favour for him. Having no other option, the chief then put Changkhatpu

---

[32] For the Kuki version, see Haokip (1998: 1–59) and Lhangum (2013: 1–7). For a Lushei version, see Shakespear and Hodson (1909: 404–8).

through some impossible tests for his daughter's hand. He was however rescued again by the range of animals and nature he had helped on the way. In refilling sesame seeds on the grass, the *gitchate* helped him out. In cutting the chief's jhum field alone, the storm came to his help. To bring home a huge boulder, the cloud helped him out. In bringing plantain leaf without tearing it from the midst of thorny bushes, the red-necked snake helped him out. Having passed the ordeals, he finally married Ahsijolneng. However, Changkhatpu had to face some more ordeals under *lhomi-nu* (tiger-woman), who killed Ahsijolneng, dressed in her apparels, and married Changkhatpu, who later killed her when Ahsijolneng reappeared from the gourd issued from lhomi-nu faeces. The story ends with the tragic imprisonment of Ahsijolneng inside a rock (issued from the head part of lhomi-nu body buried there) and the eventual release of her soul into the sky as 'twinkling star' when the rock was broken with fire in order to save her.

There were many such stories related to human relationship in the village society. But the above-cited story is sufficient to show the general contour of such stories that underpinned the undercurrent of egalitarian ideology of the hill society. They defined what it was to be a 'good' hillmen and what was not. The good was defined in the character of the poor, righteous, and compassionate boy, Changkhatpu, and Ahsijolneng. And the opposite was defined in the character of the proud, arrogant, and oppressive Punchate, Ahsijolneng's parents, and his councilmen. Thus, Changkhatpu triumphed over the arrogant band of brothers. The proud chief, father of Ahsijolneng, and his councilmen were brought to their knees by the common folks (widow, mortar-maker, and so on) of the village community. Their sinister design to sabotage the normative code of marriage was frowned upon by nature (storm, cloud, and so on) and the wild animals (like birds, snake, and rats [in Lushei tale]). The sinister design to ruin the socially sanctioned marriage by the wicked woman (lhomi-nu) was defeated. Thus, it ridiculed human vanity, domination, and social discrimination based on wealth and celebrated the values of equality, kindness, cooperation, and reciprocity. In other words, it re-enacted and encrypted the ideology of an egalitarian society.

The celebration of egalitarian ideology was more forcefully enacted by another popular tale common to most tribes in the region. This tale came in two sets; it was combined into one among certain tribes and was separated in others. It questioned: who is the 'greatest' of all? The Tangkhul's tale of 'The Story of the Bat' combined both the sets in one tale. It was the story of an integrated, egalitarian, and truthful society where justice to all was guaranteed and the wrong condemned and punished by all. In this tale, the bat started a series of violent incidents in the village by crying 'Chap, Chap' in the middle of the night. This led to his foot being cut off as punishment. It was then decided that the 'greatest of all' should eat the foot. They asked the sun, the cloud, the wind, and the rock, who pointed to the other in succession to be greater than him. Eventually, the little bird was found to be the 'the conqueror of all'.[33] In the Angami story of 'The Rat Princess and the Greedy Man', a man catches a rat and puts it into a box. The rat turns into a beautiful girl, whom the man decides to sell to the greatest man in the world with the aim of getting the highest possible price. He asked the king, the water, the wind, and the mountain, but each of them referred him to the next in succession and the little rat was finally pointed as the 'greatest' of all.[34] In the Sema story of 'The Dog's Share', a bitch was killed by the Sambhar in a series of violent events started by a crab. Her puppies vowed to avenge her death and asked god: 'Between heaven and earth who is the greatest?' God sent them to the tiger, who in turn sent them to the elephant, who sent them to the 'Spirit', who sent them finally to man. With the help of man, they took their revenge.[35]

These sets of folktales concerned a similar moral regime. Like trickster stories, they also celebrated the smallest and weakest of all things by making them the 'greatest'. The tales showed that, on the one hand, the smallest mistake could have a domino effect in the

---

[33] Shakespear (1922: 268–9). The first part was popular among the Kuki-Chin world, and was variously known as Chemtate (Kuki), Chemtatrawta (Lusheis), Chemtattepu (Hmar), Chemchongsaipa (Aimol), and so on. See Lianhmingthanga and Fimate (2006: 5–6), Shakespear and Hodson (1909: 389–90), and Shaw (1997 [1929]: 108–10). For Karbis, see Lyall (1997 [1908]: 46–8) and for Semas, see Hutton (1921b: 315–16). The second part was popular among the Nagas.

[34] Hutton (1914: 494–5).

[35] Hutton (1921b: 336–8). See also Shakespear (1922: 270–1).

society and could snowball into a series of violent events. On the other hand, in searching the 'greatest' or 'strongest' of all, the narrative eventually found the answer in the smallest one, instead of the biggest. This was a familiar statement of moral regime that centred on the egalitarian norm of the society. By making all crimes similar and justice for all, and by making the smallest the greatest, the narrative made it known that everyone was equal and no one was greater than the smallest of them. Overall, it celebrated equalitarianism in the stateless society.

Between the Worlds Upside Down: Commemorating Statelessness

Keeping in mind their egalitarian principle, how did the stateless society situate their world order within the broader cosmological plot? It is fascinating to note that the hillmen located their world within a specific 'civilizational' regime, the logocentric type. They located their world 'in between' two world orders. It was preceded and succeeded by, as they represented, the worlds upside down, the topsy-turvy worlds. This chronological view of their universe, mimicking the civilizational plot of the social evolutionists, situated their world of statelessness between the past and the future. These two worlds upside down, the topsy-turvy worlds, interestingly related to a secular world order and were different from their millenarian 'kingdom' or their spiritual 'nether land'. The tradition of world upside down was peculiarly a pan-European tradition but, in certain ways, most societies had some similar kind of tradition, perhaps with a different meaning to it. Thus, for the stateless people of Northeast India, their vague tradition (possibly because it was not recorded properly) of the worlds upside down was understood in some specific sense. Unlike its role as a 'masking mechanism', in David Kunzle apt term, in the pan-European tradition, the tradition of topsy-turvy world in stateless hill society functioned with different objectives in mind.[36] On the one hand, it was known in terms of making a 'mockery' of the past and the future by ridiculing them. On the other hand, and more

[36] Kunzle (1978).

importantly, it was understood in terms of celebrating the present, the stateless egalitarian world order. They expressed 'satisfaction' in the present and frowned upon the worlds upside down, of the past and the future.

This notion of the world upside down should not be confused with their millennial notion of the coming state, and also the metaphorical representation of their social world order with some trickster stories of animals and human characters. The world upside down was arguably a different set of stories altogether, and the two legends of the world upside down were vastly different. The first was related to the past and the second was related to the future. It is difficult to say that the past was projected to the future either, and this future should not be confused with their substantial notion of the 'nether world', the world of the dead. The future here meant the world upside down in the shape of what Angami Nagas under- stood as 'Armageddon' (*Chusenu*)—an Armageddon that was the beginning of a harsh world, not the end of the world in biblical term. Similarly, the past topsy-turvy world was understood as their 'Golden Age'. Both the legends seem to have died out completely today; and even during the nineteenth century when great efforts were made to study the culture and traditions of the hill people, very few accounts came to light.

Among the Karen of Burma, there was a 'belief in *Apu* Lagan, where everything is upside down and all directions inverted'.[37] It is suspected that such a legend once circulated more widely across the Northeast region as well. A few of these accounts do provide a clue to their notion of the world before and after the present. There were a few passing references among the Aos, Kukis, Angamis, and Khasis. While the first two represented the past world of what was seen to be the 'Golden Age', the latter three tribes provided the future 'Armageddon'. Mills, for instance, noted of the Aos tradition:

> The Aos, like other nations, had their Golden Age. In those days, there was no toiling up to the village with heavy loads of rice. All that men had to do was to cut their crops and go back up to the village,

[37] Mills (2003 [1926]: 108, fn. 1).

and call the rice. It came flying up through the air and went into the granaries of its own accord ... In that wonderful Golden Age, too, the rice grew ready husked.[38]

The Kuki tradition noted that 'not only rice, but firewood and everything else that has to be carried' came flying on its own.[39] In fact, there was one common legend in the Kuki-Chin world, though apparently for brief period, that related to the world upside down. It was called the story of 'Thimzing', the gathering darkness, caused by the *awk* (the mythical dog that swallowed the sun, the solar eclipse). The Kuki tradition talked about seven days and seven nights, but this period seems to have been quite long in Lushei and other Kuki-Chin traditions. The Kuki tradition noted that all those who slept died, so people kept awake by putting sticks between their eyelids. The Lushei tradition indicated the world upside down. Everything, except the animal skulls, became alive; dry wood revived, stone become alive and produced leaves, so men had nothing to burn. Only successful hunters had animal skulls to burn, others had to stay in the darkness. Then, a general transformation took place. All men changed into animals: some changed into 'satbhai'; some into tigers, gibbons, fireflies, monkeys, elephants, bears, and squirrel; and the chiefs turned into hornbills or king crows. All domestic animals changed into wild animals. Mithun changed into large boulders. After this terrible catastrophe, the world was repeopled by men and women issuing from Chhinlung.[40] The Lhota tradition also mentioned the great darkness in which its charming character, Apfuho, finally tuned into a stone after the darkness was over.[41] The Aos too had a vague notion of this darkness caused by the sun going to the underworld and refusing to return, as he was angry with people talking about him. But it did not mention the cataclysmic incidents of the Lushei's Thimzing.[42]

---

[38] Mills (2003 [1926]: 108).
[39] Mills (2003 [1926]: 108, fn. 1).
[40] Shakespear (1998 [1912]: 94–5).
[41] Mills (2003 [1922]: 176).
[42] Mills (2003 [1926]: 314).

This world upside down, the 'Golden Age', however, came to an end, partly due to the one-sidedness in the system that favoured the rich against the poor, and partly due to the determined effort of the poor to outwit or circumvent the system. The Aos, for instance, felt that such 'wonderful gifts of nature' ended because it favoured the rich men. The resistance of the poor men eventually broke the spell. Mills noted:

> For it was found that the flying rice always made for rich men's granaries, and never came near those of poor men. So, finding nature so unfair, some poor men determined to outwit her, and, before the rice had a chance of beginning its wonderful journey through the air, put some in baskets and carried it up, thereby making sure of getting a share at least of the fruits of their labour. But the spell was broken, and from that day all, rich and poor alike, have had to carry their crop up from their fields.[43]

Towards the end of growing a ready husked rice, Mills recorded:

> For one day Yarila, who long ago ruled Kabza as Queen, wished to give a specially fine present of rice to her lover. So she and her sister, with that strange perversity which causes men to paint the lily, set to work to pound some rice to make it even whiter than it was before. Nature resented this scorning of her gifts, and since then rice has always grown in the husk and must be laboriously pounded before it can be eaten.[44]

The Kuki tradition had it that their 'Golden Age' also ended due to certain flaws. Hutton noted: 'But every day that this was done, a woman with child died. So the practice of calling in the firewood and the paddy was abandoned.'[45]

What is significant in the notion of the world upside down of the past is that though it was considered to be their 'Golden Age', it was not really a happy moment for all. It was the world of domination relation where the fruits of someone's labour were reaped by

---

[43] Mills (2003 [1926]: 108).
[44] Mills (2003 [1926]: 108–9).
[45] Mills (2003 [1926]: 108, fn. 1).

others, or where the price of food amounted to one's life. In other words, it was the world of social stratification, domination, and oppression. What is even more interesting is the resistance from the 'poor men', who found the system 'so unfair' that they eventually 'outwitted' it. It is tempting to relate this 'Golden Age' to the system that prevailed in the valley states before the hillmen came up to their present hills. The rice flying into the granaries of the rich people and the poor not getting enough of the share of their labour was peculiar to the conditions of the surrounding valley states where larger parts of peasant's production found their ways into the granaries of the kings and rulers. Life for food under extreme scarcity was not unknown either in the valley states. Only after breaking the 'spell' with some 'act of darkness' (put some rice in baskets, as the legend put it) did the 'Golden Age' come to an end. Breaking the spell in the context of the state-evading population may be understood in terms of their flight to their present mountain massif. This was well illustrated in the 'Thimzing' story of Kuki-Chin world.

In the Thimzing story, certain world order came to an end with cataclysmic incidents and a new world appeared. New men and women came out of Chhinlung and repeopled the land. As noted earlier, the Chhinlung (Khul) story was necessarily about the great exodus from the valley states to the hills. The Kuki tradition of this exodus to the hills was preceded by the 'great fire', the 'great flood', famine, and then darkness, all connoting the world of disorderliness and hardship.[46] The Chin's Babel tower story talked about the multistorey tower made of stone and other building materials whose rubbles now formed the Chin Hills.[47] This Babel story clearly noted how people became so proud and audacious that the spirit raised a fearful storm and the tower fell down.[48] There was also, as noted earlier, a Chin (Asho) story of the 'the brick walled city' of their forefathers

---

[46] Guite (2011: 346–9).

[47] Scott (1906: 103), as quoted in Hutton (1914: 480).

[48] A vague millennial idea circulated among them on the 'Return of Chin Hill' (*Chin Hill Kithou kit ding*, meaning 'Chill Hills will rise up again') referring, I think, to the return of this great tower, connoting the return to their great days when they built such tower (*in-sang*).

in the 'level plains of the baleng and dry htoan (grasses)'.[49] In fact, the Lusheis could not forget their old fort at Khampat, in the valley of Kale–Kabaw in Burma. And there was a prophecy regarding the banyan tree planted by their forefathers before leaving that 'walled' settlement: once its branches touched the ground, their ruined kingdom would be restored.[50] Therefore, the significance of the world upside down in the context of Thimzing celebrated their flight to the new world of the hills, the new orderliness that celebrated the world of egalitarian society of the present they founded in the hills.

The newness of the new (present) world was reflected in the expression 'from that day' onwards, 'all, rich and poor alike, have had to carry their crop up from their fields'. If the rich and the poor now had to carry their crop, unlike before, it typically referred to a new world of egalitarian society where the rice stopped 'flying' and was carried over by men to their respective granaries (thus, no more only to the rich men's granaries). It also referred to a world where the poor men got the full share of their labour and stopped agitating, and where women stopped 'dying' due to rice or scarcity. The new world of the present was then immensely better than their 'Golden Age' in the sense that nature's 'fairness' was now assured to all, and did not favour any particular section of the society. Although the labour increased (as they had to carry their rice and other things on their back), such life, free of hierarchy and domination, was new and thus they were more content. Overall, the legend of the world upside down ridiculed the so-called 'Golden Age' and celebrated the new world of egalitarian society. The celebration of the present world, the world of equality and 'alikeness', as the legend put it, was also shown by their legends of the world upside down of the future, the 'Armageddon'.

The legends of some tribes had a vague idea about their future world order. It was also described to be the world upside down, something very close to a biblical 'Armageddon'. Instead of harbouring high hopes for this world upside down of the future, unlike their future millennial hope, the hillmen surprisingly warned themselves against the coming disorderliness. This was not truly a 'prophesy' in

---

[49] Fryer (1875: 46–7).
[50] See Lalthangliana (1977: 87–91).

the strict sense of the term but a kind of warning against transforming the present. It could be taken as a sort of 'heresy' to the normative order of the present. A change in the present, as the legends put it, would be followed by the world upside down, a topsy-turvy age. Interestingly, it did not intend to revive the past 'Golden Age', and was neither akin to their millennial hope of the coming state. It was the inversion of the present egalitarian society. It celebrated their present.

The Angami tradition was instructive in this respect. Hutton recorded:

> Another prophesy is that of *Chusenu*, 'Armageddon', when everyone will fight and men will become so small that they can climb up chilli plants and their ears will grow the wrong way on and wooden pestles (for pounding paddy) will put forth leaves; at that time the dead will rise and the stored grain will fly in the air and men will run about to catch it for their food, and every family in the tribe, indeed in the whole hill country, will have a dispute.[51]

Hutton further noted that this belief in men becoming small enough to climb the chilli plants was also known to the Khasis. The Kuki tradition also said that men will become so small that they will climb not only the chilli plants but also beans and other small plants. In the Kuki-Chin world, there was another vague idea about 'Armageddon' (*ninunungni*, at end of the world) where the population of men will shrink and the women will outnumber them. Men, to save themselves, will climb up the tree and women will prick them with a bamboo stick (*he*, in Kuki) from below. This was an obvious consequence of war and conflicts. Courting of men by women also implied a change of gender role, upside down.

This topsy-turvy age, of the world upside down, was also quite a contrast to their present. To summarize, it was believed that the dead will rise up. Everyone will fight against the other; every family in the hill country will have a dispute. Men will become so small that they can climb up the chilli plants. Their ears will grow in the wrong direction. The wooden pestles will produce leaves. The number of

---

[51] Hutton (1921a: 252).

men will shrink and women will outnumber them. Women will court men. And worse, the stored grain will fly in the air and 'men will run about to catch it for their food'. It was indeed a world of hardship, warfare, and conflict. In short, it was the 'Armageddon' of the state universe.

If this is taken as a 'prophesy', instead of a 'heresy', it can be said that the prophesy has been fulfilled since the occupation of the hills by the British colonial state. The proud hillmen, who had thought so highly of themselves, suddenly became insignificant within the mighty British Empire. Hutton noted that some people believed that the Angami prophesy was 'fulfilled when Khonoma was taken by the British troops, as wooden pestles are believed to have put forth leaves at that time'.[52] In fact, the Armageddon of ethnic conflict and political turmoil has for long overshadowed this upland region. People have had to run after the 'flying' grains from the valley in different shops and markets. Their traditional rice mortar has indeed been forgotten; and leaves have already grown out of it. Their ears have gone awry, with no one listening to their cultural truths but, instead, craving for the modern knowledge of jobs and opportunity. Are they listening to their traditions? Not really. From a prophetic mode, the Armageddon is on.

However, that is not the case here. The legend of the world upside down of the future is rather a 'heresy' to the egalitarian world order. Thus, when seen from a 'heretic' mode, as in the past worldview, the legend of this topsy-turvy age is also a warning to the stateless present that what they have in the egalitarian society is the best they have got. To change it would lead to a topsy-turvy world order. Therefore, they should resist any change against the stateless present. In this context, the legend of world upside down in the future also celebrates the present and ridicules the topsy-turvy future (invariably the coming of state in the hills). It is, in a way, an expression of an experienced dignity or no indignity of the stateless egalitarian society where everyone is 'normal'. Politically, they are proud people, not small enough to climb the chilli plants, the listening ear is in the right direction to their calling in the hills, and there is peace and tranquility. Socially,

[52] Hutton (1921a: 252).

everyone is equal; men and women take their normal position and have enough choice for themselves. Economically, everyone works for their food and carries their loads and people do not run after the flying rice for their living and so on. The 'flying rice' indeed indicates an economy deprived of 'food sovereignty', as noted in the previous chapter. This present egalitarian world order is, to their understanding, the best of what they could have in this world. Any change to the present would cause what the 'prophetic' mode called 'Armageddon'. Above all, it again celebrates the world of the present, the world of statelessness.

To the hillmen, folklores are, therefore, an endless store of ideas and knowledge about their past. They are a medium of social control and constitute the moral code of conduct which centres on egalitarian principle. In most cases, they act as a primary text to serve as a measure of heresy or deviation. They are the social arsenal against the One, the Mighty, and enact the deeper current of what it means to be a 'hillmen'. They have powerfully chipped away the reputation of the One, the Mighty, and the State in the minds of the hillmen, and reinforced and socialized the twin ideologies of masculinity and egalitarianism. They are the double-edged sword for the state-evading population. On the one hand, they forbid any sort of deviation from normative values of egalitarian society, and on the other, they encourage people to remain strong and alert against the One, the Mighty, from within and without. In this sense, they are the cultural capital of the stateless hill society. In short, they celebrated their present, enacted their egalitarianism, ridiculed those who deviated from the norms, and mocked against the great and mighty. In its celebration of the present, their past and future worlds (understood as state system) have been painted as the world upside down, the topsy-turvy world order. This genre of knowledge is presently not even known and people hardly care to know it, indicating that it has lost its appeal. Are the hillmen already climbing chilli plants? Are their ears growing the wrong way? Nobody can say for sure.

8

Renouncer, Restorer, and Defender

Daughters of the Hills

A woman who dare not fight her husband is not a good wife.

—Pawi saying

Speaking on the position of women in the hill society in the 1930s, N.E. Parry, the Superintendent of Lushai Hills, remarked, 'women are normal human beings, with minds and opinions of their own; they may lead hard lives, but no harder than the men, and all the time they are free.' He went on to say that 'they can lead their own lives and are in a far happier position than their sisters in the plains.'[1] This is the position taken by most colonial ethnographers on the hill tribes of Northeast India. What remains to be discussed is whether equal rights and freedom were given to the women within the dominant tribal patriarchy of stateless society. Within patriarchy, the degree of rights and freedom enjoyed by women differ from culture to culture. Besides, value judgement, if needed, should be from inside rather than outside the culture. Recent scholarship on tribal women has shown growing male domination and masculinity with time in the

[1] Parry (1988 [1931]: 278).

hill society and the corresponding decline in women's position.[2] The rapid strides of modernity projects (under colonial and postcolonial state), for instance, have been found to strengthen male dominance.[3] This is one important tool to measure the position of women in history as well. The relative proximity they shared with each other, taken in the long view, can provide a fascinating insight into the role and position enjoyed by women in stateless society. This chapter, therefore, reconstructs the position of tribal women within the growing masculinity in stateless society of Northeast India.

Notwithstanding the dominant patriarchy system in the region, it is interesting to note that the tribal women did enjoy ample amount of relative freedom and rights vis-à-vis their men. This was largely because of two significant factors. First, as in all other patriarchal societies, the rights and freedom of women in tribal society were also conceived and defined in patriarchal terms but, significantly, the same system also provided what I call the counter-culture, the conduits against male domination. If marriage institution, for instance, favoured men and became oppressive, then there were an inbuilt conduits in the form of liberal divorce and remarriage laws through which women could evade male domination with ease. Second, and even more important, was the energy with which the tribal women fought male high-handedness. In this sense, the hill woman was a renouncer of masculinity (and the patriarchy itself) and restorer and defender of the customary 'norms' which provided ample rights and freedom to her. Taking this approach into account, it is proper to begin with the history of masculinity in the hills as a comparative tool.

'The Word of Women is No Word': Man(uring) Masculinity

Legends and folklores of some tribes in the region state that woman was the 'first human being'. For instance, the Angami 'Babel tower' story, mentioned earlier, celebrated the 'first human being', Ukepenopfu,

---

[2] A general review of the important works on tribal women is given in Xaxa (2004). See also Kishwar (1987), Singh, Vyas, and Mann (1988), Nongbri (1998), and Zehol (1998).

[3] Kishwar (1987).

as the common ancestress of all human beings who was 'raised to heaven'. The tower was built by her descendants who were eager 'to communicate' and 'talk to her' and wanted 'presents' (read blessing) from her.[4] Similarly, the Karbi's creation story celebrated the mother of human race, known as a 'beautiful' wife of Ram and a 'fruitful' mother.[5] Patriarchy as the dominant form of social organization was already visible during the course of their migration (see Chapter 2) and when they settled down in their present hills, both in patrilineal and matrilineal societies. In their folk narratives, a warrior ideology was visible as one of the celebrated ideas. What was interesting in their conception of a warrior ideology was the centrality of women. If the production of masculinity was the subject of a warrior ideology, women in general, and the 'most beautiful woman' in particular, were the central object of constructing masculinity. In other words, masculinity was conceived through, and arguably inconceivable without, women taking a prime place. Thus, she must be protected from the 'enemy', revenge should be taken against an insult on her, and above all, any outrage on her body was taken to be an insult on the body of the men, the family, and the clan/community. The primary duty of men was her protection and those who did so successfully became celebrated warriors. Unlike the present notion that men have to 'earn' for the family, in the past their role was mainly to 'protect'. Thus, she was everything for a man's fame as to his defamation.

For instance, the Garos fought against the 'powerful and cruel' chief of Brahmaputra valley because he was attracted to the beauty of a Garo maiden, Juge-Silche, and wanted to carry her off by force. The battle went against them, leading to their subjection, and many Garo headmen were 'poisoned' to death.[6] In the Kuki-Chin world, as mentioned earlier, the warrior ideology was built around protecting woman and rescuing her from the powerful 'enemy', Khalvompu, who belonged to the 'village of tiger-men'. While the subject of the story was a legendary hero, Laangchal, or Hrangchala (in Lushei), or Rangchar (in Kolhen), it was invariably built around the 'most beautiful woman' Moltinchaan (Kungori in Lushei tradition) who

[4] Hutton (1914: 479). See also Hutton (1921a: 265).
[5] Lyall (1997 [1908]: 70–2).
[6] Playfair (1998 [1909]: 7–14).

was 'bewitched' and then carried away by Khalvompu. Interestingly, Moltinchaan's mother, who was deceived by Khalvompu, was blamed for the whole episode.[7] Chapter 7 also narrated the story of 'the most beautiful women' Lenchonghoi who was carried away by Khalvompu, and to avenge the insult, her six brothers died. Her youngest brother eventually succeeded in avenging Khalvompu and rescued her from him. Lenchonghoi, to her seven brothers, was not only an object of pride but also insecurity. She was put behind the ten-folded iron door whenever they went out for hunting.[8]

The Naga story of 'The Dog's Share' or the Kuki-Chin story of 'Lengbante' (vine-cutter), mentioned earlier, were another genre where mother constituted a central place in the making of men's masculinity. In the former, the Sambhar killed a bitch in a series of violent acts started by a crab. Her puppies vowed revenge and asked god as to 'who is the greatest?' They found 'man' the greatest of all, above the tiger, elephant, and the spirit. With the help of man, they finally killed the Sambhar.[9] In Lengbante, a tiger-man killed the father of seven sons. His sons also died while fighting the tiger-man for revenge. The grieving mother then gave birth to another son through the god's bow. He finally avenged the death of his father and seven brothers.[10] Woman as a site of manhood was therefore central. She was always behind the man taking a warpath. In the first case, he took to warpath to avenge the insult. In the second story, the mother's painful condition compelled her son to take the warpath. Therefore, in both the cases, women constituted the relic in the construction of men's masculinity. In this way, the making of a warrior ideology was invariably associated with masculinity and such masculinity was built around, and/or conceived from, objectifying women.

[7] See Haokip (1998: 1–91). As mentioned earlier, in the Lushei tradition, Laangchal's role was played by Hpohtir and vice versa. See Shakespear (1998 [1912]: 177–82).

[8] See, for instance, Singson (1997: 124–7).

[9] Hutton (1921b: 336–8). See also Shakespear (1922: 270–1).

[10] See Shaw (1997 [1929]: 119–28). As mentioned earlier, for a similar version of Lamkang, see Shakespear and Hodson (1909: 411–12) and for Chakesang version, see Laloo (2011: 152–7).

If oral narratives glorified the famed warriors and socialized masculinity, the hill society also trained their young men and women to be so through institutionalization process. The machination of masculinity and femininity was achieved through the morung (young man's or bachelor's dormitory) and girl's dormitory system among most tribes, some of which were still in a vibrant form in the nineteenth century, while in other tribes they were a mere trace in folk narratives. The centrality of these twin institutions in shaping masculinity and femininity was noted in Chapter 4. In brief, it trained the young boys in warrior tradition and imparted the values of esprit de corps. In other words, it helped in disciplining or 'hammering into shape' the young boys of the village. Thus, to be a warrior, a man had to, for instance, take to a warpath (of defence or offence), kill the 'enemy', and bring their heads home. At the least, he had to be a great hunter. The idea of a warrior based on masculinity, was so pronounced that a man who could not perform the so-called 'manly' activities (war, hunting, and so on) was condemned as 'boy', 'girl', 'woman', or otherwise. In Lushai Hills, for instance, Lewin (1866) noted that young men who refused to fight, hunt, or perform 'manly' activities were called *toi* (girly) and were 'dressed in women's clothes, and consorts and works with the women'. He had seen instances of this 'in several villages'.[11] To be seen as 'girl', 'woman', or 'unmanly' was the worst form of condemnation for a man. Hence, every man would strive to avoid this public ordeal, a mockery of the worst kind that chipped away at one's spine. In fact, to attain manhood as a 'warrior' became a lifetime project for the men. I will come back into this institutionalization of masculinity during the discussion on marriage institution.

The idea of masculinity also infiltrated into their everyday chores. Works were gradually defined in gendered terms, and those works which men were most proficient at were often privileged. One popular adage in the Kuki-Chin world, for instance, was: 'A man should spend his life in fighting, hunting, and drinking, whilst labour is intended for women and slaves only'.[12] Similarly, in the Naga world, it was said that women 'does everything the husband will not, and he

---

[11]   Lewin (1978 [1870]: 134).
[12]   Carey and Tuck (1987 [1896]: 134).

considers it effeminate to do anything but fight, hunt, and cheat'.[13] The idea of masculinity even entered into their everyday discourse the other way round, that is, ridiculing womanhood. A Lushei saying, for instance, stated: 'The word of women is no word just as the flesh of a crab is no meat'.[14] Similarly, it was said: 'The word of women does not go beyond the water-pent'.[15] A Lhota Naga man would often utter, noted Mills, 'What does a woman know about such things?', although he would invariably consult her when he was home.[16] Other Lushei sayings were: 'A worn-out woman and a worn-out fence should be replaced' or 'Unbeaten wife and unbeaten grass in the fields are most unbearable'.[17] This process of constructing masculinity by ridiculing womanhood reduced the women to an object of nothingness, an identity having no resemblance with men.

Interestingly, in this socialization of masculinity, women also played an active part. For instance, no girl would marry a man (or so it was thought) if he was not a 'warrior' and could not wear a warrior dress/insignia. This prevailed across the landscape. The headhunting tradition among the Nagas is most fascinating in this respect. Hutton, for instance, noted:

> It is agreed by all Angamis, as well as by other Nagas, that head-taking was essential to marriage in so far that a buck who had taken no head, and could not wear the warrior's dress at festivals, not only found it exceedingly difficult to get any girl with pretensions to good looks or to self-respect to marry him, but was held up to ridicule by all the girls of his clan.[18]

Perhaps this was one of the strongest impetus to men in the pursuit of masculinity. The idea of being 'ridiculed by all girls' for not being able to take head not only signified the positive consent given by women to his manhood but it was also a serious question of life to

---

[13] Elwin (1969: 101).
[14] Tribal Research Institute (TRI 1991: 7).
[15] TRI (1991: 7).
[16] Mills (2003 [1922]: 111–12).
[17] TRI (1991: 7).
[18] Hutton (1921a: 165).

a young man.[19] Thus, women were not only a site of articulating manhood but also the source of it. This also certainly affected the parenting process of a mother who was at the core of machinating masculinity and femininity in her children. She often frowned upon boys behaving in a 'girly' manner and girls behaving 'manly'.

These folk narratives were, as a democratic voice, a powerful tool to propagate the idea of masculinity in the society, just as they represented the growing sense of masculinity and male domination in the society. To what extent this dominant discourse on masculinity affected women's position, and how the womenfolk reacted to them, is dealt with in the following sections.

Fighting Masculinity, Challenging Patriarchy

If the dominant discourse reduced women to an object of men's anxiety and nothingness, the fact of the matter was that her actual position in tribal society was quite different. Notwithstanding the dominant patriarchal system and the growing masculinity, folklores and the early colonial accounts showed tribal women enjoying ample amount of freedom, rights, and even equality with the men. The unique customary system that provided conduits through which she could evade domination was central to this. The ease with which she could channel her discontentment through these conduits safeguarded her rights and freedom to a great extent. In this section, some of the major patriarchal institutions which demean women, such as marriage, inheritance, administration, social status, and religion, are taken up for discussion. Before I do that, it is important to dwell briefly on the counter-discourse to masculinity, taken from their social grapevine.

If masculinity projected men to be 'above' women and that she should be 'beaten' to be controlled, then there was also a very strong

[19] In her interesting study on 'headhunting' in Southeast Asia, Barbara Watson Andaya has shown that women not only saw headhunters as more virile and highly desirable lovers, husbands, and fathers, but also played significant part in headhunting rituals that guaranteed her fertility, the fertility of crops, and the good health of her children and kinsfolk. She was an active agent in the tradition. See Andaya (2004).

sense of feminism circulating among the womenfolk. For instance, it was asserted that a 'good wife' should not remain a mute spectator before an arrogant husband. A Pawi saying remarked, 'A woman who dare not fight against her husband is a bad wife' (literally, not a good wife).[20] It was also asserted that women could protect themselves from danger. In the Kuki-Chin world, for instance, Khalvompu was an imminent danger to women and men were urged to protect women from him. Against this, there was another popular story of 'Jawllhing and Jawlphal', in which the fearful Khalvompu was courting two beautiful sisters, Jawllhing and Jawlphal, who disliked him very much. They chalked out a scheme to kill him. They prepared a strong fire alongside their normal sleeping place. At night, when they were asleep, the elder sister, Jawllhing, who was sleeping in the middle, urged Khalvompu to move towards the fire, complaining that her sister was not getting enough space to sleep. She did it with the intention to push him into the fire once he was very close. With repeated urging, Khalvompu moved towards the fire. When he was very close, Jawllhing pushed him into the fire and he died.[21] This story ridiculed the idea that women were unable to protect themselves. It showed how a woman could handle her own problems.

In a more radical fashion, there were stories that directly challenged patriarchy itself. Take the case of, for instance, the Angami and Sema tale of the 'Amazons' or the 'village of women'. The Angami story stated that 'if a man go there they drive him away by shooting at him with war bows, and they raise not any males save one only, and when other male babes are born they boil water and put them therein to kill them'. These women 'do no hard work, but eat great store of starch and oil to make them strong to battle'. It was further said that 'when a man go there, the women that be there be so eager for him that in striving to possess him they tear him to pieces utterly.'[22] The idea of women using 'war bows', eating great stores to keep them 'strong to battle', raising no males, not allowing men to enter their village, and the village itself, all contested the dominant discourse on masculinity and the hill patriarchy itself and re-enacted women as

---

[20] Tribal Research Institute (TRI 1988: 50–1).
[21] See, for instance, Singson (1997: 124–7).
[22] Hutton (1921a: 263–4).

the original being. Along this line of thought, I will take up some of the forms of women's resistance to male domination in the following sections.

'A Very Real Companion' at Work

One hill practice where women were found to be most exploited was on the subject of work or labour. They were often shown to be a model of labour and industry, carrying the weight of the hill economy on their back. Lewin, for instance, remarked that 'the whole burden of the bodily labour' falls upon women who 'fetch water, hew wood, cultivate, and help to reap the crop, besides spinning, cooking, and brewing'.[23] In this context, she was shown as the relic of 'unpolished nations' where the whole domestic economy 'fall *naturally* to the share of women'.[24] But the growing burden of labour on women should be read alongside the increasing warfare and conflict in the hills since the dawn of early nineteenth century, which resulted in the shifting of men's energy from agriculture and household activities.[25] Yet, within this situation, most colonial ethnographers still argued that the burden of work was equally shared between men and women. Hutton, supported by Mills, for instance, showed that among the Nagas, hunting fell on the men and weaving and cooking fell on women, but 'agriculture and, to some degree, trade are carried on by both together'.[26] Parry even went on say that 'the household labours, whether in the fields or in the home, are very fairly divided between men and women.'[27] They all agreed that the tribal woman was 'by no means a slave or chattel, but a very real companion'.[28]

Considering the harsh geography and the livelihood pattern chosen by the stateless hillmen, it was obvious that all needed to work

[23] Lewin (1978 [1870]: 142). See also Shakespear (1998 [1912]: 16) and Stewart (1855: 636).

[24] See, for instance, Robinson (1975 [1841]: 389; emphasis mine).

[25] See, for instance, Guite (2011, 2014).

[26] Hutton (1921a: 167–8) and Mills (2003 [1922]: 111, 2003 [1926]: 213).

[27] Parry (1988 [1931]: 276).

[28] See Mills (2003 [1926]: 211) and Parry (1988 [1931]: 276).

together to make a living and idleness was frowned upon. In this respect, one interesting case was noted by Mills among the Ao Nagas. He informed that Ao girls who were educated in the American Baptist Mission did 'not meet with the approval of conservative Aos, who regard it as *useless*' [emphasis mine]. This was not because they did not like women education but because education, as per them, led to 'idleness and immorality'. He pointed out that a few girls who returned to their village after spending some time at the Impur Mission School 'refused *to demean themselves* by working in the fields like their uneducated sisters, and preferred to sit in the village during the day doing nothing' [emphasis mine]. These 'idle' girls intrigued with the village boys and he remarked, 'It was when a baby or two arrived that I heard some *forcible opinions* on female education.' [emphasis mine].[29] He went on to note how it had become a shared opinion amongst all:

> Ao Christians have themselves complained to me that girls who have had a Mission education find it hard to settle down to village life and are liable to go on the loose. I do not mean to imply that no girl educated by the Mission keeps straight; far from it. But the consensus of opinion among respectable Aos undoubtedly is that there is *grave risk* of a Mission-trained girl getting 'above herself', and so idle and immoral.[30]

While the idea of 'immorality' was purely a Christian notion of women chastity, what was central to women education was not the education per se but the 'idleness' it had developed in the girls. Anything that would impede the hands of anyone from labour was frowned upon. In this context, to remain 'idle' was to be 'above' oneself; it was a deviation from the normative economic values of the community. 'Idleness', therefore, generated 'forcible' social disapproval. In the sense noted here, work and labour as particularly exploitative to one and not to another did not arise. Similarly, gradation of work into low–high dichotomy in this context was also problematic. Truly, work, and for that matter division of work, had

---

[29] Mills (2003 [1926]: 213–14).
[30] Mills (2003 [1926]: 213, fn. 2; emphasis mine).

nothing to do with status in tribal society. Work made women a 'very real companion' of men.

'Eating' Bride Price, Contesting Marriage Institution

In Northeast India, both the matrilineal and patrilineal marriage systems existed. As noted earlier, the established marriage institution provided a system of checks and balances through a conduit or safeguard attached to it. Interestingly, it was men who contested the established marriage institution and women struggled hard to restore it. Thus, the history of marriage among the hill tribes of Northeast India was the history of men's attempt to deviate from the established marriage custom in order to control women's freedom and the women fighting against it by using the inbuilt conduits in the form of liberal divorce and remarriage laws. All tribal customs of the region left unmarried girls virtually free from control, without incurring any social reflections, besides enjoying freedom of choice for their partner.[31] The liberality of girls among the tribes having girl's dormitory was especially fascinating.[32] Control of women actually began when the girl entered a married life.

What was said to be most exploitative to hill women was the system of bride price (*man* in southern tribes). Some colonial observers felt that bride price was the source of exploitation of women and symbolized her degraded status. It turned a woman into 'property' to be 'sold' by her father and 'purchased' by her husband. It was also seen as a 'compensation' to her greedy father. However, to see this practice purely from the point of the dominant civilizational narrative is to miss some of the important local values attached to it. It

---

[31] This was noted in most colonial sources. Hutton, for instance, noted that 'Angami woman before marriage is given a very great deal of liberty ... girls are not looked after with jealousy' and 'she is allowed a freedom of choice' and cases of girls married against their inclinations 'are exceedingly rare' and she could easily evade any 'a distasteful alliance'. See Hutton (1921a: 168).

[32] The Aos called it *chiki* and the Adis called it *rasheng*. Mills noted that 'a girl is ordinarily pretty free with her favours and probably has a series of lovers'. See Mills (2003 [1926]: 212) and Roy (1997 [1960]: 197–9).

is true that the bride price implied a kind of male dominance over the women in tribal society, but it is more important to investigate the reasons for imposing a price on the daughter and how it actually affected her rights. It is also difficult to say when and how this system of bride price started. In fact, legends and folklores are surprisingly silent on the subject of bride price. They merely show that the bride was taken without any payment and, at the most, the bridegroom was sometimes put through certain tests as a precondition for the hand of his love.

Some interesting cases show that bride price was a later invention (by men) for certain political and social ends. In the old Jewish fashion, for instance, certain tribes like Mroongs (Reangs) and Mrus of Chittagong Hill Tracts had the tradition that a man should serve in the house of his father-in-law for three years before he could take away his wife to his house. However, a rich man could commute his customary labour by certain payments.[33] The Quirengs, Chirus, and Anals of Manipur also had a similar practice: Anals served for three years and Chirus too made some payment with labour.[34] Likewise, a Lhota bridegroom had to serve for one year at his father-in-law's house before he could take his wife home, the same as the Kacharis.[35] There was also a trace of this kind of practice among the Abors (Adis).[36] In the Kuki-Chin world, there was a vague idea of a man working in the in-law's house for the hand of his love. It was called *Konglo* (literally, working-for-woman's backbone).

If such a 'laborious honeymoon' could be commuted by certain payments, then the bride price probably traced its origin from such commutation. If this is true, then it can be said that bride price developed from an older tradition of commuting customary labour into certain payment. In this sense, bride price was a more convenient and simpler practice as compared to a tortuous, compulsory labour system in the house of the father-in-law. The Chiru case of paying with both labour and certain payments, for instance, can be considered

---

[33] Lewin (2004 [1869]: 114, 131).
[34] Hodson (2007 [1911]: 91).
[35] Mills (2003 [1922]: 148) and Endle (2010 [1911]: 44) respectively.
[36] See Roy (1997 [1960]: 202–5).

as the transitional phase. In this context, man was actually paying against his own labour in the in-law's house, quite contrary to what the term 'bride price' connoted. It was therefore a deviation from the normative principle of the older tradition.

As any deviation from the established custom was frowned upon, bride price also apparently generated much social disapproval if their social expressions regarding it are taken into account. For instance, the term *man* was a widely used terminology which meant 'price' in the Kuki-Chin world. In Kuki, it literally meant 'catch', which had a negative connotation of 'taking away' from someone. Thus, when a person took bride price (*numei-man*, women's price in Kuki), it was not said 'he takes' or 'he receives'; the term invariably uttered was 'he eats'. Hence, her father/brother, the receiver of bride price, was known as the 'eater of bride price' (*man-ne-pa*). When a person gave bride price, it was not said 'he gives' but 'he bolts' (the cattle inside her father's shed—*akhum* or *khum*) or sometimes 'he throws' (the price—*asep* or *sep*). Hence, the giver of bride price was known as the 'bolter/thrower of bride price' (*man-khum* or *man-sep*). The terms 'eat', 'bolt', or 'throw' thus had a negative connotation, ridiculing the taker of bride price and the bride price itself. They enacted not only the deviation but also the social disapproval of it. Yet, taking bride price became the dominant feature of marriage among all tribes across the region.

A high bride price became a prominent feature of marriage among the southern tribes in the Kuki-Chin world. Among the Nagas, the Lhotas were one of the tribes known to take pride in high bride price. In the sub-Himalayan ranges, the Abors (Adis) and Mishmis also exacted high bride price. The bride price for Adis took the form of continuous supply of meat to the father-in-law, such as part of the meat in ceremonies, rituals, or chase and whole of the chase in cooperative hunting and fishing.[37] The Mishmis gave standing animals like mithuns or pigs as well as the skulls of various animals as bride

---

[37] See Roy (1997 [1960]: 202–5). Among the Kukis also, the *tute* (son-in-law) was bound to provide the father-in-law (*pute*) the *sangong*, the neck meat of all animals killed. In case of non-payment, the tute had to give one mithun to the pute.

price, which differed from clan to clan.[38] How and why did this system become dominant then?

A look into the political formation process is instructive in this regard. As mentioned earlier, the growing masculinity in the hill society was closely related to the increasing conflict and warfare situation in the hills or the ever-preparedness they had to put up against marauders and raiders from the valley states. The emergence of bride price can be located within this growing emphasis on masculinity. It increasingly became an enabling tool for men for political and social dominance over other men, and also the women. The bride price in the rising chiefdoms in Kuki-Chin world, for instance, became a measure of the political and social importance of the woman's father. Carey and Tuck noted among the Chins:

> If a young man wishes to marry the daughter of a Haka Chief he must be prepared to pay something like 10 mithun, 50 pigs, 10 guns, a similar number of gongs, several slaves, and a large quantity of grain, and also be able to provide several score of pots of liquor to be drunk at the feast. The Haka chiefs *boast* that no other tribe has such strict marriage laws as they, and that this shows their *superiority* to all.[39]

They also noted how marriage was 'usually arranged with the *diplomatic view* of strengthening the position of Chiefs and consolidating the power of clans' [emphasis mine].

In Lushai Hills, among the Lakhers, Parry noted how bride price was an indicator of social status. It was a marker of the so-called 'higher' clans (the chiefly clans) and 'lower' clans (non-chiefly clans). Yet, what is interesting is that one could improve his social status by having a marriage relationship with the chiefly clan who had the privilege to exact high bride price. In this context, Parry noted that 'all Lakhers are social climbers, and try to marry into a clan higher than their own'. The idea was to not only have a social/political connection with the higher/powerful chiefly family/clan but also, more importantly, to raise one's own social status. Thus, if a man, his son, and his grandson, all married women from 'higher' clan, then when

---

[38] See Cooper (1995 [1873]: 235–7).
[39] Carey and Tuck (1987 [1896]: 190; emphasis mine).

the grandson married off his daughter(s), he could claim a higher clan's bride price, a distinction preserved only for the club of the chiefs.[40] In being able to demand a higher bride price, a person was actually enhancing his social status, similar to the higher clan, even if he could not change his clan and ritual status.

Thus, among all the tribes which exacted a higher price, the association of bride price with power and authority, as well as social status, was clear. It marked a person's social and political superiority over other men; and the chiefs could actually strengthen their position and consolidate their power over other chiefs or clans. In this sense, women became the object of man's pride or at least a reflection of him. Thus, bride price turned an emotional event in life into an event of subordination–superordination by men over other men. In this context, daughters were not sold by their parents but given to marriage only to reconstitute and re-enact men's position in the society.

Within the growing masculinity, bride price also became popular as an attempt by men to overawe the long-cherished custom of liberal divorce and remarriage which had acted as a liberating force for women. Some colonial ethnographers found that high bride price actually reduced domestic violence, thereby enhancing the stability of marriage. It gave security to the wife and helped her evade male harassment, and hence the marriage last longer. Parry, for instance, noted of the Lakher system:

> It is very rare to find a Lakher who is brutal to a woman ... The high marriage prices in force strengthen a wife's position, and a divorce is far less common than among the Lusheis, neither party being lightly to incur the material losses involved ... The high marriage price therefore has its good side, in that it tends to make marriages more permanent and the position of the wife more secure.[41]

Mills found the same result among the Lhotas:

> It is comparatively rare for a man to divorce his wife [among Lhotas] without very good cause, partly because he will not get his marriage

---

40 Parry (1988 [1931]: 311–12).
41 Parry ((1988 [1931]: 276–7).

price back if he does. Among the Aos, on the other hand, where there is no marriage price [*sic*], a man will divorce his wife in the most heartless manner when he gets tired of her.[42]

The argument was related to a heavy price to be paid by the one who caused the marriage to break up. If the woman returned on her own or due to her own folly, her male relations were obliged to return the bride price 'eaten' by them. If she returned home due to her husband's cruelty, infidelity, or otherwise, the bride price was not given back. Instead, more would be 'eaten' from her husband (call *daman* or divorce price in Kuki) as a punishment for causing divorce. Thus, if high bride price was an evil custom in one way, it also acted as a check and balancing factor on the other. However, simultaneously, bride price also restrained women from choosing divorce as an easy option to get away from an unwanted marriage, thereby challenging her freedom. The liberal divorce law was then restrained in a big way. How did the tribal women respond to such deviations and constraints?

Divorce and Remarriage as Counter-Culture

If men tried hard to control the liberty of women through various injunctions like bride price, the women too struggled hard to renounce such injunctions and restore their freedom. As noted earlier, liberal divorce and remarriage laws were inbuilt conduits through which women could easily evade male domination and high-handedness.[43] Despite all efforts to restrain women from choosing the divorce option, most colonial ethnographers found that divorce, as well as remarriage, was liberal and common among all hill tribes, including those tribes who 'ate' high marriage price. Among the Aos (who took nominal bride price), for instance, Mills found that: 'Divorce is amazingly common. In fact it is very rare that an Ao man or woman of any age who has only been married once. Couples part on the least provocation ... Divorced persons soon remarry, and after one

[42] Mills (2003 [1922]: 112).
[43] Divorce could also be taken for reasons ranging from mere incompatibility to adultery, impotency, and so on.

or two experiments, most people find a mate for life.'[44] Among the Angami, Hutton also noted: 'Divorce is easy to obtain; incompatibility of temper is a quite sufficient reason.'[45] Similarly, Shakespear noted among the Lusheis that the 'bonds of matrimony are extremely loose and are easily slipped off'. He went on to say that 'if a couple disagree, they simply separate'.[46]

On the one hand, Mills noted that, among the Lhotas (who exacted high bride price), divorce was very common because of the prevailing 'arranged marriage'.[47] He remarked:

> The result is that divorces, in which it is the wife who refuses to stay with her husband, are pretty frequent. Often for the slightest of causes or even for no ascertainable reason at all, a woman simply refuses to live with her husband. She will shed floods of tears over her own supposed grievances and pay not the slightest attention to his earnest entreaties.[48]

In the Ao and Lushei case, the reason for frequent divorce was said to be due to less bride price. Mills remarked that, among Aos, since 'marriage price there is very small', it 'tends to make divorce easy, for the husband has paid little for his wife and loses little if he parts with her'.[49] On the other hand, as already noted, divorce was less among the Lakhers because of high bride price.

Yet, both the arguments based on bride price seem simplistic if other facts are considered. The case of the Lusheis and Lhotas is instructive. Among the Lhotas, Mills pointed out that divorce was very common because of the prevailing male dominance over women. The freedom of girls was curbed, arranged marriages were prominent, and male arrogance increased. This resulted in frequent divorce in which it was not the husband but 'the wife who refuses to stay with her husband'.[50] Similarly, among the Lusheis, evidence

[44] Mills (2003 [1922]: 212).
[45] Hutton (1921a: 168).
[46] Shakespear (1998 [1912]: 52).
[47] Mills (2003 [1922]: 111–12).
[48] Mills (2003 [1922]: 112).
[49] Mills (2003 [1922]: 112).
[50] Mills (2003 [1922]: 111–12).

suggested that divorce was common largely because of the arrogant attitude of men towards their women. Women were seen as objects that had to be 'beaten' in order to control them and their words were 'no words'. This situation that governed domesticity and the social environment made the bonds of matrimony 'extremely loose' and it could be 'easily slipped off'.[51] Why male arrogance was central to divorce being common could also be seen from the case of Lakhers, in whom divorce was relatively less. Two factors in this regard were significant according to most colonial observers: Lakher men showed greater respect to their women and Lakher women, in turn, were powerful enough to fight back. Thus, domestic violence was less and divorce minimal.[52] In this sense, it can be said that divorce was less not because of high bride price but because of men's civility to women.

What is even more significant about the predominance of divorce across the region was that it symbolized, on the one hand, the increasing male dominance over women, and on the other hand, the persistent protest and resistance from the womenfolk. Parting ways 'on the least provocation', or for the 'slightest of causes', or even with 'no ascertainable reason' epitomized not only the persistence of a powerful mechanism to overcome unsolicited marriage at ease but also the perseverance of women to make use of the system against male domination. In other words, divorce became a powerful weapon in the hands of women. Shedding 'floods of tears' and paying 'not the slightest attention to his earnest entreaties' were subtle acts of sabotaging the unceremonious nuptial relationship before the intimidating gaze of patriarchal society. It was a powerful technique of dissent used by the women to make 'her own supposed grievances' known in the right perspective. It took refuge in the emotive space of the filial cord of her clan members and that of the larger society, whose veneration for 'motherhood' still remain unfazed.

When she did that, the woman was actually appealing to the flattering self-image of the male 'warriors' who felt that they were her 'protectors' and whose rhetorical cry for war against an insult on her body was well hyped. Thus, a swarm of her angry 'warrior'

---

[51] Shakespear (1998 [1912]: 52).
[52] Lewin (2004 [1869]: 311–12).

relatives would be soon buzzing around the ears of her husband. Her appeal was also usually heard by the emotive society. She would then promptly desert him in pain and penury. Mills, for instance, noted among the Aos:

> An Ao woman is very far from being a slave and a drudge. Her position is no whit inferior to that of a man. She always has her clan behind her, and were a bad-tempered husband to bully his wife he would soon have a swarm of angry in-laws buzzing round his ears, and his wife would promptly leave him.[53]

Divorce became an easy and effective tool in the hands of women only when they could remarry at ease. Interestingly, most tribal societies did not attach any social stigma to both the divorcees so that they could 'soon remarry, and after one or two experiments most people find a mate for life'. Hence, divorce became an easy option for a woman as she was not worried about her life post-divorce and could remarry. An interesting case of Khasi divorce custom shows why divorce and remarriage did not produce any social reflections. Here, divorce was official and required a special ceremony. After the ceremony, the village crier officially announced in public about the divorce in the following lines: 'Kaw—hear, oh villagers, that U— and K—have become separated in the presence of the elders. Hei! Thou, oh, young man, canst go and make love to Ka—for she is now unmarried (*khynraw*), and thou, oh, spinster, canst make love to U—. Hei! There is no let or hindrance from henceforth.'[54] This was a social declaration that, after divorce, a person became 'unmarried' and there was no 'hindrance' or stigma attached to her/him from the society. Thus, 'young man' and 'spinster' were asked to freely seek the hands of the divorcees for love or marriage. The absence of social stigma in divorce and the freedom to remarry were particularly significant safeguards against male domination and high-handedness.

Only in the case of widow remarriage, some control among certain tribes was evident. Among the Kukis, for instance, a widow was encouraged to marry her husband's brother in a sort of levirate, but it

---

[53] Mills (2003 [1926]: 211–12).
[54] Gurdon (2010 [1906]: 80).

all depended on her choice. Most widows, however, chose to return home or stay back with their children in a separate house. Thus, there were a good number of widows in history who chose to stay back and look after their family. In Lushai Hills, for instance, there were generations of chieftainesses who looked after the village administration after their husbands died. Similarly, the Garo custom of *akim* discouraged widow remarriage to some extent. It laid down that 'a widow or widower may not marry again without the permission of the family of the deceased husband or wife, and then, only into their respective motherhoods'.[55] Playfair remarked:

> The law is especially hard on the women. They are the owners of all property, and the relations of a deceased husband will often keep his widow waiting for years for a mere child. By the time the child is of marriageable age, the woman is already old. In such a case, the young husband is always allowed to marry a young girl as well, so the widow is kept unmarried for years *for the sake of her property*.[56]

However, in 1883, some Garo women fought in the colonial court and got it derecognized. Playfair informed: 'In 1883, fifty women of the Someswari valley appeared in court at Tura and applied to be relieved from the operation of this law [*akim*]. Their prayer was acceded to, and *akim* is no longer officially recognized, though still generally obeyed by people.'[57]

The fact that Garo women did not remain complacent to forms of domination is significant. Overall, women had to struggle hard to renounce or evade male domination, which came along with the progressive machination of masculinity. Women made use of the counter-cultural conduits provided in the system, and outside of it, to get away from unwanted marriage relationship. They 'easily slipped off' the marriage on the 'slightest of causes' and would 'soon remarry' again when their husbands became oppressive. This power not only liberated women from unwanted nuptial relationships but also strongly prevented and deterred men from becoming oppressive

---

[55] Playfair (1998 [1909]: 68–9).
[56] Playfair (1998 [1909]: 68–9; emphasis mine).
[57] Playfair (1998 [1909]: 69).

to women in the first place. In so doing, the women made their position worthy within the tribal patriarchy. In this sense, liberal divorce and remarriage customs also became the counter-culture of the stateless hill society. Along this line of understanding, a few more cases of women's movement against patriarchy are discussed in the following sections.

Gong Thrower, Merit Performer

It is often argued that women enjoyed a low social status due to the lack of inheritance. She was 'toiling without rights' on the soil of her husband. It is true that in most patriarchal societies women lost this right. Yet, in the context of traditional society, it makes little sense to argue that possession of land right was the measure of one's social status. This is particularly true for Northeast India where individual landholding right is a recent development and was virtually non-existent in the past. In the past, land belonged to either the clan (among many tribes) or the chief. But as long as a family lived in a village, they had the right to cultivate land and use the forest resources. In the southern hills, for instance, chief was the owner of the village land but all the villagers had unlimited right of access to the land for agriculture, forest resources, water bodies, and so on. As long as they lived in that village, the chief could not deprive anyone from this access right. In this context, land as a measure of social status did not arise. Indeed, it was other social parameters that located the social status of women better.

For instance, consider her participation in public feasts and ceremonies. She was not simply a part of them but often at the core of them. For instance, in the famous 'feasts of merit' common to most tribes in the region, the wife of the performer of 'feasts of merit' always constituted a central position. Among the Aos, Mills noted: 'At feasts of merit, which are perhaps the greatest of all occasions in a man's life, his wife plays a prominent and honourable part. On days of lesser festivity she acts as hostess and talks freely with the guests.'[58] In the Kuki-Chin world, this was even more significant. In the great 'feasts of merit', common to all of them and variously

---

[58] Mills (2003 [1926]: 213).

known as *Thangchhuah* feasts, *Khuangchawi, Khangchei, Khuang Soi, Chon,* and so on, the wife of the performer was at the centre of the ceremony.[59] Among the Lakhers and Pois, she was particularly famed in distinction. She was carried on a bamboo platform, called *khangang* in Lakher, by eight young men for nine rounds in front of the house, followed by all the villagers shouting: 'Is the wife performing the ceremony? Is the husband performing the ceremony? Rock them from side to side. Hurrah! Hurrah!' Then, the woman would throw down gongs, brass basins, and money from the platform.[60]

Among the Lusheis, she was joined by her husband—the performer of Khuangchawi—other members of the family, and some elders of the village on the platform. She would also throw down brass pots, clothes, money, and other things from the platform for the people. Interestingly, the great Khuangchawi began with the performer going to his *nupu's* (wife's father or brother) house with a forked piece of bamboo to which was attached white cock's feathers and ginger. This forked bamboo he fixed on the wall of his father-in-law's house. The father-in-law fed the party and the performer with the meat of one pig and paid Rs 10 to the performer of *Khuangchawi* as *thingman* (ginger price). This day was called *Thingthiak-ni* and not only reckoned the great feasts of merit (which was to begin the next day) but also signified the importance given to his wife for the grand occasion.[61]

On the lines of men's 'feasts of merit', a Kuki woman also performed her own 'feasts of merit' called *Chang-Ai* or *Buh-Ai* (rice ritual). Chang-Ai was a merit feast given to the entire village for one day by the wife of an important man. To commemorate this event, she put up a special memorial, consisting of an upright stone plate some three feet high, in front of which another flat stone plate of similar size was laid out, supported by three smaller stones on the ground. A space of about four square yards in front was enclosed by a line of stones set on the edge, with the whole of the interior being

---

[59] See Lehman (1980 [1963]: 177–86), Parry (1988 [1931]: 376–7, 2009 [1928]: 107–8), Shakespear (1998 [1912]: 87–90, 170–2), and Shaw (1997 [1929]: 76).

[60] See Parry (1988 [1931]: 376–7).

[61] Parry (2009 [1928]: 107–8).

planted with small stones which were supposed to show the number of baskets of rice consumed on the occasion of the Chang-Ai.[62] Like those men who performed the feasts of merit, these women who performed Chang-Ai feast were permitted to wear a certain cloth called *thangnang*.

The idea of 'feasts of merit' was connected not only to their social but also to their spiritual world. The performer of Chon and Chang-Ai could get a good place in *Mithikho*. This 'good place' was understood as their *Peo-gal* (*Pial-ral* in Lushei, which means beyond the Pial/Peo river on the far side of mithikho). Pial-ral or Peo-gal was 'the abode of bliss' where 'food and drink are to be obtained without labour', whereas in mithikho life was said to be more 'troublesome and difficult' and 'everything being worse than in this world'.[63] Getting a pass into the Peo-gal was, therefore, what everyone was striving for in his or her lifetime. However, as both the 'feasts of merit' involved heavy expenditure, only a rich family could afford to perform it and had the opportunity to enter Peo-gal. While men could manage to enter Peo-gal through their masculine activities, most of the womenfolk were deprived of the opportunity to enter the 'the abode of bliss'.[64] I will now show in the next section how such deprivation was a serious issue for the women and how they responded to it.

[62] Shakespear (1998 [1912]: 205). Shaw recorded that 'she puts up a platform of earth about 6 inches above the ground level which is held in position by a border of small stones placed upright. Within this border small upright stones are placed and represent the number of *bings* (woman's baskets) of paddy which is being consumed on that day. In the centre are two stones also upright with one larger than the other known as *Shong mol* (spirit stones).' See Shaw (1997 [1929]: 74–5). These stone memorials were reminiscent of the Khasi monolithic memorials.

[63] For Pial-ral concept, see Shakespear (1998 [1912]: 62–4).

[64] It was believed that one could obtain this position only by killing enemy human beings and certain animals, such as elephant, bear, sambhar, barking deer, wild boar, and wild mithun, and by giving certain feasts to people, of which the 'feasts of merit' was at the top. Since such activities were masculine in character, women were essentially at the receiving end. See Shakespear (1998 [1912]: 62–4).

God's Bridge, Dream-Women and Friend of Gods

If a large number of women were condemned to live in 'troublesome and difficult' mithikho and deprived of the opportunity to enter 'the abode of bliss', Peo-gal, traditional religion was equally harsh to women. The growing masculinity in the hills gradually excluded women from all religious affairs. Priesthood was exclusive to men, women's mere presence in rituals was profane in many cases, and she was normally prohibited from taking the meat of sacrificial animals. Yet, it is interesting to see that the women, again, did not remain complacent towards male domination in religious matter. Among the Khasis, for instance, women continued to control some of the family rituals. In different parts of the hills, generations of women contested the male priest hegemony in their religion by creating their own sacred space within the society. These pious and powerful women, at times, became very successful and influential in creating their own social and sacred sphere, in which their fellow women constituted the social base. The so-called 'dream-women', for instance, variously known by different names such as *Terhope* ('god's bridge') by Angamis, or *Khuavangzawl* ('friend of Khuavang gods') by Lusheis, or *Maibis* (image of gods?) by the Meiteis, were such influential persons in the local society that, at times, they challenged the male domination of priesthood.

Hutton mentioned one famous Terhope of Jotsoma named Whelelhuwu and another 'well-known dream-woman' named Lobeni in the Lhota village of Phiro.[65] The influence of Lampha, which is still a domestic name among the Kukis of Manipur, in the local society was undoubtedly enormous.[66] The Maibis held a large sacred space in Meitei society, and do so even in the present.[67] They all represent and symbolize the important role played by pious women among

[65] Hutton (1921a: 245–7).

[66] She was said to have been married to the reigning deity family of the Koubru Hills (shading the western plain of Imphal valley). She could tell the past and foretell the future. She even treated people for their illnesses.

[67] I would like to thank K. Bijoykumar of North East India Studies Programme, Jawaharlal Nehru University, for providing the full details of the role of Maibis in Meitei society in the present, in a discussion on 10 November 2017.

the hill tribes (who have now become Christians) in the past. In the face of such contestations, the priests had to defend their position in various ways. One dominant strategy employed by them was to declare such pious women as possessed by evil spirits. The women dissenters were condemned as heretics to the established religion, and also labelled and stigmatized variously as witches, sorcerers, wizards, necromancers, dream-women, and so on. They become the heretical image of male-dominated priesthood and tribal religion despite their claim of being the 'image' and 'messenger' of gods.

Their protest against traditional religion was also visible in the form of conversion to Christianity. In Lushai Hills, for instance, evidence showed that these pious women, the *Khawhringnei* (said to be possessed by evil spirit and can enter the body of others to devour on their vital parts), were the forerunners in embracing Christianity. Khawhringnei were invariably women (never men) who were despised by the society as almost untouchable; in fact, cases of their frequent murder have come to light from colonial records.[68] They were said to be one of the first groups of Christian converts in Lushai Hills. They also formed the famous group of local missionaries, called the 'Bible Women', for spreading Christianity in the hills.[69] Although Christianity was also a male-dominated religion, the fact that it promised women participation in religious services and the bliss of 'Heaven' to all, including women, especially appealed the spiritually deprived women of traditional society. In this context, their conversion to Christianity may be taken as another form of resistance against the male-dominated traditional religion.

First Reaper, First Litigant

With growing masculinity in the tribal society, the women also gradually drifted away from politics and administration. The men ran the village administration; they became the 'chief', 'headmen', and 'councilors'. Women were deprived of all the important political/administrative

---

[68] For *khawhring* explanation, see Shakespear (1998 [1912]: 111–12). Note that *Khawhring* is the spirit which dwelled in a person and the person who is possessed by *khawhring* is called *khawhringnei* (*nei* lit. have).

[69] See Pachuau and van Schendel (2015: 81).

positions in the village community. However, such deprivation was not complete in the past. Till about the nineteenth century, women were holding certain important positions in the village administration. Among the Angamis, for instance, women always held the village office of 'First Reaper' (*Lidepfu*). The Semas called the same office *Amthao* and this was also occupied by women. This office recognized the important role that women played in the village economy. In fact, such formal social recognition is significant in that instead of reading it as a symbol of demeaning status, it may well be taken as symbolizing a social system which recognized and celebrated the profession one was best suited for. In such system, the question of status did not arise. As noted earlier, the widows of the chiefs in Lushai Hills took up village administration as chieftainess after their husbands died, just as they always stood behind their husbands when they were alive.

Though a woman could not preside at the court or become a chief, she still influenced the decision of the village court regarding her and her family. She was not only the most litigious person but also the most vocal personality at the court whose assertion was often taken seriously. The idea that 'women and children' were excluded in politics and administration was a later invention (possibly during the colonial period). The theoretical position of the village durbar, as seen in Chapter 6, was that 'everyone', including women, children, and even 'infants', was a part of the village assembly and had to not only 'listen attentively' but also to 'deliberate' and 'give intelligence' on any matter. For instance, in the popular Kuki folktale of 'Ahsijolneng' (see Chapter 7), a poor widow of the village was most vocal in the chief's court. She fought for the poor boy, Changkhatpu (again the son of a widow), against the arrogance of the chief and his councilmen. Her powerful arguments at the village council eventually led to a majority decision in favour of the poor boy for the hand of the chief's daughter, Ahsijolneng. In another widely circulated story in the region (called 'Chemtate' or dao sharpener among the Kukis), it was another widow who first brought up the matter against a chain of conflicts that affected the whole village community. Her powerful litigation at the village court eventually brought the main culprit, the prawn, to book.[70]

[70] Shaw (1997 [1929]: 108–10).

Thus, women continued to participate in the deliberations in the village assembly among the tribes which followed democracy in the nineteenth century. This was also, to an extent, still visible among the tribes following chieftainship system. Here, the role of women as powerful litigants was visible. Parry, for instance, noted of Lakher women: 'Among Lakher women there is no false shame, they do not consider themselves as inferior beings, and take part in all matters in which the family is interested. If a man has a case, his wife comes along with him, presses her opinion, and says anything she may have to say without any shyness or reluctance.'[71] Mills also noted a similar case among the Aos: 'In litigation she is well to the fore. On asking a man in Court what his complaint is, I have often known his wife step forward, tell him to keep his mouth shut, and announce that she will state their case.' Interestingly, he even went on to say that 'hen-pecked husbands are not unknown in the Ao country'.[72]

If a woman could step forward, ask her husband to keep his mouth shut before the court, fearlessly assert her case, and forcefully press her opinion without any shyness or reluctance in public, then it is difficult to suggest that her opinion had no public significance at all. It is even more difficult to suggest that she was a junior partner in the family. Even if men considered her opinion worthless, just as 'the flesh of a crab is no meat', she still considered herself as an important person of the village community and hardly held herself as an 'inferior being'. If her husband called her an 'old fence', she had her own way of ridiculing the arrogant husband.

Thus, as women could successfully contest male domination by 'easily slipping off' marriage and 'soon remarry' again, by creating their own sacred space, by taking over administration, and by fighting their cases fearlessly in the village durbar, then it can be said that women still enjoyed ample amount of rights and freedom in the stateless patriarchal society. The woman was still a 'normal human being', with minds and opinions of her own, even if her freedom was restrained by some patriarchal injunctions.

[71] Parry (1988 [1931]: 277). McCall (2003 [1949]: 132–64) also mentioned various cases of litigation in Lushai Hills during his time, in which women were certainly at the forefront.

[72] Mills (2003 [1926]: 213).

9

Symbiotic Hill–Valley Relationship

Transactions of Space, Manpower, and Resources

The dominant colonial narrative makes us believe that the hills were historically isolated from the valley and the hill–valley relationship in the precolonial period was largely confrontational. The same discourse continues to influence our understanding even today.[1] However, evidence from the precolonial period is to the contrary. Instead of being confrontational, one can rather talk about a symbiotic and interdependent hill–valley relationship in the past. This is also the line taken by James Scott in his recent work on Zomia.[2] His understanding of state evaders is, I think, not necessarily anti-state but against control and appropriations of the state. Thus, Scott has talked about the state evaders from Han China becoming state builders in Southeast Asian mainland in time. While some remained in the hills, travelling from one hill to another, movement into state spaces in Southeast Asian mainland was a continuous process, just as many of them also escaped to the hills against the *new* state-making projects there. Therefore, there was a continuous two-way traffic between

[1] See the standard texts on this, such as Barpujari (1970) and Devi (1992 [1968]).

[2] Scott (2009: 26–32).

the hills and valleys in the long view, depending upon the situation that individuals or groups found themselves in both the hills and the valleys. Chapters 3 and 7 showed that the idea of state was very strong in the consciousness of the hill people; to prevent its control and to build one if luck favoured. The hillmen chose to be 'rulers' and not 'subjects'. In fact, their hope to become rulers lasted well into the colonial period.[3] Just as they inherited this 'hope', there was continuous movement of people, culture, and commodities between the hills and valleys in the past.

Although certain societies could survive in isolation, this was not the case with the state evaders of Northeast India as this region was surrounded by valleys on both sides and the people depended heavily on the valley resources for many of their wants.[4] They developed a certain mechanism that allowed them to procure their requirements from the valleys and, at the same time, sustain their independence in the hills. Scott also talked of Kachin's 'adopted' villages, which largely operated under the same system.[5] This chapter unpacks this unique mechanism, known in Assam as posa, that regulated the hill–valley relationship in precolonial Northeast India.

Posa: A Subscription to the Hill Polities

Posa was a term that referred to a payment given in kind or labour services by the plainsmen (who were generally known as *Bohotias*) to the hill polities of the 'sub-Himalayan tribes' in the northern frontier of Assam.[6] It literally meant 'a collection or subscription for a common purpose'. In its special sense of payment to the hill tribes, it strictly meant the subscription which the village raised in order to meet the

---

[3] Shaw, for instance, remarked of the Kukis after the Kuki Rising of 1917–19: 'I have heard it said that they hope to become a "Raj" someday' and the Kukis still believed that 'they are destined to be rulers of their earth and not to be submissive to any one'. See Shaw (1997 [1929]: 23, 50).

[4] Universal items in the hills, like common salt, iron, utensils, ornaments, cultural items like gongs, and so on, were produced in the valleys.

[5] Scott (2009: 150–53).

[6] By 'sub-Himalayan tribes', I am referring to the Bhutias, Akas, Dufflas (Nishi), Apatanis, Abors (Adis), Miris, Mishmis, and so on.

customary demands of their visitors from the hills.[7] Two-third of the rent or labour services imposed by the Ahom state under its khel system was usually given to the hill chiefs as posa; only one-third remained with the former.[8] The first mention of posa in the Ahom *Buranjis* (royal chronicles) was during the reign of Susengpha, alias Pratap Singha (1603–1641), who was designated as introducing the posa system to a section of Bhutias (Charduar Bhutias), Akas (Hazari-khowas), Dufflas , and Miris.[9] The Abors were not mentioned in the Buranjis as receiving posa, but their claim of absolute sovereignty over the Miris of the plains from whom they received payments in kind and the Ahom sovereign, like the posa, recognized labour. The Buranjis, however, mentioned that during the reign of Pratap Singha, the Abors were given, like the Akas, the Dufflas, and the Miris, some villages in the plains whose inhabitants had to cultivate paddy for them. Besides, some *beels* (water bodies for fishing) with fishermen were also granted to them.[10] Hence, the same kind of payment was accepted which was later recognized and regularized as posa by the British government. Thus, Bhutias, Akas, Dufflas (Nishis), and Abors (Adis), by and large, received posa from the inhabitants of the plains adjoining their hills which formally came under the Ahom sovereign. Cooper noted that the Abors, Dufflas, Nagas, and other hill tribes 'had levied tribute from the people of the plains from time immemorial, and accustomed to receive it as a right'.[11]

The Akas, besides their share in rice, were entitled to receive from each house in the Charduar area in the plain, 'one portion of a female dress, one bundle of cotton thread, and one handkerchief'. The term 'Hazari-khowas', a section of Akas who were granted posa, indicated a thousand paiks or cultivators set aside to cultivate paddy for, and pay posa to, the Akas.[12] The Dufflas were entitled to receive from every

---

[7] Devi (1992 [1968]: 199).

[8] NAI, FP (B): July 1877, No. 85: Capt. E.T. Dalton to Lt. Col. F. Jenkins, 19 May 1852.

[9] Devi (1992 [1968]: 216).

[10] Devi (1992 [1968]: 200).

[11] Cooper (1995 [1873]: 131).

[12] See Devi (1992 [1968]: 216). Paik generally referred to a 'foot soldier' but, in actual practice, it meant an able-bodied man under Ahom's khel system.

10 houses, one doubled cloth, one single cloth, one handkerchief, one dao, 10 heads of horned cattle, and 4 seers of salt.[13] The Abors claimed absolute sovereignty over the Miris of the plain as well as a right to tax on all the fishes and gold found in the streams that flowed down from their hills. Thus, the Beeahs gold-washers and fishermen of the plain had to constantly pay tax to the Abors.[14] Wilcox, in 1825, noted that Abors 'claim the whole of those plains [the district north of the Buri Lohit] as their domain'.[15] 'These tribes', wrote Major General Babbage who led an expedition against them in 1848, 'look on the flat country at the foot of their hills as their territory, and hunt, fish, and cut wood there freely.'[16] In the case of Bhutia rajahs, the Ahom state recognized their rights over some *dwars/duars* (passes) permanently as long as they paid a certain tribute to Assam, but the dwars in Darrang district were to be annually surrendered to Assam from July to November.[17] When posa was commuted into money payment during the early colonial period, it was calculated at Rs 9,919-14-6 in Darrang district (since 1844) and Rs 6,473-6-11 in Lakhimpur district (since 1850), which made a total of Rs 16,393-5-5 from the government exchequer.[18] Dalton remarked:

> Previous to the commutation [into money payment] now effected and submitted for confirmation the blackmail [posa] was contributed by the ryots in cloths of their own manufacture, rice, pigs, fowls, dogs, daws, & c. The hill clans with their families appeared in the plains about harvest time and encamped in the vicinity of the village from which they drew their possa or where their Bohotias lived, and there they remained often for months till they had collected their dues and sold their hill produces.[19]

[13] Dao is a broadsword commonly found throughout the region.

[14] See Mackenzie (2007 [1884]: 35–6).

[15] See Wilcox (1873: 8–9).

[16] As quoted in Hamilton (1997: 36).

[17] Mackenzie (2007 [1884]: 10).

[18] Here, Rs. 9,919-14-6, means '9,919 rupees, 14 annas, and 6 pices' as per colonial monetary system. The conversion is like this: 1 pice = 1/4 anna = 1/64 rupee and 1 anna = 1/16 rupee. The same applies to the other values mentioned here. For details of posa given to each tribe, see NAI, FP (B): July 1877, Nos 83–6.

[19] NAI, FP (B): July 1877, No. 85: Capt. E.T. Dalton to Lt. Col. F. Jenkins, 19 May 1852.

Thus, posa was a well-established revenue payment in kind and labour services collected by, or given to, the hill polities from/by the inhabitants of the plain adjoining the hill territory with the consent of, and under mutual agreement with, the Ahom sovereign of Assam.

On the origin of the posa system, there was disagreement in the sources. As noted earlier, the Ahom Buranjis claimed that Pratap Singha introduced posa in the seventeenth century. However, later investigation and other circumstantial evidences showed the possibility of its earlier origin. Posa was, naturally, a very disturbing practice in the eyes of the British colonial state since they took over the governance of Assam. For the Company government at Calcutta, payment of revenue by the subject of one sovereign country to a foreign polity was undoubtedly a blot on its notion of space, territoriality, and sovereignty. Time and again, the frontier officers were pulled up and ordered to provide detailed information on posa and the policy to be taken either to do away with it or to continue it differently. Therefore, detailed surveys on the 'origin and nature' of posa were undertaken in 1839–40 by frontier officers like Major Vetch, Lieutenant Holroyds, Lieutenant Bivar, Captain Dalton, and so on, with the assistance of some 'native' officers and informants. Brijonath Bundari Barua, the *sudder ameen* of Lakhimpur district, was one such knowledgeable 'native' who, Dalton declared, 'summarily investigated and recorded what each chief was in the habit of receiving and from whom'.[20] He investigated all the existing records, called upon information from the hill chiefs and from that of the lowland cultivators, interviewed them, and finally drew up a detailed report which included the various reports of the frontier officers.

Based on these findings, the origin of posa system was pushed back to the pre-Ahom period. In giving the full report of the survey, Dalton, for instance, noted:

> According to the traditions of the hill tribes themselves, corroborated by those of our own ryots, the former received blackmail [posa] from that part of this division now called Luckimpore, *previous to its annexation* by the Ahom Sovereign of Assam, which gives it an origin dating further back than the middle of the fifteenth century of our era, it

[20] The details of various survey reports are appended in the proceedings of Foreign Department. See NAI, FP (B): July 1877, Nos 83–6.

is however certain that the Ahom Kings *very soon found it expedient to make a compromise* with the Duphla and Meeree Hill clans to induce them to refrain from molesting the unwarlike 'Hindu' population of the plains.[21]

On the basis of circumstantial evidences too, the theory of pre-Ahom origin of posa system was acceptable. The Ahom Buranjis had it that until the sixteenth century, the northern Brahmaputra valley remained outside the imperial ambit of the Ahom state, just as it was outside the control of the Koch and Kamata kingdoms. The powerful Bhuyan chieftains (in the west) and the Chutiya kingdom (in the east), in close understanding with the hill chieftains such as the Bhutias, Akas, Dufflas, Miris, Abors, and Mishmis, virtually ruled over the frontier area. It is possible that payment of revenue to the hill tribes was already in existence during this time.

The fact that all the hill tribes claimed such shares from the valley as their 'customary' right brings us close to such a conclusion. As noted earlier, there was a Miri (Mishing, close kin of Abors or Adis) tradition that they, along with the Chutiyas, once conquered the plain of Lakhimpur, and after some centuries of ruling over this region, 'retired again' into 'their mountain fastnesses when they were finally defeated in the sixteenth century by the Ahoms'.[22] The annexation of Chutiya kingdom in 1523, followed by the subjugation of the Bhuyan chieftains, by the Ahoms up to the left bank of Mara-Dhansiri River, however, changed the existing status quo so far maintained with the hill polities.[23] The changing circumstances under the Ahom occupation, and then the promise to restore their former rights by the Koches, led the disaffected hill tribes (such as Bhutias and Dufflas) and the Bhuyan chieftains to support the latter during their victorious invasion of Ahom kingdom in 1562.[24]

---

[21] NAI, FP (B): July 1877, No. 85: Capt. E.T. Dalton to Lt. Col. F. Jenkins, 19 May 1852; emphasis added.

[22] Hamilton (1997: 85).

[23] Devi (1992 [1968]: 213–14).

[24] The Koch King, Nar Narayan, was said to have ordered that the Bhutias, Kacharis, Meches, Dufflas, etc., could follow their tribal customs within the Gohain Kamal Ali road, but from the said road till Brahmaputra River, only Brahmanical rites were to be preserved. See *Koch Beharer Itihas*,

By learning the danger of not taking the frontier chieftains into confidence, and from the way the Koches had appeased them, the Ahoms must have later changed their frontier policy by stepping into the shoes of their predecessors (Chutiyas, Bhuyans, and Koches), which was later institutionalized during the reign of Pratap Singha in the form of posa.[25] Thus, the 'expediency' of maintaining status quo, in terms of the earlier practices, became very strong with the Ahom state, just as it was also later found to be 'expedient' by the colonial state. Dalton, for instance, remarked:

> The scattered state of the population [in the frontier] and their intimate relations with the hill tribes, two thirds of whom annually resided for months in the plains, all pointed to the *expediency of adopting a conciliatory policy* towards these savages, and no resumption could have been made without involving a necessity of resorting to extreme measures of which it would have been difficult to foretell the result. Their rights to levy blackmail [posa] and to the services of the Bohotias was therefore recognized [by the British].[26]

Whatever may have been its origin, posa was a well-established revenue payment to the hill polities, with the consent of the Ahom sovereign of Assam. As the hill tribes with their families encamped in the plains, remained there for months, walked around the villages and collected their posa in person, or sold their hill items and 'gave themselves all the airs of masters' over them, it cannot be pretended that posa was a mere 'blackmail' or 'presents'. At least Mackenzie was right in saying that posa was 'really a well-ascertained revenue payment'. He felt that it was 'based upon customary and primeval rights'

107, as quoted in Devi (1992 [1968]: 272, 279). See also Gait (2008 [1905]: 49).

[25] Of their policy towards the Bhuyans, they were scattered and divided, especially in the form of transplanting most of their powerful chieftains on the southern Brahmaputra valley towards the frontier of Kachari kingdom; they were then not permitted to cross Brahmaputra River towards its northern plains.

[26] NAI, FP (B): July 1877, No. 85: Capt. E.T. Dalton to Lt. Col. F. Jenkins, 19 May 1852; emphasis added.

and 'was a distinct feature in the revenue system of the country when the British annexed Assam'.[27] The amount collected might have been trivial, but it was certainly 'a distinct feature in the revenue system of the country' and carried much political weight just as it carried a utilitarian value. The Buranjis were particularly clear in this respect in specifying the number of paiks or cultivators allotted, or the amount of revenue and other items to be given, to the hillmen by the Ahom sovereign.[28] It was this right of collection which made the hill polities not only the paramount authority over the 'Bohotias' but also obliged them to protect the people from 'raid' from other hill tribes. Non-payment of posa, on the other hand, would invariably lead to bloodshed from the hill master.

The extent of territory over which the hill polities had collected posa is evident from the existence of, for instance, the 'great raised road or barrier', known as 'Gosain Combla Allee' (or Gohain Kamal Ali), along the northern fringe of Brahmaputra valley. It was known to the local people as 'Dufflas Gurh' (gurh/garh means fortification, meaning a wall and hence Duffla's Wall), synonymous to 'barbarian wall' of the great world empires. This gurh/garh was used by Pratap Singha as a measure to prevent the Dufflas from molesting the plain dwellers inside it. It was also sometimes known as 'Rajgarh' (royal fortification). Dalton noted that the 'services of those who then resided' north of the great raised road 'were thus disposed of'.[29] A bolder policy was adopted during the reign of Pratap Singha when the hill tribes were 'not allowed to cross the barrier and transactions of barter between them and the ryots were all made through the intervention of the Bohotias'.[30] Thus, the 'Gurh' represented the limit of a zone of effective rule, the 'inside' boundary of a sovereign authority in Winichakul's apt term.[31] The area beyond this 'wall' till the foothills was, therefore, the territory from where posa was

[27] Mackenzie (2007 [1884]: 21).

[28] See, for instance, Devi (1992 [1968]: 218).

[29] NAI, FP (B): July 1877, No. 85: Capt. E.T. Dalton to Lt. Col. F. Jenkins, 19 May 1852.

[30] NAI, FP (B): July 1877, No. 85: Capt. E.T. Dalton to Lt. Col. F. Jenkins, 19 May 1852.

[31] See Winichakul (1995).

collected, where both the hills and valley polities claimed authority and where sovereignty overlapped (see Figure 9.1).

A deceptive category, 'Bohotia', meaning 'bonded' or 'indebted', was a term used to describe the inhabitants of the area from where posa was collected.[32] The Bohotias, in general, paid posa in kind and services to the hill chieftains. Thus, even in the early colonial period, they were still seen to render labour services to the hill people. 'They were not coerced to render such service', remarked Dalton, 'but they generally continued doing so in preference of paying full rates.'[33] This system was still visible when Wilcox visited the hills in 1825–28. While he was still in the plain, he saw the Abors collecting their share from the plain cultivators:

> Some of the chiefs of an Abor tribe had arrived at this time to make their annual collections from the district north of the Buri Lohit. They claim the whole of those plains as their domain ... However, from the Bhuruli to the banks of the Dihong, the whole of the hill tribes pretend to similar rights, and have never been interfered with when at the accustomed season they have descended from their strongholds and peaceably taken their dues from each separate dwelling.[34]

Beside the peasant 'Bohotias' who cultivated paddy for their hill masters and paid posa, there were also other classes of 'Bohotias' who served the hill polities in different ways: Parowas (ferrymen), Dooms (fishermen), blacksmiths, and so on. The Parowas were the peasants of Bor Dolloni and Pattalipam, who, as gold-washers, plied canoes among the rapids of the Subunsiri River in the foothills. As the said river was not fordable for the hill tribes, who were obliged to cross it in order to reach the plain, the Parowas were responsible for ferrying them to and from the plain villages or markets during their annual visit to collect posa and to sell their hill items. The Dooms supplied fishes to the hill chiefs and the blacksmiths mended daos for the same.[35]

---

[32] NAI, FP (B): July 1877, No. 85: Capt. E.T. Dalton to Lt. Col. F. Jenkins, 19 May 1852.

[33] NAI, FP (B): July 1877, No. 85: Capt. E.T. Dalton to Lt. Col. F. Jenkins, 19 May 1852.

[34] Wilcox (1873: 8–9).

[35] NAI, FP (B): July 1877, No. 85: Capt. E.T. Dalton to Lt. Col. F. Jenkins, 19 May 1852.

The cultural composition of Bohotias showed a synthesis of their two 'masters'. Dalton, for instance, noted: 'Instead of despising to the hill savages they [Bohotias] looked up to them, imbibed their superstitions, adopted many of their customs and were as servile as slaves to the chieftains, who gave themselves all the airs of masters over those from whom they collected blackmail.'[36] Sandwiched between the 'Duffla Gurh' in the south and the imposing hills in the north, the Bohotias were therefore people who connected the two worlds, who paid tribute to two masters, and who were protected by both. They were people, as the term 'Miri' implies, who were the 'go-between', and hence a 'bridge' community between the two. They were akin to what the 'core' civilizational discourse would call the 'semi-savage' of the 'civilized' plainsmen or the 'cooked barbarians' in Chinese civilizational narrative.[37] They were 'cooked' in a double sense: they adopted the cultures of both the masters, hence making them ready to go either way as circumstances may permit. In this context, the plain region where posa was collected was where a kind of sociocultural baptism took place, a prerequisite condition for assimilating into either of the two contested world orders. Consequently, they belonged to both, while they were neither of them; they were on *half-way* and hence 'Bohotias'.

As a result of posa system, there emerged a zone of shared space and overlapping sovereignty in the frontier over which both the hill polities and the valley state claimed authority and from where both extracted resources by mutual consent. This zone I have called posaland. The extent of posaland kept shifting over time depending on the fate of the valley state and/or the hill polities, but the fact remained that it was a peculiar feature of precolonial frontier politics.

Posa Subscriptions in Other Frontiers

The term posa may also be used for other similar claims made by the hill polities over the inhabitants of the plains, which the valley states

---

[36] NAI, FP (B): July 1877, No. 85: Capt. E.T. Dalton to Lt. Col. F. Jenkins, 19 May 1852.

[37] For the 'raw' and 'cooked' barbarians of Chinese frontiers, see Fiskesjo (1999) and Wang (1999).

consented to or, at the least, declined to interfere with. Thus, in the southern frontier of Brahmaputra valley (Assam), a similar kind of claim was made by the hill polities of Naga Hills and Khasi Hills. As in northern Brahmaputra valley, the Ahom sovereigns granted a large amount of land (called khats) in the plain, along with the cultivators, to the Naga chieftains. The Ahoms relationship with the Nagas went back to their invasion of Assam. For the Ahoms, Naga Hills was always a strategic resource as it connected with its original homeland, invasion from the east was expected, and was the main source of its indispensible salt (from 85 salt wells in Naga foothills). Forging a good relationship with Nagas was always important to Ahoms for these reasons. The first reference of formal grant of land to Nagas in the Buranjis came during the reign of Ahom King Sukhampha or Khora Raja (1552–1603). He rewarded the Tablungia Nagas living by the side of river Dikhow with beels, along with some fishermen paiks (Dom-bahatia or Bohotias), to supply dried fishes.[38] During the reign of Pratap Singha, 'Naga Garh' was constructed along the southern frontier of Sibsagar and Lakhimpur and the Nagas were prohibited to cross the line unaccompanied by *chaotangs* (interpreters).[39] This came along with land grants to many Naga chiefs, managed by 'Naga Katakis'.[40] During Moamaria uprisings and Burmese invasion, when most of the peasants fled, Brodie remarked that the Nagas were 'extremely anxious to get possession of the land and beels … formerly held'.[41] Most of these claims were granted. Thus, about 640 poorahs in Sibsagar district alone was in the possession of Nagas in 1853.[42]

---

[38] Devi (1992 [1968]: 37).

[39] Devi (1992 [1968]: 37).

[40] Devi (1992 [1968]: 37).

[41] Brodie recommended to the government that 30–40 poorahs (1 poorah is 2.66 acres) of land may be restored to the rajah as rent-free land in the Government Jykhumdang Khat and one or the other beels lying between the Dikho and Desang rivers. See NAI, FP: 17 August 1842, No. 186: T. Brodie to F. Jenkins, 9 April 1842; see also *Selection of Papers* (1873: 296–7): T. Brodie to F. Jenkins, 6 August 1844.

[42] Mills (1980 [1853]: cxv–cxvi).

Similarly, some Khasi chiefs too claimed certain parganahs (administrative unit) adjoining their territory.[43] Francis Jenkins noted:

> From the western boundary of Gowalparra to Gowhatty, there are ten Pergunnahs under the hills (nine Dowars and one Desh) over all which some time ago Cossiah [Khasi] Chiefs were feudal lords, paying merely a tribute to the Rajahs of Assam; the greater parts of those Districts are still held by descendants of the Cossiahs of whom the principal are the Rajah of Sokee Dowar, the Rajah of Desh Rannee and the Rajah of Munklow in charge of Bor Dowar.[44]

Likewise, the hill polities of some Khasi chiefs bordering the Bengal frontier made similar claims on their adjoining plain areas. Mackenzie noted that the Garos had, for a long time, annually collected in person a 'tribute' locally known as *matarakha* from their adjoining plainsmen, which the British later commuted into 'annual presents'.[45] Gird Garo area of the plain, in the foothills of Kurribari Hills, was one such area where the Garo chiefs claim suzerainty. It was a contested space between the zamindars (landlords) of Sherepore and the Garo chieftains of the Kurribari Hills. The inhabitants were mostly Garos who owed their allegiance to their hill chieftains; they rose up against their oppressive zamindars during 'Paghul' uprising of 1825.[46] Similarly, the Kukis of the hills bordering southern Cachar and Sylhet plains were, noted Mackenzie, 'in the habit of receiving yearly presents from the frontier zamindars', or woodcutters, 'as the price of safety' and 'failure to acknowledge their claims invariably led to bloodshed'.[47] Extreme cases of extending hill authority over the plains came in the form of Tipperah, Jaintia, and Cachari kingdoms.[48]

---

[43] Parganah or pargana was a local administrative unit of a *sarkar* or district during Mughal India. The term continued to be used in the colonial period.

[44] F. Jenkins to A.J.M. Mills, 4 June 1853, as cited in Mills (1980 [1853]: cxx).

[45] Mackenzie (2007 [1884]: 246–8).

[46] For 'Paghul' uprisings, see Mackenzie (2007 [1884]: 254–5).

[47] Mackenzie (2007 [1884]: 279).

[48] For the formation of these three states, see Bhattacharjee (1991) and Sinha (1989).

On the other side of the mountain ranges, in Burma frontier, the same sort of hill–valley relationship existed. With the consent of the Burmese court, noted Carey and Tuck, the Yokwas of the Chin Hills annually received tributes from the bordering plainsmen in the form of 'Yaw blanket and a viss [1.6 kg] of salt from all the villages on the border on the condition that raiding ceased.'[49] Similarly, the Kachins, a terror in Burma's northern and north-eastern frontier, too received regular payment from the inhabitants of the plains adjoining their hills. The fear of this tribe was especially strong. Early British observers were stunned to see that almost all settlements in the frontier, from small villages to the largest townships like Bhamo and Mogaung, had heavy stockade 'as a protection against' the Kachins. The British observers felt that the frontier population lived in a constant state of alarm and uncertainty.[50] However, they were even more stunned to see the frontier officers taking no action at all: 'local Government never interfere, and no attempt is ever made to suppress depredations.'[51]

Therefore, things went on as usual and the border population made certain arrangements by making some payments to the hill polities to defuse the tension. Thus, many small Shan villages at the foot of the Kachin Hills 'manage[d] to preserve their safety', noted Bayfield, 'by paying a kind of blackmail to the Kakhyen [Kachin] chiefs'. In the plain district of Bhamo (Bamo), for instance, 29 villages, out of the total 151 villages, were under the control of four Kachin chieftains.[52] Later British observers, after the occupation of Upper Burma, found that the plain villages in the foothills were indeed 'protected' by different Kachin chieftains. 'It appears that', noted J.G. Scott, 'there was hardly any village in the whole Bhamo district which was thus not protected and the Kachins were really masters of the country.'[53] In this way, many of the plain villages bordering the hills had literally become what James Scott has called 'adopted villages' of the hill polities who, as the tribute receiver, protected them and exerted

---

[49] Carey and Tuck (1987 [1896]: 161).
[50] See, for instance, Bayfield (1873: 134–244).
[51] Bayfield (1873: 179).
[52] Bayfield (1873: 239).
[53] Scott (1893: 49).

mastery over their affairs, to which the valley state authority invariably consented.[54]

Therefore, all along the frontiers of Northeast region, a zone of shared space and overlapping sovereignty existed between the hills and the valley polities and along the hill–valley continuum, which I have called posaland. The schematic representation of such overlapping zone is shown in Figure 9.1.

The pertinent questions then are: why did the hill polities want to control the plain areas; and why did the valley states consent to such a claim within their considered sphere of territory and sovereignty? The existence of this overlapping zone of territory and sovereignty may be best situated in two complimentary ways. First, it can be seen as the remnant of the old system, and second, it can be seen in terms of the larger environmental and economic forces which had driven the precolonial valley states and that of the hill polities. Recorded history is profound on the gradual migration of the hill tribes into the adjacent plain areas and vice versa, noting the fact that

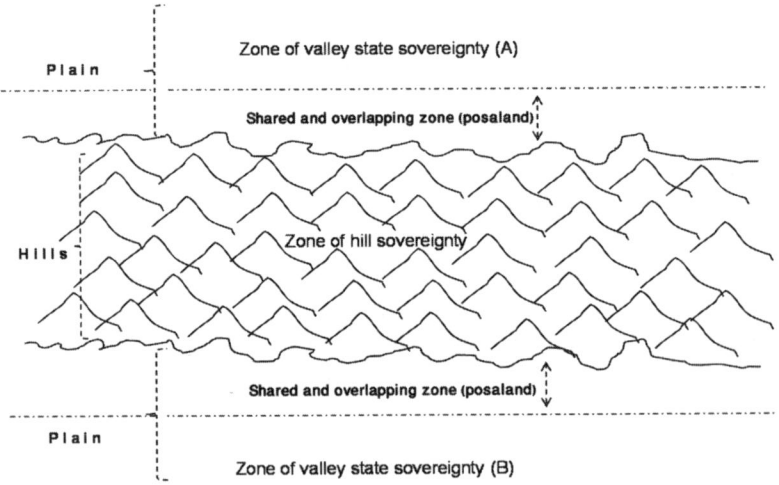

Figure 9.1　Schematic Representation of Posaland
Source: Prepared by author.

[54]　Scott (2009: 150–3).

in the long view there was a continuous two-way traffic of population movement between the hills and valleys.[55] Thus, a section of the hill tribes always remained at the margins of the valley; they were, as their tradition goes, either the remnants of the tribes who had gradually escaped the valley, or those who escaped from the hills to the plains, or both. The people who paid, or over whom such customary tribute was claimed, were mostly this section of the valley population. Considering the fact that the tribute claimed was mainly over the tribes who still *remained* in the plains, which often extended to non-tribes who settled amongst them later, it makes sense to argue that such a claim originated in what Mackenzie has called 'customary and primeval rights'.

Yet, such rights could not have existed in a vacuum, especially when the area they inhabited came under the valley state sovereign; it required a much larger force to continue the system. From the court–centre perspective, the existence of such a zone in the frontier was of paramount importance to prevent the hill tribes from raiding the directly controlled state space. It is true that such payment prevented 'raiding' (more appropriately punishing) but, from its essence, it was certainly not a means to prevent 'raid' but something much larger than that. In fact, it can well be said that such payment was not to stop raid but that raid was a means to enforce hill authority over the plain dwellers.[56] In other words, non-payment of customary dues (revenues) was considered an act of rebellion, which would invariably cause raid or bloodshed. The idea that posa was paid to the hill polities to prevent raid is not only simplistic but also buries an important historical theme that governed the hill–valley relationship in the long view. The larger environmental and economic forces that drove the precolonial states in the valley and that of the hill polities in highland massif are essential to understand this system at the frontier. A brief discussion on this will be helpful.

---

[55] The history of most of these tribes attests to their earlier settlements in the plains before they were pushed up to, or took refuge in, the hills.

[56] Thus, the Abors always asserted that they raided upon the Miri villages because they refused to return to their original village at the foothills and serve them. It was asserted as a right in various ways.

A Resource Conduit, a Buffer against Control

Chapter 3 described how the hill people had evolved a curtain of 'uninhabited and uncultivated' forested jungles around the hills adjoining the valleys to prevent the appropriations and control of the valley states. Beyond this line and towards the centre of the state core was what was an additional zone, the posaland. The relatively harsh mountainous terrain and its different ecological settings presupposed the hill economy. Few of the universal demands across the hill ranges under study were rice, common salt, iron, clothes, and beads and ornaments of various sorts. But all these items were not present equally across the landscape; surplus rice and cotton were produced in richer hill tracts inhabited by Kachins, Garos, Nagas, and in such hills like Chittagong Hill Tracts and Lushai Hills, but they were in high demand in the cold and rocky sub-Himalayan ranges, plateaux Khasi Hills, and in the leeward Chin Hills. Except in certain fringe of Naga Hills, the demand for common salt from the plain was universal. Similarly, iron was produced in plenty in Khasi Hills but, again, it was a universal demand in all the other hill tracts. The demand for luxury items such as beads and other ornaments, or cultural items like gongs, or household items like utensils, which were manufactured in the plains, was universal throughout the hills.

In case of the sub-Himalayan ranges, the rocky mountain topography did not permit adequate economic production and labour utilization was intensive for its production process.[57] Consequently, the inhabitants of these rugged mountain ranges had to depend heavily upon the plains for most of their manpower supply and material requirements. Wilcox, for instance, noted that salt, clothes, and tobacco 'were in great request among them'.[58] In the list of their demands as posa, clothes and common salt were dominant, but they also imported other basic items like iron, rice, and different protein supply from the plains. The need for clothes was especially severe as they were in a colder altitude where cotton was not produced. No

[57] For the economic life and its situation of virtual state of poverty, see, for instance, the survey report of Griffith (1873: 110–24); see also Cooper (1995 [1873]).

[58] Wilcox (1873: 12).

wonder, certain tribes were contemptuously dubbed as 'Kapachor' (stealer of cotton), a markedly significant aspect of the sub-Himalayan economy. It was under these ecological conditions of the rocky mountain that the origin of a markedly defined shared space and overlapping authority—posaland—could be located in the northern fringe of Brahmaputra valley.

In other less fertile hill tracts such as Khasi and Chin Hills, there was a similar but less vigorous case of extending the hill authority. In the plateaux landform of Khasi Hills, Lister, for instance, noted that '[r]ice of good quality is grown towards the north and throughout the centre of the hills; but, even with a few other poor description of grain, is not sufficient for the support of the people.' So the import of the district included rice, salt, tobacco, dried fish, oil, corals, brass and copper utensils, cloths of all descriptions, and cattle and goats.[59] Captain Rundall also noted the same situation in leeward mountain ranges of the Chin Hills: 'the people are extremely poor, and do not grow rice, but live on millet, Indian corn and sweet potatoes, and beans'.[60] The main imports of the Chins were, therefore, rice, salt, iron, cattle, brass utensils, and beads and ornaments.[61] Thus, there was a more aggressive demand from these hill tracts.

If the poorer hill tracts were more aggressive in their demand from the plain areas, this did not preclude other richer hill tracts from pursuing their political ambition with regard to the plain areas adjacent to their hills. The demand for some basic items of the plains, such as common salt and iron implements, and luxury-cum-cultural items was equally high across the hills. Thus, to stop the entry of these basic items from the plains would have been suicidal for the hills. This naturally induced them to bring their hill products for exchange in the plains. The Miris, for instance, brought for exchange ginger, pepper, *manjit* (madder), and wax and the Abors brought, besides copper vessels, straight swords and elephant teeth.[62] The Garos were known

---

[59] F.G. Lister to A.J.M. Mills, 1 July 1853, as cited in Mills (1985 [1853]: 38–9).

[60] WBSA, PP: File L-36 (1–6): April 1892, No. 60: Minutes of Alexander Mackenzie, Chief Commissioner of Burma.

[61] Carey and Tuck (1987 [1896]: 214–15).

[62] Wilcox (1873: 9).

for supplying cotton to their adjacent plain; the Khasis for iron, lime, and orange; the Nagas for salt, rice, wax, ivory, and cotton; the Kukis traded with beeswax and elephant teeth; the 'Joomias' of Chittagong Hill Tracts with cotton; and the Kachins brought rice, cotton, and timber to the frontier markets.

This two-way traffic of goods naturally resulted in the development of a regular trade between the two worlds. In the Naga frontier, Peal, for instance, noted: 'the traffic had worn down the rock into a narrow passage, where only one at a time could pass, and also into holes and steps, very well for Nagas to grip with their bare feet, but slippery and unaccommodating to thick-soled boots.'[63] In 1875–6, as mentioned earlier, 1,904 Nagas, of which 1,445 persons took cash, 74 persons took ponies, 3 persons took waxes, and 382 persons took cloths, passed through Samaguting (then British headquarter in Naga Hills) to trade at Dimapur, Golaghat, and other places in the Assam plain. Traders of Samaguting and Dimapur sold 2,800 maunds of salt to the Nagas and, in turn, bought rice from the Nagas worth Rs 1,000, beeswax of Rs 3,750, and ivory of Rs 4,497.[64] Dalton also noted that 600–800 Sourock tribe of sub-Himalayan region annually visited Bordolloni, bringing down manjit (Indian Mudder), wax, ginger, and chillies for sale and traffic.[65] Some tribes even turned into professional traders. Wilcox felt that every man among the Mishmis was a petty merchant.[66]

The annual visit of the Garos of interior hills to a trade fair in the frontier markets was regulated through a certain market mechanism: some plainsmen were given to them, who were taken as hostages to the hill villages and were detained there till the fair was over. This was a means to secure the safe conduct of the plainsmen when the hill people were in the frontier markets.[67] The Falams of Chin Hills even appropriated salt trade with the plain of Burma; in 1892–3, for instance, noted Carey and Tuck, 'no less than 100,000 lbs. of salt

---

[63] Peal (1873: 317).

[64] NAI, FP (A): September 1876, No. 143: *Naga Hills Administration Report, 1875–76.*

[65] NAI, FP (B): July 1877, No. 85: Capt. E.T. Dalton to Lt. Col. F. Jenkins, 19 May 1852.

[66] Wilcox (1873: 36).

[67] Mackenzie (2007 [1884]: 246–8).

were purchased at Indin and Sihaung'.[68] Bayfield too noted that the Kachins 'carry on a small trading intercourse with most of the [plain] villages on this part of the Irrawaddy, bringing rice and cotton, and sometimes timber, and taking away in exchange spirits, tobacco, salt, gnapie, & c.'[69] Besides, he also saw good number of Kachin traders in most of the frontier markets, including Bhamo.[70] The existence of such frontier markets—which were later promoted by the British authority—where the hill people annually came down for exchange was noted in several colonial accounts.[71]

If some basic needs of the hill people were produced by the plainsmen or could be procured only from them, then to ensure a regular supply of such items became the central concern of the hill polities. 'Raid' as an instrument of supplying the hills with plain items was unsustainable, although it was utilized as a last resort. Rather, the hill people generally resorted to two other possible alternatives to ensure the supply: first, encourage the free flow of goods and exchange between the two worlds; and second, control the plain areas so that they got their supplies in the form of regular revenue/tribute. Yet, there were advantages and disadvantages in both the alternatives. Encouraging the free flow of goods and exchange between the two worlds was the easier alternative but there was one major disadvantage in this. As mentioned earlier, the hill people were the 'state-evading population' who constantly struggled to discourage and evade valley state control and appropriations in the hills. In this context, allowing the free flow of goods and transactions with the valley societies was evidently a prelude to valley state control and appropriations.[72]

---

[68] Carey and Tuck (1987 [1896]: 147, 215).

[69] Bayfield (1873: 172).

[70] Bayfield (1873: 177).

[71] There were frontier markets in the various dwars, and also in Sadiya, Sibsagar, Golaghat, and Nowgong (in Assam); Silchar, Bepari Bazar, Lushai Hat, and Tipaimukh (in Cachar); Demagiri and Kassalong Bazars (in Chittagong); Talakme (in Araccan); and Yazagyo, Kalemyo, Indin, Sihaung, Myintha, and Gangaw (in western Burma), and Bhamo, Mogoung, Payenwen, and Meingkhwon (in northern Burma).

[72] This was well-illustrated during the colonial period where trade and commerce was initially employed by the colonial power as instrument of control, and for eventual occupation of the hills later.

To avoid the aforementioned problem, the hill people eventually chose the second, and much more complicated, alternative. This alternative (control over the plain villages permanently) provided a two-pronged advantage in the long run. First, the control of their adjoining plain areas ensured a regular supply of their basic needs in the form of revenue or markets for exchange of goods, or otherwise. Second, it ensured their relative independence from the valley state control and appropriations as such a zone of control acted as a buffer to encroachment from the valley potentates. The control over the plain areas by the hill polities can be, therefore, first located in the context of the economic and political imperatives of the hill people. Also, for the hill population of the chilly sub-Himalayan ranges, posaland can be regarded as their winter resort, where, as Dalton reported, 'two thirds' of the 'hill clans with their families' annually appeared 'about harvest time and encamped in the vicinity of the village' and 'resided for months' there, with 'all the airs of masters', till they had 'collected their dues [posa] and sold their hill produced'.[73]

Keeping the Peace Where State Machine Failed

Clearly, posaland not only became a channel, a conduit, through which regular supply of commodities from the plain, and the flow of hill products in exchange, was ensured but it also acted as a bulwark to prevent the valley states from becoming master of the hills. Yet, the existence of such shared space and overlapping sovereignty in the frontier cannot be explained only in terms of the economic and political imperatives of the hillmen alone; it also depended very much on the circumstances in which the valley states found themselves in the plains. In Chapter 1, it was shown how friction of terrain generated a powerful brake on the wheels of valley state machine. To overcome such friction, the valley state builders banked on concentrating population and grains around the centre of power, at an arm's length and for efficient broadcasting of power. The inconsistency that ensued due to rapid political expansion along with agrarian expansion generated

[73] NAI, FP (B): July 1877, No. 85: Capt. E.T. Dalton to Lt. Col. F. Jenkins, 19 May 1852.

multiple and contested frontiers for the state: political, agrarian, forest, and demographic. These 'rippling' frontiers competed and conspired against each other in such a way that the expansion of one necessarily went against the other. Central in this conspiracy was the low population–land ratio. Thus, concentration of population at the nucleus of the kingdom transformed those lands occupied by them earlier into vacant land, rapidly overrun by forest. For instance, Dhansiri valley in southern Brahmaputra valley and large parts of Upper Assam very soon returned to forest after Ahom occupation. At the same time, it also resulted in some population escaping to the margins of the kingdom. On being deprived of a certain number of its conquered population, the state was often forced to press further upon its grain producers, leading to further flights. This vicious circle was one of the main reasons for the rise and decline of many valley states. In all the cases, the phenomenal growth of forest frontier was significant. The forest impeded state efficiency to the extent that it halted movement during the rainy season. The predominance of this forest friction across the valley played havoc with the state builders. Thus, the broadcasting of power, which normally emanated from the core of the kingdom, rippled. As it radiated towards the frontier, it became nominal, erratic, and symbolic at the margins. It is within this inescapable reality of the nature of broadcasting of power in the valley states during the precolonial period that the importance of posa system can be located.

The daunting geography and the practical difficulties faced by the central authority in the margins of the state were real and present in the precolonial period. The Ahoms, for instance, tried hard to link their margins with networks of roads, but these were almost useless once the torrential rains started. Their occasional expeditions into the hills resulted more in humiliation than punishment of the culprits. It was within such shortcomings that confronted the valley polities that, instead of waging unrewarding wars against the hill polities, it was thought expedient to follow a conciliatory, rather than confrontational, policy. Thus, when the hill polities insisted that they had the sovereign right over part of the plain areas adjoining their hill territories, it was found beneficial to make a compromise with them, instead of fighting against it. This was especially so in a situation when such insistence was a means to ensure a regular supply in the hills of basic items produced in the plain and in keeping the valley states at an arm's length. Therefore, for the valley states, consenting to posa claims by the hill polities was part of its frontier policy, instead of a mere blackmail. Unlike the colonial state, the precolonial valley states never saw posa as demeaning to its sovereignty. It was rather considered to be the customary right of the hill people—a point of view which was indeed in stark contrast to the notion of space and territoriality in the unfolding century under the British.

The recognition of posa was not merely on the basis of it being a customary right but was more due to the frontier politics of the time. The granting of this customary right was indeed highly advantageous for the state. The area over which posa was claimed, and given, in Assam, for instance, was generally the 'illegible' terai or dooar belt of the state, sparsely populated by migratory communities, practising unsophisticated sali rice or unproductive shifting ahu rice cultivation, infested with diseases, and badly connected with the centre of power. Therefore, it was thought pertinent and wise that, instead of waging an unrewarding warfare with the turbulent hill polities over the areas where the state's rippling authority was not sufficiently felt and where its enforcement power was virtually negligible due to powerful friction of terrain, such a claim be recognized to keep the peace in the frontier at the least cost. Hence, keeping the peace, not tension, in the frontier was central to posa system. In other words, mutual reciprocity between the two polities was central to the frontier politics of the region to ensure general peace in the frontier in the precolonial period. In this context, the hill–valley relationship in precolonial period may be understood in terms of what Edmund Leach has called 'symbiotic to one another', rather than what the dominant colonial discourse would make us believe as confrontational.

It was within this symbiotic relationship that the valley states gained the confidence of the hill polities. This not only enabled them to keep peace in the frontier at the least cost but also allowed them to harness the benefits from regular trade which sometimes extended beyond those hills, towards other states. Take, for instance, the case of trade route between Bhamo in Upper Burma and Mo-myen in China. They were separated by five mountain ranges inhabited mainly by the Kachins. The Burmese authority was allowed to set up a *chokey* between Koon-kao and Kala-tsa ranges and merchants who traded between the two trading marts made their own arrangement with the Kachin chiefs by paying them 'small presents, i.e., pay a kind of black-mail for safe passage through them and for which they obtain a guide'.[74] Indeed, the valley states were able to create a chain of trading networks by being friendly with the frontier chiefs, who channelled the valley goods into the interior hills and even beyond to other countries, and back. As noted earlier, the various examples of Mishmee Hills (between Assam and Tibet/China), Khasi and Jaintia Hills (between Assam and Bengal), Naga Hills (between Assam and Burma), Bhutias (between Assam/Bengal and Tibet), and so on, show how trade between them went on through the centuries.

Abode of Power, of Immense Possibilities

Such symbiosis was not in material and cultural terms alone; it was often seen politically as well. Thus, both helped each other in times of adversity. The court chronicles of the valley states in the region were witness to several occasions in which the hill forces were sought, and usually given, to assist the valley states against their rivals; in fact, a large part of the valley forces was often composed of the hill warriors. For instance, as mentioned earlier, the support of the Bhutias and Dufflas chiefs to Koches in 1562 was decisive for their victory over the Ahoms. Likewise, the Dufflas, Abors, and Nagas often joined the Ahom Army during different battles with their rivals, just as the Chins joined the Burmese Army and the Kukis were always associated with Manipuri, Tipperah, and Kachari forces.[75] 'The Abors were', noted Robinson, 'always looked upon as the allies of the ancient Assamese government; and it is said that a large body of them, to the amount of 20,000 or 30,000, came down to assist the Bura Gohain in repelling the Maomarias, who were then devastating all the country east of Jorehat.'[76] The Manipuri kings often took the help of the Naga and Kuki warriors during wars against their enemies or on various

[74] Bayfield (1873: 176).

[75] These associations were clearly visible from the court chronicles of valley states of the region. See, for instance, Barua (1985 [1930]), Long (1850), and Singh (1995).

[76] Robinson (1975 [1841]: 363).

expeditions, say, against the Sumjok, Pongs, Avas, Suktes (1857 and 1875), and during the Lushai Expedition of 1871–2.[77]

The same court chronicles were witness to the refuge to kings and rulers (when their kingdoms were invaded and occupied by rivals), the court rivals (when they were at a disadvantage), and rebels and fugitives (when there was no place to hide in the valley). For instance, the Kukis claimed that the Raja of Manipur took shelter in the house of one Khongsat Kuki's father during the Burmese occupation of Manipur. He (Ngameingam or Chandra Kirti Singh) ate only *ga* (beans) for several months and returned after the Burmese left.[78] Raja Chingtung Komba (Joy Singh) stayed among the Kukis during the Burmese occupation of Manipur; the superior rice cultivated by the Kukis was given by him during this time.[79] The Ahom rulers also often took shelter in the hills when Assam was invaded. In 1563, for instance, King Sukhampha took shelter in Naga Hills and remained at Klangdoi Hill for three months when the Koches invaded Ahom capital.[80] Besides, thousands of plainsmen took refuge in the hills during various adversities in the plains. In Naga Hills, for instance, there were imprints of refugees from the plains during the Maomarias uprisings and Burmese occupation of Assam. Thus, Brodie noted that the chief of Hurro-moothoon was 'a very benevolent looking old man, who, I was informed, had behaved with the greatest kindness to a large

[77] In 1717–18, for instance, Raja Garib Nawaz 'invited all the Naga chiefs ... and made friendship and intimacy with them' and 'entertained the Naga chiefs with good feasts and wine and requested them to help him to attack Samjok'. See Singh (1995: 29). Shaw (1997 [1929]: 48) also noted that 1,000 Kukis helped the Manipuri forces which were said to be 1,500 in 1857 and 2,400 in 1875. See also Mackenzie (2007 [1884]: 163–71).

[78] See Shaw (1997 [1929]: 48). *Cheitharol Kumbaba* also mentioned this when both Joy Singh and Hera Chandra were hiding in Khongjai Naga village (read as Khongsat Kuki village). While Joy Singh was deceived and taken to Burma with 30,000 Manipuri captives, Hera Chandra reorganized his troop out of Manipuris and Khongjai Kukis and 'came down and attacked the Burmese, they built the fort at Takoo'. The war went on with these troops. See Singh (1995: 96–7).

[79] See McCulloch (1980 [1859]: 61).

[80] Barua (1985 [1930]: 87).

number of Assamese who fled from the plains for refuge in the time of the Burmese' occupation.[81]

In another place, Brodie came across a small piece of rice cultivation, called *boka pathar*. He was informed that 'many Assamese ryots took refuge here to avoid the exactions and oppression they were subject to in the late rule of Rajah Poorunder Sing' and a few still remained there, but they complained of the incessant demands made on them by the Nagas.[82] Part of the Burmese Army which occupied Telyne and its neighbourhood in 1824 never returned to Ava, but it was said that they settled among the Kukis in the hills south of Cachar.[83] The Moamaria rebels taking shelter in Cachar Hills, the 1857 'rebels' taking refuge in the Lushai Hills, and the Kale Sawbwa 'pretender' taking shelter among Falam Chins during the British occupation of Upper Burma in 1885 were all cases of fugitives taking refuge in the hills.[84]

With these possibilities in hand in the frontier for the states, the hills and its inhabitants were always seen as important partners during adversities, which happened quite often, and were always expected to happen, in the unquiet valleys of the region. The hill polities were a source of power and much-needed assistance in times of uncertainties, hence maintaining good relationship with the hillmen continued to be the rule in most of the valley states, as evident from the case of Manipur's annual *Haochongba* (tribal feast) festival and the granting of posa rights to Assam hill tribes and such similar recognition in Burma and Bengal frontiers.[85] In the Manipuri festival, 'men of the

[81] NAI, FP: 17 August 1842, No. 186: Capt. T. Brodie to Maj. F. Jenkins. The same is reproduced in *Selection of Papers* (1873: 256–67).

[82] NAI, FP: 19 October 1844, No. 123: Capt. T. Brodie to Maj. F. Jenkins, 6 August 1844.

[83] WBSA, JP: 27 February 1850, No. 36: Lister to Grant, 2 February 1850.

[84] See WBSA, JP: August 1872, No. 220, Appendix B: Robert Brown to Secretary, Government of India, 22 March 1869. For the escape of rebel Sawbwa 'pretender', Shwe Gyo Byu Prince, see Carey and Tuck (1987 [1896]: 20–6).

[85] The Manipuri term for tribe, *Hao*, is a very old term, which has synonyms in Kuki-Chin, such as *Hiou, Shou, Sho, Dzo, Zo, Mizo*, and *Yo*, or in Chinese use of *Miao* and *Yao*, connoting 'barbarians' or 'hillmen'.

various tribes came down to Imphal to perform feats of strength and agility' and 'the sports of the day conclude with a feast, at which they are regaled with the flesh of cows, buffaloes, dogs, cats, &c., which have died in the valley... dried and preserved on purpose for this feast, and being supplied with plenty of spirits'.[86] The appointment of Katokis, mainly from the hillmen themselves, by the Ahom rulers to keep the frontiers was another case of 'pacific approach' in border politics. The Nagas even held important positions in Ahom administration; the appointment of a certain Naga-origin person, Kanseng, from Daichili Hills to the post of Barpatra Gohain, one of the three highest officers of the Ahom administration, who was also well known for his work in expelling the 'Muhammadan' army beyond the river Karatoya in 1532, was a case in point.[87] The history of Tipperah kingdom was always associated with the hill Kukis: as soldiers, courtiers, and allies.[88] The Falams of Chin Hills even had a defensive and offensive alliance with the Sawbwas of Kale (Burma), as did the tribes of northern Assam, like Mishmis and Abors, with the highland state of Tibet.[89] Thus, the hills were source of support power as to hideouts and even lords to many plainsmen.

The fact that there was an intimate relationship between the hills and valley polities in the long view does not, however, lead to the conclusion that the hills had been conquered and were controlled by the valley states, which is often asserted, nor does it indicate that the hill people had submitted before the valley states while remaining in the hills. It only means there was a situation of mutual dependence and coexistence between the two political entities, whose relationship may be best described as symbiotic yet different. While the physical friction of terrain sustained the difference, the economic interdependency and what may be called the politics of posa sustained the symbiosis. It was this symbiosis which was at the heart of coexistence through the long span. In the long process of two-way traffic of population movement between the hill and valley societies, posaland was the gateway where social and cultural baptism took place. Thus,

---

[86] Hodson (2007 [1911]: 60), McCulloch (1980 [1859]: 24).

[87] Barua (1985 [1930]: 35). See also Acharya (2003 [1966]: 253).

[88] See Long (1850) and Mackenzie (2007 [1884]: 269–70).

[89] Carey and Tuck (1987 [1896]: 150) and Cooper (1995 [1873]: 213).

people moved into and out of the valley, but were readily absorbed within the society they were entering. This two-way movement of people between the hills and valleys was inarguably real and present in the past, which the unfolding centuries of ethnic sterilization process under the colonial mania of classificatory order overturned.

Therefore, there was a peculiar situation across the frontier parts of Northeast region during the precolonial period, a situation of dovetailing, interpenetrating, and mutually interdependent existence between the two worlds of the hills and the valleys. If the physical friction of terrain and differing cultural patterns sustained the divide, the economic interdependence and interpenetrating space of resource conduit sustained the symbiosis. Posaland, therefore, emerged not only as a 'comfort/contact zone' of shared space and overlapping sovereignty in the borderland between the hills and valley polities, but it also continued to act as a buffer to both the hills and valley polities against hostile intention of the other, as a safe resource conduit, as a contact zone of cultural assimilation, and more importantly, as a *peace zone* where both could dip their differences. It was, undoubtedly, a peculiar feature of precolonial frontier politics in the region.

Conclusion

Disowning State, Becoming Egalitarian

This book started with the simple thesis to decentre, and recast, the dominant colonial discourse on the history of Northeast upland region in the light of recent historiography that presents the highlanders as state-evading population in the hills, instead of being the 'relics' of 'prehistoric' society. The book began by examining the state-formation process in the valleys in order to find out why certain people ran away from the state. This was followed by a discussion on the migration history of the hillmen, their settlement and population distribution patterns, and their village built-up. Next, the book talked about their livelihood strategies, their social and political organizations, their ideologies, position of women within the patriarchal set-up, and then their relationship with the valley societies. What became clear from these discussions was that, before they came up to the present hills, the hill people escaped, in a sort of what we call a reverse movement, from their surrounding valleys against the hardships of state-making project there. Once they settled down in the highland massif, they refashioned their lifeways and relationship so that they could effectively preserve their freedom from coercive control and oppression.

The hillmen chose a splitting demography and settlement patterns, horizontally and laterally, across the rugged landscape and chose a secured village site that was constantly on guard. They practised an economy that ensured their food sovereignty from forcible appropriation. They also adopted multiple, fluid, and pliable social, cultural, and linguistic identities to stay safe. Even their pliable orality was studded with a warrior ideology and egalitarianism, which acted as instruments of social control. These important nonstate practices kept them away from coercive control and oppression of power from above and the centre over the centuries. Even the overarching patriarchal social setting, however hard it tried, could not force the women to submit to men's high-handedness. What was, therefore, peculiar to the hill system was the amount of physical and social mobility it guaranteed to individuals, which each system provided with what I have called a safe conduit, the counter-culture. This counter-cultural conduit helped in preventing, evading and even dismantling the systems of relationship when they have become oppressive. In so doing, it prevented the system from becoming oppressive and harmonized the system with individuals. It sustained individual rights and freedom against forms of domination which were likely to become coercive. Being mobile and being able to get away with ease from the system of domination through these conduits therefore became the main pillar of the hill system. Thus, when the chief became a tyrant, an individual could easily leave him; when a husband became oppressive, his wife could desert him with ease; and when one social system become exploitative, the individual could easily opt out and move to another social system. In this way, the unchaining of the chain was possible. Considering the extent to which the hillmen succeeded in keeping the surrounding valley states away from control over the hills, and the extent to which they could prevent state and domination relations from springing up in the hills, they were indeed people who may be called 'free'.

Overall, the book contested the existing discourse on 'tribe' in general, and the hill tribes of Northeast India in particular. The idea that they were primitive, static, and 'relic' of prehistoric society found a hard ground. Instead, this was a society that was not only without state but one that was moving on a particular path different from the state system, a direction which was not necessarily opposite to the state but one that required to be read on its own terms. If State and History demonized the hillmen and their nonstate practices, as uncivilized, regressive, and primitive, and dishonoured them as against State and History, the hillmen's narratives, the *histories* of 'unlettered race', of the voice of 'unreason', celebrated the same civilizational categories of 'uncivil' not only as the core of their cultural collective, of being 'human' or 'hillmen', but also to re-enact themselves differently from State and its History. They 'positioned' themselves to *disown* State and History. Thus, they ridiculed their past 'golden age' in the valley and their future world as the world upside-down, the topsy-turvy world, only to celebrate their present state of statelessness, the egalitarian world. In the book, this positioning, this process of re-enactment, of disowning State and History, has been referred to as 'unstate', not proto-, pre- or post-state.

Re-enactment as unstate or statelessness is understood both as a concept and process. As a concept, unstate posits that the development of stateless hill society was not completely an independent phenomenon but related to State, if not anti-state. It drew its idea and practices from the State space, only to be re-enacted to disown State and evade domination relations in the hills. It was, as noted earlier, the by-product of State making. Unstate, therefore, underpinned the state of statelessness, of an egalitarian world order, which decentred State and focused on protection of individual rights and freedom in a different way. In other words, it disowned State, demonized it, and celebrated statelessness. It positioned the stateless society antithetical to oppressive control and appropriations. It placed individuals and society at the centre of the universe. As a process, unstate connotes a society that was moving in a particular direction, alongside State, from one point of articulation to another. It was a process of becoming egalitarian or equalitarian society through a process of not only disowning State but decriminalizing and celebrating statelessness. Decriminalization of statelessness centred on individual freedom. Individual, and for that matter individual freedom, therefore became the pivot of unstate as a process. To the extent it helped individuals against domination, the process of unstate may be said to be closer to an egalitarian society.

Disowning of state was particularly in the form of freedom and resistance the hillmen projected for themselves. Thus, freedom in stateless hill society was a limited freedom, not the 'unlimited freedom' in a 'state of nature'. It was also related to individual or what I have called the 'uncivil' freedom, not the 'civil' liberty of the liberal society. In fact, freedom in stateless hill society was limited by both 'external' and 'internal' impediments or actual and potential interferences. The external impediments included, besides others, their customs, norms, village 'government', and the social structures. Internal impediments included, for instance, the fear of their celebrated idea of revenge or that of perennial fear of invasion from state conquerors and marauders. Although their society was structured, they were not structures of arbitrary power or a regime of oppressive control. There were social divisions, say, chief–commoners, men–women, husband–wife, older–younger, master–slave, and so on, but such divisions were not governed by domination relation or subordinate–superordinate relationship. Thus, the society was heading towards an egalitarian society, not a state society.

This process of disowning the state, and becoming an egalitarian society, was sustained by the vibrant counter-cultural collective. As shown in the book, the stateless hill society celebrated a vibrant culture of resistance in the open. Resistance was embedded within their various cultural collective as a counter-cultural conduit through which individuals could evade oppressive control with ease. Thus, when the village chief or council become oppressive, his villagers could easily get rid of him by deploying their migration rights and shifting to another village. Similarly, when a husband became oppressive to his wife within the dominant patriarchal system, his wife could easily slip out of the marriage and then get another husband. The embeddedness of resistance was also noticeable from the way they patterned their space, settlements, resources utilization, and so on. Thus, the dispersive settlement and population distribution pattern, villages at the top of the hills, separated by large tract of jungles, connected only by repulsive pathways, and the choice of flattened wealth systematically prevented raiders, marauders, and conquerors.

Therefore, it can be seen that being in a state of statelessness or unstate was to disown state and become an egalitarian society in which freedom of individual or uncivil was at the heart of the system and was sustained by a vibrant form of resistance culture. If personal liberty was a limited one, it was not under any arbitrary power, just as resistance was structurally embedded, open, and direct. Disowning state and becoming egalitarian was a process that could only be reversed by the political force of arms, not by any economic process. To the extent the hillmen were able to prevent the coming of state and domination relation from inside and outside, this process of disowning state would continue to move an egalitarian path on its own dynamic.

Thus, for centuries, there were always chiefs or headmen in the hills, elected or inherited, but they continued to hold the office without any 'exclusive power to take cognizance of offences against the person or property of individuals'.[1] With the entry of Western-made firearms in the nineteenth century, a few chiefs or clans emerged powerful and had indeed subdued few others into a state of 'semi-slavery'. Yet, they still could not go beyond a certain point as the migration right of individuals was strong and used so liberally that the chiefs risked their own authority. Thus, the Lushei chiefs, who became powerful in the nineteenth century, had to continuously show themselves as 'equal' members of the village community so that they were not left alone in the village without any 'subjects'.[2] It was only in later part of the nineteenth century that the British colonial state, with its military might, was able to reverse this process. If many of the stateless cultural collectives still persist in the hills today, they are certainly and gradually dying out, the process gaining momentum in the recent past due to globalization.

However, it is worthwhile to remember the cultural thrust the stateless hillmen had once found for themselves. It is even more worthy of memory considering the present state of conflict and human insecurity in the highland region of Northeast India. What is worth remembering particularly is the kind of freedom enjoyed by individuals. Even if there were some impediments against their free will, they were not living under arbitrary power and domination relation. If the individuals were under actual, potential, and psychological threats, they had embedded mechanisms to evade such threats without taking recourse to the village court. The ease with which they could prevail over oppression, the openness by which they were

---

[1] Butler (1978 [1855]: 146).

[2] I have discussed this elsewhere in the context of the southern hills. See Guite (2011).

able to resist domination, and the air of fearlessness expressed against repression were fertile grounds in which individual freedom persisted over the ages. Thus, the ozone over individual freedom was thick so that the striking capability of the political state was weak. If life in the stateless village society were history today, the ozone it offered to individuals would remain invaluable for ages.[3]

[3] 'Ozone' refers to the ozone layer of the earth atmosphere which protect us from harmful rays.

References

Acharya, N.N. 2003 (1966). *The History of Medieval Assam*. New Delhi: Omsons.

Agamben, G. 2005. *State of Exception*, translated by Kevin Attell. Chicago: University of Chicago Press.

Amin, S. 1995. *Event, Metaphor, Memory: Chauri Chaura 1922–1992*. New Delhi: Oxford University Press.

Andaya, B.W. 2004. 'History, Headhunting and Gender in Monsoon Asia: Comparative and Longitudinal Views', *South East Asia Research*, 12(1): 13–52.

Anderson, J.A. 2009. 'China's Southwestern Silk Road in World History', *World History Connected*, 6(1), available at http://worldhistoryconnected. press.illinois.edu (accessed on 13 October 2016).

Bareh, H. 1985 (1967). *The History and Culture of the Khasi People*. Guwahati: Spectrum.

———. 1989. 'Khasi–Jaintia State Formation', in S. Sinha (ed.), *Tribal Polities and State Systems in Pre-colonial Eastern and North Eastern India*, pp. 269–72. Calcutta: Bagchi & Co.

Barpujari, H.K. 1970. *Problem of the Hill Tribes: North-East Frontier, 1822–42*, 2 vols. Gauhati: Lawyers' Book Stall.

Barpujari, S.K. 1997. *History of Dimasas: From Earliest Times to 1896 A.D.* Haflong: North Cachar Hills District Autonomous Council.

Barua, G.C. (trans. and ed.). 1985 (1930). *Ahom-Buranji: From the Earliest Time to the End of Ahom Rule*. Guwahati: Spectrum Publications.

Baruah, S. 1999. *India against Itself: Assam and the Politics of Nationality*. New Delhi: Oxford University Press.

Baruah, S.L. 1993. *Last Days of Ahom Monarchy: A History of Assam from 1769 to 1826*. New Delhi: Munshiram Manoharlal.

Bayfield, G.T. 1873. 'Narrative of a Journey from Ava to the Frontiers of Assam and Back, Performed between December 1836 and May 1837', in *Selection of Papers Regarding the Hill Tracts between Assam and Burmah and the Upper Brahmaputra*, pp. 134–244. Calcutta: Bengal Secretariat Press (reprint: Vivek, Delhi 1978).

Behal, R.P. 2014. *One Hundred Years of Servitude: Political Economy of Tea Plantations in Colonial Assam*. Delhi: Tulika Books.

Bello, David A. 2005. 'To Go Where No Han Could Go for Long: Malaria and the Qing Construction of Ethnic Administrative Space in Frontier Yunnan', *Modern China*, 31(3): 283–317.

Berlin, I. 1969. 'Two Concepts of Liberty', in *Four Essays on Liberty*, pp. 131–2. Oxford: Oxford University Press.

Besnier, N. 2009. *Gossip and the Everyday Production of Politics*. Honolulu: University of Hawaii Press.

Bezbaruah, R. 2010. *The Pursuit of Colonial Interests in India's North-East*. Guwahati: Empyreal Publishing House.

Bhattacharjee, J.B. 1991. *Social and Polity Formations in Pre-colonial Northeast India*. New Delhi: Vikas.

Bhaumik, S. 2010. *Troubled Periphery: The Crisis of India's North East*. New Delhi: Sage.

Blackburn, S. 2003. 'Memories of Migration: Notes on Legends and Beads in Arunachal Pradesh, India', *European Bulletin of Himalayan Research*, 25/26: 15–60.

Braudel, F. 1980 (1969). *On History*, translated by Sarah Mathews. Chicago: University of Chicago Press.

Brown, N. 1851. 'Specimens of the Naga Language of Asam', *Journal of the American Oriental Society*, 2: 157–65.

Brown, R. 2001 (1873). *Statistical Account of the Native State of Manipur*. New Delhi: Mittal.

Butler, Maj. J. 1847. *A Sketch of Assam: With Some Account of the Hill Tribes by an Officer*. London: Smith, Elder and Co.

———. 1978 (1855). *Travels and Adventures in the Province of Assam during a Residence of Fourteen Years*. Delhi: Vivek.

Butler, Capt. J. 1875. 'Rough Notes on the Angami Nagas and their Language', *Journal of Asiatic Society of Bengal*, Part I, No. 4: 307–42.

Carey, B.S. and H.N. Tuck. 1987 (1896). *The Chin Hills: A History of the People, British Dealings with Them, their Customs and Manners, and a Gazetteer of their Country*. Aizawl: Tribal Research Institute.

Cederlöf, G. 2014. *Founding an Empire on India's North-Eastern Frontiers 1790–1840: Climate, Commerce, Polity*. New Delhi: Oxford University Press.

Census of India, Vol. II: Burma, Part II, 1931.

Chambers, O.A. 1899. *Handbook of Lushai Country.* Aizawl: Tribal Research Institute.

Chatterjee, I. 2013. *Forgotten Friends: Monks, Marriages and Memories of Northeast India.* New Delhi: Oxford University Press.

Choudhuri, D.K. (ed.). 1996. *Administration Report of the Political Agency, Hill Tipperah, 1872–1877/78 and 1878/1879–1889/1890,* vol. I and vol. II. Agartala: Tripura State Tribal Cultural Research Institute and Museum.

Chowdhury, J.N. 1990. *The Tribal Culture and History of Arunachal Pradesh.* Delhi: Daya Publishing House.

Clastres, P. 1977 (1974). *Society against the State: Essays in Political Anthropology,* translated by Robert Hurley. Oxford: Basil Blackwell.

Cooper, T.T. 1995 (1873). *The Mishmee Hills.* New Delhi: Mittal.

Crace, J.H. and J.H. Hutton. 1960. 'An Animal Tale from Assam', *Folklore,* 71(3): 180–3.

Dalton, E.T. 1960 (1872). *Descriptive Ethnology of Bengal.* Calcutta: Government of Bengal.

Damant, G.H. 1880. 'Notes on the Locality and Population of the Tribes Dwelling between the Brahmaputra and Ningthi Rivers', *Journal of the Royal Asiatic Society of Great Britain and Ireland,* N.S., 12(2): 228–58, available at www.jstor.org, accessed on 29 June 2010.

Devi, L. 1992 (1968). *Ahom-Tribal Relations: A Political Study.* Guwahati: Lawyer's Book Stall.

Dr M'Cosh. 1860. 'On the Various Lines of Overland Communication between India and China', *Proceedings of the Royal Geographical Society of London,* 5(2): 47–55.

Dun, E.W. 1992 (1886). *Gazetteer of Manipur.* Delhi: Manas.

Dunbar, G. 1916. 'Abors and Galongs. Part 1: Notes on Certain Hill-tribes of the Indo-Tibetan Border; Part 2: Anthropometric Section (by J. Coggin and S.W. Kemp); Part 3: Personal Narrative of a Visit to Pemakoichen', *Memoirs of the Asiatic Society of Bengal,* 5.

Eaton, R.M. 1993. *The Rise of Islam and the Bengal Frontier, 1204–1760.* New Delhi: Oxford University Press.

Elton, H. 1996. *Frontiers of the Roman Empire.* Bloomington: Indiana University Press.

Elwin, V. (ed.). 1959. *India's North-East Frontier in the Nineteenth Century,* Delhi: Oxford University Press.

Elwin, V. (ed.). 1969. *The Nagas in the Nineteenth Century.* New Delhi: Oxford University Press.

Endle, S. 2010 (1911). *The Kacharis.* New Delhi: Akansha.

Fiskesjo, M. 1999. 'On the "Raw" and the "Cooked" Barbarians in Imperial China', *Inner Asia*, 1(2): 139–68.

Foucault, M. 1977. *Language, Counter-memory, Practice: Selected Essays and Interviews*, translated and edited by D.F. Bouchard. New York: Cornell University Press.

———. 2008. *The Birth of Biopolitics: Lectures at the College de France, 1978–79*, translated by Graham Burchell and edited by Michel Senellart. New York: Palgrave Macmillan.

Fr. Sangermano. 1966 (1833). *A Description of the Burmese Empire*, translated by Willian Tandy. London: Sushil Gupta.

Freid, M.H. 1975. *The Notion of Tribe*. Menlo Park, CA: Cummings Pub.

Fryer, G.E. 1875. 'On the Khyeng People of the Sandoway District, Arakan,' *Journal of Asiatic Society of Bengal*, 1: 39–82.

Gait, E. 2008 (1905). *History of Assam*. Guwahati: EBH Publications.

Ghosh, K.K. 1969. *Indian National Army: A Second Front of the Indian Independence Movement*. Meerut: Minakshi Prakashan.

Gimson, C. 1926. 'Notes on the Marings', *Man in India*, 4(6): 39–56.

Goody, J. and I. Watt, 1963. 'The Consequences of Literacy', *Comparative Studies in Society and History*, 5(3): 304–45.

Goswami, T. 1985. *Kuki Life and Lore*. Haflong: North Cachar Hills District Autonomous Council.

Grierson, G.A. 1928. *Linguistic Survey of India*, Vol. 2, Delhi: Low Price Publications, 2005.

———. 1994 (1904). *Linguistic Survey of India*, Vol. 3, Part III. Delhi: Low Price Publications.

Griffith, W. 1873. 'Journal of a Trip to the Mishmi Mountains, from the Debouching of the Lohit to about Ten Miles East of the Ghalums', in *Selection of Papers regarding the Hill Tracts between Assam and Burmah and the Upper Brahmaputra*, pp. 110–33. Calcutta: Bengal Secretariat Press (reprint: Vivek, Delhi, 1978).

Guha, A. 1991. *Medieval and Early Colonial Assam: Society, Polity, Economy*. New Delhi: Bagchi & Co.

Guha, B.S. 1953. 'The Abor Moshup as a Training Centre for the Youth', *Vanyajati*, 1(4).

Guha, R. 1994. 'The Prose of Counter-insurgency', in N. Dirks, G. Eley, and S.B. Ortner (eds), *Culture/Power/History: A Reader in Contemporary Social Theory*, pp. 336–71. Princeton: Princeton University Press.

———. 1999 (1983). *Elementary Aspects of Peasant Insurgency in Colonial India*. New Delhi: Oxford University Press.

Guite, J. 2011. 'Civilisation and Its Malcontent: The Politics of Kuki Raid in Nineteenth Century Northeast India', *The Indian Economic and Social History Review*, 48(3): 339–76.

Guite, J. 2014. 'Colonialism and Its Unruly?—The Colonial State and Kuki Raids in Nineteenth Century Northeast India', *Modern Asian Studies*, 48(5): 1188–232.

———. 2018. 'Marginalized Ethnicity: Colonial State and Ethnogenesis in India's North-East', in Sajal Nag and Ishrat Alam (eds). *Blending Nation and Region: Essays in Honour of Late Professor Amalendu Guha*. Delhi: Primus Books.

Gurdon, P.R.T. 2010 (1906). *The Khasis*. Delhi: Low Price Publications.

Halbwachs, M. 1992 (1925). *On Collective Memory*, translated by Lewis A. Coser. Chicago: University of Chicago Press.

Hall, D.G.E. (ed.). 1955. *Michael Symes: Journal of His Second Embassy to the Court of Ava in 1802*. London: George Allen and Unwin.

Hamilton, A. 1997. *In Abor Jungles of North-East India*. New Delhi: Mittal.

Hamilton, W. 1993 (1828). *East-India Gazetteer*. Delhi: Low Price Publications.

Hannay, S.F. 1873. 'Abstract of the Journal of a Route Travelled by Captain S.F. Hannay, of the 40th Regiment, Native Infantry, in 1835–36, from the Capital of Ava to the Amber Mines of the Hukong Valley in the South-East Frontier of Assam', compiled by Captain R.B. Pemberton, in *Selection of Papers regarding the Hill Tracts between Assam and Burmah and the Upper Brahmaputra*, pp. 83–109. Calcutta: Bengal Secretariat Press (reprint: Vivek, Delhi, 1978).

Hannerz, U. 1996. *Transnational Connections: Culture, People, Places*. New York: Routledge.

Haokip, J.V. 2011. *Mythology of North East India*. Shillong: Don Bosco Centre for Indigenous Cultures.

Haokip, P. 1998. *Thusim Thum: Ahsijolneng, Gaalngam and Moultinchaan*. Imphal: Private Circulation.

Haokip, P.S. 2008. *Zalengam: The Kuki Nation*. Private Circulation.

Harvey, G.E. 1925. *History of Burma from the Earliest Times to 10 March 1824*. London: Longmans, Green and Co.

Herbst, J. 2000. *States and Power in Africa: Comparative Lessons in Authority and Control*. Princeton, NJ: Princeton University Press.

Hodson, T.C. 2007 (1911). *The Naga Tribes of Manipur*. Delhi: Low Price Publications.

———. 2009 (1908). *The Meitheis*. Delhi: Low Price Publications.

Hollander, J.A. and R.L. Einwohner. 2004. 'Conceptualizing Resistance', *Sociological Forum*, 19(4): 533–54.

Hunter, V. 1990. 'Gossip and the Politics of Reputation in Classical Athens', *Phoenix*, 44(4): 299–325.

Hutton, J.H. 1914. 'Folk-Tales of the Angāmi Nāgas of Assam', *Folklore*, 25(4): 476–98.

———. 1921a. *The Angami Nagas*. Bombay: Oxford University Press.

———. 1921b. *The Sema Nagas*. Bombay: Oxford University Press.

Jenkins, H.L. 1873. 'Notes on a Trip across the Patkoi Range from Assam to the Hookoong Valley, 1869–70' and 'Notes on the Burmese Route from Assam to the Hookoong Valley', in *Selection of Papers regarding the Hill Tracts between Assam and Burmah and the Upper Brahmaputra*, pp. 245–54. Calcutta: Bengal Secretariat Press (reprint: Vivek, Delhi, 1978).

Johnstone, J. 1987 (1896). *Manipur and the Naga Hills*. Delhi: Gian.

Kabui, G. 1991. *History of Manipur: Pre-colonial period*. Delhi: National Publishing House.

Keivom, L. n.d. *Hmar Hla Suina*. Private Circulation.

Kishwar, M. 1987. 'Toiling without Rights', *Economic and Political Weekly*, 22(3): 95–101; 22(4): 149–55; and 22(5): 194–9.

Konow, S. 1902. 'Notes on the Languages Spoken between the Assam Valley and Tibet', *Journal of the Royal Asiatic Society*, 34(1): 127–37.

Kunzle, David. 1978. *World Upside Down: The Iconography of a European Broadsheet*. Cornell University Press.

Kuper, A. 2005. *The Reinvention of Primitive Society: Transformations of a Myth*. London: Routledge.

Lahiri, N. 1991. *Pre-Ahom Assam: Studies in the Inscription of Assam between the Fifth and the Thirteenth Centuries AD*. New Delhi: Munshiram Manoharlal.

Laloo, B. 2011. *Folktales of North East India*. Shillong: Don Bosco Centre for Indigenous Cultures.

Lalthangliana, B. 1977. *History of Mizo in Burma*. Aizawl: Zawlbuk.

Le Goff, J. 1992. *History and Memory*. New York: Columbia University Press.

Leach, E.R. 1960. 'The Frontiers of "Burma"', *Comparative Studies in Society and History*, 3(1): 49–68.

Lehman, F.K. 1980 (1963). *The Structure of Chin Society: A Tribal People of Burma Adapted to a Non-Western Civilization*. Aizawl: Tribal Research Institute.

Lenthang, K.M. 2005. *Manmasi Chate (Kuki-Chin-Mizo) Thulhun Kidang Masa*. Moreh: Hill Tribal Council.

Levi, Jerome M. 1998. 'The Bow and the Blanket: Religion, Identity, and Resistance in Raramuri Material Culture', *Journal of Anthropological Research*, 54(3): 299–324.

Lewin, T.H. 1978 (1870). *Wild Races of South-Eastern India*. Aizawl: Tribal Research Institute.

Lewin, T.H. 2004 (1869). *The Hill Tracts of Chittagong and the Dwellers therein*. Aizawl: Tribal Research Institute.

Lhangum, L. 2013. *Thu Goulu: Thusimlui leh Paochamtuh*. Silchar: Private Circulation.

Lianhmingthanga and V.L. Fimate (eds). 2006. *The Mizo Folk Tales*. Aizawl: Tribal Research Institute.

Long, J. 1850. 'Analysis of the *Raj Mala* or Chronicles of Tripura', *Journal of Asiatic Society of Bengal*, 533–57.

Lumsden, D.M. and Noel Williamson. 1911. 'A Journey into the Abor Country, 1909', *The Geographical Journal*, 37(6): 621–29, available at http://www.jstor.org, accessed on 19 October 2015.

Lyall, C. 1997 (1908). *The Karbis: From the Papers of the late Edward Stack*. Delhi: Spectrum.

M'Cosh, J. 2000 (1837). *Topography of Assam*. New Delhi: Logos.

Mackenzie, A. 2007 (1884). *The North-East Frontier of India*. New Delhi: Mittal.

Macrae, J. 1919 (1801). 'Account of the Kookies or Lunctas', *Asiatick Researches*, vii: 183–98.

Mauss, M. 1966. *The Gift: Forms and Functions of Exchange in Archaic Societies*, translated by Ian Gunnison, London: Cohen & West.

May, A.J. 2012. *Welsh Missionaries and British Imperialism: The Empire of Clouds in North-East India*, Manchester: Manchester University Press.

Mayaram, S. 2003. *Against History, against State: Counterperspectives from the Margins*. New York: Columbia University Press.

McCall, A.G. 2003 (1949). *Lushai Chrysalis*. Aizawl: Tribal Research Institute.

McCulloch, W. 1980 (1859). *An Account of the Valley of Manipore and of the Hill Tribes*. New Delhi: Mittal.

Mills, A.J.M. 1980 (1853). *Report on Assam*. Delhi: Gian.

———. 1985 (1853). *Report on the Khasi and Jaintia Hills*. Shillong: NEHU Publication.

Mills, J.P. 1982 (1937). *Rengma Nagas*. Kohima: Government of Nagaland.

———. 2003 (1922). *The Lhota Nagas*. Delhi: Spectrum.

———. 2003 (1926). *Ao Nagas*. Kohima: Government of Nagaland.

Misra, P.S. 1978. 'Historical and Linguistic Aspects of the Dimasa Kacharis', *Souvenir of Haflong Government College*, vol. II.

Misra, S. 2011. *Becoming a Borderland: The Politics of Space and Identity in Colonial Northeastern India*. New Delhi: Routledge.

Misra, U. 2014. *India's North-East: Identity Movements, State, and Civil Society*. New Delhi: Oxford University Press.

Misztal, B.A. 2003. *Theories of Social Remembering*. Open University Press.

TRI. 1991. *Mizo Women Today*. Aizawl.

Nag, S. 2007. *Pied Pipers in North-East India: Bamboo-flowers, Rat Famine, and the Politics of Philanthropy, 1881–2007*. New Delhi: Manohar.

———. 2016. *The Uprising: Colonial State, Christian Missionaries, and Anti-slavery Movement in North-East India (1908–1954)*. New Delhi: Oxford University Press.

Nath, J. 2000. *Cultural Heritage of Tribal Societies, Vol. 1: The Adis*. New Delhi: Omsons.

Nongbri, T. 1998. 'Gender Issues and Tribal Development', in RGICS Paper No. 47: *Problems in Tribal Society—Some Aspects*. New Delhi: Rajiv Gandhi Institute for Contemporary Studies (RGICS).

Nora, P. 1984. 'Between Memory and History: *Les Lieux de Memoire*', *Representations*, 26(Spring): 7–25.

Nyori, T. 1993. *History and Culture of the Adis*. New Delhi: Omsons.

Ostrom, Elinor. 2015 [1990]. *Governing the Commons: The Evolution of Institutions for Collective Action*. Cambridge: Cambridge University Press.

Pachuau, Joy L.K. 2014. *Being Mizo: Identity and Belonging in Northeast India*. New Delhi: Oxford University Press.

Pachuau, Joy L.K. and W. van Schendel. 2015. *The Camera as Witness: A Social History of Mizoram, Northeast India*. Delhi: Cambridge University Press.

Parker, B.J. 2006. 'Toward an Understanding of Borderland Processes', *American Antiquity*, 71(1): 77–100.

Parratt, S.N.A. 2005. *The Court Chronicle of the Kings of Manipur: The Cheitharon Kumpapa*. London: Routledge.

Parry, N.E. 1931. 'Notes on Lushei', in J.H. Hutton (ed.), *Census of India 1931: With Complete Survey of Tribal Life and System, Vol. I, Part III: Ethnographical*, pp. 126–30. Delhi: Omsons.

———. 1988 (1931). *The Lakhers*. New Delhi: Omsons.

———. 2009 (1928). *A Monograph on Lushai Customs and Ceremonies*. Aizawl: Tribal Research Institute.

Peal, S.E. 1873. 'Notes on a Visit to the Tribes Inhabiting the Hills South of Sibsagar, Asam', in *Selection of Papers Regarding the Hill Tracts between Assam and Burmah and the Upper Brahmaputra*, pp. 316–35. Calcutta: Bengal Secretariat Press (reprint: Vivek, Delhi, 1978).

———. 1893. 'On the "Morong" as Possibly a Relic of Pre-marriage Communism', *Journal of the Royal Anthropological Institute*, vol. xxii: 244–61.

Pemberton, R.B. 2000 (1835). *The Eastern Frontier of India*. New Delhi: Mittal.

Phayre, A.P. 1967 (1883). *History of Burma: Including Burma proper, Pegu, Taungu, Tenasserim, and Arakan*. London: Sushil Gupta.

Playfair, M.A. 1998 (1909). *The Garos*. Delhi: Spectrum.

Pudaite, R. 1963. *The Education of the Hmar People: With Historical Sketch of the People*. Sielmat: Private Circulation.

Ramirez, P. 2014. *People of the Margins: Across Ethnic Boundaries in North-East India*. Delhi: Spectrum.

Recoeur, P. 2004. *Memory, History, Forgetting*. Chicago: University of Chicago Press.

Reid, A.S. 1976 [1893]. *Chin-Lushai Land: A Description of the Various Expeditions into the Chin-Lushai Hills*. Aizawl: Tribal Research Institute.

Robinson, W. 1975 (1841). *A Descriptive Account of Asam*. Delhi: Sanskaran Prakashan.

Roy, S. 1997 (1960). *Aspects of Padam Minyong Culture*. Itanagar: Directorate of Research.

Roychowdhury, N.R. 1976. 'Kuki Disturbances in Tripura, 1860–61', *Social Scientist*, 4(9): 60–5.

Saikia, A. 2011. *Forests and Ecological History of Assam, 1826–2000*. New Delhi: Oxford University Press.

———. 2014. *A Century of Protests: Peasant Politics in Assam since 1900*. New Delhi: Routledge.

Sangma, M.S. 1981. *History and Culture of the Garos*. New Delhi: Books Today.

Scott, J.C. 1985. *Weapons of the Weak: Everyday Forms of Peasant Resistance*. New Haven: Yale University Press.

———. 1990. *Domination and the Arts of Resistance: Hidden Transcript*. Yale: Yale University Press.

———. 1998. *Seeing Like a State: Why Certain Schemes to Improve the Human Condition have Failed*. New Haven: Yale University Press.

———. 2009. *The Art of Not Being Governed: An Anarchist History of Upland Southeast Asia*. New Haven: Yale University Press.

Scott, J.G. 1893. *Gazetteer of Upper Burma and the Shan States, Vol. I, Part 2*. Rangoon: Govt. Printing Office.

———. 1906. *Burma: A Handbook of Practical Information*. London: Alexander Moring, the De La More Press.

———. 2002 (1886). *Burma: As It Was, As It Is, and As It Will Be*. Kolkata.

Shakespear, J. 1892. *Diary of the Superintendent, South Lushai Hills*, NAI, FEP (A), March, No. 201. Kolkata: R.N. Bhattacharya.

Shakespear, J. 1922. 'Tangkhul Folk Tales and Notes on Some Festivals of the Hill Tribes South of Assam', *Folklore*, 33(3): 265–81.

———. 1998 (1912). *Lushei Kuki Clans*. Aizawl: Tribal Research Institute.

Shakespear, J. and T.C. Hodson. 1909. 'Folk-Tales of the Lushais and their Neighbours', *Folklore*, 20(4): 388–420.

Shakespear, L.W. 2004 (1914). *History of Upper Assam, Upper Burmah and North-Eastern Frontier.* Delhi: Spectrum.

Sharma, J. 2011. *Empire's Garden: Assam and the Making of India.* New Delhi: Permanent Black.

Shaw, W. 1997 (1929). *Notes on the Thadou Kukis.* Delhi: Spectrum.

Shimray, R.R. 1985. *Origin and Culture of Nagas.* New Delhi: Pamleiphi Shimray.

Sing Khaw Khai. 1995. *Zo People and their Culture: A Historical, Cultural Study and Critical Analysis of Zo and its Ethnic Tribes.* Lamka: Private Circulation.

Singh, J.P., N.N. Vyas, and R.S. Mann (eds). 1988. *Tribal Women and Development,* Jaipur: Rawat.

Singh, L. Joychandra (ed.). 1995. *Cheitharol Kumbaba* (Manipur Chronicle: From 33 AD to 1897 AD), translated by Bama Charan Mukherjee, in *The Lost Kingdom: Royal Chronicle of Manipur.* Imphal: Prajatantra Publishing House.

Singson, T.S.A. 1997. *Guollui Sanakhang.* Private Circulation.

Sinha, S. (ed.). 1989. *Tribal Polities and State Systems in Pre-colonial Eastern and North Eastern India.* Calcutta: Bagchi & Co.

Skaria, A. 1999. *Hybrid Histories: Forests, Frontiers and Wildness in Western India.* New Delhi: Oxford University Press.

Smith, W.C. 2002 (1925). *The Ao Naga Tribe of Assam.* New Delhi: Mittal.

Soppit, C.A. 1976 (1887). *A Short Account of the Kuki-Lushai Tribes of the North-East Frontier.* Aizawl: Tribal Research Institute.

Berlin, I. 1969. *Four Essays on Liberty.* Oxford: Oxford University Press.

Srivastava, L.R.N. 1990. *Social Organisation of the Meyongs.* Itanagar: Directorate of Research.

Stewart, R. 1855. 'Notes on Northern Cachar', *Journal of Asiatic Society of Bengal,* XXIV(3): 582–701.

Thakur, A.K. 2003. *Slavery in Arunachal Pradesh.* New Delhi: Mittal.

Thompson, L. and Howard Lamar (eds). 1981. *Comparative Frontier History in the Frontier in History: North America and Southern Africa Compared.* New Haven: Yale University Press.

Tribal Research Institute (TRI). 1988. *Pawi Chanchin.* Aizawl.

————. 2008 (reprint). *The Lushais.* Aizawl.

Sarma, Ratna Kandali and Arjun Das Bairagi. 1938 [1724]. *Tripura Buranji, or A Chronicle of Tipperah.,* trans. & ed. by S.K. Bhuyan. Gauhati: Government of Assam.

van Schendel, W. 1992. *Francis Buchanan in Southeast Bengal (1780): His Journey to Chittagong, the Chittagong Hill Tracts, Noakhali and Comilla.* University Press: Dhaka.

van Driem, G. 2001. *Languages of the Himalayas: An Ethnolinguistic Handbook of the Greater Himalayan Region*, 2 vols. Leiden: Brill.

van Schendel, W. 2002. 'Geographies of Knowing, Geographies of Ignorance: Jumping Scale in Southeast Asia', *Environment and Planning D: Society and Space*, 20: 647–68.

Vansina, J. 1985. *Oral Tradition as History*. London: James Currey.

Verghese, C.G. and R.L. Thanzawna, 1997. *A History of the Mizos, Vol. I*. New Delhi: Vikas.

von Fürer-Haimendorf, C. 1938a. 'Through the Unexplored Mountains of the Assam–Burma Border', *The Geographical Journal*, 91(3): 201–16, available at www.jstor.org, accessed on 16 July 2010.

————.1938b. 'The Morung System of the Konyak Nagas, Assam', *Journal of the Royal Anthropological Institute*, 349–78.

————. 1969. *The Konyak Nagas: An Indian Frontier Tribe*. New York: Holt, Rinehart and Winston.

Vumson, 1986. *Zo History*. Aizawl: Private Circulation.

Wang, Q.E. 1999. 'History, Space, and Ethnicity: The Chinese Worldview', *Journal of World History*, 10(2); 285–305, available at www.jstor.org, accessed on 11 June 2011.

White, R. 1991. *The Middle Ground: Indians, Empires and Republics in the Great Lakes Region, 1650–1815*. Cambridge: Cambridge University Press.

Wilcox, R. 1873. 'Memoir of a Survey of Assam and the Neighbouring Countries, Executed in 1825-6-7-8', in *Selection of Papers Regarding the Hill Tracts between Assam and Burmah and the Upper Brahmaputra*, pp. 1–83. Calcutta: Bengal Secretariat Press (reprint: Vivek, Delhi, 1978).

Wilks, I. 1992. 'On Mentally Mapping Greater Asante: A Study of Time and Motion,' *Journal of African History*, 33(2): 175–90

Winichakul, T. 1995. *Siam Mapped: A History of the Geo-body of a Nation*. Chiang Mai: Silkworm Books.

Woodthorpe, R.G. 1882. 'Notes on the Wild Tribes Inhabiting the so-called Naga Hills, on our North-East Frontier of India. Part I', *The Journal of the Anthropological Institute of Great Britain and Ireland*, 11: 56–73, available at www. jstor.org, accessed on 16 July 2010.

————. 1980 (1873). *The Lushai Expedition, 1871–1879*. London: Hurst and Blackett.

Xaxa, V. 2004. 'Women and Gender in the Study of Tribes in India', *Indian Journal of Gender Studies*, 11(2): 345–67.

Yerushalmi, Y. 1982. *Zakhor: Jewish History and Jewish Memory*. Seattle, WA: University of Washington Press.

Zehol, L. (ed.). 1998. *Women in Naga Society*. New Delhi: Regency.

Index

About the Author

Jangkhomang Guite teaches modern Indian history at the Centre for Historical Studies, Jawaharlal Nehru University, New Delhi. He was previously at the Department of History, Assam University, Silchar. His research explores the history of the long-neglected borderland of India and Myanmar, commonly known as Northeast India. He is interested particularly in tribal studies, economic, social and cultural history, memory studies, and war and military history.

He has published some original articles related to his area of research in different refereed journals. His works includes colonial and postcolonial period of Indo-Myanmar borderland. These include themes related to colonial frontier policy, tribal 'raids', ethnicity, politics of remembering, and First and Second World War in the Northeast. He is presently working on British colonial rule in the Northeast, monuments and memory in postcolonial Northeast, social history of jhum cultivation, and response of Northeast Indians to First World War.